GERMAN, JEW, MUSLIM, GAY

RELIGION, CULTURE, AND PUBLIC LIFE

RELIGION, CULTURE, AND PUBLIC LIFE

Series Editor: Matthew Engelke

The Religion, Culture, and Public Life series is devoted to the study of religion in relation to social, cultural, and political dynamics, both contemporary and historical. It features work by scholars from a variety of disciplinary and methodological perspectives, including religious studies, anthropology, history, philosophy, political science, and sociology. The series is committed to deepening our critical understandings of the empirical and conceptual dimensions of religious thought and practice, as well as such related topics as secularism, pluralism, and political theology. The Religion, Culture, and Public Life series is sponsored by Columbia University's Institute for Religion, Culture, and Public Life.

For a complete list of titles, see page 301.

GERMAN, JEW, MUSLIM, GAY

The Life and Times of Hugo Marcus

MARC DAVID BAER

Columbia University Press

New York

Publication of this book was made possible in part by funding from the Institute for Religion, Culture, and Public Life at Columbia University.

Columbia University Press
Publishers Since 1893
New York Chichester, West Sussex
cup.columbia.edu

Library of Congress Cataloging-in-Publication Data

Names: Baer, Marc David, 1970– author.
Title: German, Jew, Muslim, gay : the life and times of Hugo Marcus / Marc David Baer.
Description: New York : Columbia University Press, [2020] | Includes bibliographical references.
Identifiers: LCCN 2019032664 (print) | LCCN 2019032665 (ebook) | ISBN 9780231196703 (cloth) | ISBN 9780231196710 (paperback) | ISBN 9780231551786 (ebook)
Subjects: LCSH: Marcus, Hugo, 1880–1966. | Gay men–Germany–Biography. | Muslim converts from Judaism–Germany–Biography. | Holocaust survivors–Germany–Biography. | Jews–Europe–History–20th century. | Muslims–Europe–History–20th century. | Europe–Ethnic relations–History–20th century.
Classification: LCC HQ75.8.M326 A3 2020 (print) | LCC HQ75.8.M326 (ebook) | DDC 306.76/62092 [B]—dc23
LC record available at https://lccn.loc.gov/2019032664
LC ebook record available at https://lccn.loc.gov/2019032665

Columbia University Press books are printed on permanent and durable acid-free paper.
Printed in the United States of America

Cover photo: bpk Bildagentur / Staatsbibliothek zu Berlin, Stiftung Preussischer Kulturbesitz, Berlin, Germany/Photograph by A. Alberino, Capri, Italy, July 1901/ Art Resource, NY

Contents

Acknowledgments

I conducted the research for this book in Basel, Berlin, Bern, Los Angeles, and Zürich between 2009 and 2019.

In Berlin the greatest pleasure was working at the library of the Zentrum Moderner Orient (ZMO)—despite having to pass under a "pre-Nazi-era" swastika above the early-twentieth-century Mittelhof villa's main door. In forested Nikolassee, colleagues and I skinny dipped in the ice-cold Schlachtensee on summer lunch breaks but skidded across icy paths in winter, anxious about the wild boars snorting in the blackberry bushes. At the ZMO library I benefited from the rich collection of the Gerhard Höpp archive, which contains key archival and secondary sources revealing the history of Muslims in Weimar and Nazi Germany.

I had the misfortune to take the S-bahn from Nikolassee to the end of the line at Oranienburg on a hot summer day to walk to the Sachsenhausen concentration camp. After many bizarre spells of disorientation, I managed to find the library and consult copies of the records of Hugo Marcus's incarceration—near where inmates were gassed—and located his former barracks (marked only by a numbered stone).

I visited Berlin's Landesarchiv (State Archive), located in a gigantic, brick, former weapons and munitions factory complex in the far north of the city, to read files on Weimar and Nazi-era Muslim organizations.

Garish Potsdamer Platz's serenely quiet Staatsbibliothek (State Library)—whose student canteen's Berliner specialties such as *Eisbein* and wine and beer never failed to intrigue me—was a peaceful place to read through Marcus's early-twentieth-century philosophical, avant-garde, and pacifist publications. The library also surprised me with a tiny portrait of a young Marcus.

Most important, I attended Friday prayers in a tiny, crumbling, painted jewel, the Ahmadi mosque in Wilmersdorf at Fehrbelliner Platz, which gave me a sense of the intimate space where much of this narrative took place.

My understanding of German converts to Islam has been greatly shaped by accompanying anthropologist Esra Özyürek on her ethnographic journey, which culminated in *Being German, Becoming Muslim: Race, Religion, and Conversion in the New Europe* (Princeton, 2014). How much of her voice and analysis is in this book I cannot really determine. I especially remember the "only in Berlin" scene where the gracious and welcoming participants at a mainly German converts' gender-segregated Muslim picnic in Tiergarten had to chase dogs away from their prayer mats during prayer while averting their eyes as nude couples made out in the grass. Also in Tiergarten, I read fundamental texts in the gay rights struggle as dust settled at the recently completed library of the expanded Schwules (Gay) Museum, near where prostitutes continue to walk the same streets sex workers have frequented for a century. But I actually had to travel back to California to find all of Marcus's gay writings published after World War II in *Der Kreis* at the ONE National Gay & Lesbian Archives at the USC libraries in Los Angeles.

In Zürich I conducted research mainly at the stately Zentralbibliothek (Central Library), which owns Marcus's Nachlass (estate), including his private letters exchanged with a kaleidoscopic array of Jews, gays, and Muslims; autobiographical texts; personal documents such as Nazi-issued travel document and Swiss police files; unpublished works, including typewritten or handwritten mosque lectures; copies of published works including his hard-to-find early-twentieth-century homoerotic novella; and private photos with passionate inscriptions pasted into private letters spanning his entire life.

I also visited the Thomas Mann Archives at the new, wind-swept mountaintop campus of the ETH Zürich in a blazing, pink sunset.

I examined Marcus's police file at Basel's City Archive, located in the over-the-top, brilliant red, frescoed sixteenth-century Town Hall complex. I was fortunate to visit at the same time as the archive's extraordinary exhibit, "Magnet Basel," featuring photocopies of entire personal police dossiers, annotated and contextualized, striking examples of the very type of file I was reading. Documenting a century of migration to the city, curated for the one hundredth anniversary of the Swiss Federal Foreigners' Police, the exhibit offered moving tales about the lives of migrants ranging from Jews during World War II to Syrian Kurds today.

Staff at the Jüdisches Museum der Schweiz (Basel) revealed further unknown, dramatic stories about German Jewish arrival in the city during World War II.

When I walked to Marcus's surprising final resting place in Basel, I finally realized why the funeral directors had sent me a photo of a strand of trees taken from a distance. May Hugo Hamid Hans Alienus Marcus rest in peace, and forgive me for exposing his private life in this book.

Following Marcus's paper trail also took me to beautiful Bern, the turquoise-green, river-wrapped medieval Swiss capital, to examine Marcus's dossier at the Federal Archive. It was impressive to be able to register myself and order documents online, selecting the date on which I would read the material. And, indeed, when I arrived at the archive on the specified day, the friendly and helpful staff presented the documents as I had ordered and provided a Swiss adapter for plugging in my laptop. To top it off they pointed out the machine dispensing free water and coffee! Incomparable. If only all archives were like this. The sweetened coffee served to offset the depressing impact of holding Marcus's swastika-laced Nazi passport and looking in the eyes of the terrified man in its photograph.

I am especially grateful to individuals who made this research possible. Tireless researcher, former Ahmadi, and all-around fun-loving motorbike and *Fasching* enthusiast Manfred Backhausen first introduced me to Marcus and generously shared Ahmadi archival sources, photographs, and a copy of the Qur'an translation edited by him. At the beginning of my research Gerdien Jonker offered me other Ahmadi sources and uploaded (most of) her collection of the near-complete run of the *Moslemische Revue* to the Ahmadi website. My understanding of Islam in interwar Europe is greatly indebted to conversations especially with Umar Ryad. My knowledge of Goethe's approach to Islam was enlightened by email conversations with Katherina Mommsen. Esra Özyürek and David Motadel read a draft of the entire manuscript. My analysis was greatly improved by the editors and anonymous readers of *New German Critique* and the *American Historical Review*. Much of the material in chapter 2 was originally published in an earlier version as "Protestant Islam in Weimar Germany: Hugo Marcus and 'The Message of the Holy Prophet Muhammad to Europe'" in *New German Critique* 44, no. 2: 163–200. © 2017, New German Critique, Inc. All rights reserved. Republished by permission of the copyright holder and the present publisher, Duke University Press. A prior version of chapter 3 was originally published as "Muslim Encounters with Nazism and the Holocaust: The Ahmadi of Berlin and German-Jewish Convert to Islam Hugo Marcus," in the *American Historical Review* 120, no. 1 (February 2015): 140–71, © American Historical Association and Oxford University Press. Reprinted material from *Secret Germany: Stefan George and His Circle*, by Robert E. Norton, copyright © 2002 by Cornell University, is used by permission of the publisher, Cornell University Press. I am grateful to the entire team at Columbia University Press, especially Wendy Lochner and Lowell Frye, and to former LSE colleague Matthew Engelke, who agreed to publish it in his exciting book series.

I would not have been able to conduct this research had it not been for research and sabbatical leave, or generous funding provided by the University of California, Irvine, and the London School of Economics and Political Science, the ZMO, the Alexander von Humboldt Foundation, and the Leverhulme Trust.

Research was carried out during extended periods of research leave granted by Carolyn Boyd, Robert Moeller, and Jeffrey Wasserstrom, successive chairs of the History Department at the University of California, Irvine between 2009 and 2012. I initially conducted research in Berlin and Zürich from 2009 to 2011 thanks to a fellowship at the ZMO directed by Ulrike Freitag. A follow-up visit to Berlin in 2013 and 2014 was made possible by a continuation of a Research Fellowship from the Alexander von Humboldt Foundation received in 2006 and 2007 (my academic hosts at that time were Maurus Reinkowski at the University of Freiburg and Gudrun Krämer at the Free University, Berlin), and by renewed affiliation with the ZMO. I was able to continue my research in Berlin in 2013–2014 thanks to a sabbatical granted by the LSE before I began my teaching duties. I was able to take many research trips to Switzerland between 2014 and 2018 due to generous annual LSE research funding from the International History Department. I completed the final version of the manuscript in 2018–2019 thanks to a yearlong Research Fellowship from the Leverhulme Trust.

I am indebted to Bekim Agai, Umar Ryad, and Mehdi Sajid for including me in the International Symposium on Islam in Inter-War Europe and European Cultural History at Leiden University, the Netherlands (2012); to Jasmin Khosravie, who invited me to participate in the International Research Colloquium, Institut für Orient- und Asienwissenschaften, University of Bonn, BMBF Research Group "Europe from the Outside" (2013); to Moez Khalfaoui, for inviting me to give the keynote address at the Workshop Islamisches Recht und die Herausforderungen moderner Gesellschaften, Zentrum für islamische Theologie Tübingen, Graduiertenkolleg Islamische Theologie, University of Tübingen, Germany (2014); to Ben Fortna, organizer of the Near & Middle East History Seminar at the School of Oriental and African Studies, University of London (2014); to Janet Hartley, who invited me to give my inaugural lecture sponsored by the International History Department at the LSE (2015); to members of the panel "Muslim Destinies in Inter-War Europe: Laying the Foundations for European Islam" that I organized at the American Historical Association annual meeting (2015); to panel and audience members at two panels organized by Umar Ryad: the Lecture-Cum-Seminar, ERC Project "Muslims in Interwar Europe," Religious Studies, University of Utrecht (2016), and "New Muslim Communities in Europe, 1918–1945," Glaubensfragen: 51, Deutscher Historikertag at the Üniversitat Hamburg (2016); to participants in the international workshop I co-organized with Esra Özyürek at the LSE, "Connected Pasts and Futures: Jews and Muslims of Europe" (2017): David Feldman, Esther Romeyn, Brian Klug, Aomar Boum, Nassar Meer, Josef Meri, Humayun Ansari, Nora Şeni, Damani Partridge, Kimberly Arkin, Marcy Brink-Danan, and Ben Gidley; and to the audience at the talk I gave at the Jewish History Seminar, Institute of Historical Research, London, organized by Michael Berkowitz, Francois Guesnet, and Nathan Kurz (2018). Maurus Reinkowski invited me to present my research at the Seminar für Nahoststudien at the University of Basel (2018), which coincidentally is located very close to one of Marcus's final abodes, the Adullam Care Home. I am grateful for the thought-provoking questions with which he and his colleagues challenged me and for the delicious homemade borscht with horseradish crème and red wine we enjoyed afterward. And thank you for the Basler Läckerli.

I am grateful for the assistance of Muhammad Ali, imam of the Berlin Mosque; Dr. Zahid Aziz, webmaster of the Berlin and Woking Ahmadi missions; Father Placidus Kuhlkamp, Order of Saint Benedict, librarian at Beuron Abbey, Germany; Robert Parzer, archivist, Stiftung Brandenburgische Gedenkstätten, Gedenkstätte und Museum Sachsenhausen; Thomas Ripper, librarian, Bibliothek ZMO; and the directors and staffs of the Handschriftenabteilung, Zentralbibliothek Zürich, the Landesarchiv Berlin, and the Staatsarchiv Basel-Stadt. The staff at the Zentralbibliothek graciously made PDF scans of material from Marcus's estate for me when I was unable to travel to Zürich. Email communications with Elke von der Lieth, Kommunale Galerie Berlin, Villa Oppenheim; Dagmar Seemel, Universitätsarchiv der Humboldt-Universität; Susanne Grulich Zier, university archivist, University of Basel; and Hermann Wichers, head of user services, Staatsarchiv Basel-Stadt, provided answers to questions concerning details of Marcus's life.

My understanding of the many difficult to decipher and even more difficult to comprehend German sources is thanks to several native German speakers, German and Swiss, including Susanne Hillman, Katrin Simon, Teresa Schlögl, and Tobias Pester, as well as several student research assistants provided by the ZMO. Laurence Krupnak carried out research into the membership rolls of the Nazi Party for me at the National Archives and Records Administration, Washington, D.C. After a long and fruitless search, I finally located the portrait of Marcus's friend Roman, thanks to art collector Ernst Ferman of Mönchengladbach, Germany, who shared an image of it with me. This book could not have been written without all of their graceful assistance. Whatever errors of translation or errors of fact or interpretation that remain are my own.

GERMAN, JEW, MUSLIM, GAY

Introduction

Goethe as Pole Star

German, Jew, Muslim, Gay offers an astonishing perspective on the history of modern Germany and German-speaking Central Europe from the vantage of a man who united multiple marginal identities in himself, devoted his life to promoting religious utopias and secular brotherhoods, and considered himself as part of a spiritual elite that held the key to Germany's salvation. Hugo Marcus (b., 1880, Posen [today, Poznań], Poland; d., 1966, Basel, Switzerland) was an extraordinary individual. He is the only figure to have played an important role in the gay rights movement *and* in establishing Islam in Germany. He was one of the most prominent German converts to Islam and one of the most significant Muslims in Germany prior to World War II. He was one of the few Jewish converts to Islam, and the only one who remained in Germany after conversion, leaving involuntarily. His life offers an example of the unexpected outcomes of the Muslim-Jewish encounter and a new aspect on Muslim experiences of the Holocaust. Above all, he created a unique synthesis of being German, gay, and Muslim modeled after the life and work of Johann Wolfgang von Goethe (1749–1832).

A novelist, poet, philosopher, political activist, and writer, Marcus committed to many different circles, movements, and ideologies over the course of his eighty-six years. His choices speak to a desire to find a utopia or to join universal brotherhoods. After completing *Gymnasium* in Posen in 1898, he migrated to Berlin and around that time—before his parents arrived in 1901—he joined the first organization in the world to campaign for the rights of homosexuals, the Wissenschaftlich-humanitäres Komitee (Scientific Humanitarian Committee), founded by his friend Magnus Hirschfeld (b. 1868, Kolberg [today, Kołobrzeg], Poland; d. 1935, Nice, France), who was also of Jewish background.[1] Like many other scions of German Jewish provincial families in Imperial Germany, Marcus then studied philosophy at Berlin's university, where he befriended Kurt Hiller (b. 1885, Berlin; d. 1972, Hamburg), another leading homosexual rights activist of Jewish background, whose 1922 book *§ 175: Die Schmach des Jahrhunderts!* (Paragraph 175: The disgrace of the century!) is a seminal work in the homosexual rights struggle, aimed at winning "the liberation of a human minority that, although harmless," is "oppressed, persecuted, and tormented."[2] Their academic mentors included Georg Simmel (1858–1918), himself the son of Jewish converts to Christianity, who, although renowned today as one of the founders of sociology, in his day was known as "the philosopher of the avant-garde" and played a leading role in the left-wing, pacifist, feminist, and homosexual rights movements.[3] A countercultural iconoclast, Simmel "sought to undermine the status quo by social critique, opposing accepted tastes, hierarchies and conventions"; "believing there was no such thing as self-evident and universal Truth," he sought "to construct a new morality and spirituality."[4] Marcus found two pathways to what he conceived of as divinity. He first joined the George-Kreis (George Circle), a quasi-religious group composed of the rapturous middle-class youth disciples of the poet and "prophet" Stefan George (b. 1868, Büdesheim, Germany; d. 1933, Minusio, Switzerland), who thought of themselves as avant-gardes waging a cultural and spiritual war of redemption to renew Germany, and whose membership overlapped that of masculinist homosexual circles.[5] He was either introduced to the circle by his well-known historian cousin, Ernst Kantorowicz (b. 1895, Posen; d. 1963, Princeton, N.J.), or he was inspired to do this by Simmel, who was George's close friend.[6] Then, however, Marcus went on to join the Ahmadiyya Anjuman Ishaat-e-Islam (Ahmadi Movement for the Propagation of Islam), an Islamic confessional minority born in British India, becoming their only Jewish convert and member in Berlin.[7] Prior to World War I, Marcus earned some renown with a half-dozen philosophical works.[8] In one of these, *Meditationen* (Meditations)—written while the precocious twenty-year-old was still a doctoral student, and whose writing, like that of George, is marked by "an elitist, philhellenic homoeroticism,"[9] whose major themes are pederasty, the master-disciple relationship, and a search for a new utopia—we catch a hint of his openness to joining a new spiritual community.[10] Marcus's utopia includes "a new, lay priest order devoted to the purpose of spreading a uniform worldview and a truthful social doctrine."[11]

Marcus did not have the luxury of being able to devote himself to philosophical and poetic pursuits alone. Like other Jewish youths sent to the capital to seek higher education to facilitate their families' social climbing, he was expected to work in the business established by his grandfather. World War I would change that. During the war, Marcus worked with Hiller in the latter's pacifist organization, the Aktivistenbund (Activist League) and served on the staff of his pacifist-socialist journal, *Das Ziel: Jahrbuch für geistige Politik* (The aim: Yearbook for spiritual politics, 1916–1924).[12] After the war, Marcus's father lost his fortune when Prussian Posen became Polish Poznań.[13] But Marcus considered this a lucky break, freeing him of the unbearable obligation to inherit his family's wood-finishing business.

It was also as a result of this that he found Islam, presented to him as a universal brotherhood that united men of all nations and races and that, as he quickly discovered, promotes homosocial bonds. To support his family, he began working as a German tutor to young Muslim men from the Ahmadi mission, a community not unlike the George Circle, in that both consisted of disciples who were devoted to the teachings of a charismatic master originally seen as a prophet and who perceived themselves as a select few waging a war to redeem the soul of Germany.[14] He made a strong impression on the mosque community. In 1923 the Ahmadi hired him *for life* as editor of all of its German-language publications. He formed an especially close bond with the chic, handsome bachelor Maulana Sadr-ud-Din (1881–1981). Inspired by the imam, Marcus converted to Islam in 1925. It would be mistaken to consider the pre- and postconversion phases of his life to be entirely distinct. He viewed Islam in a "Jewish way," as rational and a pure expression of Jewish monotheism and, reflecting the fact that he was gay, promoted the idea that one of the core pillars of Islam is "purity," which includes pacifism, love and beauty, brotherhood, and tolerance of exceptional cases (like himself). For a dozen years, under the adopted name Hamid (Arabic: the praised one, a variant of the name Muhammad), he was the most important German in Berlin's mosque community. As the Ahmadi boasted, "The West is destined sooner or later to witness *the sunrise of Islam*, and we hasten to congratulate Dr. Marcus on his being one of the few chosen ones who are the harbingers of that sunrise."[15] Referring to Marcus as "one of the few chosen ones" speaks to his Jewish heritage. Nevertheless, he did not terminate his membership in the Jewish community or cut his ties to Jewish friends and family. Despite his conversion to Islam, Marcus did not end his attachments with friends in the homosexual rights movement or with his younger, blonde-haired Polish Catholic "friend," Roman Malicki (sometimes spelled Malecki, a fellow native of Posen), either. The year of Marcus's conversion he helped craft and signed a petition that was organized by

Hirschfeld's Institute for Sexual Science and sent to the justice minister urging repeal of Paragraph 175 of the criminal code, which penalized, in the law's language, "unnatural sexual acts" between men.[16]

DR. HAMID MARCUS

Marcus was the leading German Muslim in the Islamic community centered on the first mosque in Germany established by Muslims, the Berlin mosque completed in 1927 by the Ahmadi. Marcus played a key role in articulating the meaning of Islam for Germans, a European Islam, in his capacities as chief editor of the Ahmadi journal *Moslemische Revue* (Muslim review, 1924–1940, circulation about one thousand), in which he published nineteen articles between 1924 and 1933—the most by far by any German author; chairman of the Deutsch Muslimische Gesellschaft (German Muslim Society, 1930–1938); frequent lecturer at the society's monthly public "Islam Evenings" (attended by audiences of up to four hundred including two of his acquaintances from gay rights and literary circles, Thomas Mann and Hermann Hesse, and other German intellectuals, or so the Ahmadi claimed); and editor of a Qur'an translation, commentary, and introduction (1939, in three thousand copies).[17]

In 1932 Marcus proposed a remedy for his country's ongoing crisis: mass conversion of Germans to Islam and the establishment of an Islamic state. More allegory than solution, Marcus's essay "The Message of the Holy Prophet Muhammad to Europe" is an imaginary dialogue between two old friends—a Christian European and a Muslim longtime resident in Europe. Holding up this mirror to society to illuminate its shortcomings, Marcus uses the Christian to explain how the crisis from which Germany suffers is not merely political and economic but religious, intellectual, and cultural. The Great War of 1914–1918 has left Europeans with "shattered faith in mankind." In the subsequent upheaval, "How many millions of Europeans have just now lost their old line of direction and are looking about anxiously for a new source of guidance among the ruins of their erstwhile beliefs? Where do they find it?" The Christian turns for this to his friend's faith: "There is, however, an old saying: *Ex Oriente Lux* [Light comes from the East], and there are, more especially at the present time, many people throughout the Western countries who are looking to the East for the satisfaction of their religious hunger."[18]

But the Christian understands that religion not as an "Eastern" Islam but as a surprisingly Eurocentric, even German, one. Europe, "in its greatest times and through its greatest men, got so close to Islam as almost to shake hands with it."[19] During the era of Goethe, German Europe had reached the heights of its spiritual development. Its thinkers gathered in all the wisdom of humanity, promoted tolerance and religious freedom, and "looked on all humanity as a big brotherhood, just as Islam did."[20] None of the Enlightenment thinkers, moreover, "was a better Muslim than the greatest man of those days, the German Goethe." Goethe's poems about Muhammad, and his claim that all the monotheistic religions were equally valid paths to God "sound like the words of a real Muslim." Islam is not only the religion of the German past, Marcus concludes, but also, given its faith in the intellect and in progress, "the religion of the future."[21]

A proposal for mass conversion to Islam and establishment of an Islamic state does not figure in the historiography of Weimar Germany. While many of the new political notions of the future that Weimar writers contemplated have been explored, scholars have paid less attention to the spiritual and religious utopias envisioned in the 1920s. But as Peter Gay observes, for the "outsiders" of Imperial Germany—a group in which he includes Jews—who became the "insiders" of the Republic, "the most insistent questions revolved around the need for man's renewal, questions made most urgent and practically insoluble by the disappearance of God." Seeking answers, they "turned to whatever help they could find, wherever they could find it."[22] This book engages with the question of German responses to the rupture of World War I and the realm of imagined political possibilities in Weimar Germany by focusing on one such utopia overlooked in historiography, the German-Islamic synthesis that Marcus advocates.

In his mosque lectures and publications, including his own conversion narrative, Marcus promoted the utopian project of an Islam for Germany, demonstrating the similarities between Muslim and German values and philosophy—especially as represented by Friedrich Nietzsche—and presenting the "Muslim" views of Muhammad and Islam held by Goethe—expressed in his poems "Muhammads Gesang" (Muhammad's song) and "Hymn," and *West-östlicher Diwan* (*West-East Divan*), including its *Noten und Abhandlungen zu besserem Verständnis des west-östlichen Divans* (Notes and Essays for a Better Understanding of the *West-East Divan*) as well as his incomplete "Mohammed-Drama" (Muhammad tragedy)—as a precedent for his own. Although scholars have grappled with Goethe's views of Islam, none have explored how members of the first generation of German

Muslims engaged with his work.[23] Marcus used Goethe's "conversion" to make a bold argument about German and Islamic cultures. What Marcus envisioned was an Islam rooted in Goethe's Weimar classicism in the Enlightenment era. He saw being German as viewing the world in the Muslim Goethe's terms; for Germans, being Muslim was to read Islam in a Goethean way.

Rather than see converts such as Marcus instrumentally, as "mediators" between foreign Muslims and local Christians, we should see these new Muslims as playing an active role in responding to the crisis in German society.[24] Marcus's astonishing analysis of the crisis reflects the broader debate about the future of German society and historical revisionism that marked Weimar Germany. Facing utter and complete change, Germans debated how to rebuild society.[25] According to Marcus's acquaintance Hesse, Germans—affected by "the death and dismantling of the culture into which the elder among us were raised as children" and by the loss of "religion and customary morals"—longed for a way to satisfy their own and society's search for "new forms of religiosity and community," meaning, and harmony.[26] What could best speak to the general "impatience and disillusion with both received religious creeds and scholarly philosophies" and the "demand for new formulations, new interpretations, new symbols, new explanations"?[27] If the war's end served as a historical rupture, "at once the site of the invalidation of the past and the point of departure for the future," then what should that future look like?[28]

Peter Fritzsche observes that, in Weimar Germany, "renovation and crisis went hand in hand," and that the era's "consciousness of crisis" produced a sense of "exuberant possibility."[29] Rather than perceive Weimar "crisis talk" as defeatist, Kathleen Canning notes its "positive and productive associations," providing Germans with "confidence in their own capacity to change, innovate, and even surmount crisis."[30] In other words, "a crisis can evoke not only the pessimistic sense of a threat to the old order but also the optimistic scenario of a chance for renewal."[31] In this turbulent era, marked by its iconoclasm and syncretism, just as radical artists created "the multiperspectivism of montage" and people with wildly divergent aims deployed the Nietzschean transvaluation of values, intellectuals blended contradictory elements into blueprints for the future.[32] One such paradoxical utopian vision brought Islam together with German Enlightenment culture and romanticism. Marcus, rather than accept that Enlightenment values had been proved false or that German culture was bankrupt, reevaluated the ideas and contributions of the greatest German thinkers, especially Goethe, to make them relevant and useful for stepping back from the moral abyss and providing for a spiritually and politically sound future. Islam, "the religion of eternal self-renewal," belonged both to Germany's past and to its future, according to Marcus. It was the country's only salvation. His envisioned potential future for Germany, which had European-wide implications, was not to be. A year after Marcus made these arguments, the Nazis seized power.

Marcus was incarcerated in the Sachsenhausen concentration camp not as a Muslim or a gay but as a Jew in 1938, following the November 9–10 pogrom. He was brutalized and held in the barracks newly constructed for the thousands of recently arrested Jewish men.[33] He claimed to have remained there until a delegation led by his imam, Dr. Sheikh Muhammad Abdullah (1889–1956), gained his release ten days later. Abdullah obtained a visa for Marcus to travel to British India, where a sinecure at a Muslim organization awaited him. Just before the outbreak of World War II, using travel documents secured by the imam and with the assistance of his international network of gay acquaintances—especially his fellow liberal journalist Dr. Max Jordan—Marcus was able to escape to Basel, Switzerland, instead, where he intended to establish an Islamic cultural center and edit its journal.[34]

These facts do not fit our available frames of thinking about Muslims and Jews. Yet these facts alone challenge many deeply ingrained preconceptions about Muslim attitudes toward Jews, and even toward gays. Who were these tolerant Muslims who created an intellectual and spiritual home for Marcus and allowed him to rise to be the representative of their community? What was their understanding of Islam and religious conversion that attracted German intellectuals yet offended the Nazis? Why did they risk the standing of their community in Nazi Germany to save Marcus's life? Hugo Marcus and Muhammad Abdullah do not figure in academic and popular narratives of Muslims during World War II. Why is their extraordinary story of Jewish-Muslim interaction practically unknown? What are its implications for the history of Muslims in Europe?

The history of the Berlin mosque community and the life of its leading convert shed light on two interconnected topics: Muslim responses to Nazism and Muslim-Jewish relations. Largely because of the tendentious politics of history and memory produced by the Israeli-Palestinian struggle, we do not yet have a complete answer to the question of how Muslims responded to Nazism and the persecution of Jews. Until recently, few academic and popular responses to this question have focused on Muslims who came from Germany or had resided there for decades; most look at Muslims in the Middle East or those who were temporarily located in Berlin during World War II.[35] In fact, research on Muslims in Nazi Germany has overwhelmingly focused on Arabs and, for that matter, on a single Palestinian, the grand mufti of Jerusalem, Al-Hajj Amin al-Husayni (1897–1974), who was the guest of Hitler in Berlin and whose notoriety for working closely with the Nazi regime has overshadowed the activities of all other Muslims in Germany and, indeed, elsewhere as well.[36]

Scholarship on Muslim-Jewish relations has been seen as part of Middle Eastern history, shaped by the conflict in Palestine.[37] Immediately after World War II, supporters of the establishment of a Jewish state began campaigning to delegitimize the competing Palestinian national movement by claiming that al-Husayni's anti-Semitic views and collaboration with the Nazis were representative of the sentiment of all Palestinians and, consequently, of all Arabs.[38] Referring to the Israeli Holocaust memorial Yad Vashem's *Encyclopedia of the Holocaust*, Peter Novick notes, "The article on the Mufti is more than twice as long as the articles on Goebbels and Göring, longer than the articles on Himmler and Heydrich combined, longer than the article on Eichmann—of all the biographical articles, it is exceeded in length, but only slightly, by the entry for Hitler."[39] After recognizing nearly twenty-five thousand people over fifty years, only in 2013 did Yad Vashem accept its first Arab "righteous gentile," Dr. Muhammad Helmy, an Egyptian physician who saved the lives of four Jews in Berlin.[40] Recently Israeli prime Minister Benjamin Netanyahu even claimed the mufti gave Hitler the idea to annihilate the Jews.[41] Such preconceptions about Arabs—and Muslims—still prevail even in academic circles today. Jeffrey Herf's recent study uses al-Husayni's actions to implicate all Palestinians, Arabs, and Muslims in the perpetuation of the Shoah. He depicts Arabs as uniformly pro-Nazi and anti-Semitic, citing the "fateful collaboration" of Arab exiles in Berlin with the Nazis and the alleged widespread acceptance of Nazi ideology in the Middle East, then and even now.[42] The appetite for biographies of the mufti of Jerusalem and conspiracy theories about ties between Nazis and Islamists appears insatiable.[43]

Other scholars have rejected such a one-sided depiction, finding that Arab intellectual elites—Christian, Jewish, and Muslim—overwhelmingly rejected fascism and Nazism as ideology and practice and condemned the persecution of European Jewry, and that al-Husayni's views were peripheral in Palestine, Egypt, Syria, and North Africa.[44] Moreover, they have presented evidence that Arabs—especially Jewish Arabs—were also victims of the Nazis.[45] Yet by focusing on the

Arab Middle East and Arabs in Germany, this scholarship, too, implicitly takes the Arab experience to represent the Muslim experience more generally.

In fact, al-Husayni did not reach Berlin until 1941, eight years after the Nazi seizure of power. Pro-Nazi Muslim exiles did not take over the Berlin mosque and leadership of the only recognized Muslim organization in the Third Reich until 1942, twenty years after Muslims had first established Islamic institutions in the city. Few have yet asked how those who built the mosque responded to the Nazis and anti-Semitism.[46] For what has been largely missing from the debate until now is a "prehistory" of al-Husayni's collaboration, an introduction to the diverse Muslim groups present in the city beginning in the 1920s, a discussion of how their rivalries affected their responses to the Nazi takeover, and a narrative of the spectrum of Muslim responses to Nazism in Germany from 1933 until al-Husayni's arrival, including that of German converts to Islam.

The Muslim encounter with the Holocaust is not just a Middle Eastern story or one that concerns only Middle Easterners in wartime Europe.[47] It also is not limited to Muslims of the majority Sunni denomination. After World War I the Muslim population of Berlin included Afghans, Arabs, Persians, Tatars, Turks, South Asians, Germans and other Europeans, Sunnis and members of other Islamic confessions, secularists and Islamists, nationalists, and socialist revolutionaries.[48] Islam in Germany was first established by non-Arab Muslims, especially South Asians, including those of a minority Islamic confession, the Ahmadi. That they were not Arab, Sunni, or Middle Eastern; not connected to any nation-state's politics of memory; and not in conflict with Israel are among the many possible reasons for that neglect. Moreover, South Asia is not the usual focus of research into the relations between Muslims and Jews.[49] None have yet provided a satisfying answer as to whether they were victims, resisters, accommodators, or collaborators during the Nazi era. Also obscured in the debate is the crucial role played by German converts in the establishment of Islam. Just as not all Muslims in Germany were Arabs, neither were they all foreign. And not all German Muslims were former Christians. A question previously unexplored is the fate of German Muslims of Jewish background during the Nazi reign of terror and how other Muslims responded to their persecution. Answering this final question enables us to simultaneously explore both Muslims *and* the Holocaust and Muslims *in* the Holocaust.[50]

An analysis based on an examination of the publications and archival records of the first German Muslim communities and the personal documents and private correspondence of their leading members can address these lacunae and add something new to the literature on Muslims in Germany. From its establishment, the Ahmadi mission in Berlin attracted German avant-garde intellectuals, partly by promoting conversion as a kind of double consciousness, preaching interreligious tolerance, practicing inclusion of gays, and speaking out against racism, nationalism, and war. When German society was Nazified, the Ahmadi—like the other Muslims in Berlin—found themselves needing to make accommodationist overtures to the regime. Yet in helping Marcus to escape from Germany, they managed to thwart the Nazi reign of violence. Their actions in saving the life of their formerly Jewish co-religionist call into question the claim that Muslims shared the Nazis' deep-rooted anti-Semitism.

A close examination of Marcus and his mosque community thus moves the debate away from the Sunni Arab al-Husayni, sheds light on the history of the diverse Muslims of prewar Germany, and contributes to a growing body of literature focusing on the "lost stories" of European Muslims and Muslims of Europe who saved Jews from Nazi persecution.[51] By acknowledging Marcus's life, we can help change not only how the Muslim encounter with Nazism is depicted but also how the history of the Muslims in Europe is portrayed—when it begins, who it includes—and whose interpretation of Islam is remembered.[52]

A focus on Marcus also provides insights into two broader issues. First, it offers historians a methodological approach to the broader issue of relations between Muslims and Jews. Scholars have been inclined to examine the Muslim-Jewish encounter in terms of "cultural interaction" and "religious exchange," and the impact of that exchange across the border between different faiths. Positing clear-cut religious borders but nonexistent cultural boundaries, they have often focused on the ideas, practices, innovations, and "goods"—the secular and religious culture—that passed back and forth between the two groups.[53] Studying religious texts, language, law, ritual, sacred spaces, intellectual and spiritual movements, art, architecture, and literature, many scholars have concluded that the Muslim-Jewish relationship can be characterized as "creative coexistence," "cultural symbiosis," or even a common "Judeo-Islamic civilization" or "Judeo-Islamic tradition."[54] The best recent example of this approach is the impressive collection of state-of-the-art research edited by Abdelwahab Meddeb and Benjamin Stora, who present "points of intersection and mutual influence" between Jews and Muslims.[55] Their aim is to enable readers to figuratively cross borders, to break free of communitarianism and nationalism and think about Jews and

Muslims not in isolation but as two peoples engaged in an intimate historical relationship. Such an aim raises the question, however, of why historians should visualize Jews and Muslims crossing imaginary borders when we can look at the actual experiences of those originally of one faith who converted to the other. The liminal space between religions is also a "crossing point for people."[56]

By examining the postconversion lives of formerly Jewish Muslims instead of framing the interrelated histories of Jews and Muslims as an encounter between two distinct groups or civilizations, we can contribute to an emerging field of scholarship that renders more complex the lines that have traditionally shaped historiographical accounts of the nature of their interaction. Studying religious conversion and its aftermath is a useful strategy for moving "beyond religious borders," seeing the history of Jewish-Muslim relations from within, and recognizing the literal points of convergence between these two faiths as well as the unexpected outcomes of that encounter.[57] Conversion opens a window into the historical experience of individuals and groups of men and women within the larger framework of intercommunal relations.

Including Jewish converts to Islam and their descendants within the history of Muslim communities helps break down the reified frameworks of "Muslim" and "Jew" in two ways. First, recognizing the significant role these individuals could play despite their background brings the diverse creative forces that forged Islam and Islamic history into focus, making it possible for us to recognize the full participation of Jewish converts in Muslim political, intellectual, and religious life. Studying them also helps us move beyond borders because converts played a historical role out of proportion to their limited numbers. As leading Muslims, they formulated Islamic thought and practice through lectures and publications on Islam. Through their Qur'an translations and commentaries—still in wide use today—they have had an impact on successive generations of Muslims.[58]

Second, exploration of the new spiritual and social lives that converts created changes how we think about religious, cultural, and national boundaries. The fact that converts adopted a mix of Jewish and Muslim beliefs, practices, and identities challenges their conventional depiction. This historical approach addresses issues that cut across disciplines, illuminating the complex social and historical processes behind ontological classifications.[59] Hugo Marcus can be used to illustrate both of these points. Marcus was not an isolated case. Other Jewish intellectuals, including Muhammad Essad Bey, alias Kurban Said (Lev Nussimbaum, 1905–1942) and Muhammad Asad (Leopold Weiss, 1900–1992), converted to

Sunni Islam in Berlin in the 1920s.[60] Unlike these men, however, Marcus became a prominent Muslim in Germany while retaining membership in the Jewish community. His religious identity should give us cause to rethink where the boundary between "Muslim" and "Jew" lies, especially in historical eras when the definition of belonging was a matter of life and death.[61]

A JEWISH READING OF ISLAM, CONVERSION, AND RESPONSES TO THE "JEWISH QUESTION"

To understand Marcus's conversion to Islam, one gains little insight from scholarship that views conversion of Jews as an act of "radical assimilation" and integration.[62] Todd Endelman argues convincingly that most Jews who converted to Christianity in modern Europe did so as "a strategic or practical move," leaving the fold primarily for "nonspiritual reasons," driven by ambition, a search for fame, or a desire for status.[63] They converted to Christianity to overcome "social discrimination and cultural stigmatization" as well as "legal disabilities" and even violence.[64] Rather than become Christian, a road taken by thousands of German Jews for careerist, romantic, cultural, and nationalist motivations—in the words of Deborah Hertz, "a complex mix of opportunity and discrimination" from the end of the seventeenth century through his conversion—Marcus chose to become Muslim.[65] He was secure enough in his Germanness to choose a very newly established minority rather than the majority religion, which other Jews thought offered them the surest path to feeling that they were becoming more German and to full acceptance as a German by others. Marcus was convinced that in becoming Muslim he would not have to give up being German, unlike other Jews who became Christian to escape who they were. Marcus maintained membership in the Jewish community of Berlin for over a decade after converting to Islam. His conversion is thus atypical and hardly an act of radical assimilation, for he did not cease to legally identify himself as a Jew or end his formal ties to Judaism and Jews.

If Marcus's conversion to Islam was somewhat unusual for German Jews, his understanding of that religion was not. Susannah Heschel and others have written of the cultural identification and fascination with Islam by the German (or, more correctly, German-speaking) Jews.[66] Jews played a leading role in Islamic studies in nineteenth-century central Europe, and Jewish orientalists "tended to be more favorably inclined toward Islam than their Christian counterparts," lending their research "a more respectful" character.[67] As John Efron observes, their orientalism was colored by "Jewish sensibilities—namely, their desire for Jewish civil equality, their antipathy to Christianity, and their rejection of Orthodox Judaism" as well as their "Islamophilia, which saw them tirelessly promote the idea of a genuine Muslim-Jewish symbiosis."[68] Writing against the grain of orientalist scholarship—which denigrated Judaism and Islam alike—pursuing complete integration in German society, waging their own personal battles against professional exclusion and anti-Semitism, they aimed to reform and "de-Orientalize" Judaism and "de-exoticise" Jews.[69] The path to doing so led them to present Islam as a rational and tolerant relative or product of Judaism. They contrasted an idealized image of medieval Muslim tolerance—Muslim Al-Andalus and the Ottoman Empire as "golden ages" of Jewish-Muslim harmony, interfaith utopias of *convivencia*—with eternal Christian intolerance to chastise contemporary Germans.[70]

From the early nineteenth century, German-speaking Jewish scholars and writers such as Abraham Geiger (1810–1874), Heinrich Graetz (1817–1891), Ignaz Goldziher (1850–1921, who was Hungarian but wrote mainly in German), and Gustav Weil (1808–1889) felt deep affinities with Muslims, perceiving Islam as rational, tolerant, and philosophical; the religion that promoted science, reason, and a free spirit of enquiry; and the religion closest to the ideals of pure monotheism first introduced by prophetic Judaism, as it was "assembled from the building blocks of Jewish ideas and religious practices."[71] They contrasted Islam, in which they saw "a pure essence" that was "the living embodiment of prophetic Judaism," with contemporary Orthodox Judaism—in their view, "an affront to reason."[72] Accordingly, they "aligned Islam with Judaism in opposition to Christianity," contrasting Christian persecution of Jews especially with the tolerance granted Jews in Muslim societies.[73]

Geiger, a rabbi who played a leading role in developing Reform Judaism, was "remarkably sympathetic to Islam."[74] He criticized Christian scholars for their approach to Muhammad, finding their opinions to be the product of "outright bias and misunderstanding of the human heart."[75] He analyzed Muslim-Jewish intertextuality, influence, and parallels—such as in his 1833 study, *Was hat Mohammed aus dem Judenthume aufgenommen?* (What did Muhammad adopt from Judaism?)—promoting Muhammad as a religious reformer, expressing great respect for Islam's "pure monotheism" and "free spirit of enquiry."[76] Viewing Muslim Al-Andalus as a golden age in Jewish history, where worldly pursuits flourished, he contrasted Muslim cultivation of science and philosophy with the Church's opposition to science and reason, adding that Islam was far more tolerant than Christianity.

Graetz, the most significant Jewish historian of the nineteenth century, author of a very influential, eleven-volume *Geschichte der Juden* (History of the Jews, 1853–1876), also contrasted Muslim tolerance of Jews with Christian persecution. In his view, Jewish life in Christendom "was an unremitting Leidensgeschichte, a history of suffering."[77] In contrast, whether writing about early Islam, Muslim Al-Andalus, or the Ottoman Empire, Graetz consistently depicted the "unalloyed happiness" and "happy condition" of Jews under Muslim rule.[78] He contrasts "the happy lot of Jews under the crescent" with "their hard fate under the shadow of the cross," where they "were savagely hunted," facing "relentless persecution."[79] A Jew "who would have been burnt at the stake without ceremony in the countries of the cross, occupied a very influential position in the land of the crescent."[80] "Free to raise their heads," not having to "look out with fear and humiliation," Jews "were allowed to develop their powers."[81] Seeing in it a model for modern Jews and Germans alike, he simply imposed the view of the cultural assimilation of German Jews that he wished German Christians to adopt when he declared anachronistically of the Jews of Al-Andalus: "The Jewish inhabitants of this happy peninsula contributed by their hearty interest to the greatness of the country, which they loved as only a fatherland can be loved."[82]

Goldziher, a prominent orientalist scholar of Islam and proponent of Reform Judaism, argued that Islam, based on Jewish ideas of monotheism, became "the most important manifestation of the Semitic genius ever made."[83] Goldziher was much influenced by Geiger, viewing Islam as the proponent of scientific understanding. But he went much beyond the mere academic affinity with Islam depicted by his predecessors. After attending prayers at a mosque in Damascus in 1890, Goldziher declared, "I truly entered in those weeks into the spirit of Islam to such an extent that ultimately I became inwardly convinced that I myself was Muslim and judiciously discovered that this was the only religion which, even in its doctrinal and official formulation, can satisfy philosophical minds."[84] After attending prayers at a Cairo mosque, he said, "I only wish I could elevate my Judaism to the same rational level as Islam."[85] As Efron concludes, Geiger's "hopes for his own Jewish identity lay in Islam, his love of which saw him become a Muslim in all but name. He testified, 'Although I never pretended to be a Muslim, I termed my monotheism Islam, and I did not lie when I said I believed the prophecies of Muhammad.'"[86]

Weil was another nineteenth-century promoter of reformed Judaism and Islam, rationalism, and *Bildung*—the individual journey of self-improvement and refinement best articulated by Goethe. Holder of a chair in oriental studies, he wrote a very positive biography of Muhammad (1843), presenting him as a rational reformer.[87] Weil even went further than the other writers in comparing Judaism and Islam, for he did not claim that Islam was but a branch of Judaism but rather that it was a purified version of it, the Enlightened religion.[88]

Positive views of Islam compelled some Jewish contemporaries of Marcus—most famously, the writer Essad Bey and the philosopher and writer Muhammad Asad—to formally and publicly convert to Islam. Lev Nussimbaum was the son of a wealthy Russian Jewish oil baron from Baku who emigrated with his father to Berlin in 1921, where he studied beginning in 1922 at the Seminar for Oriental Languages at the Friedrich Wilhelm University.[89] "Driven by a mysterious compulsion" and an attraction to all things "Oriental," and "Orientalizing" himself completely, this Easterner converted to Islam at the Ottoman Embassy in Berlin that same year, becoming Essad Bey (adding Mohammad later).[90] He enjoyed wearing "full Muslim drag"; photos show him in a "white turban, with a stone ornament and a spraying feather in the center, enormous multi-hoop earrings and rings" on his fingers, "eyeshadow and lipstick and even a painted mole above his lip," and classmates considered his a "romantic conversion to Islam."[91] He viewed himself as a "complete cosmopolitan" and an "Oriental," who "based his life and career on an urgent desire to explain the East to the West, all but rhapsodizing on the superiority of the former to the latter," a place free of anti-Semitism, imagining Jews and Muslims sharing a "common, harmonious past and future together," like other Jewish writers in Weimar Berlin seeking "refuge from the new political realities in esoteric visions of sympathetic Orientalism."[92] After the Nazis turned against him, he fled to Positano, Italy, in 1938 where he passed away. His turban-topped tombstone, inscribed in Arabic, faces Mecca.[93]

Essad Bey may have been one of the founding members of the Islamische Gemeinde (Islamic Community) in Berlin in 1923 and its affiliated student group; he gained international fame as an "expert on the East," with over a dozen works and two novels (under the pen name Kurban Said) about "the Orient," including a biography of Muhammad, but his publications drew the ire of the city's Muslims who accused him of slander for "discrediting the orient in the eyes of Europeans."[94] His former Muslim friends turned against him for "having insulted 'the feelings of the Islamic world with his literary scams.'" Worse, they called him a Jewish swindler, casting doubt on the validity of his conversion.[95]

As Essad Bey was vilified by Muslims in his own day, scholars and German-speaking Muslims today have taken Asad to be the prototypical "Western" convert to Islam and have imagined that his experience was normative and representative; considered "Europe's gift to Islam" and even "a Martin Luther for Islam," he has been the subject of film. A prolific writer, journalist and intellectual, religious reformer and diplomat, Asad has long been the subject of popular and academic writing.[96]

Asad, however, is an ironic choice for a model German-speaking Muslim. To become Muslim in 1926, Asad "cut all mental and emotional ties to Western civilization, which he denounced as decadent and in decline."[97] "Infatuated with almost everything Arab," and motivated by a belief that to accept a way of life as binding, one must "pursue it among like-minded people," Asad spent his postconversion life outside Europe.[98] He became fully Muslim and left his Europeanness behind. Rather than serving as a bridge between East and West, Asad traveled from West to East and never looked back. For decades he lived like an Arab, wearing only Arab dress, speaking only Arabic, and marrying Arab women to become Muslim, perceiving an intractable chasm between the materialist "West" and the Muslim "East."[99] Asad's "self-orientalizing"—his preference for being "clad in Bedouin garb and riding a camel through the pristine deserts of Arabia"—and views of Muslims were marred by European orientalist prejudice.[100] Such an exoticizing, ethnic or race-based approach to religious belonging was not unusual for an era in which a European convert to Islam could boast that his change of religion was motivated by the fact that he would be happy only with dark skin and that he looked forward to becoming browned by the sun after making the hajj so that he could paint his self-portrait, as a brown man in a white turban.[101] The only thing brown about Marcus were his eyes.

Marcus would be a better standard for German converts to Islam to follow, for Marcus came into contact with Muslims in Germany, and he never doubted that one could be German *and* Muslim, seeing correlations in basic approaches to life, and could live as a German Muslim, never leaving German-speaking Europe. Marcus used the same tropes as earlier Jewish writers—reform, rationalism, science, philosophy, and tolerance—to "de-exoticise" and "de-orientalize" Islam and Muslims (rather than Judaism and Jews). Unlike earlier Jewish scholars such as Geiger, he neither aimed to redeem Judaism in the eyes of Jews and Christians alike by reforming it nor was inspired to return to reinvigorate Judaism after investigating Islam. Marcus interpreted Islam to show that it is compatible with German culture, values, and philosophy, rooted in Germany and German history. Unlike Asad, who sought to leave his previous central European life behind to begin anew elsewhere as a Muslim, Marcus sought to reveal the convergences in German and Muslim history, culture, philosophy, and values.[102] Marcus rejected a number of paths taken by other Jews like himself. Rather than "self-orientalize" by making himself into an Arab, like Asad, or by migrating to Palestine and having relations with and writing explicit, erotic, orientalist-soaked verse about Arab youth, like the gay and *haredi* (Orthodox) Dutch Jewish poet Jacob Israel de Haan (b. 1881, Smilde, the Netherlands; d. 1924, assassinated in Jerusalem[103]), and rather than seeing himself as a "noble oriental" straddling East and West, like an earlier generation of German-speaking Jews fascinated with Islam and his contemporary Essad Bey, Marcus never doubted his ability to remain German and live in Germany after becoming Muslim.[104] Unlike Essad Bey, who proudly sat for a portrait in red fez following his conversion, Marcus was nearly always photographed in "Western" dress, bareheaded.[105]

This Jewish man's life marked by an embrace of Islam and by his becoming a proponent of a new way of life raises the question of how his participation in universal movements compares with that of other German Jews. In one sense Marcus's move is familiar when we consider how German Jewish men of his generation have long been depicted by scholars. George Mosse famously argued that in response to "the Jewish Question," these Jews sought "a personal identity beyond religion and nation," which led ultimately to a left-wing identity, as socialism offered egalitarianism.[106] Adam Sutcliffe concurs that Jews have played a disproportionate role in left-wing political movements and "have almost always been vigorously anti-clerical and are usually considered as antithetical to religion in every way." Yet, "despite their hostility to all traditional religious practice and their ambivalent or even hostile attitude to the Jewish collectivity," the thought of a long line of intellectuals from Baruch Spinoza, Saint-Simonist Gustave d'Eichtal, Heinrich Heine, Ludwig Börne, and Moses Hess to Karl Marx was infused with "the trace of a Jewishly religious approach to the ethical meaning of history."[107] This was more evident for a later generation of Jewish intellectuals, including Martin Buber, Walter Benjamin, Georg Lukács (who had studied with Simmel), and Gershom Scholem, who combined redemptive Jewish messianic religious thought and radical secular utopian beliefs.[108] David Biale argues that from the seventeenth century through the twentieth century, the most important modern Jewish secular thinkers rejected particularism associated with Judaism and embraced secular universalism instead.[109] He argues that "the vehemence with which some secular Jews reject Judaism and embrace abstract universalism certainly appears to be peculiarly—if not uniquely—Jewish."[110] Thus, as Sutcliffe argues, Jewish espousal of universal views should be seen in dialogue with Judaism, "as an inversion of normative Judaism, rather than as an exit from it."[111]

Where does this depiction of German Jews leave Marcus? Why should Jewish utopianists only be associated with the Left and with secularism? And why should faith in eighteenth-century ideals culminate in a turn to nonreligious universalism known as socialism? Marcus, who was rather conservative, did not construct an identity beyond religion, for he converted to Islam.

Educated in a humanistic Gymnasium, Marcus remained devoted to the classic liberal formulation of Bildung as individual self-development leading to the transcendence of difference culminating in universal harmony and tolerance.[112] Yet, unlike other Weimar-era Jews, Marcus saw Bildung's perfect expression in Islam. Marcus's writings, especially his discussions of Goethe, are similar to Weimar-era German Jewish adulation of the writer who first formulated the concept of Bildung.[113] Dissimilar to other Germans of Jewish background, however, Marcus analyzed Goethe's connections not with Judaism but with Islam. He asserted that he was attracted by Islam's Bildung, its encouragement of individual cultivation of reason and spiritual potential leading to a society founded on race-blind universalism. As many Weimar Jews adopted the antirational ideals of modernism, romanticism, kabbalah (Jewish mysticism), haredism (Jewish orthodoxy), and Zionism (Jewish nationalism also imagined as a form of self-orientalization, a return to the Orient to revive the Jewish spirit) instead, ironically, it is the anti-Zionist, Muslim convert Marcus (minus the socialism) who best illustrates Mosse's German Jew who remains loyal to Bildung and dedicated to rationalism to the very end.[114]

HANS ALIENUS

Marcus's life was saved by his taking refuge in Switzerland in 1939. He refused to return to the Federal Republic of Germany, which persecuted gay men by implementing Paragraph 175's harsher version introduced by the Nazis. Just as he was known as "Hamid" to Muslims, Marcus was called "Hans Alienus" (Latin: Hans the Stranger) by other gay men, a reference to his being a German exile. Writing under that pseudonym, he was a frequent contributor to the international gay—or, in the language of the day, homophile—journal *Der Kreis—Le Circle—The Circle*, first published in Zürich in 1943, the only (primarily) German-language gay journal (until 1951), which featured articles "from members of the prewar German homosexual rights movement."[115] At its height in the late 1950s it had a subscription of two thousand, nearly half outside Switzerland. Everywhere, it was a forbidden magazine, read in secret, passed from hand to hand; the lifeblood of a secret organization that hosted costume balls. It was as an island of continuity from Weimar Germany.[116] Marcus published fiction, sometimes containing Islamic elements, and nonfiction in the journal from the age of sixty-eight to eighty-five, from 1948 to 1965.

Marcus's decades-long association with Hirschfeld and Hiller, his life-long activism fighting for gay rights, and his nonfiction writing on homosexuality—including a post-World War II essay on Goethe's approach to homosexuality and a piece he penned at the age of eighty-five in commemoration of Hirschfeld—point to his support of the "Jewish" and "liberal" model of gay identity. That model minoritized gays as members of a biologically determined, distinct subculture with a fixed nature that was homosexually inclined; promoted gender inversion to explain their desire; relied on the sciences and medical research; and emerged from progressive, emancipatory, and liberal politics seeing homosexuality as a subculture analogous with race and ethnicity and especially comparable to Jewishness, deserving legal protections.[117] Marcus argued that Goethe anticipated sexologist Hirschfeld's scientific theory of sexual intermediaries (*Zwischenstufentheorie*). Yet Marcus's homoerotic fiction writing—from a novella he published as a twenty-year-old to his last short story published when he was seventy-five—show that he also identified with the competing version of gay identity, the "Hellenist" and "illiberal" model. That model, linked with Adolf Brand (1874–1945, killed in Berlin in an Allied bombing) and Hans Blüher (1888–1955) and spurred by Nietzsche's illiberal rereading of the Greek tradition, was universalizing, presenting gay desire not as the province of a numerical minority but of all men, a building-block of masculine society especially in the military and schools as exemplified by the ancient Greeks; it was an understanding of homosexuality that was cultural rather than biological and masculinist; it objected to medicalization and psychologization; and it was intertwined with conservative thought.[118] Synthesizing both models, various writers and artists created a gay literary culture with its own understanding of sexuality and gay identity and focusing on the cultural aspects of same-sex desire.[119] Marcus was one of them, for in his work we find attention to the aesthetic nature of homosexuality that reflects Thomas Mann (b. 1875, Lübeck; d. 1955, Zürich) as much as Goethe.

Just as he had modeled his own conversion narrative on the "conversion" narrative of Goethe and sought precedent in his own appreciation for Muhammad and Islam in his, Marcus turned to the writing and life of Goethe as personal and literary precedent and legitimizer for his own gay feelings and identity. For just as Goethe's poetry and prose exhibit unmistakable praise for Muhammad and Islam as well as apparent adoption of Islamic views, compelling German Muslims to consider him to have been a Muslim, so does Goethe's writing—particularly his early poetry, such as "An den Mond" (To the moon), and "Ganymede," written around the same period as his "Muhammad's Song" and "Erlkönig" (The elf king), as well as his prose, including *Faust*, *Italian Journey*, *Letters from Switzerland*, *Wilhelm Meisters Wanderjahre* (Wilhelm Meister's journeyman years), and then *West-East Divan*, written when he was mature—offer explicit homoeroticism, admiration of male beauty and love between male friends, and the theme of pederasty, giving rise to queer readings of the man and his age.[120] Marcus is the first and perhaps only writer to maintain that Goethe was Muslim and gay like him.

Scholars have found that while Goethe and those like him could not have had a gay identity, which emerged in the late nineteenth century, they were part of a subculture based on same-sex desire whose signifiers prefigured the identity of the modern homosexual. Among the signifiers were art history, Greek antiquity, and culture, particularly the propensity for male-male love (such as the figures Adonis [god of beauty and desire, shorthand for an extremely attractive youthful male] and Ganymede [model for the Greek social custom of *paiderastía*, the socially acceptable erotic relationship between a man and a youth]), Biblical traditions, orientalism (a region stretching from the Muslim world to Italy where one found classical civilization and sexuality perpetuated), Switzerland, and the cult of friendship.[121] Friendship between men, which surpassed a man's love for a woman, was seen as an effusive, passionate, and intimate relationship. If these were signifiers of homosexuality for Goethe, so are they in the fiction of Marcus, where one finds the erotic themes of the beauty of the male nude, the superiority of male-male unrequited desire to male-female consummated love, temptation and awakened yet never consummated desire, the meaning of true friendship, Christian imagery, and ancient Greek mythology.

Queer Muslims are hardly conceivable in most discourse about Islam and homosexuality in Europe today. How much more is this the case for a Muslim man before gay liberation.[122] Unlike as is often the case for Muslims in Europe today, however—following the mass migration of Muslims to the continent after World War II—no one could ask Marcus, "Where do you come from?" as he was German. But as with the Far Right today, the Nazis told him, "You do not belong here," but because he was also Jewish, not because he was Muslim. His answer, "I am from here," was as unacceptable to the Nazis then as it is to Islamophobes in Europe today.[123] A biography of Hugo Marcus helps us to queer Jewish and Islamic Studies simultaneously.

Marcus is relatively unknown beyond a tiny circle of historians of Islam in interwar Germany and an equally small group of people knowledgeable about the history of the gay rights movement.[124] What is published about him, however, is factually incorrect and does not encompass all parts of the man: German, Jewish, Muslim, and gay. A proper accounting of his life illustrates the limits of scholarship, which does not take into account the intersectionality of legal, political, and social frames affecting a figure with multiple identities like Hugo Marcus. *German, Jew, Muslim, Gay* is the first biography devoted to examining the life of the German born as Hugo Marcus who became the Muslim Hamid (chapter 2), who the Nazis forced to be renamed Israel (chapter 3), a gay man who never called himself gay but fought for homosexual rights (chapter 1), who chose to write gay fiction under the pen name Hans Alienus during his decades of Swiss exile (chapters 4 and 5). He saw Goethe as his pole star: model German, model gay, and model Muslim, whose life and writing offered a solution to Germany's cultural crisis.

CHAPTER 1

Fighting for Gay Rights in Berlin, 1900–1925

We do not ask whether the devotion of . . . Goethe's Ferdinand to Egmont . . . has anything to do with a witch-hunting section of the law or a silly medical category: rather, we have always believed that we find in these relationships an essential, constitutive element of German culture.

Stefan George[1]

That which is natural cannot be immoral.

Friedrich Nietzsche, quoted in Magnus Hirschfeld, *Sappho and Socrates* (1896), the founding manifesto of the gay liberation movement[2]

To celebrate his twenty-first birthday, Marcus traveled to the Isle of Capri in the summer of 1901, prior to enrolling at Berlin University. He had his portrait taken, the size of a passport photo, at the nineteenth-century luxury hotel in the center of the pedestrian area, the Grand Hotel Quisisana, "a veritable oasis of relaxation, immersed in a luxuriant park," and "the perfect expression of Capri's *Dolce Vita*." Middle-aged German steel magnate Friedrich Alfred Krupp (b. 1854), a friend of the kaiser, spent several months at the hotel each year.[3]

In the portrait, the brown-eyed Marcus wears a dark wool, three-piece suit, vest jacket buttoned, a striped ascot over a starched white shirt.[4] He sports a thin mustache and turns his head to his left, eyes raised. The picture is not flattering, displaying all of Marcus's angular features. The viewer gets a full profile of Marcus's large right ear, bony right cheek, and large sharp nose. He has a full head of hair, mussed on top, yet with clear razor line above his right ear.

He chose to visit Capri because men like Marcus considered Italy to be part of the "Orient," where love between males could be expressed without reprobation. In so doing, he was following his role model, Goethe. Goethe chose *Et in Arcadia ego* as his *Italian Journey*'s (1816) motto, although he first used the German translation, *Auch ich in Arkadien*: "Even I managed to get to paradise." Arcadia is a link "between homosexuality and the Orient," which reaches as far north as Italy, "a homo-utopia, an Arcadia, where sexuality was freer."[5] Goethe's Italian journey can be interpreted as a journey of sexual awakening in a land that was "a site of homosexual desire in the minds of many eighteenth-century Europeans," especially those men who loved men, known as "warm brothers."[6] Goethe declared how "morally salutory" it was to live "in the midst of a sensual people."[7] Along with his artwork from the trip, including "images of male nudes with prominent genitalia" and erupting volcanoes, he included such couplets as this in his Venetian epigrams: "Boys I have also loved / But I prefer girls / If I'm tired of her as a girl / She can serve me as a boy as well!"—which provides evidence of either his own experience or at least his knowledge of gay sex practices.[8]

The connection between Italy and love that had been prohibited in central Europe continued into the early twentieth century when Marcus visited. The Napoleonic Code (1804) had eliminated antisodomy laws in Italy and thereafter "specific resorts in particular—Taormina or Capri, for example—became playgrounds for wealthy elites who had been disgraced and forced into exile from England or Germany."[9] And for sex tourists. Goethe describes Taormina as "paradise on earth" in his *Italian Journey*. As the French Revolution gave Jews equal citizenship in France, Napoleon emancipated Jews in the territories he conquered, liberating them from ghettoes in Italy. In 1928 Marcus's lifelong friend of Jewish background, Kurt Hiller, noted that "love between man and youth was no more excluded from the heroic and golden ages of Ancient Greece, than it was from the most illustrious period of Islamic culture, or from the age of Michelangelo."[10] Gays situated homosexuality in the Orient, and traveled to the Orient or had relations with people from the region visiting Europe because engaging in such practices there or with people from there was seen as less taboo.

As Marcus recalled, his fellow hotel guest, Krupp, "was the first person, whom I heard about, that felt as I did."[11] Marcus had "mystical ideas about such a man of 'this' type: how he should look and his probable lifestyle. Although I, too, was a youth of 'this' type, it did not occur to me to compare [myself to him]. And now he was the first that I saw, and no less a person than Krupp." Marcus wondered whether the industrialist was a living Goethe. He saw him instead, as so many crowded about seeking his attention and patronage, as a Roman emperor.[12] He imagined Krupp as Hadrian, and himself as Antinous, his beautiful Greek youth beloved, after whose tragic death the Roman emperor built a city in his honor in Egypt and made him into a God. In Marcus's eyes, "Our relationship would be no less dignified" than the famous homosexual couple of antiquity.[13]

He felt Krupp and he shared a secret bond. Marcus was ashamed, "not that I could have a relationship [with him], but that I played with an idea that had no prospect [of becoming reality]. But I was twenty years old, I always went [to the island] alone."[14] Knowing that Krupp had relationships with other young men made it a real possibility. Rather than demanding money and gifts like the others, Marcus fantasized giving himself to "powerful Alfred" *as* the gift. He was enticed by the idea of "for once being able to give something to the man who always only gives and is sought."[15] But what if Krupp offered him a ring, or some other precious object? Marcus mused how "I would say: what should I do with rings? I don't garland myself with golden things. Better: it is too little! . . . my father, you know, gives me 150 Marks per month spending money." He came up with a plan for the industrialist to give his money to an artist friend instead. Better: out of love for Marcus, he would improve the lot of his tens of thousands of factory workers. Having the ear of the kaiser, he would ensure that the eight-hour workday became universal: "That would be a gift, worthy of you and also me. Aren't you also interested in the school question, the peace question?" he asked him rhetorically in his mind. He imagined Krupp thinking about these issues, long after he had forgotten about Marcus, who would not have crossed his path in vain.[16] But such conversations never occurred. The shy Marcus observed Krupp from a distance, a wealthy man surrounded by a circus of ambitious, pleading artists, painters, and singers. The young man felt frustrated for living a "fantasy life. At home [in Germany] I had led a fantasy life. I came to Italy to finally experience reality. And now in Italy I also only experienced fantasies."[17]

The fantasy turned to nightmare. A little over a year after Marcus's stay at the hotel, in November 1902, the Social Democratic journal *Vorwärts* outed Krupp in an article titled "Krupp on Capri," alleging that he had sexual relations with local boys and men, and that his boyfriend was an eighteen-year-old barber and musician named Adolfo Schiano. Italian newspapers were also filled with these claims. A week later Krupp committed suicide.[18] As Marcus later wrote, "One can be against the Paragraphs" (175 of the German Criminal Code, which penalized homosexual relations), as were the Social Democrats, "yet nevertheless use them to drive supposed opponents to their death."[19] Marcus remembers his brother telling him about the *Vorwärts* article and then "the next morning called to me: Krupp is dead!"[20] Marcus thought of how "I sat down quietly, said nothing. For him Krupp was the cannon king in Essen; for me he was a person. I knew him though, had experienced so much with him," if in his fantasies. "I was as if hit [in the gut], terribly upset for weeks; now for the first time I felt very close to him. Perhaps I loved him now." Seeing a silver lining in the cloud of his bereavement, Marcus realized that "at last, because of the Krupp Affair, our cause, our secret—associated with powerful people and kings—for the first time was shouted out loud throughout the whole world, on all the streets of every city." While he could not openly express his mourning to anyone, "for me it was a blessing at least to be able to speak with some neighbors about the sensational news and to be able to express my grief behind this mask."[21]

JOURNEY FOR SELF-UNDERSTANDING, SEARCH FOR UTOPIA: GAY, JEWISH, AND GERMAN IN EARLY-TWENTIETH-CENTURY BERLIN

Similar to many other scions of bourgeois, liberal, and highly Germanized Jewish provincial families from Posen in Imperial Germany, Marcus migrated to Berlin. Like other Jewish youths sent to the capital to pursue higher education to expedite the rise in the family's social status—Marcus chose to study philosophy at its university, where Jews were overrepresented—Marcus was also expected to be employed in the family business. After graduating from the Friedrich Wilhelm Gymnasium in Posen in 1898, Marcus moved to Berlin for vocational training in the Office of Heavy Industry "with the aim of taking over the wood finishing business handed down from my grandfather."[22] Alone in Berlin, in 1900 he became an early member of the Wissenschaftlich-humanitäres Komitee (WhK; Scientific Humanitarian Committee, 1897) the first organization in the world to campaign for gay rights.[23] In the first decade of the twentieth century, Marcus became a close friend of Magnus Hirschfeld, one of the WhK's founders and chairman, and its leader for three decades, whom he admired and adored.

To try to understand his own feelings for and friendships with other young men, Marcus wrote his first novella, *Das Frühlingsglück: Die Geschichte einer ersten*

Liebe (Spring luck: The tale of a first love) in 1900.[24] The turgid tale is an extended meditation on the superiority of homosexual to heterosexual relations. The main protagonist, fourteen-year-old Guido Erhard, is confused by the strong feelings he has both for a young woman, Adeline, and his classmate, Ernst. Guido loves Adeline but does not care if his love is reciprocated, quoting Goethe: "So what if I love you, that is none of your business."[25] The love is more about himself than his object. What also stands in his way is the fact Guido is a self-absorbed idealist who wants to fight for a cause such as human rights, Napoleon's revolution (implying the new freedoms granted Jews and men who love men), and social justice.[26] For all of his interest in her, Guido is unable to become close to Adeline. More than custom and propriety separate them. He is much closer to Ernst. Guido confesses he would often become distracted from his homework by erotic, perhaps homoerotic "dreams that confused and frightened him so that he blushed involuntarily."[27] The youth revolt against religion, forsaking belief in God for the science of the natural world. Guido expresses his admiration of Ernst's courage to open himself up to him, "but with that their friendship ended."[28] After this they avoid each other, scared of how vulnerable they had become from sharing their most intimate secrets regarding their true feelings about society's values. Perhaps it is their parents who want to separate them; Ernst is sent away to another Gymnasium. Years later they find themselves studying philosophy at the same university, happy to be reacquainted.

Just as Guido is appalled at the thought of men and women having sex, Ernst criticizes possessive, romantic, heterosexual love. He declares heterosexual love to be "the greatest misfortune of humanity."[29] Just when you feel good about yourself, and are satisfied with life, he explains, along comes a beautiful girl, and you fall in love, which is like being imprisoned. Love brings passion and jealousy, but then the love quickly ends, and you are left weak and listless, all your greatest powers exhausted. Why bother? He consoles his friend, saying they should feel lucky never to have personally experienced the disappointment of (consummated heterosexual) love.[30] At the same time, Guido dreams of having a relationship with Adeline. He imagines she can fulfill his "youthful dream of love," which for him is no different than friendship between two men, defined as where two "comrades" love each other and go through thick and thin together.[31] Guido and Adeline grow sentimentally attached and yearn for each other's touch. But when both are driven by "an endless yearning," when she is in his arms and both desired to be even closer—he is incapable of taking that step.[32] Perhaps it is the photograph of Guido's friend Ernst in his wallet that serves as a reminder of where his heart lay, a reminder of the superiority of homosocial relationships.[33]

The theme of the inferiority of heterosexual love is best illustrated by a conversation between Guido and Adeline where he discusses a Pole "who spoke only of his fatherland"—which had been partitioned out of existence—"like a dead bride."[34] Adeline responds by sharing with him how she had considered converting to Judaism when she had read Heinrich Heine's poetry and considered how the "unlucky" Jewish people, and especially the poet Judah Halevi, "had longed to return to their beautiful, lost fatherland, which they loved like a far-away lover. . . . Can you imagine a greater misfortune than such a love?" "Oh yes," Guido responds, "loving a beautiful young woman." He explains that "it is a great misfortune when one loves his fatherland as a young bride, when the young bride is dead, and lies in her coffin, and the man lives his entire life with his yearning unfulfilled." He continues, "There is only one misfortune that is greater. . . . Loving a beautiful young woman."[35] To Guido, heterosexual relations are as hopeless as pining for a lost homeland.

As Guido is incapable of consummating his desire for Adeline, they agree to separate so as not to ruin the ideal of platonic love, ensuring that "young love remains pure, unadulterated by everyday life and hot passion."[36] He considers their intimacy a great gift.[37] It is an intimacy without any physicality, a love he deems superior. Illustrating the catastrophe of heterosexual relations, the novel ends with a duel caused by competition for the love of a young woman, where Ernst is seriously wounded. He and Guido have to flee.[38] Guido and Adeline were comrades, but their spring love was over and so was their youth.[39]

The novella exemplifies Goethe's principles of Bildung, the physical as well as the "psychological, creative, and artistic development" of an individual.[40] As described by Wilhelm in *Wilhelm Meisters Lehrjahre* (*Wilhelm Meister's Apprenticeship*, 1795), that path to self-development, striving for betterment, and rejection of illusions about the self is a journey of self-discovery. The path entails Wilhelm's "irresistible desire to attain the harmonious development of my personality such as was denied me by my birth," through efforts to improve his physical powers, the development of his mind and taste, and the ability to discern what is good and beautiful, to the point where "a cultured human being can appear in the full splendor of his person," where "mind and body keep step in all one does."[41] *Wilhelm Meisters Lehrjahre*, often named the prototype for the *Bildungsroman*, dominated by its protagonist's search to find himself, "showed the processes whereby its young protagonist sets aside misleading social and cultural influences to discover who he really is and develops himself to the best of his abilities to rejoin society as a productive member."[42] Discovering "who he really is," the protagonist comes to terms with his desires, particularly those for members of the same sex. For this reason Marcus chose a quote of Mignon from *Wilhelm Meisters Lehrjahre* as *Das Frühlingsglück*'s motto: "I lived indeed untouched by care / And yet I felt deep sorrow there."[43] Marcus dedicated the book to "all" like him, "who are young" and facing the same confusion about the border between love and friendship. As in Goethe's *Wilhelm Meister's Journeyman Years* (1821), the sequel to *Wilhelm Meister's Apprenticeship*, on a hot summer day the two male friends undress and swim together.[44] Wrestling on the riverbank their reverie is broken when they spot a female figure from afar. As she comes closer, Guido suddenly jumps back into the water and is gripped by a "hot ire against the woman" because she had spoiled their bliss.[45]

A year after he published his novel, Marcus's own paradise was lost when he was joined in Berlin by his parents. He served as an assistant to Joseph, his industrialist father, in the family business while continuing to write. In June 1902 a twenty-two-year-old Marcus published a short article in the *Allgemeinen Deutschen Universitätszeitung* (General German university newspaper) in the "Religion and Science" column entitled "In Sachen eines philosophischen Gymnasiums" (On the matter of a philosophical gymnasium).[46] He may have based his ideas on his own experience, been influenced by Stefan George's ideas about educational reform, or been inspired by Thomas Mann's character Hanno Buddenbrook, from his first novel, *Buddenbrooks*—a delicate, effeminate, precocious piano virtuoso tormented by his manly classmates. Marcus proposed the establishment of a philosophical Gymnasium as a third type of secondary school alongside those devoted to either the classical or mathematic and natural science tracks. He reasoned that, while every care is taken to develop the minds of students inclined either toward the humanities or the sciences, no educational institutions existed for those with a philosophical and artistic tendency and that "the given paths of education are inadequate for all personalities." For this third type of student, a philosophical education would be necessary where, "after being taught a moderate amount of mathematics and a single foreign language, at the sixth form philosophy would become the focal point of their education."[47]

Prior to publishing this piece Marcus wrote to a number of people asking their opinion on his proposal. Among them were a twenty-six-year-old Thomas Mann, who received his letter in April 1902, half a year after publishing *Buddenbrooks*, which would earn him the Nobel Prize in literature.[48] Marcus, who had read *Buddenbrooks*—revealing himself as having the same surname as one of the book's characters (the confidential clerk and future partner of the firm, Herr Marcus), had also recently published his first novel, *Das Frühlingsglück*, with E. Pierson's which also published the monthly *Das Zwanzigste Jahrhundert* (The twentieth century), to which Mann contributed.[49] Nevertheless, he signed his letter under a pseudonym, Dr. Hans Marco.[50] Writing under a pseudonym and changing his name would be lifelong habits for Marcus.

In his response, Mann discusses how at the end of his novel he "ironizes" the modern Gymnasium through his depiction of the weakling, weepy Hanno, passionate only about his music, the last, yet never to be realized hope of a "socially, economically, and psychologically declining," decayed family.[51] What he aimed to show was the "contrast between the timid incapacity of this nervous-artistic individual and how life is," as manifested at school. He expresses how he was sympathetic to sensitive Hanno, "and I directed my ridicule and bitterness toward the stupid and brutal power that frightened his poor soul."[52] But he continues with the stark thought that "life itself is stupid and brutal, and is always right, not those who are too weak or too good for it." He asks Marcus to recall a section of the novel where he portrays a student condemned as the "shame of the class" by the teacher, a judgment accepted by all the other students—except for sensitive Hanno, who responds with "abhorrence, fear, and revulsion."[53] In his novel, Mann writes, "Most of this class of twenty-five young folk, being of sound and strong constitution, armed and prepared to wage the battle of life as it is, took things just as they found them, and did not at this moment *feel any offence or uneasiness*. Everything seemed to them to be quite in order." Mann comments how this passage expresses his "total skepticism and pessimism," which is also his personal view of the much-discussed school question. He opines that "school is preparation for life, as it actually is, which is good and rightly so." Mann accepts this is "a melancholic truth," but that "it is a truth."[54] Then he turns to ridicule Marcus's call for a philosophical Gymnasium.

Mann labels a Gymnasium for artists, poets, and exceptional people, "if you'll excuse me—a utopia," and states that Marcus must himself be "a poet and an exceptional person himself to believe that there is any need" for such a school. He asks whether "the state is obliged to take care of a minority of musically-inclined posh individuals *who will never be of any use to it*?" He claims that "we poets and artists are already seen as a very dubious tribe." He argues that if Marcus's proposal were to be realized, "even at the age of fifteen we would behave badly at the most philosophical gymnasium," and even in an improved world "we would always be full of opposition, protest, and irony, always alien, different, and 'better' than the others, unfit to be bourgeois." Turning ever nastier, Mann ends his letter with the fiendish remark that "those among us who cannot compensate society for their total uselessness by the delight of their talents, would do well to perish as soon as possible, instead of astonishing the public by means of such immodest demands as 'philosophical gymnasiums.'"[55]

After reading *Buddenbrooks* Marcus was not wrong in assuming Mann would have supported his idea; he must have been bitterly disappointed to have received such a response rejecting the philosophical high school as a utopian idea.[56] Mann's rejection of the idea culminates in the demand that such exceptional people "perish as quickly as possible," a verdict sparing only those who can "compensate for their total uselessness to society by the delight of their talents." One scholar has expressed being "almost frightened" by the directness of the statement, not alleviated by irony, and directed not toward a fictional character as in one of his novels but toward a real person whom Mann does not even know. Perhaps sensing how harsh he had responded, Mann hastens to end the letter praising Marcus for his "noble-minded endeavors," which earned Mann's "heart-felt sympathy."[57]

Ever the utopian, the following year Marcus responded to Mann's rejection in print in his study of the education problem, *Die Allgemeine Bildung in Vergangenheit, Gegenwart und Zukunft: Eine historisch-kritisch-dogmatische Grundlegung* (General education in the past, present, and future: A historical-critical-dogmatic foundation), where he argues philosophy can be used "to complete and deepen education."[58] Although he does not attack Mann's response directly in the study, he must have had it in mind when he argues, for example, that "the goal of all education is to produce useful members of society."[59] There are also hints of a response to Mann's rejection in Marcus's 1904 work, *Meditationen* (Meditations, discussed below), such as where he writes, "It fills us with regret when we read that great men were hostile to great trends of their time. The reason for such a negative attitude was not the content of a trend, but the Nietzschean feeling of opposition."[60] Nevertheless, Marcus remained an admirer of Mann's work. Marcus includes Mann's *Buddenbrooks* among his long list of favorite authors and works. Others include Plato's *Dialogues*; Goethe's *Faust*, *Werther*, and *Letters from Switzerland*; the lesbian novelist and WhK member Sophie Höchstetter's (1873–1943, murdered at

Dachau) *Sehnsucht, Schönheit, Dämmerung* (Desire, beauty, twilight), which links "the artistic production of women and love between women"; and Friedrich Paulsen's (1846–1908) *Geschichte des gelehrten Unterrichts* (History of learned teaching).[61] More significant than the effect that Mann's letter had on Marcus is the effect Marcus's letter had on Mann: one scholar claims that it is one of the earliest, if not the earliest, documentation of Mann perceiving of himself as a writer and the first appearance in this letter of certain motifs such as the "exceptional situation of the artist" that will appear and play a significant role in his later work.[62]

Among Marcus's other early major publications is a study that would foreshadow his entire life and work. Published when he was a twenty-four-year-old doctoral student, Marcus's *Meditationen* consists of his reflections from the period 1895–1903, when his father finally allowed him to study at university. The themes that predominate are those already encountered in his coming-of-age novel and article on the education problem: love between men and boys; the master-disciple relationship; the ideal of male friendship; and a search for a new utopia.

The theme of pederasty—intergenerational love between men and young boys, expressed in a pedagogical and physical relationship—appears most explicitly in a Mediterranean-themed homoerotic poem about a Greek boy, "Teacher and pupil," where the author gazes upon a beautiful boy, dressed in white, and compares him to a Christian saint:

> My boy stood in the waves
> Like the thinnest Greek boy,
> dream of Samian shores.
> Gods rejoiced at the image!
>
> And my boy stood on the shore.
> In the long, white cloth
> he seemed like a young saint,
> Saint Thomas or Saint Francis!
>
> And in heavily pleated shirt
> he seemed to me a youthful
> lay priest, spring frankincense
> the wind carried through his curly hair.

But as a blonde page
he snuggles in the pale silk
of his half soft garments
against a tall tree.

Hearken the bells ring from afar
and now the dream about
all the beautiful ancient times is over.
And now my boy is back

As a charmingly silent youth
in day garments,
and in silent conversation we stride
through broad, silent country.

In the well-hidden *loggia*
with the old oak tables
our books that we want to read today
beckon.[63]

The attraction is spiritual and intellectual, hence erotic, an illusory fantasy that is not realized. The poem's repetition of silences (the boy is the silent object of older men's affections, "silent youth," "silent conversation," "silent country") and implications of love as a shared secret ("well-hidden loggia") speak to the fact that, in that era, gay inclinations were not spoken of openly, and gay relationships were entered into in secret because they were outlawed and subject to harsh punishment. Many gays were driven to commit suicide rather than face social death and incarceration. The criminalization of sexual acts between men had been established in the first General Law for Prussia of 1794, which replaced the sixteenth-century Holy Roman Empire death penalty with imprisonment, corporal punishment, and banishment.[64] With the founding of the German Empire in 1871, the Prussian Civil Code, including Paragraph 175, which went into effect a year earlier, was extended to cover all of Germany. Paragraph 175 prohibited sex between men, which was seen as being as "unnatural" as sex between humans and animals: "Unnatural sexual offenses committed between persons of the male sex or by persons with animals is to be punished by prison. Loss of civil rights may also be imposed."[65]

In his early poetry, fiction, and nonfiction, Marcus promotes *Freundschaft* (friendship) between men as a type of love that is superior to love between men and women. Friendship is oriented to like rather than difference, as in love. Friendship and love resemble each other in that through both sentiments a "richer, higher unity in multiplicity" is aspired. When Marcus writes of love, he implies heterosexual, romantic relationships. He reserves friendship for the pursuit of the enrichening unity with another person who is the same, a partner of the same sex. In *Meditationen* he promotes a hierarchy of sentiment where friendship (homosexuality) is higher than love (heterosexual romantic relationships).[66]

Like other young gay men, Marcus found that Berlin—with its gay bars and drag balls, its legions of male prostitutes, its public baths and rail stations, its woods and lakes, where Hirschfeld enjoyed naturism—offered myriad spaces for alternative sexual practices. As Hirschfeld relates in *Berlins drittes Geschlecht* (*Berlin's Third Sex*, 1904), which was also the subject of several homoerotic novels of the era, Berlin was "an intimate connection between the geography of the city and the possibilities it allowed for the explorations of alternative desire. The city of Berlin, he argued, with its multitude of tunnels, train stations, and public baths, was able to install a richly functional and diverse architecture of homoerotic desire." As a city packed with inhabitants yet spread out across a large territory, much of which consisted of secluded lakes and forests, Berlin offered same-sex couples "anonymity, legions of hiding places, a communal sense of like-affected individuals, and the possibility to live at great distances from the nuclear family without needing to relocate to another city."[67] Berlin was so vast that it easily afforded the opportunity for gays to live two lives, as Hirschfeld notes: "It was possible for native Berliners who were homosexual to continue living in Berlin and not encounter family members for over two decades."[68]

In the view of Thomas Mann's gay son, Klaus Mann (b. 1906, Munich; d. 1949, suicide in Cannes), Weimar Berlin (1919–1933) was "Sodom and Gomorrah in a Prussian tempo," a city that offered a "circus of perversities," a "department store of assorted vices," and "an all-out sale of brand new kinds of debauchery!"[69] The city was unique in the world for having an open gay culture, despite the prohibition of gay sex. It had a vibrant gay press, at the time consisting of up to thirty titles sold openly including at the city's two busiest newspaper kiosks, at

Potsdamer Platz and the Friedrichstrasse train station, displaying full male and female nudity and gay singles ads.[70] It boasted an estimated eighty to one hundred gay and lesbian bars or clubs open around the clock, undisturbed by the Berlin police.[71] Klaus Mann expresses the exuberant, anything goes attitude toward sex in that era: "Let's go to bed with each other! Or fool around in the parks if there are no beds. Boys with girls, boys with boys, girls with girls, men with boys and girls, women with men or boys or girls or tamed little panthers—what's the difference? Let's embrace each other!"[72]

Today we do not hesitate to label such men as Klaus Mann and Marcus as gay. But this is not a term that most would choose for themselves. One of Marcus's guides and mentors, Stefan George, for example, never clearly and unambiguously articulated his sexual leanings: "For that he was too proud, too secretive—and too wary," considering the legal penalties and social stigma such admission would entail.[73] George was a pseudomessianic gay lyric poet, an aristocratic "mystagogue," the "idolized center of an esoteric circle" devoted to his "concepts of beauty and morality."[74] George's writing—such as *Alqabal* (1892), which seemed to celebrate love between men—included explicit, passionate, homoerotic passages, paeans to Greek love—namely, the deification of the body of the beautiful boy, in the words of Klaus Mann, "the worship of an effulgent youth, Maximin, whom he glorified as a sort of bacchantic saint."[75] According to Peter Gay, he was "a modern Socrates who held his disciples with a fascination at once erotic and spiritual. There was a certain type of German to whom George was simply irresistible."[76] Walter Benjamin defined that type: "German-Jewish intellectuals with a more conservative political outlook."[77] Marcus was one such man who fell under his spell, one of those "fastidious young men" who sought to "cultivate their inner life, articulate their religious yearning, and satisfy their dim longing for human and cultural renewal."[78] George aimed to restore "true" Germany in part on a Hellenic model, replacing "false" bourgeois values and society; he was the spiritual forefather of an imagined new nation (which seemed to be realized in Nazi Germany), and his male circle of disciples—which ironically, despite George's and some of his followers' explicit anti-Semitism—included a large number of Jews, such as Marcus's famous younger gay cousin, Ernst Kantorowicz.[79] These disciples "followed him wherever he went and whenever he wanted them to come, ready to do his bidding and grateful just to be in his presence. To them, he was literally everything. He was their leader, their father, their ruler; their priest, their wise man, prophet, king, and creator. He was their god; he was their Master."[80] To his disciples, George's "word and gesture was absolute law."[81] The master "repaid his beloved followers with emotional verses of—to mere outsiders—embarrassing warmth."[82] Although George may "never have called himself 'a homosexual,' the main subject of his texts is love of men and boys."[83]

George and Hirschfeld, as did Marcus and men of his generation, studiously avoided calling themselves gay, although their sexual orientation cannot be described today by any other term.[84] Hirschfeld saw the term "*schwul*" (gay) as a swear word used by "normal" people to insult and belittle men who loved men. Although around the turn of the century very few activists publicly declared themselves homosexuals, by the 1920s younger men in Berlin used the term "gay" to describe themselves, although Hirschfeld urged them not to do so. One can speak of a generational divide.[85] For Hirschfeld and other early members of the WhK, it was a difficult balancing act, presenting themselves as fighters for the emancipation of gays and as having nothing personally to do with homosexuality, as if it were only for scientific and humanitarian reasons that they fought on behalf of the unjustly persecuted. Almost all of these early activists hid their sexual identity, which, for most, was gay. Hirschfeld used the term "*das drittes Geschlecht*" (the third sex) to encompass gays and lesbians.[86] This is not to overlook that members of the WhK itself debated whether a massive self-outing would have the greatest effect in spurring change. Unlike Hirschfeld or Marcus, however, the younger Hiller used the word "gay" to describe himself.[87] In 1905 at the annual meeting a proposal was made for one thousand gays to publicly self-identify, but it was rejected.[88] Hiller supported the idea in theory but knew it was unworkable.[89]

Along with attraction to boys and superiority of homosocial relations, Marcus also writes of alienation from his ancestral Judaism. At the turn-of-the-twentieth century, Marcus could not have foreseen the horror that would befall Germany Jewry in his lifetime when he wrote: "The misfortune of Jewry today stems not from the fact of its being persecuted—indeed, for the most part, earlier, less sensitive generations witnessed much worse—but rather in its loss of the feeling that it is fortunate to be persecuted: the loss of belief." This loss in turn "divides Jewry into two groups, inflexible fathers and unbelieving sons, where the sons, who lately often have to serve two masters, tradition and the state, daily get into danger of sacrificing themselves and the future of the beliefs of their fathers, which for them are only a phantom." Marcus finds this "an irony of fate, for Jews had been the people who took the greatest precautions for their progeny. Nota bene: To want to devote all one's strength uninhibitedly to solve the greatest social problems, including those that cause those from both the pro- and contra- sides to burn with so much hatred, was that not noble enough a reason to abandon an old, exalted, and evermore reviled tradition?"[90] Marcus would seem at that age to answer in the affirmative. Yet for what cause would he fight?

In Judaism's place he searches for a utopia, "a new, exclusively social, non-democratic, non-revolutionary party, that unites all socially inclined members of all parties, of whatever leaning and belief, not in their aims, but in their means—a new, lay priest order devoted to the purpose of spreading a uniform world view and a truthful social doctrine."[91] This is not left-wing utopianism. While Hiller was a socialist and radical revolutionary, and Hirschfeld wavered between social democracy and socialism, Marcus was antirevolutionary, never becoming a socialist or even social democrat. He was a lifelong liberal. World War I made all three men into pacifists.[92] As I explore below, Marcus, like Hiller, promoted the rule of an aristocracy; like Hirschfeld, he was a German patriot.

Marcus also had conflicting feelings regarding his Germanness. He describes his conflict with his own patriotic feelings, which he feels he is not entitled to feel as a Jew, but which he nonetheless feels toward the fatherland. Marcus was a member of an all-male Wandervogel youth organization in which, according to its historian and proponent Hans Blüher, homoeroticism and homosexuality were fundamental and natural features.[93] As Klaus Mann notes in his autobiography about the youth movement, "I suppose that never before in history—not even when the wise men of Athens worshipped and inspired the adolescents—were young people as consciously and arrogantly young as were the German generations preceding and following the [First] World War."[94] Peter Gay observes that as "alienated sons sought out other alienated sons" and rebelled against their fathers, seeking "purity and renewal" as well as "warmth and comradeliness, an escape from the lies spawned by petty bourgeois culture," many found it in the youth movement, where they were able to form, in Blüher's terms, a "confederation of friendship."[95] Marcus reflects not on friendships formed but on feelings aroused on one such hiking trip with his group in 1899: "When I was nineteen and hiking in the Harz mountains I was suddenly overwhelmed with the feeling 'oh Germany, beloved land, beautiful country, father and motherland!' Was that patriotism? Perhaps." The feeling hit him at once when he had hiked to an overlook where he could see many beautiful valleys. Marcus felt "suddenly overjoyed" by the new feeling. At the same time, he felt guilty, for "it came with a secret protest that I was really experiencing what others felt, [a feeling] that did not come to me, as a Jew, as a cosmopolitan." Nevertheless, the "sudden beauty" of the illicit feeling and the feeling itself were stronger than him, so he embraced it, as it took him over. He found it sorrowful, however, that he was not allowed to possess the strongest, most beautiful feeling of patriotism without at the same time being violated by his feeling of protest. Yet he declares that the feeling of patriotism was stronger than his protest and the experience proclaimed to him that "secret powers are hidden within you, that you do not yet know, that are more formidable than the ones you know. And there are things within, that one can not think, calculate, or picture beforehand . . . Wait, just wait!"[96] Marcus was a proud German patriot but not a nationalist. What mattered more than what Marcus felt about his homeland was what other Germans felt about Jews. Concerning Jewish national feeling, his master Stefan George would declare, "The soul of a nation [*Volk*] is its language, but they [the Jews] have lost [theirs]."[97] He is implying Jews can have no national feeling because they have no national language. What of German Jews like Marcus? Is German not their national language? Can they not feel German?

According to Klaus Mann, "conceived as a sort of romantic revolution against our mechanized era," the youth movement "contained inspiring, truly progressive elements along with the germs of evil."[98] The Wandervogel would later forbid Jews from membership.[99] The anti-Semitic Blüher became one of the most popular authors in Weimar Germany to promote the concept of the homoerotic *Männerbund*, associations of healthy, virile, masculinist, nationalist homosexuals united behind a führer, as manifested in ancient Greece, in the Wandervogel, or in the German state. He defined the *Männerbund* as "non-Jewish and distinctly German," arguing that "one cannot be a Jew and a German."[100] The choice would soon no longer be Marcus's to make.

That Marcus rejected his father does not mean that Marcus rejected his mother, Cäcilie (sometimes spelled Zäzilie), who may have approved of or at least looked the other way at his homosexuality, for as we shall see, they lived together, and she was in contact with his friend Roman.

Today we would also not hesitate to call such men Jewish and German. But Hirschfeld would not have identified himself simply as Jewish, for he was completely assimilated and thought of himself as a German and a cosmopolitan, a citizen of the world promoting panhumanism.[101] The only time he ever identified as Jewish was his first semester at university.[102] He did not identify as a Jew after that, seeing it as a label given him by anti-Semites and racists; at the end of his life, he apparently stated,

> I object to being called a Jew now and because of it being villifed and persecuted by the Nazi swines. I am a German, a German citizen, as German as a [General Paul von] Hindenburg or [General Erich] Ludendorff, Bismarck and the kaiser! An honest German, born to German parents in Germany! And what happened to me is what happens to every new born child in Europe: you are stuck in a religious straitjacket by your parents, baptized or circumcised and raised in their beliefs. Because my parents were of the Mosaic persuasion, I was given the Mosaic stigma![103]

Marcus would also try to escape the "stigma" of being Jewish in his own way, bringing together homosexuality, German philosophy, and Islam as "lived" and interpreted by Germany's greatest poet, Goethe.

INTELLECTUAL AND POLITICAL AWAKENING: MARCUS'S MENTORS GEORG SIMMEL AND MAGNUS HIRSCHFELD

Marcus studied philosophy at Friedrich Wilhelm University in Berlin from 1903 to 1906, although he did not earn a doctorate.[104] While a student, Marcus got to know Hiller, who studied philosophy with the same advisor, Georg Simmel, before enrolling at the University of Freiburg and then earning a law degree at the University of Heidelberg in 1907. Hiller joined the WhK in 1908 after his published dissertation, discussed below, won Hirschfeld's respect. Hiller became the WhK's publicist and then second director from 1929—possibly due to a split over whether to support the parliamentary committee's vote to abolish Paragraph 175 while cracking down harshly on male prostitution—to its closure in 1933.[105] In his autobiography, *Leben gegen die Zeit* (Life against the times, 1969), Hiller mentions, "It is worth noting that in the course of working for Hirschfeld's Committee [WhK] I got to know a number of precious personalities," including "the philosopher Hugo Marcus (1880–1966; author, for example, of the unsung volume, *Philosophie des Monopluralismus*)."[106] Hiller considered Marcus a worthy reviewer of his work, including him among those who offered appreciation that was "wise and deserving of thanks."[107]

Marcus's professor and Hiller's doctoral advisor was Georg Simmel, the son of two Breslauer Jews who had converted to Christianity.[108] Simmel was a *Dozent* (private lecturer) at Friedrich Wilhelm University in Berlin from 1885 to 1900, when he received an honorific title, Extraordinary Professor, but no professorship or salary; he could not supervise dissertations. What blocked his attainment of a permanent post was his "feminist politics, Nietzschean morality, antibourgeois ethics, and sociological investigations of social hierarchy."[109] His Jewish origins and the students he attracted also played a role. As a government administrator wrote opposing Simmel's appointment to the University of Heidelberg in 1908, "He is an Israelite [Jew] through and through. . . . His academic audience sits together. The ladies constitute what is, even for Berlin, a strong contingent. The remaining are students from the oriental world who have become residents, and those who stream in from eastern countries are extremely well represented."[110]

Although renowned as one of the founding fathers of sociology, in his day Simmel was a towering figure of philosophy, known as "the philosopher of the avant-garde" by his contemporaries and as an academic activist for his role in the left-wing, pacifist, feminist, and gay rights movements: "What made his thought so powerful and appealing to the expressionistic generation was its combination of modernist aesthetics, antibourgeois sexuality, and anticapitalist philosophy. Consequently, his critical penchant drew a variety of radical students to his seminars at Berlin University."[111] Simmel was an iconoclast, "a countercultural member of the upper bourgeoisie," swept up by the bohemian Naturalism movement, which sought to undermine the status quo by social critique, opposing accepted tastes, hierarchies, and conventions.[112] Influenced by Nietzsche, believing there was no thing as self-evident and universal Truth, to construct a new morality and spirituality, he turned to aesthetics as a way of life as opposed to a mere art form.[113] Simmel combined Nietzschean philosophy (aesthetic resistance to social fate) and critical sociology, identifying capitalism as Nietzschean slave morality: he was a Nietzschean anticapitalist who urged individuals to resist convention, specifically bourgeois culture.[114] He was the first to fashion a critical philosophy from "the antibourgeois thought of Nietzsche" and "a socialist critique of bourgeois economics" to reject the values of economic individualism, the State, and the Church, as is seen in his critique of capitalist culture, *The Philosophy of Money* (1900).[115] His "critique called forth countercultural political practice. His anticapitalism . . . was ethical. His language of *Geist* (spirit) and *Seele* (soul) was uniquely suited to influence those radical students for whom secular language was inadequate to express the existential affinity of knowledge, anticapitalist culture, and aesthetic self-creation."[116] Simmel criticized capitalism, economic inequality, bourgeois values, Christian morality, and conventional hierarchies while at the same time promoting sexual equality and the cultural elitism of a spiritual elite.

Simmel introduced his middle class students, including Marcus and Hiller, to aristocratic radicalism, which allowed them to combine Nietzschean critique of bourgeois values and socialist critique of capitalist culture from an avant-garde position: they savaged bourgeois worldviews and freed themselves from convention, yet without surrendering "the sense of superiority that redounded from their class position and cultural capital. In taking up intellectual arms against bourgeois life, they did not want to identify with egalitarian socialism."[117] This describes Marcus's writings on philosophy and Islam in the 1920s and 1930s, discussed below. While liberated from the hegemony of tradition and given a sense of superiority to the working class, they saw themselves as a cultural nobility, offering a "polemic against both the ancient noblesse of blood and the bourgeois aristocracy of wealth," a "meritorious royalty of spirit."[118]

Simmel's disciples absorbed his ideas, learned in part at his Friedrich Wilhelm University in Berlin seminars. These included "Philosophy of the Nineteenth Century from Fichte to Nietzsche," "Social Psychology: Ethics and Social Problems," "Sociology with the Consideration of Social Problems," "Aesthetic Practices: The Fundamental Characteristics of Psychology as a Human Science," "Introduction to Philosophy with Consideration of the Philosophy of Society and History," and "Greek Philosophy and Philosophy of Culture-especially Aesthetic and Social Culture."[119] Marcus took "Philosophy of the Nineteenth Century from Fichte to Nietzsche" and "Sociology with the Consideration of Social Problems."[120] Simmel's students translated his ideas into political action. For Hiller this meant literary expressionism, which combined antiestablishment critique and a new culture of spirituality, as he founded a literary club (The New Club, 1909) at the university, whose manifesto included quotes from Nietzsche, Oscar Wilde, and Goethe; organized readings at West Berlin cafés; and established two journals, *Pan* (1910) and *Aktion* (1911).[121] The Hillers and Marcuses of the day dominated the counterculture: "With doctorate in hand, but lacking academic positions, these intellectuals began to advocate a practical relationship between radical thought and political activity."[122]

Hiller took Simmel's feminism, which promoted liberated heterosexuality, to a new level, taking aim at "the hegemony of heterosexism" and proposing "an apollonian vision of dionysian freedom." Inspired by Nietzsche's call for the individual to develop his or her erotic instincts in the process of becoming, Hiller legitimized his own homosexuality, defending personal freedom and the right to self-determination. "I want to be free" Hiller proclaims in his 1908 dissertation, "Das Recht über sich selbst" (The right over oneself), which challenges the criminalization of male homosexuality.[123] The thesis also discusses suicide, self-mutilation, bestiality, and abortion, asking where the line can be drawn between personal freedom and societal regulation. Concerning homosexuality, Hiller mentions that men who love men may have high social, intellectual, and cultural standing; argues against the assertion that homosexuality contravenes natural law and nature; and contends that procreation need not be the intention or outcome of heterosexual desire and thus is not the exclusive telos of affection—because it is most prevalent does not mean it is the natural law of desire. Homosexuality did not damage the race or harm the state and was not pathological, dirty, ugly, or immoral; after all then, he interjects, the Greeks must have been a nation of criminals! He concludes there was no reason to outlaw sex between consenting adult men.[124]

Closely connected to the naturalists and Stefan George, and married to a feminist philosopher, Simmel denounced patriarchal culture and rejected the male-dominated world, including bourgeois marital conventions, imagining feminine culture (and female eroticism) to have its own rightful place.[125] George was a close friend of Simmel; George praised Nietzsche, a man whose work was symbolic of Simmel's philosophy: "the artist-outsider, through the vatic struggle of creation, transcends intimate and passionate subjectivity and fashions an elite civic morality."[126] Simmel's students carried his ideas into developing expressionism and gay rights (Hiller), and feminism (Helene Stöcker, 1869–1943, his student from 1896 to 1899 and among the first cohort of female students).[127]

The year Marcus completed his studies, the Eulenburg affair riveted the attention of the German and international public. Marcus came of age in an era where several sensational public scandals involved gays, including the Oscar Wilde trial in England and the Krupp affair in Germany.[128] The first decade of the twentieth century "was punctuated by scandals involving male homosexual public figures" such that "the general cultural awareness of homosexuality and the existence of modern homosexuals is inseparable from these stories and images."[129] These scandals put a face to homosexuality, made people aware of actual gays and homosexual practices and the men and boys who engaged in them, and stigmatized such men further. The legal persecution and verbal and physical violence directed against gays and the violence that outed homosexuals inflicted on themselves—suicide—must have also left an emotional impact if not traumatized young men like Marcus and shaped the way they expressed their gay selves.[130] Hirschfeld, who repeatedly returns to the emotional theme of suicide to support his promotion of sex reform and the abolishment of discriminatory legislation, "claims to have known personally over half of the one hundred homosexual suicides that had taken place in recent years."[131]

Marcus attended the three well-publicized trials of the Eulenburg affair (1906-1909). The scandal erupted when Maximilian Harden (1861–1927)—a journalist of Jewish background born as Felix Ernst Witkowski, who had converted to Christianity and changed his name at the age of sixteen ("an ambitious henchman of Bismarck's" according to Marcus)—accused many members of Kaiser Wilhelm II's (r. 1888–1918, d. 1941) entourage, including the kaiser's friend and advisor Count Philipp zu Eulenburg (1847–1921), of homosexuality and treason.[132] Marcus narrates how he "got to know Magnus Hirschfeld better as his success and fame were at their peak. His appearance at the Eulenburg trial had made him famous all around the world," having served as a medical expert on homosexuality.[133]

Despite Marcus's assertions, Hirschfeld became notorious as much for his claims—in the first trial, that homosexuality was not an abnormality but an inborn disposition, and, in the second trial, that the intimate friendship between men had not been uncommon in the age of Goethe—as for altering his own testimony. He argued in the first trial that defendant Gen. Kuno Graf von Moltke (1847-1923) was homosexual and in the second trial that he was not.[134] Eulenburg defended accusations against being gay by attacking Hirschfeld:

> I have been an enthusiastic friend in my youth and am proud of having had such good friends! Had I known that after twenty five to thirty years a man would come forward and develop such a system, according to which such potential filth in every friendship lurked, I would have truly forsaken the search for friends. The best that we Germans have is friendship, and friendship has always been honored! I have written letters that overwhelm with friendly emotions, and I will not reproach myself for that. As examples we

> have the letters of our great heroes, such as Goethe, etc., which are also effusive.[135]

Despite his effort, the trials helped cast such formerly tolerated "effusive friendships" as obsolete and "regarded as homosexual."[136] Moreover, while as a result of the scandal the word "homosexuality" and "homosexuals" became "mentionable," so too were they often accompanied by vocal expressions of homophobia, ruining the possibility of revoking Paragraph 175, convictions for violation of which nearly doubled between 1907 and 1911.[137] As "public homophobia first took form" during the trials, so too was it connected to the rise of anti-Semitic conspiracy theories positing a struggle between moral "Germans" and degenerate "Jews,"—the former represented by the anti-Semitic kaiser and Eulenburg (until they too were brushed with the accusation of being "tainted" by Jewishness), the latter by Harden and Hirschfeld—pejoratively linking Jews and homosexuality.[138]

Hirschfeld's claims at court earned him harsh attacks in the press across the political spectrum, harmed his reputation, and caused the WhK, until then "a respectable and growing association," to lose a large proportion of its members and supporters.[139] Its membership fell from its maximum of around five hundred in 1907 to around half that in the succeeding years.[140] The entire scandal had an antihomosexual tone and gave the Social Democratic Party of Germany (SPD) an opportunity to abandon its efforts at repealing Paragraph 175; when the WhK petitioned in the aftermath of the trial in 1907, the Reichstag committee decided to "arrange a quiet funeral for the petition."[141] Hirschfeld needed a break from the attacks. Guided by Goethe's *Italian Journey*, he made a pilgrimage to the grave of open homosexual Hellenist Johann Joachim Winckelmann (1717–1768), whom Goethe admired.[142]

Marcus remembered how, after they met during the trials, "Hirschfeld often summoned me to be at his side. I came to him early at nine a.m. for a walk through the wonderful flowering Tiergarten," or "around noon he might suggest I join him on his walk" to Unter den Linden, "which had the reputation of being a meeting place of male prostitution. There I saw him immediately negotiate with a young man clad in scanty elegance. There appeared to be a matter of blackmail, but it seemed a success for Hirschfeld. After fifteen minutes he was back at my side."[143] Such strolls through the Tiergarten to visit the promenade where male prostitutes waited for customers was a form of gay voyeurism.[144] As the police reports of the time amply illustrate, men sought erotic contacts with other men on Unter den Linden and the bars and clubs leading to it; in a grove of trees east of the university; and in certain sections of Tiergarten park, especially by the goldfish pond in its southwest corner, accessed along the *schwuler Weg* (gay path).[145] Hiller reports that in 1904, while a nineteen-year-old university student, he paid a gay prostitute in Tiergarten for his first homosexual experience.[146] For the next three decades he would pay male prostitutes to have sex while loving other men through chaste friendships, distinguishing between "animal practice" (sex) and "eros" (eroticism and loving devotion belonging to the mental and spiritual realms).[147] When he first came to Berlin as a seventeen-year-old in 1923, Klaus Mann learned that "to be in Berlin meant a constant thrill in itself . . . [Berlin was] a labyrinth swarming with mysteries and adventures. What fun!—to stroll along those fabulous streets whose very names were charged with risky allurements . . . Unter den Linden, Tauentzien-Strasse, Kurfürstendamm."[148]

NIETZSCHE, PACIFISM, EROTICISM, AND WORLD WAR I

Despite initial support of World War I, Simmel inspired a leftist, anticapitalist, anti-Christian reading of Nietzsche, "the antiwar philosophy of the neo-Nietzschean avant-garde."[149] His stance was in distinction to others, such as Thomas Mann, and the German high command, which distributed *Thus Spoke Zarathustra* to soldiers, where Nietzsche was linked to the right wing: German conservatism, masculinity, antifeminism, antiradicalism, nationalism and militarism. Hiller and Stöcker, however, Simmel's spiritually inclined students, "led the anti-war movement and opposed the war from a Nietzschean perspective," turning against their mentor for his having at first supported the war.[150] Hiller founded the antiwar Aktivistenbund (Activist League), an offshoot of expressionism, in 1914; the Internationale des Geistes (International of Spirit) in 1917; and the pacifist-socialist journal *Das Ziel: Jahrbuch für geistige Politik* (The aim: Yearbook for spiritual politics, five volumes published between 1916 and 1924). In his autobiography Hiller lists Marcus among the staff of *Das Ziel*, whose other contributors included Hirschfeld, Stöcker, Max Brod, Walter Benjamin, and Marcus's acquaintance Dr. Armin T. Wegner (1886–1978).[151] The "Simmelian model of the engaged intellectual reached its zenith" in Hiller and Stöcker, "the next generation of left-wing avant-gardists who, like Simmel, espoused a countercultural politics which unified Germany's two most powerful critiques of bourgeois society: Nietzschean and socialist."[152] With the exception of Hirschfeld (with whom they worked closely at the WhK), the Institute for Sexual Science (which republished his thesis in 1926), and the Kartell für die Reform des Sexualstrafrechts (Cartel for the Reform of the Sexual Penal Code, made up of communists and social democrats), Stöcker and Hiller "were Germany's unsurpassed titans of an alternative gender politics for over three decades."[153] Their working relationship was consolidated during the war. The political program of their International of Spiritual Workers shows how they saw themselves as the cultural vanguard of social revolution calling for socialist radicalism, an anticapitalist vision of human rights fighting against war service and the suppression of workers, and promoting personal freedom and social justice, a model of cultural revolution that was Simmelian in its promotion of a spiritual avant-garde leading the way to societal transformation.[154] Their program was not only antimilitarist and communist but promoted sexual freedom.[155] The socialist republic would be directed by a spiritual avant-garde, governed by an assembly of spiritual intellectuals, a Platonic republic led by an intellectual-moral elite and where homosexuality was given free rein.[156]

Marcus supported this vision of a society guided by a pacifist, homosexual, intellectual, spiritual avant-garde throughout his life.[157] He may have also been affected by the loss of his brother Otto in 1919.[158] During the war or immediately after, Marcus penned a homoerotic, pacifist ode that turns from fantasizing about a youth's body to Christian imagery, to an impassioned antiwar plea, an elegy to the fallen youth of war in whose honor he imagines dedicating "Die Kirche zu den heiligen Brüsten der Jünglinge" ("The church of the hallowed chests of youth"). Although the piece was not published until after World War II, its language and perspective, belying Marcus's later postconversion beliefs and relation to God, provide internal evidence that it was written three decades before it appeared.[159]

One sunny summer afternoon the author takes pleasure in observing the handsome chest of a young man, whose shirt is unbuttoned to his waist: his "chest burst out of the blue shirt like a huge ray of light, like a sun." But then Marcus immediately imagines "the millions of luminous, sun-like chests of youth that were pierced in the war. I saw them far and wide lying in state in the brightest afternoon light, all dead suns, bursting out of blue shirts. Tears well in my eyes for so many sent to Paradise." He turns his anger toward God: weeping, he clasps the slain youth "with both arms, shaking him, for all the dead that the world war [World War I] had murdered. The pain of so many precious chests pierced by this world war [World War I] came to me every now and then." He curses the fact that "this pain will stay with me my entire life." The pain does not return when he visits the graves of the fallen but rather when he sees "the candles of millions of blossoming chestnuts and the gold light of the sun."[160]

Suddenly he hears an awful dirge arising from empty factory buildings. The stones, windows, and chimneys murmur "De Profundis," Oscar Wilde's epistle written during his imprisonment. In it Wilde recounts his relationship with Lord Alfred Douglas, which led to Wilde's conviction and imprisonment for gross indecency, indicting both Lord Alfred's vanity and his own weakness in acceding to those wishes, and then charts his spiritual development in prison and identification with Jesus. The author of "Die Kirche zu den heiligen Brüsten der Jünglinge," in great contrast, does not reconcile with the Christian God but is so angry he hears how "even the stones raised their lament to God: against God." He responds to the cries of the stony lips: "O hallowed chests of youth! I want to build a church from plaintive stones—an anti-war church, the Church of the Hallowed Chests of Youth—to search for friends on both sides who are opposed to the murder of friends."[161]

Driven by an "iron pacifism," he sets off, "following the command to the Church of the Hallowed Chests, a *miles ecclesiae* [soldier of the Church]." He asks how one can tolerate that the chests of youth are split apart: "Friends, you often ask what is your purpose in life. I believe today that it is only possible for us to feel. And this leads to a worldly purpose. Eternal peace. A thousand paths lead to eternal peace. But I believe this way points only to us. Points only to us! Come, o son of man, establish the Church of the Hallowed Chests of Youth!"[162]

The work echoes the sentiment of Stefan George, who "feared and loathed the war precisely because it was killing off his young men," those "lovely boys who served the pleasures of older men."[163] It also reflects Marcus's engagement with the pacifist movement led by classmate Hiller, which brought together pacifism, socialism, Nietzschean antibourgeois spirituality, and demands for sexual liberation. According to the manifesto of Hiller's International of Spiritual Workers (1917) "the guiding star of all future politics must be the inviolibility of life," against "the subjugation of the totality of people through war service and against the oppression of workers through the capitalist system."[164] They established seven main aims, the first three of which are "1. The Prevention of War: the abolition of military service in all countries and the prohibition of all military establishments, 2. The Just Distribution of All Earthly Possessions: the transformation of capitalist enterprises into a productive worker's association, 3. Freedom of the Sexual Life Within the Borders of Responsibility: through control of all men and women over their bodies."[165] Hiller also used spiritual language in his pacifist activism, directly confronting the supposed moral authority of the Church, and offering an alternative: "Spirit [*Geist*] is the unavoidable detour to the happiness of paradise," for "Spirit is the striving for responsibility—to stir others and make them jointly responsible. . . . Spirit would be the moment of the birth of paradise. . . . Spirit is the goal. . . . As spiritual intellectuals, we embrace association. . . . What do we want? Paradise. Who will gain it? *Geist*. What does it need to succeed? Power. How will spiritual intelligence win power? Through union."[166]

The overwhelming support for the war by Germany's Christian churches sparked an antiwar response "that claimed the same level of spiritual authority. There was no way for Hiller to express the intensity of his ethical opposition to war culture without resorting to spiritual language." Hiller had used such terms as "soul" and "spirit" before the war in "the struggle for moral authority against Christianity. . . . Hiller's mobilization of the trope of paradise was an intensification of this cultural strategy. Hiller's discourse of paradise and spirit highlight the fact that the German avant-garde referenced their spiritual intelligence [*Geistigkeit*] in an attempt to usurp the cultural hegemony of Christian spirituality [*Geistlichkeit*]."[167] He also added the following as a plank in the platform for social revolution: "Struggle against the Churches, as long as they continue to oppose the will of spirit [*Geist*]."[168]

We see these themes reflected in Marcus's homoerotic pacifist piece. Rather than a church devoted to God, he imagines a church devoted to young men who have gone to paradise. Instead of church music, disused factories call out a tune penned by a persecuted gay writer. The lament cries out against God, not for God. The church does not hallow God, it hallows young men. It is a temple to men. It is a replacement for Christianity, dedicated by a disillusioned church member. It alludes to Jesus's pierced, tortured body, but rather than drawing the Christian to his faith, it repels him. Instead of the Church, only pacifism and eroticism will unite men across borders in a brotherhood of friendship.

In the immediate postwar period, Marcus wrote frequently for *Das Junge Deutschland* (Young Germany), a monthly for literature and theater established in 1918.[169] In a typical homoerotic piece, "Mein toter Freund erzählt sich selbst seine Knabenzeit" (My deceased friend narrates his youth), Marcus explores the theme of love between young men.[170] He describes his experience at the Gymnasium, focusing on the secret love he felt for classmate Alfred Roller and, years later, his crush on his professor, Friedrich Paulsen, author of one of Marcus's favorite works.

He states explicitly: "At Gymnasium I loved Roller."[171] Marcus expresses frustration, asking "why cannot one go up to the one that impresses you so, and say to him, 'I think so highly of you: should we not try to consort with one another?'" Marcus uses the verb "*verkehren*," which also can mean sexual intercourse. The passage can be read as Marcus propositioning a fellow student to have anal intercourse. He continues: "why can't one be so direct?" But realizing such direct speech and action are inconceivable, Marcus uses Hiller's conception of eros and instead comes up with a high-minded way to seduce Roller: he establishes an art and science club at his Gymnasium and invites Roller to join. He finds it a simpler plan to bring together all intellectually minded students, among whom is his object of affection, rather than to speak to the object of desire more directly about his wishes. Marcus imagined that the club would offer him and Roller a cover for their relationship, one that was "worthy" of them. Disappointedly, perhaps, he concludes that nothing came of the club, and nothing of the acquaintance with Roller, either.

Later, as a university student, Marcus "adored" Professor Paulsen, who was more than twice his age. Marcus attended Paulsen's philosophy course in the winter of 1903–1904 and in the summer of 1906. He could have simply visited him during his office hours, "as did hundreds of others," but that idea would never occur to him. Instead, Marcus again came up with a more complicated and intellectually exciting, thus erotic, way to meet his male object of desire. He suddenly decided the way to meet and impress him was to write a long analysis of theodicy, a philosophical discussion of why, if there is a God, there is evil in the world. To his mind "only a great work would be the worthiest and quickest path to reach such a man." Later in the piece, when describing how he lost his feelings for Roller, he refers to how he "only wanted to love a young Greek," as, one suspects, he had depicted in *Meditationen* over a decade earlier.[172]

Near the end of Marcus's life, with the assistance of friends in the gay community, he published a collection of his writing from the immediate post–World War I period. *Einer sucht den Freund: Gedanken zum Thema das Ewige und der Freund* (One seeks a friend: Reflections on the theme of the eternal and the friend), of which some reflections had appeared in *Das Junge Deutschland* and other similar journals, explores friendship, companionship, erotic love, and the ever-changing boundaries that distinguish them.[173]

In a period of his life when he had turned away intellectually from Judaism but not yet joined another religion, Marcus describes his own search for the friend, explaining how "searching for God and the friend, I found my intellect, which I was not seeking."[174] Turning his back on religious life, he argues "It is not that the intellect kills God, but the reverse: the God who dies gives birth to the intellect."[175] Less interested in the intellect than in male beauty and love, he mentions Goethe, Venice, and ancient Greece (Adonis, Icarus), references to homosexual desire and identity, expressing the ideal of pederasty: "I idolize you, youthful boy, as if you were an ancient, eternal god." Adonis, the god of beauty and desire, may have died, he argues, but his young male object of desire is the reborn Adonis. He hints of living in the closet, as he mentions how "the companion [*Gefährte*] is the sweetest fruit of danger [*Gefahr*]."[176] Throughout the book he discusses two university students, male sweethearts Heinrich and Eduard, who will figure as main characters in Marcus's homoerotic fiction penned in this era but published after World War II.[177]

Salvation for Marcus comes not from political solutions but from friendship. He expresses a turning away from the search for a political utopia in the world. Strife and agony will never end, he argues, and the only hope lies in friendship. While large-scale utopia will not be built on earth, the friend serves as "the littlest bond, as the smallest island and last resort and refuge for saving humanity."[178] Long after humankind, the nation, and the state have failed him, there will be the friend: "Once you and I should have been the primeval cell of a world community, and we would have been companions in the struggle for the wider, world-wide society. Now you and I [Marcus and the male friend] are the last remnant of the dream of a world community. The last remnant of utopian lands."[179] He reveals that his best friends are Goethe, Nietzsche, and Plato.[180] Why Plato? Like George, Plato was a "leader-master-poet-lover-educator, who reforms society by reforming its art, and simultaneously by inculcating new values through the erotic cultivation of an elite group of youth, as both preparatory to and constitutive of a broader political revolution."[181]

Marcus brings together friendship, love, and eroticism. Engaging in a play on words, he writes, "The word friend [*Freund*] comes from the word for joy [*Freude*]; the comrade [*Genosse*] awakes pleasure [*Genuss*] in you; there are helpmates [*Gefährten*] who help you in times of danger [*Gefahr*]; mates [*Kameraden*] who share your room [*Kammer*]."[182] Just as there are so many words for "friend," so, too, are there many different manners of friendship. Most remarkable to Marcus's mind is how "one, who was initially only your friend, whose nature gave you joy, blossoms one day into a companion in ecstatic enjoyment. And later, the danger [of secret same-sex love] makes you companions . . . or from the companions of danger grows the comrade who shares your room, and comrades in the room become comrades in pleasure."[183] Indeed for Marcus, a friend becomes "an entire invisible collective of friends, an entire secret society," a network of men engaged in relations that society forbids.[184]

He links friendship and erotic love and elevates the love between two men above that between men and women: "Erotic love and heroism. Love for a girl: I want you, and I want to make myself as rich as I can, to win you over."[185] By contrast, he defines love for a friend as defined by the motivation "I will not have you—no, but to be like you! I want to be equal with you . . . I want to belong to the same band and rank of mind and spirit as you . . . and by virtue of our community of shared values we remain forever companions of the same band and the same rank, companions in the face of eternity," a band of gay pacifist brothers.[186]

PARAGRAPH 175: THE DISGRACE OF THE CENTURY!

The core activity of the WhK was petitioning for the abolition of Paragraph 175. The petition is seen as the founding charter of the German (if not European, and world) gay rights movement.[187] In the words of cofounder Max Spohr, it was "an act of justice" to work for "the abolition of a penal regulation which is no longer compatible with the most advanced knowledge," or, as Hirschfeld put it in his motto, "Durch Wissenschaft zur Gerechtigkeit" (Justice through science), emancipating gays by using scientific findings and the latest research to convince politicians to change the criminal code.[188] According to the WhK's constitution, published a decade after its founding, first, "the *aim* of the Committee is research into homosexuality and allied variations, in their biological, medical and ethnological significance as well as their legal, ethical and humanitarian situation. The WhK gives its members every assistance in the spirit of true humanitarianism." Second, "the Committee wants to change public opinion about homosexuality through publications like the *Jahrbuch für sexuelle Zwischenstufen unter besonderer Berücksichtigung der Homosexualität* (Almanac for sexual intermediaries with a special focus on homosexuality, 1899–1923), pamphlets and petitions, scientific talks and popular lectures."[189] One of the main claims of Hirschfeld and that which his organization promoted was that "sexual orientation was biological."[190] Hirschfeld sought to reassure gays and educate the public that homosexuality is "an innocent, inborn orientation, which is not a misfortune in and of itself but rather experienced as such because of unjust condemnation."[191] As Hirschfeld's and WhK members' lectures and publications strove to assert based on their own current research, homosexuality was "a natural variant of sexuality," "natural and unalterable," so that any prohibition was "absurd."[192] The petition, first composed in 1897 and resubmitted over three decades, reads:

> The undersigned men and women, whose names guarantee the seriousness and purity of their intention, inspired by the pursuit of the truth, justice, and humanity, declare that the current version of Paragraph 175 is incompatible with advanced scientific knowledge, and ask for the legislation as soon as possible to amend this paragraph, so that just as in the abovementioned countries [France, Italy, Holland and many others] sexual acts between persons of the same sex likewise between people of different sexes homosexual as heterosexual shall only be punishable when they are compelled by force, conducted with a person under the age of sixteen, or made in an offensive way as a public nuisance.[193]

The WhK petitioned the German Reichstag in 1897, 1900, 1904, 1907, 1922, and 1926.

After World War I the new Social Democratic government gave Hirschfeld permission to establish the Institut für Sexualwissenschaft (Institute for Sexology / Sexual Science, or IS) in Berlin (1919), the first in the world, whose aim was scientific exploration into all forms of human sexuality and the utilization of this research for the public good.[194] The WhK became incorporated into the IS as its division for sexual reform. Because it was inconceivable in that era for a German university to establish a chair in sexology, Hirschfeld created the IS with his own funds, appointing himself its director.[195] The main work of the IS focused in general on sexual politics and sexual reform. The IS team Hirschfeld assembled included experts from the fields of medicine, biology, psychology, psychiatry, ethnology, and anthropology, and their primary mission was devoted to research and teaching, as in any interdisciplinary academic department. Unlike a university department, the IS, in addition to providing academic research and education as well as outreach counseling professionals and public information, offered medical treatment of and counseling sessions for married couples, gays, and transvestites. Its surgical unit offered the first experimental and ultimately dangerous hormone treatments and sex-reassignment surgeries.[196] The IS offered classes, lectures, conferences, training, and counseling to doctors, lawyers, teachers, social welfare workers, and police.[197] It served as a community empowerment center, helping gays and lesbians meet and find help and employment, and enabling men and women to accept who they were and to live according to their desires and identity. Thousands of people passed through its doors every year: individuals seeking counseling, pedophiles undergoing court-ordered castration, physicians and medical students attending clinical demonstrations, the public attending classes and individual lectures, Germans and foreigners taking guided tours of the erotica collections, those accused of crimes seeking expert opinion that could free them of prison terms, couples seeking therapy or divorce seeking expert opinion, couples seeking fertility treatment, men and women seeking treatment for sexually transmitted diseases, and doctors and students of medicine and law pursuing training.[198]

The IS was housed in a palatial mansion decorated like a private home, "aristocratic style married to scientific functionalism."[199] Its central Tiergarten location, with quarters for foreign guests, such as French author André Gide, was "one of the attractions of Berlin."[200] Gide was taken on a private tour by Hirschfeld, who introduced the patients and guests; "one of these [patients] was a young man who opened his shirt with a modest smile to display two perfectly formed female breasts."[201] The institute's museum contained "whips and chains and torture instruments designed for the practitioners of pleasure-pain; high-heeled, intricately decorated boots for the fetishists; lacy female undies which had been worn by ferociously masculine Prussian officers beneath their uniforms . . . Here were fantasy pictures, drawn and painted by Hirschfeld's patients. Scenes from the court of a priapic king who sprawled on a throne with his own phallus for a scepter and watched the grotesque matings of his courtiers."[202]

According to novelist Christopher Isherwood, who resided at the institute in 1929, it "was by no means exclusively concerned with homosexuality. It gave advice to couples about to marry, based on research into their hereditary backgrounds. It offered psychiatric treatment for impotence and other psychological problems. It had a clinic which dealt with a variety of cases, including venereal disease. And it studied sex in every manifestation."[203] In addition, the institute's legal department "advised men who were accused of sex crimes and represented them in court. Hirschfeld had won the right to give them asylum until their cases were heard."[204] As a "place of education for the public, its lawmakers, and its police," it offered film nights, showing and leading discussion of such films as the pedantic silent film, banned one year after its release, *Anders als die Anderen* (Different from the others § 175, 1919), directed by Austrian Jew Richard Oswald (1880–1963), who collaborated with sexologists such as Hirschfeld on "enlightenment films" aiming at sexual education, of which this was the most famous, the first film to deal explicitly with homosexuality.[205]

Anders als die Anderen is a vehicle for the promotion of Hirschfeld's scientific, medical, and political views. The film was cowritten and partially funded by Hirschfeld, who is credited for "scientific-medical advising" and who costars as "the physician and sexologist." Hirschfeld even gave a minor role to his lover, thirty years his junior, his personal secretary and institute archivist Karl Giese (1898–1938, by suicide in Brünn/Brno, Czechoslovakia).[206] Giese appears in a flashback as the young Paul, expelled from boarding school after being caught having intimate relations with his roommate. Hirschfeld lectures Paul's parents: "You must not think poorly of your son because he is a homosexual. He is not at all to blame for his orientation. It is neither a vice, nor a crime. Indeed, not even an illness. . . . Your son suffers not from his condition, but rather from the false judgment of it."

The film's main plot centers on the love between the mature violinist Paul (played by one of Germany's most famous actors, Konrad Veidt) and his young male student, Kurt. But Kurt leaves Paul due to the threats of a blackmailer. Paul sees the sexologist, who assures him, "Love for one's own sex can be just as pure and noble as that for the opposite sex. This orientation is to be found among many respectable people in all levels of society. Only ignorance or bigotry can condemn those who feel differently. Do not despair! As a homosexual, you can still make valuable contributions to humanity." Paul attends a public lecture by the sexologist, who explains, "Nature is boundless in its creations. Between all opposites there are transitions, and this is also true of the sexes. Thus, apart from man and woman, there are also men with womanly physical and psychological traits, as well as women with all sorts of male characteristics." He argues that sexual intermediates are physically determined. He narrates how the persecution of homosexuals "belongs in the same sad chapter of human history as the persecution of heretics and witches." The French Revolution and the Napoleonic Code changed all that, for laws against homosexuality were abandoned "because they were seen as a violation of the fundamental rights of the individual. In Germany, however, despite fifty years of scientific research in this area, legal discrimination against homosexuals continues unabated." Finally, "May justice soon prevail over this grave injustice, science conquer superstition, love achieve victory over hatred!"

Paul appears in court against his blackmailer, charged under Paragraph 175. The blackmailer is sent to prison for his crime. The judge, persuaded by the expert testimony of the sexologist that Paul "is an honorable individual who has hurt no one," nonetheless declares, "A judge can only carry out the law. As long as Paragraph 175 exists, we are not entitled to grant acquittal." Paul is sentenced to a brief prison term. Devastated, his social and professional life ruined, rejected by his family, he commits suicide. Kurt breaks down at the sight of his lover's corpse and attempts to commit suicide, but the sexologist dissuades him, "If you want to honor the memory of your friend, then you must not take your own life, but instead keep on living to change the prejudices whose victim—one of countless many—this dead man has become. This is the life task I assign you . . . what matters now is to restore honor and justice to the many thousands before us, with us, and after us. Justice through science!" The movie closes with an open German law book, turned to Paragraph 175, as a hand holding a brush crosses it out.

The film, with its overt political message and scenes of gay men, lesbians, and transvestites dancing at a gay bar and a masquerade ball, "made history; it was a breakthrough in the dramatic presentation of unorthodox love."[207] It had an impact; thereafter, "the number of films with explicitly homosexual themes of characters is remarkable."[208]

Along with such films, the IS also published journals. Marcus served on the staff of the Institute of Sexology's monograph series, SEXUS, which published three collections of essays edited by Hirschfeld in 1921 and one in 1926.[209] In 1922 Marcus appeared together with Hirschfeld and professor Ferdinand Karsch-Haack (1853-1936)—like Marcus, an early member of Hirschfeld's WhK, and author of *Das gleichgeschlechtliche Leben der Naturvolker* (The same-sex life of primitive peoples, 1911)—as expert witnesses in a trial against the newspaper *Die Freundschaft* (Friendship), the world's first popular entertainment magazine for gays openly sold at kiosks from its establishment in 1919 until 1933. Marcus recalls the start of the trial as follows: "The hearing took place on the day when from 6am a special issue of *Die Welt* cried out the murder of Walter Rathenau [Weimar Germany's Jewish foreign minister], and which casually stated that he was condemned to be a great man in the field of friendship [i.e. he was homosexual]."[210] He then turns to describe Hirschfeld in a reverential way: "In court the chairman could not cope with the many technical sexual medical terms of the day.

You cannot imagine how Hirschfeld intervened with such delicate acumen. He not only completely transparently answered the questions posed to him by the Court Director, but also allowed the content of ancient Greek ideas to arise directly from the words themselves, as no philologist could have done better." As a result, "we all suddenly felt our ignorance; not as painful, but rather as beautiful shame. And this feeling embraced equally the judges, defending counsel, experts, the accused, and even the prosecutor. It was well to remember how it linked us all for a few moments in an unusual spiritual community. Hirschfeld left the room after half an hour crowned the victor of the courtroom. The atmosphere had changed after the path over the great eternal Greek gods had been shown to us."[211]

As seen in this passage, Marcus revered Hirschfeld and believed the erotic homosexual spiritual path of the ancient Greeks could pave the way to an enlightened future. But his love for men and motivation to fight for the gay cause was not only philosophical, political, and literary. It was personal. He had a relationship with a younger Catholic man, Roman Malicki. Until the end of his life Marcus saved a letter Malicki had written him from the Baltic Sea resort of Karlshagen in the summer of 1922:

> Sweetheart!
>
> A grey rainy day hangs over my summer. Nevertheless, it is beautiful here, despite the damp, leaden skies. And yet . . . one ought to be coupled up here, not alone! One ought to have someone, to whom one could say: how wonderful everything is . . . someone with whom one could look for mussels on the beach, and the silent paths through the forest . . . someone whose hand one could clasp! Someone, with whom one could also remain silent, silently sit and daydream. And when night falls and shadows rise from the forest and completely enshroud everything in their cloak, then one should have someone, whom he is fond of, and should not have to go home alone. I never traveled together with anyone. The rule for me is hard. Alone for ever. The trees in the forest whisper it. And the waves of the sea whisper "alone alone." And rain drops alone, alone, alone . . . and I wobble tired and misty-eyed like a butterfly in autumn . . . and I watch how the sun sets. This is how the days pass here. They appear to me sometimes like dead Sunday [the Sunday before Advent on which the dead are commemorated], like grey, taunting autumn days. And when the wind rustles stormily through the forest like a heavy sigh, then to

me it is like . . . a person you know . . . is in fear and agony and cries "help me, come, I am pleasure, I am the best that you have." And all around me is silence. The rain drops alone, alone and sad, I return home. . . . If I indulge by writing down everything and telling you my mood, well, sorry, sweetheart, that I did it first today. For days I had difficulty breathing and heart trouble so that I was incapacitated. Also, thanks for the two love letters. I like your letters so much. Like yellow tea roses I wanted to carry them with me like on Sundays. I am so fond of you. For today, so much.

Goodbye, I think of you in all your sorrowful days.
Your Roman.[212]

That same year saw the publication of Hiller's *§ 175: Die Schmach des Jahrhunderts!* (Paragraph 175: The disgrace of the century!). It aimed "for the liberation of a human minority, which, although harmless," is "oppressed, persecuted, and tormented," a call to arms that gained much attention to the cause, partly through its witty tone, for example, ridiculing the phrase used to denote homosexual sex, "unnatural fornication," for, referring to Nietzsche, he argues "how can something, which occurs in nature, and which is the ineradicable disposition of many people (people of all time periods and all nations), be called unnatural"?[213] Explaining why he used the term "shame," Hiller, considering the well-established integration of German Jewry, reasons that a German kaiser "had named antisemitism as the shame of his century. Yet when were the Jews in Germany ever as persecuted as the homoerotics? Does the criminal law contain an exceptional provision against that racial minority as the notorious exceptional provision against this sexual minority? The shame of the century is anti-homoeroticism [homophobia]; the shame of the century is Paragraph 175."[214] Like Marcus, he could not have predicted what would befall German Jewry the following decade.

In March 1925 Marcus helped craft and signed the petition organized by Hirschfeld's Institute for Sexology sent to the justice minister urging repeal of Paragraph 175. The original petition of 1898 cited in its support that homosexual intercourse was "in no way different from other sexual relationships which, to date, had never been threatened by court proceedings, be it masturbation, or love between women, or love between men, as well as intercourse between men and women," and that abolishing such punishments has not lowered moral standards in other countries. Progress in scientific knowledge based on the latest scientific research has confirmed that this way of love is natural, and occurs at all times all over the world, that gays throughout history have included people of the highest mental quality, and that the criminalization of homosexuality leads to madness, suicide, blackmail, and prostitution. Hirschfeld estimated that "nearly 30 percent of Berlin's homosexual community was blackmailed at some point."[215] The petition demanded that "homosexual actions should be treated in the same way as those between people of the opposite sex, and are punishable only: a) when force by one partner is exercised against the other, b) when either person is under the age of sixteen, c) when their activities offend public decency."[216] Paragraph 175, it continues, "contradicts the demands of a just society, which allows punishment only for unlawful actions. If two consenting adults have a secret sexual affair the rights of a third person are not involved."[217] Moreover, "those who made this law were scientific ignoramuses. It is highly probable that this law would never have been made if the fact that homosexuality is inborn had been known to the legislators."[218]

In the March 1925 petition Dr. Kurt Hiller and Dr. Helene Stöcker appear along with president of the Reichstag, Paul Löbe, and Reich justice minister Dr. Gustav Radbruch—who had been one of Hiller's professors at the University of Heidelberg—among the list of "Philosophers, Jurists, and Politicians."[219] Marcus—not listed as "Dr."—appears under the rubric "Poets, Artists, and Art Scholars," along with Max Brod, Maximilian Harden, Hermann Hesse, and Höchstetter, for whose novella *Lord Byrons Jugendtraum* (Lord Byron's youthful dream) Marcus wrote an afterword including a discussion of the meaning of friendship.[220] His signature is beneath that of Thomas Mann and along with Armin Wegner and Dr. Max Jordan. Jordan at the time was an editor of the prestigious, liberal *Berliner Tageblatt*, owned from its nineteenth-century establishment until 1933 by the German-Jewish Mosse family (the forebears of the influential historian George Mosse), for which Marcus also wrote.[221]

As Marcus relates, "we applied ourselves to the newly published draft of a new criminal code, to which we wanted to offer a counter proposal. Then we began to compose letters to prominent men in the opposing camp, followed by visits to suitable persons. This included Professor Kahl, president of the majority party in the former Reichstag. Years of effort [by Hirschfeld] managed to get him to radically change his view. Hirschfeld got a hearing with the Minister of Justice."[222] This was an impressive achievement, as Dr. Wilhelm Kahl (1849–1932) was leader of the anti-Semitic and socially conservative Deutsche Volkspartei (German People's

Party). Yet in October 1929 the Reichstag committee that Kahl chaired, set up to revise the criminal code, voted to eliminate the antisodomy statute. He cast the deciding vote, reasoning that the law was unenforceable and that it caused more criminality—namely, blackmail—than it deterred.[223]

In October 1925 Hirschfeld asked his friend Marcus to accompany him to the Jury Free Art Exhibition at the Lehrter train station in Berlin, serving as his guide. He wanted to see the portrait of Marcus.[224] Marcus led Hirschfeld past works by Hannah Höch, Wassily Kandinsky, Paul Klee, and Georg Kolbe. They passed a work of Thea Schleusner (1879–1964), who painted Albert Einstein and Nietzsche, arriving at her portrait of Hugo Leichtentritt, German-Jewish musicologist and philosopher from Posen. He is the wrong Hugo. They finally entered the right room.

Hirschfeld's friend Julie Wolfthorn (b. 1864, Thorn [today, Toruń], Poland, d. 1944, Theresienstadt) had completed the portrait by February. Wolfthorn was a well-known Jewish feminist painter, cofounder of the Berlin Secession. She was an artist who gained fame mainly for her portraits of girls, nude bathing nymphs and damselflies and bosomy redheads as well as modern women who were emancipated, self-confident, sporty, and employed in the arts and academy. She considered the portrait of Marcus, one of her very few portraits of men, to be one of her best works.[225] She chose to paint him because Marcus was a friend and was devoted to sexual freedom and equal rights for gays. Wolfthorn was Hirschfeld and Hiller's acquaintance through Helene Stöcker, the leftist, pacifist, feminist activist, sexual reformer, and student of Simmel as well as Hirschfeld's co-campaigner in the successful challenge to the proposed criminalization of lesbian relations (1909–1912).[226] Marcus attended the philosophy course of Wilhelm Dilthey, a strong proponent of the women's movement who also counted Stöcker among his students.[227] Hirschfeld, Wolfthorn, and Marcus hailed from Prussia's Polish provinces, lost after the war. After the Nazi rise to power, Hirschfeld, Marcus, and Wolfthorn would again be denied the right to call themselves citizens, this time as Germans. Two would die for it. But Marcus escaped their fate. What was the secret to his survival?

A clue arises from the coincidence that the portrait of Marcus hung in the same room as Jewish artist Martha Wolff's "Hagar and Ismael," published a year earlier in the Jewish journal *Menorah*, which depicts the affectionate embrace of Abraham's concubine and her tiny son. It evokes the relationship between Muslims and Jews. Both call Abraham their forefather. Muslims say they are descended from Ishmael, and Jews claim to be descended from Isaac. The Torah records how Abraham was compelled to attempt to sacrifice Isaac, whereas the Qur'an implies that son is Ishmael. Along with the biblical scene was pacifist Gert Heinrich Wollheim's portrait of an angelic Tatjana Barbakoff, née Tsipora Edelberg, a famous model and dancer who would be murdered in Auschwitz.

When we look at the portrait of Marcus, we notice he is uncomfortable. Marcus and Hirschfeld had known each other a quarter century. Hirschfeld was always in the limelight, a world-leading sexual rights activist and researcher. Marcus was often at his side, twelve years his junior. They were two men who fought for the right for men to love other men without being persecuted for it. Neither would live to see victory in this battle of a hundred years' war. In October 1925 the spotlight shone on Marcus. What did he look like? Wolfthorn always captured the psychology of her subjects as well as their likeness, as they gaze back at the well-known painter.

Wolfthorn's portrait depicts Marcus sitting uncomfortably in a chair in front of a bookshelf with haphazardly stacked oversized books. Marcus's forehead is lined, and his face wrinkled. His hair is mussed; his angular facial features, including a long, sharp nose, are striking. He almost scowls, if not looks impatiently at the viewer, as if to say, "Just get on with it!" His sharp nose is depicted almost as an arrow, pointing to his thin mustache. He appears restless, somewhat leaning toward the viewer at the same time as he seems to draw back. He crosses his right leg over his left, placing his right elbow on the arm rest, long and bony middle and ring fingers pressed against his cheekbone, the other fingers floating, while the left arm incongruously forms an inverse "D," elbow straight out, fingers touching his left hip. His black jacket is either too small or too tightly buttoned over his white shirt. The odd position makes his necktie and jacket collar slip to the left, adding to the sense of impatience. While simultaneously glaring at the viewer, he looks as if he is absent, deep in thought, asking himself why he is wasting time sitting for the portrait in the office of the imam of Germany's first mosque built by Muslims. Is that why he was uncomfortable? Had not that religion, like Judaism, banned the depiction of the human form?

Marcus had converted to Islam less than half a year earlier, in May, after the portrait had been completed, after he had helped bring to fruition the petition to repeal Paragraph 175.[228] Like Judaism, Islam is generally interpreted to forbid sex between men. At the same time as he edited Hirschfeld's journal, *Sexus*, Marcus also served on the staff of the Muslim community, editing its journal,

Moslemische Revue (Muslim review). And here he was, a Muslim, accompanying Hirschfeld, the well-known sexologist and naturist.[229] Hirschfeld was the author of a popular ethnography of gay Berlin—"from the subterranean gay bars and drag balls to the public baths and railway stations"—a book cataloging the "colorful patchwork" of erotic variety and desire in Berlin.[230] Hirschfeld coined the term "transvestite," provided medical evaluations to allow cross-dressers to obtain licenses so they would not be prosecuted, and supervised the world's first sexual reassignment operation. Americans labeled him the "Einstein of Sex," a sexual reformer who advocated emancipation for homosexuals and women's rights and suffrage and promoted sexual education, sex therapy, the "liberalization of contraception, the right to legal and safe abortions, the enhancement of sexual pleasure."[231] How could such a relationship and such views be reconciled with Islam?

Hirschfeld had left his ancestral Judaism behind, declaring his religion to be "dissident" rather than "Jewish," refusing membership in the community but without becoming Christian. Like other German Jews of his generation, he celebrated Christmas with a Christmas tree and Santa Claus at home.[232] However, while studying the natural sciences, he came into contact with monism. Monism was "a kind of natural science replacement for religion."[233] Hirschfeld promoted the view that "science is not there for its own sake, but for all humanity."[234] In the words of their younger friend Hiller, "Science *per se* is godless. Hirschfeld's humanity is religious—much as he may be a 'Monist.'"[235] Marcus, despite his conversion, did not leave the Jewish fold for over a decade. In his later years he reclaimed being Jewish. How can we comprehend the kaleidoscopic identities and beliefs of this man?

One answer is suggested by his philosophical writing. In one of his earliest works, *Meditationen*, Marcus wrote, "Paradox has played the most important role in the history of the human spirit."[236] For *Die Philosophie des Monopluralismus: Grundzüge einer analytischen Naturphilosophie und eines ABC der Begriffe im Versuch* (The philosophy of monopluralism: The main features of an analytical philosophy of nature and an attempt at an ABC of the term), Marcus's most important philosophical work, Marcus coined the term "monopluralism."[237] The neologism unites the terms "monism" (the idea that all life is part of one basic element in the world) and "pluralism" (the idea that there are many basic elements in the world). Marcus argues that all things in the world are united through the interaction of unity and multiplicity. In this sense they form a unity. They are not different manifestations of a single basic element, as in monism, but rather a "multiplicity of parts" that relate to each other. This *Einheit der Vielheit* (unity of multiplicity) Marcus sees also in the basic elements of the world that exist next to one another but are at the same time dependent (force, time, space).[238] His claim that the world consists of a multiplicity of things, that through their cooperation form, regardless, a unity, contains a contradiction. Unity and multiplicity appear unassociable, but they cannot be conceived without the other: a whole is made of different parts.

He pursued this thesis further in a book published five years later, *Die ornamentale Schönheit der Landschaft und der Natur als Beitrag zu einer allgemeinen Ästhetik der Landschaft und der Natur* (The ornamental beauty of the landscape and nature as contribution to a general aesthetic of landscape and nature).[239] In this work he argued that just as the world is based upon the principle of "the unity of multiplicity," beauty is also a composite made up of the repetition of individual elements. Together the elements are perceived to form a beautiful whole. Beauty is found in nature but also manifests itself in what is true, what is good, and the social.[240]

"Unity of multiplicity" serves as an accurate description of a man who over the course of eighty-six years lived as a German and a Jew, a man who loved men and fought for the right to do so, a man who took the unusual path to become a Muslim.

CHAPTER 2

Queer Convert

Protestant Islam in Weimar Germany, 1925–1933

The religious person attaches his heart to love in every form, to that power whose root is Eros.[1]

Weimar Germany witnessed a "thousand different forms and degrees" of religious and philosophical speculation, "a gigantic wave" encompassing "American Christian Science and English theosophy, Mazdeanism and Neo-Sufism, Steiner's anthroposophy, and a hundred similar creeds," new doctrines of faith, and, according to Hermann Hesse, an "awakening of the soul, burning resurgence of longings for the divine, fever heightened by war and distress."[2] After World War I, Germany "was filled with saviors, prophets, and disciples," some of whose ideas reflected transnational intellectual interactions between Germans and South Asians.[3]

One such new creed was Islam. After World War I, during which millions of Muslims fought for the European powers and the Ottoman sultan launched a jihad encouraged by Germany, Muslims established their first institutions in Europe, including mosques in Paris, London, and Berlin (the latter two founded by Ahmadi).[4] Muslims—especially Bosnians and Tatars—had lived in Germany and given their lives in Prussian wars since the eighteenth century; Ottoman diplomats, soldiers, and war college students likewise had a presence for two centuries, concentrated in Berlin and Potsdam.[5] Coincidentally, Berlin had been known for its male prostitution since the eighteenth century, as male prostitution served as an additional income source for garrisoned soldiers.[6] What was new was Berlin's nondiplomatic civilian Muslim population, numbering between two thousand and three thousand Germans and foreigners—businessmen, physicians, doctoral students, anticolonial activists, intellectuals, and university lecturers.[7] Despite constituting only a tiny percentage of the population—less than 1 percent of the four million residents of the metropolitan region known as Greater Berlin—Muslims became visible in the early 1920s. They established a Muslim institute, library, publishing house, schools, and clubs, and more than a dozen Muslim journals and newspapers appeared, published in German and other languages.[8] Nile Green describes Muslims as making German into "a new Islamic language," with Germany becoming "a Muslim publishing center" and parts of Berlin transformed into "Muslim space" through the establishment of a mosque.[9] While Green is correct in noting Islam's new linguistic, spatial, and geographical configurations, he flattens diverse interpretations of Islam into one generic category and fails to consider the confessional diversity and political differences of Muslims in Berlin.

The Muslims who established themselves in Berlin after World War I were highly heterogeneous. According to Marcus, "in those days there was no Islamic people that did not have its representative in Berlin."[10] They divided into a number of camps, most prominently the two self-described as Ahmadi and Sunni. They competed to build and then control the Berlin mosque, to gain public recognition as the single group representing Muslims, to disseminate their interpretation of Islam through preaching and publishing journals and a Qur'an translation and commentary in German, and to gain converts. Their disputes and differences spilled from the street into the courtroom and forced the reluctant involvement of German authorities. The Ahmadi engaged in a universal mission to renew Islam, defend it from Christian missionaries, and propagate a tolerant, rational, and progressive Islam to Muslims and non-Muslims alike. The Ahmadi believed that Muslim reformer Mirza Ghulam Ahmad (1839–1908) of Qadian, near Lahore, Punjab, in British India, was Jesus Christ reincarnate and a prophet.[11] The Ahmadi emerged in the context of several trends affecting Muslim-majority societies in that era: the birth of new religions—including Bahai'ism (emerging in the 1840s in Iran through the preaching of the Bab, and established in 1852 by Baha'u'llah, believed by his followers to be a prophet); the scriptualist reformist trend in Egypt; and the modernist Islamic movement in South Asia, exemplified by Syed Ahmed Khan (1817–1898), who promoted science and reason in place of orthodoxy and dogma.

After Mirza Ghulam Ahmad's death, followers took his message to the colonial metropole, where they established a mission at England's only mosque, at Woking in Surrey, near London, in 1913.[12] In 1914 the movement split into two branches.[13] The leader of the branch of the Ahmadi that rejected Ahmad's claims to prophecy, Muhammad Ali (1879–1951), sent Maulana Sadr-ud-Din, who had been imam at the Woking mosque during World War I, as a missionary to Berlin in 1922.[14] Within two years of his arrival, he laid the foundation stone of the city's first mosque, completed in 1927 in a well-to-do district.

The year of Sadr-ud-Din's arrival also witnessed the establishment of the Islamische Gemeinde zu Berlin (Islamic Community of Berlin), founded by Abdul Jabbar Kheiri (1880–1958) and Abdul Sattar Kheiri (1885–1953), who were also Muslims from British India.[15] The Kheiri brothers were Sunni Muslim socialist revolutionaries who, while earning doctorates at Friedrich Wilhelm University in Berlin during World War I and introducing Islamic studies there, worked with the German Foreign Office—and especially the head of its section covering Islamic regions, the Jewish orientalist Max von Oppenheim—to secure independence for the Muslims of British India.[16] Archenemies of the Ahmadi, they used their German-language journal, *Islam* (1922–1923), to attack the legitimacy of the group's mission and its right to build a mosque.[17] The Kheiris and their organization, which was led from its founding to 1930 by one or the other of the brothers and never had a building constructed specifically for prayers, promoted normative Sunni Islam.[18] They challenged the Ahmadi's Islamic credentials, considering them sectarians who sowed discord among Muslims by promoting heretical beliefs. As anticolonial activists, the Kheiri brothers labeled the Ahmadi British agents.[19] In campaigning to have Muslims in Berlin boycott the Ahmadi mosque or to have other Muslims take possession of it, they were joined by their close associate, the Egyptian nationalist Mansur Rifat, who quoted from the Qur'an (9:107–110) in condemning "those who build a mosque to cause harm and for unbelief and to cause disunion among the believers," urging Muslims "never to stand in it."[20] The Ahmadi rejected these charges, noting that such differences did not prevent individual Sunni Muslims from praying at their mosque and celebrating the major Muslim holidays in it, or from publishing in their journal.

MAKING CONVERTS: CONVERSION AS DOUBLE CONSCIOUSNESS

The Ahmadi had their sights set on larger goals, seeing themselves as "missionaries" devoted to propagating Islam around the globe. This modern religious movement is an example of conversion emerging out of the colonial encounter not as "a unidirectional process of cultural influence and adaptation" but rather "as resistance to ideological domination," for its members viewed it as a counter response to Christian missionizing.[21] The first of their missionaries to Europe was the barrister Khwaja Kamal-ud-Din (1870–1932), a leading disciple of Mirza Ghulam Ahmad, who claimed to have been on the verge of converting to Christianity before he joined the Ahmadi. After arriving in England in 1912 he established the mission and began to publish its journal, *Islamic Review*. He also took over the Woking mosque. Britain's first purpose-built mosque—built in 1880 by Dr. Gottlieb Wilhelm Leitner (1840–1899), a Hungarian Jew who taught Arabic and *sharia* at King's College, London, and served as principal of Government College University in Lahore—had fallen into disuse before being converted into the headquarters of the Muslim Woking Mission in 1913. The mission had many influential converts and used its journal "not only to spread the message of Islam but also to inform and encourage the converts in their new religion." As of 1924, of the estimated ten thousand Muslims in England, one thousand were converts—all of Christian background, they claimed.[22]

Interested primarily in encouraging conversion and seeking the same success elsewhere in Europe, the leader of the Ahmadi, Muhammad Ali, "resolved to extend its work of the propagation of Islam to Germany" and accordingly "sent two missionaries to Berlin." One of them was Sadr-ud-Din; born in Sialkot, Punjab, British India, and companion of Mirza Ghulam Ahmad, he was a member of the first Ahmadi council (1914), the second missionary to England, and editor of *Islamic Review* (1914–1917) and of the Ahmadi English translation of the Qur'an (1918).[23] Sadr-ud-Din explains how Mirza Ghulam Ahmad's "enthusiasm for Islam and its propagation lit a fire in the souls of those who followed him," such that his disciples "aimed to spread knowledge of Islam to the whole world."[24]

The Ahmadi missionaries in Germany followed the same strategy they had followed in England: establish a mosque and a journal in the local language, win over high-profile converts, set up an organization headed by converts to propagate their vision of Islam, and translate the Qur'an into the local language. They built their mosque in the well-to-do Wilmersdorf district of Berlin, and it remained the only mosque built by and for Muslims not just in Berlin but, indeed, in all of Germany.[25] In 1924 Sadr-ud-Din established *Moslemische Revue*, modeled on the *Islamic Review*, with the express aim of "explaining the teachings of Islam to Germans" in German.[26] Many articles in both journals were written by converts, including the Qur'an translator Muhammad Marmaduke Pickthall (1875–1936; conversion in 1917) in *Islamic Review*, and professor Baron Omar Rolf von Ehrenfels (1901–1980; conversion in 1927 or 1931) in *Moslemische Revue*. Converts played a leading role in the Deutsch Muslimische Gesellschaft (German Muslim Society), a mosque-based organization whose aim was "to promote understanding of Islam through educational work, lectures, and intensive community life in Germany."[27] For the entire eight years of its existence, converts were always in the majority on its board.[28] Since the society "mostly consisted of new German Muslims," it "played an effective role in making the activities of the mission vibrant and known to Berlin's literary circles."[29]

All of these efforts served to proselytize. In 1925 the editor of the Ahmadi's United Kingdom-based *Islamic Review* boasted that in the new "mission field" in Berlin, "twenty-five converts have already turned to Islam."[30] By 1932 the missionaries claimed the number had grown to one hundred.[31] Just as significant is the Ahmadi understanding of religious conversion, something that has largely escaped scholarly analysis.

Borrowing Christian proselytizing techniques—especially autobiographical conversion narratives—the Ahmadi deployed double consciousness as a strategy to win over converts in Europe.[32] Sadr-ud-Din did not demand that converts make a clean break from their former religious beliefs and practices. On the contrary, he asserted: "No ceremony is required to become Muslim. Islam is not only a rational, widespread, and practical religion, it is also fully harmonious with the natural human disposition. Every child is born with this disposition. This is why no one needs to convert to become a Muslim. One can be a Muslim without telling anybody. Committing to Islam is merely an organizational formality."[33] At the same time, however, using a technique favored by British missionaries in India, the Ahmadi boasted of the new converts the community had won, splashing their photos and conversion narratives across the opening pages of the same journal that declared in every issue from its founding in 1924 through 1929 that one did not need to convert to become Muslim.

The autobiographical conversion narratives of these new Muslims, which promote the self-identity they and the missionaries aimed to create, reveal this understanding of conversion.[34] For example, the founder of the Ahmadi Mission in Vienna, the Austrian convert von Ehrenfels, who had also been involved with Magnus Hirschfeld's efforts at sex reform, was described by the Ahmadi as a "great success achieved," inasmuch as he and his wife were "members of an aristocratic family."[35] Von Ehrenfels and his sister Imma married sibling duo Fridl and Willy Bodmershof, and the four became acolytes of German guru and spiritualist painter Bô Yin Râ (Joseph Anton Schneiderfranken, 1876–1943) after World War I.[36] But in the early 1920s the four "didn't know what to do with themselves," so Imma wrote an open letter to Hermann Hesse asking for his advice. They turned to "the Orient." Von Ehrenfels converted to Islam and, like his close friend Essad Bey, enjoyed "looking the Muslim," making a home movie in pajamas "about leaving Europe to find himself in 'the East.'"[37] Indeed, he left Europe for India in the late 1930s. According to von Ehrenfels, "the Islamic teaching of successive revelation implies in my opinion the following: The source from which all the great world religions sprang as one. The founders of these great paths, prepared for peace-seeking mankind, gave witness to one and the same basic divine teaching. Acceptance of one of these paths means searching for Truth in Love, but it does not imply the rejection of any other path, i.e., another religion." He concludes from this that "the acceptance of Islam and the path of the Muslims by a member of an older religion thus means as little rejection of his former religion as, for instance, the acceptance of Buddha's teaching meant the rejection of Hinduism to Buddha's Indian compatriots," for "the differences of religion are man-made. The unity is divine."[38]

The foreign Muslims in Berlin formed an "Islamic middle class."[39] Most of them were university students financially supported by their homelands or were professors, diplomats, businessmen, journalists, doctors, and other professionals.[40] The leaders of the Ahmadi and the Islamic Community—South Asian Muslims with doctorates—used German middle-class values such as simplicity, practicality, a thirst for knowledge, reason, and intellect to attract members of the middle class and intellectuals, who were facing severe financial and spiritual distress.[41] As a result, German converts who came from the same educated middle class as the missionaries made up a significant proportion of the Muslim population.[42] Nathalie Clayer and Eric Germain claim that a third of Germany's Muslim population in the 1930s consisted of converts, despite the fact that the exact numbers of Muslims and converts cannot be determined since Islam was not a recognized religion in Germany and not given community status.[43] As Germain notes, the social status of the aristocrats, professionals, and scientists who did convert was of greater importance than the number of converts.[44] For as Humayun Ansari points out, they were best able to establish "consonance" between Islam and the "native" religions (Christianity and Judaism), making Islam "indigenous."[45] Hugo Marcus, referred to by the Ahmadi as "the most valued prize of our Mission in Berlin," was one of those converts.[46]

Marcus's impact was significant throughout the time the missionaries were active in the city. For over a decade and a half, he helped shape the expression of Islam and presented it to the German public. The monthly "Islam Evenings" at the mosque were, along with Muslim holidays, not for Muslims to celebrate alone but were mass media events as well; the Eid al-Fitr sermon in 1931 was broadcast live on radio. The mosque was an "in" place to see and be seen, and the events it hosted were frequently written up in the German press, including the *Berliner Illustrirte Zeitung*, which had a circulation of nearly two million, and in society papers.[47] Marcus introduced foreign Muslim dignitaries at the mosque to crowds of German guests and embassy officials from Muslim-majority lands.[48] He was on good terms with politicians of the Weimar Coalition—the bloc of the Social Democratic Party of Germany (SPD), the liberal German Democratic Party, and the Catholic Centre Party (BVP)—as well as with Protestant and Catholic clergy and German royalty.[49] According to the last imam of the mosque, Sheikh Abdullah, Marcus "made our community life bloom through many new endeavors and his broad initiative."[50] What has not previously been explored is his interpretation of Islam.

MARCUS'S PROTESTANT, OCCIDENTAL ISLAM

Although Muslims introduced Marcus to Islam, with one notable exception, Marcus's Islam is strangely devoid of Muslims. It includes nothing from the Islamic past, save Muhammad's era, and no Islamic thinkers, aside from the reported speech (in the Qur'an and the hadith) of Muhammad. Not only is Marcus's Islam reduced to the founding text and founder's life, but the analysis and interpretation of them are based on a single source: Goethe. Thus, for example, Marcus's discussion of the difference between prophets and reformers in his analysis of Muhammad is similar to Goethe's discussion of the difference between prophet and poet in the "Notes and Essays" section of Goethe's poetry cycle *West-östlicher Diwan* (1819; *West-East Divan*).[51] Although Muslims had been present in Germany for centuries—namely, Muslim royal retainers and soldiers fighting on behalf of various German princes and Prussia, including against Napoleon—Marcus never mentions the actual Muslims praying, fasting, battling, dying, and being buried in German soil during Goethe's era. Marcus refers to no Muslim but the Prophet. He never quotes from a single Muslim philosopher. He takes the Qur'an and the life of the Prophet as everything one needs to know to be a Muslim. Writing in the *Moslemische Revue* to middle-class seekers like himself, he advocates a German Islam without a Middle Eastern component.

Marcus's is a very Protestant Islam because he crafts his own interpretation of Islam based solely on the Holy Book and the life of the Prophet. In "Islam und Protestantismus" ("Islam and Protestantism"), he divides religions into two types, the "mystical" and the "rationalistic."[52] Doing so enables him to make an analogy between the great schism between "mystical" Catholicism and "rationalistic" Protestantism and the supposed rupture between "mystical" Buddhism and "rationalistic" Islam. Calling Islam the "Protestantism of the East," he argues that "Islam is the earliest Protestantism, a Protestantism appearing one thousand years before Protestantism in the West."[53] To make the comparison more concrete, he draws contrasts between rationalistic religions, which unite worldly and sacred power, and mystical religions, which focus only on the sacred.[54] He draws parallels between Islam and Protestantism, noting that these two rationalistic religions stripped religion of miracles and magic and abolished ceremony, music, and icons. Similar to "Islam und Protestantismus" in his short biography of Muhammad, he draws parallels with Martin Luther by claiming Muhammad is the "First Reformer."[55] Crucial to understanding his vision of Islam is his claim that Islam and Protestantism both established "a priesthood of all believers."[56] With this statement Marcus explains why he is able to jettison thirteen hundred years of Islamic thought. The believer reads the holy text, finds his own personal interpretation, and passes over all others in silence.

Without naming a single Muslim philosopher or theologian, Marcus overlooks the succeeding millennium of Islamic thought after Muhammad's era, picking it up again as the Islamic heritage passed from the Arabs in Spain to the Spanish Jew Baruch Spinoza.[57] The Muslims in Spain shared their intellectual treasures and their philosophical and scientific culture with Jews such that it is "no wonder that the descendants of the expellees kept alive the intellectual heritage that their ancestors had gained from the Muslims."[58] Spinoza then influenced all subsequent German philosophers, including Goethe. As Marcus writes, "Goethe venerated Spinoza, Lessing endorsed him. And Hegel and Schelling would be unthinkable without him. Indeed, precisely the specifically German profoundness [*Tiefsinn*] characteristic of these philosophers is largely rooted in Spinoza."[59] The Islamic heritage—passing through Spinoza—"entered the German spirit and helped to determine German destiny," because Bismarck read Spinoza.[60] And then Marcus, born only a decade after the founding of the Second Reich, read Goethe. Marcus perceives of himself as a latter-day Spinoza, the un-Jewish Jew presenting Islam, as filtered through Goethe and his own philosophic lens, to Germany.

NIETZSCHE AND ISLAM

In "Der Islam und die Philosophie Europas" ("Islam and European Philosophy"), published in *Moslemische Revue* in 1924 (an English version appeared in *Islamic Review* in 1925), Marcus reflects a liberal Jewish approach to Islam but then takes it a step further. Marcus argues that Islam is the most modern, progressive, advanced, and rational of religions. Muslims are taught to use their reason to choose a practical path between extremes, and he notes parallels between Immanuel Kant's ethics and the ethics of Islam as well as drawing other parallels to G. W. F. Hegel and Nietzsche.[61] If Hegel envisioned history as a process of steadily advancing consciousness, thus making all progress rational, Marcus argues that Islam is the culmination of the progress of the intellect, for it "demands nothing of you which cannot be brought to agree with the human intellect," as "all of its teachings are necessarily derived from Intellect."[62] Moreover, he argues not only that Islam is the natural religion promoted by Kant but that it is also in concord with Kant's conception of cosmopolitanism since its moral teachings offer a plan for the good of society and the love of humanity and promote peace and world citizenship.[63] Referring to Nietzsche's concept of the *Übermensch* (superman), Marcus argues that, like Nietzsche, Islam promotes self-discipline and self-reflection, leading to self-perfection. Islam is based on the control of the passions and emotions through a good will, analogous to Kant's good will, the only real good in the world. As Marcus concludes, "One sees that there are everywhere points of coincidence between Islam and the deepest European [read: German] thought."[64]

Having briefly presented the alleged affinities between Islam and Nietzsche's concept of the *Übermensch* in his 1924 overview of philosophy, Marcus develops in "Nietzsche und der Islam," published two years later, what he perceives as further equivalences. Here again Marcus's writing asserts that Islam is part of German cultural history. Between 1890 and 1945 Germans with extremely different utopian aims—anarchists, the artistic avant-garde, conservative revolutionaries, expressionists, feminists, futurists, nationalists, religious reformers, sexual libertarians, socialists, vegetarians, *völkisch* groups, youth movements, and Zionists alike—selectively appropriated Nietzsche's critical ideas to suit their widely diverging political and cultural projects for overcoming Germany's problems.[65] Marcus did likewise and adopted Nietzsche's method of syncretizing various strands of thought to create new values and norms. Moreover, Marcus's turn-of-the-twentieth-century literary and formal education had been shaped by people inspired by the early Nietzsche, particularly the ideas in *The Birth of Tragedy out of the Spirit of Music* (1872). Marcus participated in the circle around the "prophet" and "poet-seer" Stefan George, which was inspired by Nietzsche's call for a "rediscovered German spirituality on a new creative basis," and then studied at Friedrich Wilhelm University in Berlin with the "Nietzsche enthusiast" Georg Simmel, who argued that Nietzsche had "criticized traditional morality . . . to make way for a superior morality."[66] Nietzsche's rejection of Christian morality was interpreted by many homosexuals as endorsing their nonnormative sexuality. What also attracted homosexuals was belief in the rumor that Nietzsche was gay.[67] More than that: Nietzsche inspired two wings of the homosexual movement, Hirschfeld's "Jewish," "liberal," medical approach supported by Marcus and especially Adolf Brand's antiliberal, antifeminist, nationalist, masculinist homosexual movement whose concept of *der Eigene* "overlapped extensively" with Nietzsche's *Übermensch*.[68] For both wings, the attraction was to an individual who "created his own morality, including in the sexual realm."[69]

In "Nietzsche und der Islam," Marcus correlates Nietzsche's best-known concepts—including the notions of the Dionysian and Apollonian spirits and the *Übermensch*—with Islamic ideas. In *Thus Spoke Zarathustra* (1883–1885), Nietzsche "established a bridge to the Orient" (i.e., the Islamic world), Marcus asserts, just as Goethe had done with his *West-östlicher Diwan*. Notwithstanding that the two authors had very different outlooks, both works' central thrust is a reinterpretation of the thought of key Persian figures: Zoroaster for Nietzsche, Hafiz for Goethe.

To explore the connection to the Orient, Marcus discusses Nietzsche's *Birth of Tragedy*. Marcus presents Nietzsche's distinction between the Dionysian and the

Apollonian spirits. The former embodies the passion of a heroic and tragic man, who, to experience ecstasy, does not shy away from misery, death, and disappointment, which leads to both happiness and suffering. In contrast, the idyllic and ascetic Apollonian man, to avoid tragedy, forgoes moments of supreme happiness, shunning extremes, "moderating his drive with reason to escape great suffering."[70]

Whereas Nietzsche argues that ancient Greek tragedy was the apex of art because it perfectly harmonized these two elements, Marcus, fitting his aim to reconcile German philosophy and Islam, claims instead that Islam is where "both perspectives are united. They complement each other."[71] Bringing together Nietzsche's finding that the culture of the Islamic world had a Dionysian core with Goethe's depiction of an Apollonian East, Marcus then explains how Islam unites the two German writers' approaches and the two fundamental principles:

> The spirit of holy ecstasy fills Islamic devotion. It elevates the soul to a Dionysian condition that other religions lack. In the Muslim religious service, each participant takes an active part, with body and soul. By encompassing the entire human being, Muslim devotion elevates man to a Dionysian condition. By limiting ecstasy to religion, it remains within safe bounds. On the other hand, we notice in Muslim moral teachings a distinctly Apollonian attitude. Rational moderation is key here. Alcoholic intoxication is forbidden. Providing for others is demanded. Channeled into devotion, the Dionysian is banished from daily life. Daily life is under the sign of Apollonian thinking. In this way, Islam reconciles the two great perspectives.[72]

Reconciling the two opposite emotional states of indifference and passion is difficult, if not unresolvable.[73] Because it is unresolvable, it is tragic. And while it is tragic, it underpins the heroic. The heroism of war—"when entire nations engage in criminal indifference"[74]—however, belongs to the past.[75] Religion fulfills this mission in the postwar period, establishing a new kind of heroism, reconciling idealism and realism, the "warm heart" and cool dispassion, our Dionysian and Apollonian sides.

The reader senses that one reason Marcus is drawn to Nietzsche is the latter's celebration of non-Christian culture. For Marcus, what was most attractive about Nietzsche's philosophy was his criticism of Christianity for its pessimism, its self-denial, as a religion that "says a 'no' to life," Subhash Kashyap writes. "It is a religion of decadents. It elevates the slave-virtues—meekness, humility, compassion, mercy, pity. It denies all the good, life-promoting instincts."[76] Nietzsche's criticism of Christianity, particularly its otherworldliness, its focus on suffering and pity, and its Christian-based morality, reflected and contributed to a widespread crisis of faith and search for other sources of spirituality in Germany. It led some Germans to "redirect and regenerate the religious impulse," to develop "new configurations of faith."[77]

Marcus directed this impulse toward what was a new cult in Germany, Islam. A tragic-heroic rather than a superficial, rose-colored optimism is common to both the great German philosopher and Islam, he observes. "Make wings from your suffering!" Nietzsche writes. "We grow through those things that almost kill us." Likewise, Islam "teaches that we have to struggle hard to realize the good. God has given us all the conditions to excel. But we have to freely use them and intensify our powers." Humanity must rise above simple contentment and the desire for self-preservation. "This is the same as Nietzsche's teaching of man as something that has to be overcome through man himself," Marcus claims. Islam believes in the unending possibilities of inward spiritual development, self-awareness, and self-mastery, in other words, in Nietzsche's *Übermensch*.[78] Seeking convergences with this journey of self-cultivation, Marcus comments that "Islam, too, conceives the progress of humanity as the realization of God," even though Nietzsche denied a progressive course of history, asserting instead a kind of entropy where, in the natural course of events, the weak and herd-like conformers and their deadly and stultifying morality and tradition and institutions prevail. More important, Nietzsche explicitly linked the superman—who was beyond traditional Christian morality and measures of good and evil—with the *death* of God. But by the death of God, Nietzsche meant that the God of European Christianity had outlived His usefulness, for the "truths" of that religion were actually falsifications because they were otherworldly and utopian rather than life-enhancing, which Marcus agreed with.[79] Moreover, slavish conformity to the church and its dogma had led to a society that was "empty, materialistic, and despiritualized."[80] Facing this crisis, Marcus would have Europeans adopt the God of Islam as the life-affirming principle that would enable people to live a vibrant, purposeful, spiritual life, a solution with which Nietzsche probably would not have agreed. As another scholar has noted regarding a more recent Muslim adoption of Nietzsche, "Rather than seek to rehabilitate a decadent religion, Nietzsche's free-spirited experimenters would attempt to hasten the process of its creative destruction."[81]

Nevertheless, Marcus appears as both "Islamist" and Nietzschean. This is revealed when one looks carefully at his envisioned utopia. The political aspect of Marcus's utopia consists mainly of claims that all laws are spelled out in the Qur'an, and the governmental model is that of the leadership of Muhammad and the first community of believers in seventh-century Medina. For Marcus, Muhammad was a democrat, ruling only as "the first among those of equal birth."[82] Reflecting the influence of Simmel—and perhaps the antidemocratic sentiment of the masculinist homosexual movement and of George—the government Marcus envisions is a "democracy of aristocrats," combining Nietzsche's pagan aristocracy, a "community of nobles," with Muhammad's Islamic aristocracy, an aristocratic democracy, which is "an aristocracy of achievement" rather than an inherited aristocracy of class.[83] He calls for an elitist form of rule where the nobles consult the leader, not a state based on the will of the people.

Mass conversion and the introduction of an Islamic state, Marcus contends, would transform Europe, bringing about a new era of peace, an end to party politics and to strife. It was also a way to revitalize Europe's spiritual life. Christianity not only brought about mass death and destruction in the Great War but is itself "dead"—Christians killed their own construct of God and religion. Islam, on the other hand, is "the religion of eternal self-renewal," the path to revitalization.[84] He argues that "only religion has the power to shake people from their indifference, to disturb us from our sense of balance," to "awaken our warm heart."[85] Nothing like religion "undermines our daily bourgeois security, allows us to expel the Philistine from our own innermost temple, frees us from indifference, brings the heroic in us to life," and arouses our "passionate enthusiasm."[86] Islam, he claims, is the antidote for indifference, for living life without feeling.

Writing for a German middle-class audience seeking solutions for its cultural crisis, Marcus envisages not the annihilation of the past, however, but a return to the high point of German culture—Weimar classicism. Goethe, the titan of the Weimar Enlightenment, or *Aufklärung*, had effectively converted to Islam, he contends—and modern Germans would be well advised to do likewise. Marcus devotes more time to describing the past, detailing the affinities between Germanness and Islam, than to a very elaborate blueprint for the future, which is why it should be read as an allegory rather than as a remedy, although he does advocate an Islamic state. But his understanding is based on his interpretation of Goethe's approach to Islam.

GOETHE AS MUSLIM AND HOMOSEXUAL ROLE MODEL

For German converts to Islam like Marcus, Goethe attracted a considerable amount of attention, for the greatest German poet had a strong personal affinity for the Qur'an and Muhammad.[87] His praise legitimized Islam for Germans. Goethe has been called "the role model for a German Islam" for good reason.[88] While a few other German Enlightenment intellectuals, such as Gottfried Wilhelm Leibniz (1646–1716), Gotthold Ephraim Lessing (1729–1781), and Johann Gottfried Herder (1744–1803) depicted Muslims in a positive light in their work, Goethe surpassed them, as "his statements are more daring and provocative than anything previously heard in Germany," expressing "an exceptional empathy" for Islam and an "extraordinarily positive attitude toward it" throughout his life.[89] As a twenty-three-year-old, he composed "Muhammads Gesang" ("Muhammad's Song," 1773), as a seventy-year-old, he declared publicly that he contemplated "devoutly celebrating that holy night, when the Qur'an, in its entirety, was revealed to the Prophet from on high."[90] In between, he "testified in various ways to his admiration for Islam," such as in his incomplete "Muhammad Tragedy," the "most remarkable act of homage that a German poet had ever rendered the founder of Islam."[91]

Above all, this sympathy is seen in one of Goethe's greatest works, the *West-östlicher Diwan*, written to inspire "a spiritual bridge from West to East," which "includes the astonishing sentence: the writer of the book 'does not even reject the supposition that he may be a Muslim.'"[92] Adopting several Muslim pseudonyms for himself in this collection, Goethe writes as a Christian, German European, and a Persian, Middle Eastern Muslim, "a thoroughly *hybridized* cultural figure."[93] Goethe enjoyed "playing the Muslim," toying with the assumed boundaries separating Christians and Muslims:

> Who knows himself and others well
> No longer may ignore:
> Occident and Orient dwell
> Separately no more.

'Twixt two worlds I love the way
Back and forth a man may sway;
So between the East and West
Moving to and fro's the best."[94]

The poet enjoyed wearing a white turban of muslin (a symbol of conversion to Islam) and claimed in the *West-östlicher Diwan* that it was better to wind a muslin cloth (as a Muslim emperor) than wear a crown (like a Christian king), for "muslin looks much better."[95] *Wilhelm Meister's Apprenticeship* (1795) may therefore contain autobiographical detail, as Goethe describes youthful poet Wilhelm in his bedroom:

> He had put a [prayer] rug in the middle of the room. . . . A white cap would be fastened on his head like a turban, and he turned up the sleeves of his dressing gown in oriental fashion, asserting that the long sleeves got in his way when he was writing. Of an evening, when he was alone and without fear of being disturbed, he would girdle himself with a silk sash, and sometimes stick a dagger in . . . and, thus accoutred, rehearse the tragic roles that he had assigned to himself. He even knelt on the carpet to say his prayers.[96]

In the last book of the *West-östlicher Diwan*, when at the gate of Paradise the poet (Goethe) is asked "Have you sure and certain ties / To our Muslim doctrine dear?"–he replies in the affirmative, "No more quibbling or delay! Go ahead and let me in."[97] Most famously, the *West-östlicher Diwan* includes this poem:

I find it foolish, and quite odd,
That stubborn folk seek to deny:
If "Islam" means we all serve God,
We all in Islam live and die.[98]

In "Notes and Essays for a Better Understanding of the *West-East Divan*," Goethe expresses admiration for Muhammad, an "extraordinary" man, whom he considered a prophet and not merely a poet, and says that the "truly sublime" Qur'an "attracts me, astonishes me, and in the end elicits my admiration."[99]

What has been largely overlooked until now is that in the 1920s and 1930s Marcus (and other German Muslims, as today) took Goethe's encounter with and sympathetic view of Islam as precedent for their own, modeling their embrace of the religion on his "conversion."[100] In fact, Goethe's religiosity was an extraordinarily complex phenomenon—despite professions such as those quoted above, he did not feel that he belonged to any religious institution, not even the Lutheran Church, into which he was born, and he did not confess to any organized religion.[101] In considering him a secret Muslim, German converts overlooked the objections the poet raised, ranging from his critique of misogyny as expressed in the Qur'an, and in the sunna and hadith (practices and sayings attributed to Muhammad), to the prohibition of wine and inebriation, and to Muhammad's (and subsequent Muslims') antagonism toward poets and poetry.[102] German converts also remain silent about the fact that wine, women, and song and the celebration of man-boy love are the main themes of the *West-östlicher Diwan* (discussed below). They avoid engaging with the German poet's ambivalence, his "displaying attraction and repulsion," and his explicit denial of core Islamic beliefs, some of which they also repeat.[103] Irrespective, however, of whether Goethe was a "secret" Muslim (an issue mainly for German converts to Islam) and of his representations of Islam and the Orient (a concern for literary scholars), the subject considered here is how Marcus used Goethe's reading of Islam to construct a vision of a German utopia.[104]

The Ahmadi translation and commentary of the Qur'an (1939), for which Marcus served as editor, includes many quotations of Goethe. Explaining Sura 21:32, "And we made the sky a protected ceiling," the editor sees fit to turn to Goethe, *Faust* I, "Prologue in Heaven," where the three archangels step up; first, Angel Raphael:

> The Sun sings out, in ancient mode,
> *His* note among his brother-spheres,
> And ends his pre-determined road,
> With peals of thunder for our ears.
> The sight of him gives Angels power,
> Though none can understand the way:
> The inconceivable work is ours,
> As bright as on the primal day.

The commentary quotes Goethe again in relation to 39:4, "If God had intended to take a son, God could have chosen from among God's creation," explaining that God can have no relations, for prophets are his "sons" only metaphorically.

It proclaims "the Qur'an and even Jesus himself deny his divinity, but this idea cannot be stated better than by Goethe":

> Jesus purely, thoughtful, awed,
> Felt One God, when all was still.
> Who'd make Jesus into God
> Would but pain his holy will.
> Right it seems, and bright as sun—
> What Muhammad knew so well;
> Through the concept of the One
> All the world could he compel.[105]

Regarding 52:34, "Then let them produce a statement like it, if they should be truthful," referring to the singularity of the Qur'an, the commentary sees fit to quote Goethe asking "what hinders us from mounting Muhammad's miracle-working horse to swing us through the sky? Why should we not devoutly celebrate that holy night in which the Qur'an in its entirety was revealed to the prophet from on high?"[106]

Marcus compares himself to Goethe in his own conversion narrative. "In 1947," he begins, "a German newspaper wrote that although I am a staid middle-aged man who carefully considers every step, after having read the Qur'an, I imprudently converted to Islam." However, Marcus declares, "already as a youth, when studying an old translation of the Qur'an in my hometown, I had felt it to be my innermost desire to learn about Islam. It was the same edition from which Goethe had become acquainted with Islam. Already back then the absolutely rational and at the same time lofty construction of Islamic doctrine made a profound impression on me, no less the powerful spiritual transformation that it effected in Islamic countries." Thereafter, in Berlin, "I then had the opportunity to work with Muslims and to hear the enthusiastic and inspiring Qur'an commentaries that Maulana Sadr-ud-Din taught us. After years of active participation in the ideal efforts of this excellent intellect, I converted to Islam, which deprived me of nothing, for it allowed me to preserve the worldview that I had formed for myself. But in addition it gave me several of the most path-breaking human thoughts that have ever been conceived."[107]

Marcus's conversion narrative is typical of the conversion narratives of his European and German contemporaries insofar as he depicts Islam as a religion "avoiding all dogmas that are incompatible with modern science" so that "in Islam there is no conflict between faith and knowledge."[108] Marcus cited the same reasons as other converts of that era for accepting Islam: its rationalism, its compatibility with modern science, its lack of a clash between belief and science, its practicality as opposed to idealism, and its tolerance.[109]

Yet Marcus's narrative is unique in the way it describes the initial encounter with Islam. Other converts usually recount an experience from adulthood, narrating an initial meeting with Muslims and Islam in an exotic, non-European locale, sometimes in the service of the empire in Africa or while stationed in the Middle East during World War I, usually set to a backdrop of the Arabic call to prayer in a mosque.[110] As one scholar notes, "The most prevalent genre of conversion accounts are those embedded in pilgrimage narratives," and the most famous among them is Asad's *The Road to Mecca* (1954) where the author contrasts the "strangeness" of Islam with the familiarity of Europe.[111]

In great contrast, Marcus's initial introduction is during his youth, when he studied a German translation of the Qur'an in his hometown library in provincial Posen. Not only does Marcus not have to travel to a Muslim-majority society to meet Islam for the first time, but Islam has already been made meaningful and understandable to him, for the Qur'an has been translated into German. There is no need for him to learn Arabic; Islam is manifest in his own language, without mediation. Moreover, Islam has been in his town for over a century: the Qur'an translation dated back to 1750 and was the edition from which Goethe also drew his knowledge on Islam. Thus, the initial encounter is not mediated by an Arab or a Muslim in the Middle East but is legitimized by Germany's greatest poet.

Marcus's narrative then moves from teenage encounters in the German provinces to meeting actual Muslims—at first the foreign students he tutored—in the German capital as a man in his mid-forties.[112] Two more steps were required before he became a Muslim. First he worked with Muslims and listened to the "inspiring" Qur'an commentaries of Sadr-ud-Din, the founder of the first Ahmadi Muslim Mission at Berlin. Again we see that Germanness is primary in his account. Having already read the Qur'an in German translation on his own as a teen, as an adult he listened to sermons in German about the Qur'an in Berlin in Germany's only mosque. Finally, after years of working together with Sadr-ud-Din—as editor of the German-language mosque publications—Marcus embraced Islam.

According to Asad, taken as the typical European convert, what is demanded is the exchange of "familiar habits of thought for new, unfamiliar ones": "you have to set out to exchange one world for another—to gain a new world for yourself in exchange for an old one which you can never really possess."[113] In great contrast to such an approach, Marcus claims that adopting Islam allowed him to preserve his former worldview. His conversion narrative, echoing his philosophical writing, argues that Islam and German values and philosophy converge.

At the same time, we see in his conversion narrative, as in that of von Ehrenfels, conversion as a kind of double consciousness. Converting to Islam "deprived me of nothing," Marcus wrote, "for it allowed me to preserve the worldview that I had formed for myself. But in addition it gave me several of the most pathbreaking human thoughts that have ever been conceived."[114] Similarly, Marcus wrote: "Islam is the only religion that recognizes all prior revelations of all other peoples likewise as divine. For example, for a Muslim, the Vedas, the teachings of Buddha and Zoroaster, the Old and the New Testament are likewise holy and binding books. And for a Muslim, Buddha, Zoroaster, Abraham, Moses, and Jesus are also prophets sent on a divine mission."[115] "In the Berlin mosque," he confirmed, "adding the Muslim religion which I embraced to my Judaism was permitted . . . since there are no fundamental doctrinal differences between the two confessions."[116] This interpretation may explain why Marcus did not leave the Jewish community of Berlin for nearly a dozen years after his conversion, and then did so only when he thought it might save his life.[117] Nor did he immediately sever ties with Hiller and Hirschfeld, accompanying the latter to an art exhibition six months after his conversion in 1925 to show the famous sexologist a portrait of Marcus done in the mission house of the Berlin mosque.[118] It is also significant that being of Jewish background and retaining membership in the Jewish community did not hinder Marcus from becoming the leading German in the Ahmadi mosque community's intellectual and administrative life.

In a lengthy lecture delivered at the mosque in the 1920s and then reworked two decades later, Marcus explores Goethe's main writings on Muhammad and Islam.[119] He notes that "Goethe was rumored to have become a Muslim in his advanced age. Heinrich Heine [the famous German poet of Jewish background who converted to Christianity] talks of him as the grand old Muslim. Other, very different voices declare the same thing." While "those voices have faded," it is commonly known and accepted "that Goethe maintained a relationship with Islam that was very close, sometimes downright intimate. And for Islam, this is a fact of no little significance." After World War II Goethe "was still being celebrated alike in Western as well as in Eastern Europe and America as the humanly richest and most interesting personality produced by the West, and as Germany's greatest poet."[120]

Marcus notes that Goethe concerned himself with Islam in two periods of his life: "As a young man of twenty-three, he began his studies of Islam. . . . As an old man of sixty-five, he picked them up once more and completed them," according to Marcus, by becoming Muslim.[121] Marcus is referring to Goethe's composition of the Muhammad poem while young and the *West-östlicher Diwan* when mature. To Marcus, Goethe's encounter with Islam was anything but superficial, for it was lifelong and exactly like that recounted by Marcus in his own conversion narrative, for "already as a young man (Goethe) studied the Qur'an and assembled a collection of Qur'anic sayings, which he deeply engraved in his memory." One of the Qur'ans that Goethe studied was the German translation published in his hometown, Frankfurt, "the city where the German emperors were crowned." To Marcus, "this demonstrates that Islam was already beginning to attract the attention of Europe's elite," a group in which he includes himself.[122]

Scholarly consensus holds that Goethe understood Islam as a "mystical" and not a "rational" religion. Most scholarship focuses on his *West-östlicher Diwan*, in which the German poet engages with and imitates a Persian mystical depiction of the divine. Marcus did not publish an analysis of this work. Instead, among Goethe's works he chose to write about an early work, "Muhammads Gesang" (Muhammad's song), which is by all scholarly accounts a depiction of mystical union with God.[123]

Marcus, however, reads into the poem the Islamic theme, absent from the original, that humanity has distanced itself from God yet still harbors a yearning for God, which God also shares. God therefore sends a prophet who can lead humanity back to God, but only when people actively endeavor to follow God's path do they find success and salvation. As increasing numbers of people follow the Prophet, the poem says—first his family, then his tribe, then his people, and finally the entire continent—all "blossom; mosques, castles, palaces, cities rise up from the earth; even a fleet connects the continents and carries the Prophet's and God's fame throughout the world." Marcus comments that Goethe celebrates Muhammad "as humanity's greatest cultural carrier, and it is demonstrated how the submission to the will of God renders peoples great and fosters progress," which is not quite what the poem is saying.[124] Marcus, insisting on his "Jewish view of Islam," which sees in Islam a rational system, misses the poem's ecstatic, spiritual depiction of the faith. He does not grasp its main message of mystical union, as

Muhammad, depicted as a river, sweeps all of humanity to "the eternal Ocean," to "his awaiting Creator/And in a torrent of joy/On to His very heart," symbolizing uniting with God.

Marcus explains that to grasp this poem in its full meaning, one needs to know that Goethe wrote it the day after he had finished reading the [most] famous work of poetry German literature then knew: Friedrich Gottlieb Klopstock's (1724–1803) "Der Messias" ("The Messiah").[125] Marcus claims that "Muhammad's Song" is Goethe's response to Klopstock's adulation of Jesus as Christ and the path to Heaven and God through Jesus's divine mediation. It is obvious to Marcus that Goethe's point of view is "also the Islamic point of view. And Goethe is right to proclaim it through the prophet Muhammad."[126] Marcus asserts: "In conversations and letters at that time, Goethe resisted nothing as bitterly as the teaching of Christ's divine nature and the Pauline crucifixion." For Goethe, Christ was entirely what he is for every Muslim: "a prophet and an excellent, extraordinary human being thoroughly worthy of admiration, but no God." Marcus concludes "Goethe opposes the idea of Jesus being God's son as much as any other superstition. . . . Goethe is entirely on the side of Islam, [he] is indeed Muslim."[127]

Marcus presents other writings in which Goethe appears to identify himself with Islam but avoids noticing his Sufi interpretation of that religion. One is the "Hymn," based on the sixth sura of the Qur'an, in which God reveals himself to Muhammad by way of the sun, moon, and stars.[128] Rather than seeing in it a mystical vision, Marcus explains that the poem's significance lies in understanding Goethe's opposition to "the dogmatism of Christianity" and "above all against superstition." Marcus uses this poem to present Islam as a religion of reason. Goethe "demands a modern worldview that does not contradict scientific insight," which is "something he has in common with the rationalism of his era," that of the Enlightenment. Marcus criticizes the adherents of the rationalistic Enlightenment, however, for to them, "the world changes, by way of scientific natural observation, into a vast soulless apparatus, into a great mechanical engine without feeling." For Marcus, Goethe had a different worldview. Because God is revealed in nature, faith, and science, reason and religion are interdependent. While Goethe "is against false superstition and for a scientific worldview," this "leads him not to a world-machine but to a loving God, whom one may gradually approach through contemplating the miracle of creation." Thus, for Goethe as for Muslims, "God does not disappear behind his works but brilliantly steps forward in them. And while rationalism only perceives a mathematical problem instead of the miracle, for Goethe it is clear that behind the mathematical problem there are final things that will never be soluble by scientific calculation." With such thoughts, Marcus notes approvingly, "Goethe walks the path of the human being [who is] at once self-confidently knowing and acting, and reverently bowing down and worshipping."[129]

Goethe, according to Marcus, wages the struggle against dogmatism in the two Muhammad poems. This was already conventional wisdom. But what makes Marcus's argument unique is his claim that "what Goethe professes in these poems is also the perspective of Islam, which pursues its path to God between superstition and mechanical worldview."[130]

"Muhammad's Song" and the "Hymn" were precursors to a prose work, a tragedy, about the Prophet that Goethe began but never completed. Marcus had to find a way to explain how Goethe, who had "never been capable of regarding Muhammad as an imposter,"[131] could agree to translate Voltaire's ostensible attack on Muhammad and the Qur'an, *Le fanatisme, ou Mahomet le Prophete* (1736)—which depicted Muhammad as "a tyrant and deceiver who abuses the credulity of his followers for his own egotistic purposes"[132]—but fail to complete his own tragedy.[133] To Marcus, "Goethe thought so highly of Muhammad as to equate him with genius par excellence. . . . [Yet] tragedy represents the tragic downfall of a man; which occurs as a consequence of his own guilt. Therefore, a dramatic hero is always burdened with a guilt that demands atonement and [that] finds it by way of his downfall."[134] Marcus perceives that as a believer in Islam, Goethe could not accuse Muhammad of any kind of guilt. Goethe was "only capable of profound appreciation, and divine praise of the Prophet." Goethe was thus unable to write the Muhammad tragedy because a tragedy always contains an indictment. And the charge he wanted to bring against the Prophet Muhammad "crumbled in his hands." The great drama remained unwritten. For Marcus, its fragments were poetic compositions of high intrinsic value, which, rather than indict, offer "the most profound appreciation and the highest praise of the Prophet."[135]

Katherina Mommsen offers a similar assessment of the work, as the best tribute to Muhammad paid by a German poet up until that time.[136] Contra Marcus, Mommsen argues that to understand why Goethe did not finish this drama, one has to consider the context of the poet's life and work. Goethe was fascinated by "great men" and tried to compose dramas about Julius Caesar and Socrates, which he never completed. He was also enthralled by characters in the Bible and aimed to write dramas about Ruth and Joseph, and several others. But he burned the fragments of dramas that he had written before he went to the University of Leipzig in 1765. In 1770, before continuing his studies at the University of Strasbourg, he again burned most of his poetic works. He was still very young and full of ideas when he tried to create a "Muhammad" drama while busy working as an attorney in Frankfurt.[137]

Marcus not only ignores these practical reasons but also fails to discuss how Goethe, in his autobiography, *Poetry and Truth*, explains why he attempted to write the tragedy. Part of the attraction to the life of Muhammad lay in Goethe's own experience with itinerant preachers and would be prophets, such as Johann Kaspar Lavater (1741–1801) and Johann Bernhard Basedow (1724–1790) and—although he does not mention it—the fact that many saw the charismatic Goethe as worthy of being a prophet. Much of his interest in Muhammad and "his work," the Qur'an, can be seen as part of his exploration of the line dividing the spiritual from the earthly, prophet from poet. Goethe perceived that, in Muhammad's case, "violent pursuit of his purposes" inevitably casts a shadow on the divine doctrine and "was convinced that the poet, limiting himself to artistic creativity, is better able to preserve the essence of the divine in its purity" than the prophet.[138]

Marcus, who had argued that Islam is the perfect synthesis of Dionysian and Apollonian cultures, held the opposite view. He argued that whereas poets are driven by feeling and thinkers by reason, only prophets such as Muhammad "possess both and in perfect equilibrium. The result of the marriage between feeling and reason is wisdom. . . . Wisdom is the characteristic element of religious life, equidistant from feeling and reason yet containing both in a new synthesis."[139] A poet aims to be concrete, enthusiastic in describing such things as the scent of a flower, yet he cannot describe higher concepts. It is the religious person who is enthusiastic about elevated concepts, which the poet has no talent expressing.

Marcus's attraction to Islam and his insistence that Goethe was a Muslim may also have been rooted in his own homosexuality and his perception that Goethe was a homosexual too.[140] This perspective shaped Marcus's life and work. We have already described how Marcus traveled to Italy to celebrate his twenty-first birthday in the summer prior to enrolling at Friedrich Wilhelm University in Berlin in 1901 because in his day, as in Goethe's, it was considered part of the Orient, where men loved men without fear of castigation. Goethe describes his *Italian Journey* as an experience that transformed him morally and aesthetically.[141]

On the occasion of Goethe's two hundredth birthday in 1949, Marcus published "Goethe und die Freundesliebe" (Goethe and homosexuality) in the world's leading homosexual journal, *Der Kreis*.[142] As was common in an era in which homosexuals were persecuted, Marcus, like the other authors, including Kurt Hiller, wrote under a pseudonym; Marcus's was Hans Alienus. He used a term for homosexuality (*Freundesliebe*) that was popular among early-twentieth-century German homosexuals and that connoted "an erotic relationship between adult men and adolescent boys," as in ancient Greece.[143] Recall that in 1907 a young Marcus had declared that *Freundschaft* (homosexuality) is superior to *Liebe* (heterosexual romantic relations).[144] Marcus would agree with the assessment that "the German Romantics lived in a golden age (1750–1850) when relationships between men that were potentially sexual were (mis)recognized as mere friendships."[145] Marcus reflects his era: early-twentieth-century homosexual German journals had already discussed homosexual eroticism and sexuality in the work of Goethe. Marcus begins with Goethe's motto: "I decided, in order not to envy others, to love boundlessly." The article is a detailed analysis of homosexual themes in Goethe's work, including the admiration of male beauty and homoerotic sensibility in *Letters from Switzerland*, *Wilhelm Meister's Journeyman Years*, and the poem "An den Mond" (To the moon), and the theme of pederasty in *Faust* and "Erlkönig" (The elf king). He applauds Goethe for having boldly stated, "'In actual fact, Greek pederasty is based on the fact that, measured purely aesthetically, the man is after all far more beautiful, more excellent, more perfect than the woman. . . . Pederasty is as old as humanity, and therefore it may be said that it is rooted in nature, although at the same time it is against nature.'"[146] If the desire for a younger man by an older man, Greek antiquity and culture (particularly the propensity for male-male love), and the cult of friendship were signifiers of homosexuality for Goethe, so too are they in the homoerotic fiction that Marcus published in *Der Kreis* (discussed in chapter 5). Many of the stories appear in the Weimar genre of "queer Bildungsroman," which chart the transplanted provincial protagonist's (read: Marcus's) journey from hometown and bourgeois family relations (German Jews in Posen) to Berlin and homoerotic entanglements.[147] Marcus discovered Goethe at a young age, "at a time when passionate friendships [read: homosexual relationships] could not be talked about anywhere."[148] Goethe's works "have shone a light from his youth on all phases of his life and provided something unforgettable, since they touch on the highest meaning friendship may achieve." Goethe's words "are pole stars" that "provide direction and orientation."[149]

EASTERN WISDOM, GERMAN WISDOM

In Weimar Germany writers sought to comprehend the cataclysm of the Great War of 1914–1918, perhaps especially defeat. "Into a middle-class world of order and stability, the brutal fact of millions of casualties had ruptured the historical narrative of progress and optimism that had reigned over European life in the pre-war epoch," Charles Bambach writes. "The unspoken bourgeois faith in both the meaning and coherence of history had been shattered. The Great War brought in its wake a profound disillusionment with the pre-war liberal worldview of academic *Bildung* and a heightened awareness of the power and necessity of 'destruction' for any project aimed at cultural renewal."[150] To reconfigure the cultural, political, social, and spiritual order, many sought to annihilate the past, which had brought them such defeat and catastrophe, and to immerse themselves instead only in "the new" and "the now" while innovatively mapping out the future.[151] Others like Marcus, one of the first German Muslims, took part in the same innovative historical reevaluation but, rather than cast off the inheritance of the past, sought to reclaim one era, Goethe's other Weimar, and use its supposed Islamic values as a blueprint for a future utopia.

Marcus defined Islam in German ethical, philosophical, and cultural terms. His effort is distinct from that of other Muslims in Germany, such as the Sunni Muslims affiliated with the Islamische Gemeinde zu Berlin, who also offered Islam as a panacea for Germany in crisis, presenting Islam as a roadmap to perpetual peace, security, and prosperity, and for the rebuilding of a shattered world, for their Islam was not correlated with German culture in any way.[152] Marcus's interpretation is also distinct from that of his well-known contemporary, the South Asian Muslim philosopher, poet, and politician Muhammad Iqbal (1873–1938), whose *Payam-e-Mashriq* (1923; The message of the east), was composed as an answer to Goethe's *West-östlicher Diwan*, as a dialogue between civilizations.[153] For when the Muslim Marcus wrote about Islam, like other German intellectuals, he was staking a claim in the raging Weimar-era debate "over the most basic political values and beliefs, over what precisely should be the character of Germany in the twentieth century."[154]

Even if his Islam was a decidedly German one, Marcus's promotion of Islam can be seen as part of the great fascination with "Eastern wisdom" in the Weimar Republic.[155] Marcus observed how "the Westerner is eternally restless and hungry for happiness, whereas the Easterner lives peacefully and calls himself happy."[156] This was an era of intellectual and spiritual crisis, when works such as Oswald Spengler's *Der Untergang des Abendlandes* (1918; *The Decline of the West*) and Hermann Hesse's *Siddhartha* (1922) were best sellers. Lecture series and novels about the Orient and translations of Eastern classics, mainly Indian and Chinese, such as Richard Wilhelm's translation of the *I Ching* (1924), and the works of the Buddha and Confucius became popular.[157] This was partly due to their critique of European culture, religion, and the Western sense of confidence and superiority, which had been deflated by the Great War. Believing the spiritual world of their fathers to be dead, Germans sought consolation in a different way of knowing, in "Eastern wisdom."[158] Scholars have even called this "therapeutic orientalism," endeavors that helped Germans achieve salvation rather than gain true insight into "the East."[159] It is no coincidence that the first Buddhist and Islamic communities were established in Germany in these years.

The Austrian novelist Joseph Roth observed, "I had long ago set aside the habit of seeing in every Berlin mosque a Muhammadan house of worship"; as the city's movie houses were often built in oriental style.[160] It did not escape the attention of society newspapers and the many German visitors at the actual Berlin mosque—modeled after the Taj Mahal—that the first Muslims wore turbans as part of their formal dress and came from the East. The quirky bohemian and Eastern aspects of the Ahmadi mosque community may indeed be an accurate account of what attracted German intellectuals, including Hesse and Thomas Mann (so the Ahmadi claim), to attend an occasional "Islam Evening" lecture given at the mosque by Marcus.

Marcus argued that as a Muslim one did not have to accept extra-European values as guidelines for life; rather, he localized Islam by interpreting it in ways that made it commensurate with his German worldview. As Suzanne Marchand points out in reference to other Germans who sought Eastern wisdom, "It would, from our perspective, be relatively easy to find lingering Eurocentrism in all this work."[161] But she does not emphasize it, as Hermann von Keyserling (1880–1946), for example, founder of the Schule der Weisheit (School of Wisdom, Darmstadt, 1920), which was "half Platonic academy and half Buddhist outreach program," insisted on "Western confrontation with 'Otherness,'" contrasting "Western spiritual shallowness" with "Eastern spiritual depths."[162] Marcus's take was not only Eurocentric, but German.

Like that of other Weimar-era Germans, the cultural work of Marcus was characterized by "first . . . casting aside older cognitive templates, then . . . retooling and recalibrating new ones."[163] Rather than jettison the older cognitive templates of German history en bloc, however, he celebrated and retained the memory of one era: Goethe's Weimar. Unlike other salvation-seeking bohemians of his day, Marcus seems anything but countercultural, affirming Germany's cultural heroes and the supremacy of German thought. "The Message of the Holy Prophet Muhammad to Europe" favors a "conservative revolution" that would bring to power a great leader who ends party politics and class division and establishes a society run by an aristocratic elite. However, his imagined utopia is based, too, on the liberal principle that "all human beings are equal" and that "fights against all prejudices and barriers and demands equal opportunities for all," presumably, including members of society like Marcus—a homosexual Jew.

CHAPTER 3

A Jewish Muslim in Nazi Berlin, 1933–1939

But I am different than this. I await always that the worst will come. I know how things are in Germany today, and suddenly it can be that my father lose all. You know, that is happened once already? Before the War, my father has had a big factory in Posen. The War comes, and my father has to go. Tomorrow, it can be here the same.

Natalia Landauer, daughter of Jewish department store owner in Berlin[1]

Marcus and the Ahmadi consistently presented Islam as a tolerant religion that allowed its members to rise above national and racial sentiment. From the founding of the mission, the Ahmadi used their public message to stress interreligious tolerance, emphasizing the unity of humankind—based on the idea that all people, no matter their race or nationality, are created by the same God—and pointing out the similarities between Judaism, Christianity, and Islam and the affinities between members of the three religions.[2] The Ahmadi claimed that Moses, Jesus, and Muhammad, as progeny of Abraham, were related by blood—in the language of the day, Christians, Jews, and Muslims were all "Semites." Displaying a complete lack of anti-Jewish sentiment, they appealed directly to Jews to convert to Islam and join their community.[3]

Throughout the Weimar era, the Ahmadi spoke out against nationalism and racism, condemning Europeans for being blinded by hatred and prejudice. According to Sadr-ud-Din, when people accepted that the same God is lord of all people, that no one people is favored or preferred by God, they would be freed of the curse of national pride and prejudice and would promote the international brotherhood of man.[4] Asserting that the world had seen enough of "the bitter consequences of national hatred and religious prejudice," Sadr-ud-Din condemned Christians' persecution of Jews and anti-Semitism.[5] He argued that Europeans should heed the suffering that hate begets, as witnessed in the misery of World War I. In a report on the mosque's opening ceremony on Eid al-Fitr in 1925, an Ahmadi newspaper proclaimed: "It is on such occasions that you see Muslims from all parts of the world, of all shades of complexion from the white European to the dark African, embrace one another like members of the same family. It is such scenes that in these days of racial hatred present a broad silver-lining to an otherwise dark over-clouded horizon."[6]

In 1929, on the occasion of the two hundredth anniversary of the birth of Gotthold Ephraim Lessing, Marcus delivered a prescient lecture in the Berlin mosque about tolerance, prejudice, anti-Semitism, and war.[7] Marcus refers to Lessing as "the man who advocated tolerance like no other."[8] He immediately reminds his audience that "Islam is also unconditionally committed to tolerance, as it follows in the footsteps of the holy Prophet, who was a shining example of tolerance. And so we German Muslims also rightly celebrate Lessing." To honor the Enlightenment thinker, Marcus tells his audience that rather than casting their gaze backward to the historical past, he aims "to ask how the idea of tolerance is doing today. Has it been realized? Has Lessing obtained his aim?" Marcus answers with a resounding no, for "we are even further away today from realizing true tolerance than he was in his day."[9]

Marcus distinguishes among three kinds of intolerance: religious, racist-nationalist, and socioeconomic. Although religious intolerance is the oldest form of intolerance, it was still encountered in his day in "highly civilized countries such as Germany." But along with the historical intolerance, he discusses "aesthetic dislike which cloaks itself in the form of religious intolerance, although it has nothing to do with religion." Unfortunately, to illustrate this point, the assimilated German Jew refers to his own prejudice against *Ostjuden* (Eastern European Jews) that reflects contemporary anti-Semitism. He argues that "intolerance against Jews is in part based on our aversion to the abject and vehemently gesticulating *Ostjuden* that strike us today as a caricature, and nothing other than a medieval type, transplanted without change, to our time. One thinks of the famous [Matthias] Grünewald altar in Colmar [Isenheim Altarpiece, 1512–1516] where one sees depicted in it bodily movements that one can also observe in the Łódź and Warsaw ghettos."[10]

Marcus uses Islam as a foil, a utopia of tolerance to compare with the intolerance found in Christian Europe. He argues "one must keep in mind the holy Prophet's stance regarding religious tolerance. He was for the strictest tolerance and exercised it at all times.... In point of fact, during the entire medieval period Jewish and Christian communities lived unchallenged in Muslim lands." Thus, when Muslims came into contact with European political ideas in the modern period, relations between Jews and Muslims in the Middle East began to deteriorate. His concern, however, is with present-day Europe where religious intolerance is no longer the predominant form of intolerance, for it has been transformed into racist-nationalist intolerance. And just like religious intolerance, "nationalist intolerance was also directed especially against the minorities in the country."[11]

Perhaps to counter claims that the Ahmadi were the tool of British imperialism, Marcus turns to the European colonies: "Racist intolerance in its most severe form manifests itself in the world as hatred of dark-skinned peoples, Negroes, Mulattos, Indians, Chinese, and so on. Islam also has every reason to fight against this hatred. This is because it is exercised by almost all the colonizing nations against the inhabitants of their colonies, and among them especially Muslims suffer." The relationship between the metropole and the colony, moreover, "is by its very nature basically permanent war on peace, a permanent state of intolerance." Only when colonies "either achieve political equality with the metropole, where they are emancipated and completely tolerated, and cease to be a colony, or become free" will racist-nationalist intolerance end, for "at the completion of all of these emancipation movements, racist-nationalist intolerance will thus fade away."[12]

Marcus reasons that if religious intolerance belongs to the past and racist intolerance to the present, then in the future intolerance will take the form of socioeconomic intolerance, which has existed a long time under the mantle of religious or racist intolerance. Marcus warns that socioeconomic intolerance "is directed toward certain minorities, which rightly or wrongly, are called 'exploiters of the masses.'"[13] In this way it differs from the other two forms of intolerance because "the other two are based on the idea that the minority which they judge is inferior, that the downtrodden embodies a lesser stage of humanity and have less right to life. But socioeconomic intolerance is something else: here the embattled minority is by no means depicted as being inferior, but rather on the contrary, as somehow superior, perceived as more economically clever and capable." Discrimination against Jews is on his mind. He mentions how "they express intolerance of an entire group, although it is based on the actions of one individual from that group." One speaks of "blood-sucking merchants," or, "'the rich bankers,' whereas the majority of bankers are not rich, although individual bankers count among the richest people in the world."[14] In his view, socioeconomic intolerance is where "one acts as if among all individual members of a minority there is a covenant, a conspiracy, and therefore assumes the right to make one individual atone for that which other individuals have done. But it was not enough, one then identified an individual of the now dubious profession with individual populations." He opposes the killing of a large landowner justified by saying it is committed against the entire baronial class. He finds that even here that religious and racist intolerance plays a role. If, for example, the most prosperous profiteer "belongs to a certain race and confession, the entire race and confession, although innocent, are considered to be more unscrupulous than the others."[15]

Marcus's warning about socioeconomic intolerance is as much a reflection of his condemnation of anti-Semitism and racism as his own opposition to the Left and violent political revolution. Robert Gerwarth observes that "between 1917 and 1920 alone Europe experienced no fewer than twenty-seven violent transfers of political power, many of them accompanied by latent or open civil wars," as well as national and social revolutions, so postwar Europe became "the most violent place on the planet."[16] As W. B. Yeats famously wrote in "The Second Coming" (1919), "Things fall apart; the center cannot hold; / Mere anarchy is loosed upon the world, / The blood-dimmed tide is loosed."[17] Marcus was likely repelled by the successful Russian Revolution of 1917; the short-lived socialist Free State of Bavaria of 1918–1919 led by the Social Democrats under German Jew Kurt Eisner (assassinated 1919); followed by the even briefer Munich Soviet Republic led by Russian Jew Eugen Leviné (executed 1919); the seizure of power by revolutionaries in Berlin in the same period, which his cousin Ernst Kantorowicz, who had served as an officer for four years during World War I, helped put down; the ongoing street battles between communists and Nazis; and the rise of mass socialist movements across Europe. Months after Marcus's speech in the mosque, Berlin would witness days of massive Communist May Day protests met with excessive police violence. Marcus may have recognized that rather than being conventional battles, battles between Right and Left were "*existential* conflicts fought to annihilate the enemy, be they ethnic or class enemies."[18] Distinctions between civilians and combatants had first begun to collapse in World War I and then "completely vanished" between 1918 and 1923 (and would again in the 1930s and World War II) as internal and external opponents of the Far Right and radical

Left alike were "portrayed and perceived as criminalized and dehumanized enemies undeserving of mercy."[19]

Marcus, the converted Jew speaking to an audience of Muslims, offers self-examination as a "cure" for religious, racial, and class intolerance. While warning his listeners not to generalize about the morals of an entire group based upon the actions of one of its members, he also admonishes that "everyone who acts immorally nourishes with every immoral act the intolerance spread by prejudice, speech, word, example and deed. Therefore every individual must from time to time examine himself to determine to which circles and classes he belongs, and determine whether in these classes there are mores, in which as an individual one often quite naively takes part." Groups that are on the receiving end of intolerance should also police their own behavior so as not to promote damaging stereotypes that will haunt them. Just as members of the targeted group must avoid unseemly behavior, so too is "individualizing the greatest means to obtain tolerance. One should not say 'the barons,' when one means the large landowners, and not 'the Jews,' when one wants to indicate merchants. When one encounters an immoral act or attitude, one vilifies this act or attitude as such, but not the class of population from which the single culprit originates."[20]

The cure for intolerance, anti-Semitism, racism, and prejudice is self-criticism and open criticism of society. He returns to Lessing, "the greatest critic of the eighteenth century," who engaged in "justified criticism." Marcus distinguishes between two forms of criticism: "ameliorative criticism," like Lessing's, that aims to make things better, and "condemnatory criticism," which is nihilistic. Whereas the former shows "what is bad and provides the means to obviate the damage," the latter "does not wish to better anything" and seeks only a path for destruction. Ameliorative criticism "speaks directly to the criticized," while condemnatory criticism engages in willful deception. The former speaks through the press, in the regional and national parliament (Reichstag), while the latter "is undisciplined, is progenitor of lynchings, pogroms, and civil wars."[21] The latter type of criticism is intolerance in disguise, and intolerance always leads to civil war.

If antiracism and anti-anti-Semitism were their values, how did Ahmadi respond to the rise of the Nazi regime of violence and its targeting of "racial mixing" and Jews? If "tolerance is the main feature of Islam," as Sadr-ud-Din claimed, and if the mosque was open to all, then what happened to it while it was controlled by the Ahmadi between 1933 and 1939, as the Nazis consolidated their power?[22] Did the society remain "equally open to members of all confessions and races"?[23] It was easy for these Muslims to practice what they preached in Weimar Germany, but how did they act after the Nazi takeover, and how did they respond to the persecution of one of their own?

A JEWISH MUSLIM IN NAZI BERLIN

The Nazi seizure of power shattered Marcus's dream of establishing a Goethean Islamic state in Germany. His promotion of the rationalism of "Semitic" religion, here Islam, the inheritor of Judaism, fell on deaf ears in an era in which everything people such as Marcus considered "un-German—brutality, injustice, hypocrisy, mass suggestion to the point of intoxication"—flourished.[24] Like his contemporary and German Jewish convert (to Christianity) Victor Klemperer (1881–1960)—who believed that the Nazis were "un-German" while he himself was "German through and through" and who sought escape amid persecution in eighteenth-century Enlightenment thought (his "a Voltairean cosmopolitanism")—Marcus failed to understand how Germany could have changed so completely. Klemperer and Marcus could not comprehend how Germany could be taken over by a regime that "sees education, scholarship, enlightenment as its real enemies."[25] Indeed, what would have Kant, Lessing, and Goethe have said of an era in which Goethe's work was declared off limits to Jews?[26] As Klemperer notes, a history of Jewish efforts "on behalf of Germanness" after 1933 is "nothing short of tragic."[27]

Despite their understanding of tolerance, conversion, and religious belonging, Marcus and the Ahmadi were compelled by the Nazi takeover to rethink this Muslim's membership in the Jewish community and his relationship to homosexual activists. As early as 1897 opponents perceived Hirschfeld's efforts on behalf of the emancipation of gays as part of a Jewish conspiracy.[28] His role in the Eulenburg trials—at first labeling men close to the emperor as homosexuals—proved to anti-Semites that Jews could never understand the true meaning of German male friendship, which was obviously not gay.[29] He was attacked—once beaten unconscious and left for dead—by Nazis three times at the beginning of the 1920s.[30] By 1929 *Der Stürmer* was calling him "the apostle of indecency."[31] The Nazis made a connection between Jews and various campaigns for sexual liberalization: legalizing abortion, decriminalizing homosexuality, promoting contraception and family planning, premarital sex, sexual pleasure, and tolerance of consensual homosexual relations.[32] This was based in part in truth, as with Hirschfeld, but was also a racist construct, as one sees in anti-Semitic cartoons published in *Der Stürmer*; Jews were out to destroy the German soul and race through advocating these sexual practices. In short, Jews, with Hirschfeld as the main exhibition, were constructed as "the primary proponents of contraceptive use and as the main celebrants of sexual pleasure and of diversity and perversity."[33] Nazis responded by both demonizing Jewish men and outlawing sexual relations between Jews and non-Jews (and then separating Jews from the rest of society and murdering them). The Nazis also responded by making sexuality (heterosexuality) the privilege of "Aryans" and an integral part of their racist and homophobic sexual politics.[34] Ernst Röhm, a proponent of the *Männerbund*, who had been a member of the Human Rights League in the 1920s, became leader of the Sturmabteilung beginning in 1930 and the second-most powerful man in the Third Reich but was murdered during the purge of the organization in 1934.[35] After the demise of Röhm, Heinrich Himmler, the most homophobic Nazi official, instigated the persecution of gays in the Third Reich, establishing an office to "combat homosexuality" and promulgating a new, harsher version of Paragraph 175 that criminalized "coitus-like" behavior between men. The Nazis "expanded the scope of the law to all same-sex activity between men," including kissing, touching, and mutual masturbation; applied it retroactively; and "significantly sharpened and expanded the scope of punishments" to include "longer prison and workhouse sentences, sentences to concentration camps, and castration."[36]

In 1922 Hiller had written that "a German Kaiser . . . had named antisemitism as the shame of his century. Yet when were the Jews in Germany ever as persecuted as the homoerotics [homosexuals]? Does the criminal law contain an exceptional provision against that racial minority as with the notorious exceptional provision against this sexual minority? The shame of the century is anti-homoeroticism [homophobia]; the shame of the century is Paragraph 175."[37] Hiller could not have foreseen what would occur after 1933: he was beaten nearly to death in the Sachsenhausen concentration camp at Oranienburg, Germany, and then took refuge in Prague and, finally, in England in 1938. Hirschfeld embarked on a world tour from 1930 to 1932 and never returned to Germany. He wrote in his diary, "For a freedom-loving person of Jewish origin it appears to me that life in Germany, when not absolutely obliged, is a moral impossibility. I have inwardly found myself resigned to the idea of never seeing Germany, my homeland, again."[38] When he returned to Europe, he fled to France; his Institute for Sexual Science was looted and plundered, and its library, as he related, was "thrown into an auto-da-fé and burnt to cinders."[39] After the book burning, Hitler personally attacked Hirschfeld as a "Jewish swine" who "perverted German culture."[40] These personal attacks made Hirschfeld wonder how to answer the questions "Where do you belong, what are you really?" He did so by reformulating the question: "'Are you a German—Jew—or World Citizen?' My answer in any case is 'World Citizen' or 'all three.'"[41]

Marcus's own family suffered, as did he. He narrates how, after the Nazi takeover, his brother, district captain of Leipzig Dr. Richard Marcus, "was immediately dismissed as first officer of Sachsen, afterwards even spied upon, and driven to his death."[42] Two years after his suicide, Marcus's other brother, "attorney Dr. Alfred Marcus of Berlin-Charlottenburg, was condemned by the Nuremberg Laws to give up his practice and needed our support."[43] As for Marcus, "on racial grounds I was denied membership in the Reich Chamber of Writers, in which then all writers were consolidated, and allowed to work." He had written primarily for liberal newspapers including the *Vossische Zeitung*, *Berliner Tageblatt*, *Tägliche Rundschau*, *Magdeburgerische Zeitung*, *Braunschweigische Ländeszeitung*, and *Gegenwart*; "all of these papers had to cease publication." Marcus's being dismissed as a writer "had an effect upon my students, the German ones as well as the many foreigners, so that they gave up their lessons with me."[44] He also had to confront the new reality in his mosque community.

The tone and content of *Moslemische Revue* changed. For the first time articles expressed anti-Semitic sentiment, claiming that Islam and Nazism shared basic principles.[45] In an article published in 1934 young German convert and Nazi Party member Faruq Fischer argued that National Socialism and Islam shared the same "modern" values.[46] He wrote that Islam rejected Judaism's claim that there is "a chosen people," which had "created much bad blood and made Jews unjustifiably egotistical and conceited."[47] He asked how Islam could be considered "arrogant" when "it is the Jews who repudiated and libeled Jesus and crucified him for being a false prophet," whereas Muhammad declared him a prophet sent by God. He concluded by arguing that "Islam recognizes the Führer of each nation." And "just as the Qur'an declares, 'For every nation there is a messenger' (10:47), one can also claim that the political Führer of a nation is chosen by God."[48] That issue also included a congratulatory letter from Muhammad Ali, the Ahmadi world leader based in Lahore. Ali welcomed "the new regime in Germany" because "it encourages the same simple life principles that Islam emphasizes."[49] He claimed that "the new Germany" and Islam were of the same mind, and he predicted that someday all of Europe would follow the German model.

German converts who belonged to the Nazi Party also became more visible in the mosque community. In 1934 Fischer attended the German Muslim Society's annual meeting for the first time and was also elected to the board.[50] That same year, Nazi Party member and convert Hikmet Beyer (b. 1907) received the second-highest number of votes for chairman, initially receiving only one vote less than Marcus, who had been chairman of the society since its founding.[51] Marcus obviously still had the support of society members, despite his Jewish background, but there was significant and increasing preference for converts who were party members.

What we are also witnessing is a generational clash. The older German Muslims considered themselves German patriots and did not join the Nazi Party. However, the younger German Muslims, like their generation, were more likely to join the party and considered themselves nationalist revolutionaries. Men of Marcus's generation who had served in or experienced the devastating Great War maintained their friendships with him; it was the younger German men in the mosque against whom he had to be on his guard.

The Gestapo reported that, rather than being closed down due to "subversive activities," as was rumored, the mosque actually featured an imam (deputy imam Sheikh Muhammad Abdullah) who, while conducting tours of the mosque, spoke "only glowingly" about the Nazi seizure of power and expressed goodwill toward the regime.[52] Abdullah also made a crucial change in Sadr-ud-Din's 1925 lecture "What Has Islam Given to Humanity?" when he presented it at the mosque after the Nazis came to power: he replaced the word "democracy" with "*Volksgemeinschaft*" (national community).[53]

As the mosque community began to succumb to the Nazification of society and then to the new anti-Semitic legislation, Marcus resigned as chairman and member of the board of the German Muslim Society.[54] Before the election was held for a new president in 1935, the prominent members of the organization were summoned "to renounce their membership in a society that still tolerated Jews, or bear the consequences, for their careers and political lives, if they remained." So Marcus relinquished his positions "to save the Society from further troubles."[55]

Despite an atmosphere in which "antisemitism became a principle governing private life as well as public," Marcus participated in the society's annual meeting barely a week after the notorious 1935 Nazi Party rally, where the Nuremberg Laws were proclaimed.[56] The board needed a new member. Disregarding the anti-Semitic laws, another non-German member of the society, assistant imam Dr. Azeez Mirza (1906–1937) of British India, proposed that Marcus again play a leadership role.[57] The board also proposed that Marcus give two of the monthly "Islam Evenings" lectures to be held at the mosque the following year. Were they not aware of the laws separating Jews from other Germans? Were they defying them?

It is unlikely that Marcus actually gave any lectures at the mosque in 1936 since Jews were being attacked both in print and in person.[58] In March, at the behest of Propaganda Minister Joseph Goebbels, a Nazi press release declared that the German Muslim Society "should not be acknowledged, as first and foremost it is made up of Jews."[59]

As Jews were increasingly isolated and made to feel like unwelcome guests in their own land, Marcus, having converted to Islam eleven years earlier, finally gave notice in May of his withdrawal from membership in the Jewish community of Berlin, effective the following month.[60] Having officially renounced his connection to the Jewish community, Marcus appeared at the society's annual meeting in autumn 1936.[61] Attendees included senior civil servants of the Third Reich. It is remarkable that he participated in the event, for a recent decree for civil servants had prohibited them from "consorting with Jews."[62] Even more astounding, one vote was cast for Marcus as chairman.[63] Did he vote for himself? Or was it another member? Was it a silent act of resistance?

The fellow convert whom Marcus had chosen to succeed him as chairman died suddenly in September 1936.[64] He was replaced instead by convinced Nazi and convert Hikmet (Fritz) Beyer.[65] During his two years as the society's head officer, Beyer used National Socialist racist principles to reinterpret a crucial Islamic tenet that promotes interracial harmony. Muslims had always endorsed the idea that what matters to God is not one's origins but one's piety. Qur'an 49:13 states that God divided humankind into different peoples so that they might know one another, not because any is better than the rest. The best are those who are most pious. Referring to this verse, Beyer proclaimed instead that "the sign of a truly advanced culture is not its interbreeding, but rather its recognition of [different] peoples!" pledging that "the German Muslim Society will act in the coming year with this in mind."[66]

In 1936 the society "had to redouble its efforts to prove its right to exist anew" and control the only mosque in Germany in the face of a sustained campaign by the Islamic Community of Berlin, which continued to challenge the Ahmadi's Islamic credentials.[67] After 1933 the Islamic Community was led by supporters of the Third Reich: by 1934 its executive director was Habibur Rahman, a veteran anticolonial nationalist revolutionary and Sunni Muslim journalist from India who later became a major figure in Nazi broadcast propaganda.[68] In the new climate, the Islamic Community reframed its attacks against the Ahmadi, attempting to convince Nazi authorities that the society was a Jewish Communist organization, unworthy of any claim to the mosque.

Unfortunately for the society, the ensuing period brought continued conflict with the Islamic Community and scrutiny by the police, the Nazi Party, and the Gestapo.[69] The Berlin police reported on the society to "special representatives" charged with "monitor[ing] the spiritual and cultural activities of Jews in the German Reich."[70] The Nazi Party reported to the chief of police in the spring of 1937 that "the Society is made up of members from the most varied races and nations," claiming that at their gatherings, "when the participants believe they are among comrades, they have apparently made derogatory comments about National Socialism and its Führer." In addition, "quite a few Jews belong to the Society. Most notably, the Society became a lair and flophouse for Kurfürstendamm Jews, especially in the years 1933–4."[71] The Kurfürstendamm, where Jews made up a quarter of the population, and Berlin West, where the mosque was located, had long been targets of Nazi rhetoric.[72]

Since only members and Muslims could attend the German Muslim Society's functions at the time, it is apparent that German converts or Muslim members were reporting to the party or the Gestapo. Fischer? Beyer? Or was it members of the Islamische Gemeinde, who also prayed at the mosque? The Nazis seem to have believed that many Jews were members of the society, although the only known one, Marcus, had ceased playing any public role in the organization, and even attending its meetings, the previous year. He does not appear in a photo taken on the front steps of the mosque on the occasion of Eid al-Adha in 1936.[73] Perhaps he continued to show up at the mosque out of the public eye; we know that he maintained a relationship with the imam. Despite the "racial laws" in Germany, his article "Moslemischer Schicksalsglaube," a long discourse on Islam and fatalism including Goethe's interpretation of Islamic fatalism, was published in

Moslemische Revue that same year.[74] Whether or not Marcus surreptitiously continued to visit the mosque, the report that it was a flophouse for Jews has been misinterpreted by Muslims in Germany, who claim that, like the members of the Grand Mosque in Paris, Muslims at the Berlin mosque saved Jews during the Shoah. But Nazi rhetoric should not be mistaken for fact. Nor were Jews in mortal danger in 1933–1934 such that they would have sought refuge.[75] During this period of scrutiny, Sadr-ud-Din, the founder of the mosque and community and the architect of its tolerant interreligious and interracial message, left Berlin.[76]

It is surprising, given the fact that contact between Jews and Germans had been forbidden and Jews had been removed from public life, that in November 1937 Jewish convert Marcus spoke at the mosque again. He was given the honor to deliver the Ahmadi community's farewell address to Sadr-ud-Din. Marcus used the opportunity to allude to the fallen status of the Jews of Germany by discussing the untouchables of India, thanking the Ahmadi for raising their position in society through conversion to Islam. In the context of the times, it is not surprising that Marcus referred to the greatness of the German nation and alleged pro-German feelings of the Ahmadi. Yet what he referred to was an elitist, aristocratic, "true" Germany based on a Hellenistic, homoerotic model, converting the Ahmadi into followers of Stefan George. Marcus speaks of having had his first contact with Ahmadi students in 1921, when "during Germany's most low-spirited moment they came to Germany because it was always their desire." They came to Germany "because during the world war they had felt pro-German, because they did not want to believe that Germany was defeated." Even "after the defeat they still believed in a *secret Germany*, whose strength yet existed, and for which they waited. They saw in an insulted and vilified Germany a destiny that they as nationalist Indians felt as their own destiny."[77] "Secret Germany" is an important term found in Stefan George's poetry, referring to his disciples, "a small, selective group of men, imbued with a higher calling and touched by (or at least in correspondence with) a divine entity" (George himself) who will bring about "redemption, the coming of a new world," a realm of the spirit.[78] The task of George's exclusive club of elected disciples "was to perpetuate cultural values" and "to renew the aristocratic sense of life," building "a secret empire for the sake of the new Reich to come, to find strength and possible inspiration in warm friendships (read: homosexuality) and among the choice spirits of the past," including Goethe.[79] Accordingly, Marcus then claims the Ahmadi felt an affinity to Germany due to their love of Goethe and Nietzsche. He even slips in mention of

German Romantic author Jean Paul, who had coined the term *Freundesliebe* (love of friends) to connote homosexuality.

Having worked his favorite German thinkers and themes into the speech, Marcus claims that while in India Sadr-ud-Din missionized to the untouchable class, gaining thousands of converts for Islam: "They were converted from being members of the lowest class of humans to becoming equals in the worldwide brotherhood of Islam." In fact, he claims, "not only Sadr ud Din, but all Ahmadi in India worked to advance humanity by bringing these fellow humans out of Untouchable status."[80] Marcus argues that Islam restored their human dignity; perhaps he was implying the same about himself, a German Jew in Nazi Germany, whose earlier conversion to Islam and more recent resigning from membership in the Jewish community, so he thought, would spare him from being treated as a Jew. Referring to the untouchables of India to make his audience consider the fallen status of Jews, the new "untouchables" of Germany, he also may have been making a plea for the Nazi members of the congregation and the Gestapo spies among them to recognize that the brotherhood of Islam pays no heed to race.

In a melancholy, unpublished homoerotic piece written around the same time, Marcus explored his relationship with his departing imam and the secret bonds between homosexual Muslim men.[81] Marcus waxed nostalgic for the Muslim community's first years in the interwar period, when the mosque was crowded with men driven by the war and economic crisis to Berlin from "Arabia, Persia, India, Malaysia, Turkestan, Afghanistan, Iraq and Japan," when the German capital was as filled with diverse Muslims as was Mecca.[82] Marcus felt the absence of the men, who had long since "scattered all over the world," leaving only a few devouts to pray the midday Friday prayer in an empty hall, which was far too large for the small number of praying men, whose voices echoed in the mosque's interior arches. Those who remained were as if "a handful of the left behind, survivors following a great catastrophe," where a feeling of "melancholy always floats over our communal prayers, as if we were a community in mourning."[83]

The short piece turns from despair to erotic confession as he described the prayer service. Marcus depicted the bond formed between two young men whose synchronized movements are expressions of their love for each other. When the congregation begins its silent prayer movements, every man praying for himself, one stands with arms folded across the chest, another moves into the kneeling posture, while yet another bows down on the carpet. All carry out their prayers in quiet movements. Nevertheless, among the small crowd, "one can find unexpected agreement between devouts who do not know each other." A young man notices that he and another young man happen to be the only ones in the standing position at that moment, while the others are in the middle of their prostrations. A "distant, hovering bond grows between them. The two alone stand over the bent backs of the others."[84] The two "continue to pray at their own separate pace," secret comrades who

> kneel, rise, stand, kneel again at the same moment. And in this way they stand at the same moment together before God. First one notices, then the other, that there is a bond between them. One of them could destroy it, without saying a word, merely by holding back one of the prescribed prayer movements, as the other one moves into the next position. He could end the togetherness of the movement, without the other one feeling hurt, but neither decides to break the tender bond that is woven between them. Perhaps one of them also notes that the other quietly waits for him or follows him in his prayer movements. That would mean that he secretly—wordlessly and silently—makes him his prayer leader, führer, imam, and master in the silent confession of love. And that he honors him in the presence of Allah.[85]

For Marcus, such "voluntary obedience" is the defining act of both Islam and love, uniting one's own natural inclination, deepest conviction, and conscience.[86] As he conceives it, "in voluntary obedience we experience the voice of God in deepest agreement with our own nature."[87] At the same time, he argues that symmetry ("the binary of similar forms") is the fundamental law of beauty and thus of its expression in love.[88] For beauty "consists of nothing but secret covenants of love" between two symmetrical forms, two homosexual men with their corresponding, "equally shaped members."[89]

After the individual prayers end, the communal prayers begin, as all the men stand in a row next to each other, which "allows for only comradeship of all, no more relationship between two single devouts," as if their synchronous agreement never occurred.[90]

Marcus makes the story confessional, describing the private yearning of two men:

> But once a year, during the Eid al-Fitr festival, you can hug each other, Sadi [Sadr-ud-Din] and you, Hussein [Marcus]; and you can silently thank Sadi for

> his love and obedience. . . . Because while all believers are hugging, you only need to approach him smiling, with open arms; you have not yet forgiven anything and have not betrayed anything to anyone, or promised anyone anything. Because it is a general need to embrace each other after the Festival prayers.[91]

A stolen hug expressed their homosexual love and voluntary obedience to each other. While perhaps the pair "are destined only to stand together before God, but not outside the holy space of the mosque and the sound of the call to prayer," Marcus hoped that one day "maybe God will walk with you and bring you closer together than you think possible through one of His wonderful divine providences."[92]

Marcus was unlikely to form such an erotic relationship with the new head imam, Sheikh Muhammad Abdullah. Born in British India, in Rasul Nagar, Punjab, he had earned bachelor of science and master of science degrees at Forman Christian College in Lahore.[93] After serving as joint secretary of the Ahmadi in Lahore in 1927, he was appointed deputy imam of the Berlin mosque in 1928 and subsequently earned a doctorate in chemistry at Friedrich Wilhelm University in Berlin in 1932.[94] Imam Abdullah praised the regime while leading public tours of the mosque, and he made important changes to stock lectures, incorporating Nazi neologisms. He made further overtures to the Nazi regime in the summer of 1938. He offered to give lectures at the Kulturpolitisches Archiv, an institute sponsored by the self-proclaimed Nazi ideologist Alfred Rosenberg (1892–1946, executed at Nuremberg). The proposed lectures would prove that there were "numerous points of contact between the Islamic and National Socialist worldviews."[95] This attracted the agency's attention.[96] The Reich Foreign Ministry certified that he posed no danger to the state, and the Public Education Agency approved him as a lecturer for winter 1939.[97] But the Kulturpolitisches Archiv was tipped off by a Gestapo agent that Abdullah "in his capacity as leader of the Muslim Society had been under Communist influence until the Nazi takeover, and until recently under Jewish influence," specifically "the Jew Dr. Hugo Markus [*sic*]," who "had founded the society, and who had played a not insignificant role in society life until 1936."[98]

Abdullah's overtures may reflect a change in philosophical orientation or a strategy for survival in the face of a totalitarian regime that brooked no dissent. At any rate, in those years *Moslemische Revue* published articles that reflected the former, such as "The New Germany According to a Muslim: Hitler Is the Appointed One," which appeared in the August 1938 issue and was written by Dr. Zeki Kiram (1886–1946), a member of the rival Islamic Community.[99] Kiram was a former Ottoman army officer and a longtime Berlin resident.[100] A Turkish citizen who maintained close relations with the Turkish embassy, which was dominated by pro-Nazi officials, Kiram was employed as an interpreter of Turkish in the Reich Foreign Ministry and worked for the Sicherheitsdienst des Reichsführers-SS (the SS intelligence agency) for years, but his main job was dealing German arms.[101] In 1936 he wrote an ecstatic letter to Adolf Hitler, his "highly esteemed Führer."[102] In the 1938 article, Kiram asks, "Is this man not sent by God to save the German people from the trap that the Jews and their various organizations, established ostensibly in the name of humanity, have set? These Jewish organizations, which appear to bring benefits, in fact pursue destructive ends."[103]

Reflecting this sentiment, on November 9, 1938, the Nazis unleashed the nationwide pogrom, signaling the beginning of the Shoah. Fellow Jewish convert to Islam Essad Bey had fled to Italy earlier in the year, but Marcus, defined as a Jew according to the Nuremberg Laws, was among the six thousand Jewish men from Berlin and northern and eastern Germany who were subsequently imprisoned at Berlin's main concentration camp, Sachsenhausen.[104] Gay Jewish men who were incarcerated at Sachsenhausen in the wake of the pogrom were arrested for being Jewish, not for their homosexuality.

After passing through the black iron gate inscribed at the top with the Nazi's cynical slogan, "Arbeit macht frei" (work sets you free), the fifty-eight-year-old was forced by the SS to stand absolutely still on the roll-call ground for twenty-four hours. He and the others were "crammed into the 'small camp,'" recently built to handle the influx of Jewish prisoners, "where they suffered continual mistreatment."[105] Marcus was held in prison block 18, an overcrowded wooden barrack.[106]

Fortunately, he did not have to remain there long. Most Jews arrested following the November pogrom were released by the spring of 1939, although two thousand died in detainment. Gay Jews arrested then—even those marked as "Jude 175" (Jewish violator of the anti-homosexual law, Paragraph 175)—were not persecuted further but were released like most others, if they survived. Prisoners were freed on condition that they would leave the country immediately, surrendering their financial assets. Marcus was slated for release on November 19, 1938, and inmates with release orders were typically let go the following day.[107] Like other former detainees, he was given a stern warning about the horror that awaited him should he remain in Germany. As Marcus recalled after the war, "On the day of their release, former detainees were urged to leave Germany posthaste, because otherwise they would disappear forever in a concentration camp."[108] Jews marked as gay who were incarcerated at Sachsenhausen after the war began in 1939 were isolated in separate barracks along with other gay prisoners and not in the barracks assigned to Jews (where Marcus had been detained). None of these gay Jews survived. Almost all of the other gays were also murdered.[109]

Facing this reality, Marcus asked Imam Abdullah to defend him, which might seem an odd choice since Abdullah had earlier praised the regime and promoted the idea of the consonance between Nazism and Islam. But to whom else could Marcus turn? Abdullah, probably responding to the shock of the November 9–10 pogrom—when the flames of burning synagogues and Jewish-owned businesses would have been visible from his residence in the mission house at the mosque—and Marcus's incarceration, worked on an exit plan.[110] It quickly bore fruit. Within a week of his release from Sachsenhausen, Marcus was informed by the Albanian consul in Bern, Switzerland, that he could obtain an entry visa for King Zog's Muslim-majority officially secularized kingdom, still an independent monarchy at that time, if he submitted a valid passport to Albanian authorities in Switzerland.[111] British India, the headquarters of the Ahmadi, for whom Marcus had worked for fifteen years, was a better option. Abdullah sought to help Marcus obtain a visa for India. On December 1, 1938, he wrote the British passport control officer in Berlin, assuring him that Marcus "is known to us personally and intimately."[112]

By January 1939 the Nazi Party was "increasingly and ever more openly" emphasizing that its principal duty was "the solution of the Jewish question."[113] German news reports broadcast Hitler's Reichstag speech of January 30, in which he "threatened the annihilation of the Jews in Europe."[114] In February a Gestapo agent repeated a claim he had been making for years: that the German Muslim Society was "without a doubt an international organization wholly under Jewish-Communist influence."[115] Moreover, according to the agent, "even today the [German] Muslim Society, and especially Dr. Abdullah, maintain close relations with various followers who due to their political views have had to leave Germany." Accordingly, he opposed any "domestic recognition" of the society.[116]

In this atmosphere, new rivals to the society emerged. Foremost among them was the Mahad al-Islam (Islam Institute).[117] Unlike the German Muslim Society, the Islam Institute was outspoken in its Nazi sentiment. Its board members included a variety of Muslims who served as Nazi propagandists and agents.[118] And while the society had never included such language in its constitution, despite having had the opportunity to do so, the Islam Institute's constitution contained the following provision: "A German who applies to be a member must present documentation that he is not a Jew, in accordance with the fifth decree of the Nuremberg Laws (of 30.11.1938)."[119] The organization was on such good terms with authorities that in the summer of 1939, the Nazi Party's foreign policy office informed the Berlin police that it had no objections to the Islam Institute, or to its board members.[120] Its chairman would soon be Habibur Rahman, one of the Islamic Community's earliest members and its leading member after the departure of the Kheiri brothers.[121] Rahman continually urged Nazi authorities to view the Ahmadi as false Muslims and the German Muslim Society as a Jewish organization, in part motivated by a desire to take over their mosque.[122]

The situation worsened for Marcus. Having already surrendered his German passport, on March 16, 1939, he was fingerprinted like a criminal and given a new identity card under the name "Hugo Israel," marked with a large "J" for "Jude" (Jew).[123] Four days later he was issued a new German passport, valid for one year, marked with a red "J" and identifying him by his new "Jewish" name.[124] And with an earlier decree having declared that Jews who converted to Christianity were still Jewish by race—from which one could infer that the same would be true for conversion to other religions—he would no longer be able to escape the consequences of his origins.[125] Remarkably, however, in spite of the fact that his life was in danger, Abdullah asked the British to postpone the date of Marcus's Indian entry visa so he could stay in Berlin to finish editing the German translation of the Qur'an: "Mr. Hugo Marcus has been indispensable for this work and thus his presence here in Berlin has been unavoidable. The climatic conditions in India combined with the above mentioned work entrusted to him here in Berlin, necessitated his departure to be postponed."[126]

Was it better to remain in the eye of the storm in Berlin and avoid the heat of India? Was this Marcus's wish, or Abdullah's? Abdullah may have been aware that others who employed Jews on similar projects were able to save their colleagues from deportation at that time. For example, Hans Wehr employed the German Jewish Arabist Hedwig Klein (1911–1942)—who was denied her doctorate in 1938 due to anti-Semitic legislation—from 1939 to 1942 to assist him with his German-Arabic dictionary project, deemed essential for the German army and Nazi propaganda. It prolonged her life; at one point she was spared from a deportation thanks to the efforts of her University of Hamburg employers.[127]

But why would Marcus choose to remain in Berlin at a time when talk of impending war filled the air, war measures were already being taken, and converted Jewish contemporaries were wondering, "Will they beat us to death.... Will they come for me tonight? Will I be shot, will I be put in a concentration camp?"[128] Was Marcus so single-mindedly determined to edit the Qur'an that he considered nothing else, that he was able to look past the violence and humiliation to which he had already been subjected? As a Jew, he was completely isolated from the rest of society. In addition to all the other regulations, he was now "banned from well-known restaurants, luxury hotels, public squares, much-frequented streets and smart residential districts" (including Wilmersdorf, where the mosque was located); forbidden from entering all public facilities, including parks and gardens, beaches and resorts, swimming pools, public baths and sports facilities; prohibited from driving or going to the cinema, theater, concerts, and exhibitions.[129] He would have had no interest in attending the segregated Jewish cultural activities, for he had renounced his attachment to the Jewish community. He was forced to surrender all assets, cash, securities, and valuables.[130] Marcus's father had passed away in 1930, his brother Richard had committed suicide three years later, his surviving brother Alfred was also prohibited from employment, and relatives in the British Mandate of Palestine, in Switzerland, and in the United States were unable to send financial assistance. Had it not been for his salary from the mosque community, which he received until August 1939, and for the one-time fee he was paid for editing the Qur'an, all of which he used to support himself and his mother, he would have been destitute.[131]

We can gain insight into Marcus's seemingly irresponsible decision to stay when we compare him to other German Jews of his generation. A majority of the Jews who remained in Germany at that time were over the age of fifty and—like Marcus, who was fifty-nine—could not imagine leaving their homeland, for, despite the violence, "ostracism, and a loss of rights" they had experienced in the past five years, they remained German patriots and still considered themselves Germans.[132] In any case, even if they had wanted to flee, there were few countries willing to take them in, especially since they would arrive penniless, as Jews had to forfeit all their wealth and property when they left Germany. Like other German Jewish men of his age, Marcus had been honored as a veteran of World War I, despite having served in only an unsalaried desk job for nine months in the heart of Berlin (at the Central Certification Bureau of the War Ministry from March to December 1917) and offering his services in the city as a voluntary nurse (as

Hirschfeld had served the Red Cross as a doctor).[133] In recognition of this minimal wartime effort, in April 1936 the Wilmersdorf police personally delivered a swastika-stamped document to his home: he had been awarded the Honor Cross for War Veterans by Reich president and war hero Field Marshal Paul von Hindenburg, "*in the name of the Führer*," while he was still officially a member of the Jewish community.[134] Perhaps thinking that such recognition could protect him, Marcus sat in his room in Wilmersdorf—the Berlin district that had the second-highest Nazi vote total in 1932—and improved the Qur'an translation, delaying his departure by six months.[135] Burying himself in his work and relying on the love of friends and his inner spiritual world gave him a sense of comfort and normalcy. Continuing to work enabled him to provide for his mother. Yet even remaining in his home was no guarantee of safety: as of the end of April 1939, Jews were "stripped of their rights as tenants, thus paving the way for their forcible ghettoization. They could now be evicted without appeal."[136] Once thrown out of their homes, they could be moved into a shared apartment, a "Jews' House," which was "stuffed full of people who all share the same fate," where "everyone's nerves fray in this ghastly situation."[137] Marcus feared being forced to vacate the family apartment that he shared with his elderly mother located at Führterstrasse 11a, close to bustling Lietzenburgerstrasse and a five-minute walk to the KaDeWe department store on Tauentzienstrasse.[138] In the Weimar era Tauentzienstrasse was "a famous strip for male and female prostitutes," including boys in drag, "an elite cruising area" connecting Wittenberg Platz and the most famous gay bars at Nollendorfplatz.[139] His friend Roman lived nearby in the other direction, at Kantstrasse 30 in Charlottenburg, near Savigny Platz, a twenty minute walk crossing Kurfürstendamm.[140]

Convinced to quit Germany by the pogrom and his incarceration at Sachsenhausen, Marcus was also busy making great efforts preparing for his departure and, presumably, that of his mother. At the end of April he went to the Swiss embassy in Berlin, located in the shadow of the Reichstag, and obtained an assurance of permission to reside in Switzerland at Oberwil in Baselland Canton with the aim of preparation for onward migration, assumedly to India.[141] This permission was valid only until July.

Sadr-ud-Din had settled safely in Lahore, British India. From the Ahmadiyya buildings he addressed Marcus a series of letters referring to him by his Muslim name, Hamid; encouraged him to be strong despite the awful circumstances; debated whether it would be best for Marcus to settle in India or Switzerland; and worried about his financial circumstances. In an undated letter from 1939, prior to Marcus's escape, Sadr-ud-Din offered him cheer: "Dear Brother Hamid, Painful news from you! May God be with you in these trying times! Please keep your head up and be comforted, a Muslim will draw comfort from such trials and will submit to God. . . . Please be ensured that I will do everything" to get him out of Germany. The question was whether following his spiritual guru to India would be wise: "The climate during winter time is glorious and pleasant for you (only Summer is hard). But you already know that life in India is very simple and natural. I am simple too, you won't find a lot of furniture in my house. But tranquility. Yes, enough tranquility. . . . Everything that is possible will be done. Your permit to obtain. Hopefully it will be fast. . . . Your brother Sadr ud Din."[142] In April, after conferring with other Ahmadi in Lahore, Sadr-ud-Din wrote to inform Marcus that travel to India was not advisable due to the climate and the lack of funds to support his guest: "The Indian circumstances and the Indian heat from May to September are hard to bear. And the congregation does not have enough money to be able to house you in a villa. More than the 75 Rs. you are receiving now the congregation is not willing to pay." Sadr-ud-Din reported to Marcus that he had told the others, "One possibility to house Mister Marcus comfortably would be that I take him in. I cannot let him down. Right now I live not in a villa but in the house where the eminent Mister Maulana [Muhammad Ali] lived. I will do anything to make him feel comfortable. May God make the nice winter time here do him well!"[143] Soon after, the Ahmadi invited Marcus "to stay permanently" at their headquarters in Lahore, India, offering to be responsible for his maintenance and defraying all expenses.[144] Assured that he would be gainfully employed translating Ahmadi literature into German, several weeks later the British government of India granted him a visa.[145] But he remained in Berlin, working on the Qur'an translation, which was finally published a month before World War II broke out. In its foreword, Sadr-ud-Din wrote, "Throughout the entire duration of my work on the translation, a great German friend exerted himself working for me, bestowing upon me the greatest help imaginable. His assistance was both indispensable and invaluable. His love of Islam is boundless. And accordingly the labor was his sacrifice and duty. May God bless and reward him."[146] That "great German friend" was Marcus.[147]

Marcus may not have been mentioned by name in the Qur'an translation, yet in light of the context in which it was published, it was a remarkable accomplishment. The commentary that accompanies the Qur'anic text often takes up to 90 percent of a given page, with one line of Arabic text and German translation accompanied by more than fifty lines of commentary. What is most noteworthy is the strident criticism of the European society that Christianity produced, whose worst symptom of violence is manifested in the brutality of World War I and in colonialism: "The Christian nations have proved their hate and hostility toward one another," for which World War I is an example; prior to World War I the Christian nations also engaged in "diabolically savage religious persecution"; "such religions are not the propagator and promoter of peace. If their followers cannot love their own brother, how can one expect them to love their enemy?"[148] Befitting the origins of the Ahmadi in British India, there is harsh criticism of colonialism in India and Africa. One finds a subtle pacifism as well. Regarding Qur'an 5:28, "If you should raise your hand against me to kill me I shall not raise my hand against you to kill you. Indeed, I fear God, lord of the worlds," the commentary declares: "Perhaps one can recognize the character trait of Cain in the character trait of Europeans today."[149] Commenting on 2:178, which calls for measured retaliation for the murdered, the editors note that Islam prohibited the gruesome and bloody vendettas that were once the norm. Yet Europeans in the early twentieth century in their eastern colonies and in Africa use similar violent and unjust methods as a deterrent; when a single European or European soldier is slighted, they take revenge by "exterminating a large number of men, women, and children by machine gun fire. On unarmed and unprotected civilians they unleash a hail of bullets and drop bombs upon them." Yet 1,400 years ago "Islam condemned such devilish arrogance and established equal rights for all."[150] Concerning 2:193, which prescribes rules for war, the editors also note that "the twentieth century has much to learn from Islam."[151] Kings, presidents, and prime ministers are condemned for their empty talk and for going back on their word to represent the interests of the oppressed and guarantee independence to small states.[152] The editors condemn imperialist racism, the "imperialist theories of white nations that allow them to draw blood from the colored nations, and to deprive them of the possibility of existence."[153]

The commentary builds to an apocalyptic crescendo regarding the impending world war. Rather than heed lessons from the Great War, the editors comment that the European nations are hurtling toward a new war, which in the end will destroy them all. Sura 18:99, 100, and 101 concern "the differences among the nations of the West. One nation will rise above the others like the billowing waves of the ocean that will engulf everything and leave no trace of itself."[154] The verse "we will assemble them in one assembly" means that all European nations will be entangled in a dreadful war; "We will present Hell that day to the unbelievers until they see it," every European nation today admits and states publicly "that a war today would mean the absolute annihilation of all who participate. The last war created Hell on earth, but this Hell is only a weak foretaste of what the next war will bring." So why, they ask, "is European civilization certain to end in such a way?" The only way out, they argue, is for Europeans to turn to God, to the morals and belief of Islam. This is what Marcus had argued in his 1932 essay, "The Message of the Holy Prophet Muhammad to Europe."

More pertinent for Marcus's situation, the commentary for Sura 2:256, "there shall be no compulsion in religion," expresses the conviction that one should not be persecuted for confessing a particular religion, including having one's wealth and property confiscated and being targeted for belonging to a particular faith.[155] Explaining the verse that refers to people protecting churches, monasteries, and synagogues from destruction by others, the editors state their hope that Europe will take this verse to heart and act upon it, to protect the houses of worship of all believers in which prayers are made to God.[156] This is an astonishing statement in the wake of the November 9–10 pogrom and the persecution of Jews. Such passages and others that condemn racism and blind submission to leaders show the Ahmadi's perseverance in articulating their core beliefs despite living in the Nazi metropolis: "Goodness and excellence must be promoted, in whatever race and community they are found; on the other hand, evil and maliciousness must be combated, wherever they are found. Help the one who does good, even if he is a non-Muslim! And whoever proves himself evil, refuse to assist him, even if he is a Muslim!" Furthermore, "even if you are led astray by a *Führer*, you will also be punished, for you have followed him blindly."[157]

What mattered most for Marcus personally was S. M. Abdullah's testimony on his behalf. At the end of August 1939 the imam gave Marcus the following letter in German, to be used to secure his exit:

> Mister Hugo (Hamid) Marcus worked for our mosque and our Berlin neighborhood from 1923 as syndic and academic staffer. During that sixteen-year time he has rendered us invaluable services and advised us tirelessly and with great success in legal and academic matters. For many years he was president of the German-Muslim Association and as such has brought congregational life to blossom by way of many new facilities and farsighted initiative. He worked at *Moslemische Revue* as a permanent staffer in its editorial room and

> brought every publication in German to their publishable form. We will miss him a lot, but hope that he will find a new sphere of activity within our congregation and its branches.[158]

Ten days before the outbreak of war, Marcus submitted the imam's certification of Marcus's good character.[159] With this testimony and a new Swiss guarantee of temporary residency, Marcus was permitted to leave Germany—without his mother—just one week before the Nazi invasion of Poland.[160] He left not on the long and precarious journey by ship to India, however, which may have been a life-saving decision, but rather headed for Switzerland.

Hedwig Klein, employed by Hans Wehr's German-Arabic dictionary project, sought to flee to British India thanks to contacts through her Oriental Studies Department in Hamburg. She obtained a visa in June 1939 and was set to sail from Hamburg to Antwerp, and from there on to India, on August 18, 1939. But as the German trade ship sat in the harbor in Antwerp, it was warned to return to Hamburg because an international voyage would be too dangerous at the time. Accordingly, on August 27 it returned to Germany. As of September 3, 1939, India was at war with Germany. As a result, Klein was eventually deported to her death in July 1942 on the first direct train from Hamburg to Auschwitz.[161]

Rather than work at Ahmadi headquarters in India, the plan for Marcus was to open an Ahmadi "cultural center" in Lausanne and publish *Moslemische Revue* there, serving as the editor. He accomplished neither of those objectives, however; nor did he continue on to India.[162] Had he traveled there, he would have been arrested as an enemy alien and spent the war in a British internment camp, sharing the fate of fellow converts von Ehrenfels and Asad.[163] His entry into Switzerland was facilitated by the intervention of a German convert to Catholicism (from an unnamed religion), wartime European director of the U.S. radio station NBC and postwar monk Dr. Max Jordan.[164] Jordan and Marcus were acquaintances from the homosexual rights movement and the early years of the mosque, when Jordan covered the German Muslim Society's "Islam Evenings" as a journalist.

After World War II erupted, Abdullah, who was a British subject and thus an "enemy national," had to leave the country or face incarceration.[165] In one of his last written communications with the Nazi regime, he used the notorious phrase, "Heil Hitler!"[166] It is not clear why he chose to do so, having had avoided using the Nazi greeting for the previous six years. In October he traveled to Copenhagen, and a month later to India.[167] Even in mid-November, after his departure, the mosque community was still promoting the brotherhood of man, regardless of race or religion, as in the Eid al-Fitr sermon given by the imam appointed by Abdullah before he left the country, the Egyptian Dr. Ahmed Galwash.[168] Refuting the 1936 lecture by Nazi Party member and German Muslim Society chairman Beyer, Galwash gave the traditional Islamic interpretation appreciating human diversity, based on Qur'an 49:13, which states that if any people can claim to be superior to others, it is only by virtue of their piety. Galwash concluded by beseeching "the God of all people and nations" to fill the hearts of all people "with respect toward one another so that peace and well-being for all will yet remain on earth."[169]

SLICES OF LIVES

"Slices of lives" can be used "as tracers, to illuminate aspects of the past that would otherwise remain obscure, hidden, or even misunderstood," just as the histories of individuals, no matter how unique, can "yield global stories that challenge conventional narratives."[170] Hugo Marcus may have been an idiosyncratic historical character—homosexual, Jewish, and Muslim—yet the questions raised by his life are salient for understanding the interrelated issues of Muslim responses to Nazism in Germany and the history of Muslim-Jewish relations.[171] Like Christians, Muslims responded to Nazism and its persecution of Jews in a variety of ways. They expressed opinions ranging "from outright refusal to fascination [with Nazism], with sympathy and scepticism often being voiced by one and the same person." Everywhere Muslim responses were conditioned by local conditions and conflicts.[172]

The religious and political rivalries that dominated Muslim life in Berlin contributed to German Muslims' response to the Nazis in the 1930s. Ahmadi beliefs about prophecy and the messiah were condemned by Sunni Muslims centered in the Islamic Community of Berlin, who challenged the Ahmadi's Islamic credentials and labeled its members British agents. Throughout the 1920s, the Islamic Community of Berlin tried to wrest control of the city's only mosque from the Ahmadi for these two reasons. When the Nazis rose to power and presented themselves as liberators of Muslim-majority lands, protectors of Islam, and enemies of British, French, and Soviet imperialism, they found a natural ally in the Islamic Community—whose leaders had worked with the German Foreign Office since

World War I to gain India's freedom—just as the Ahmadi, seen as too pro-British and too cosmopolitan to fit Nazi aims, began to voice alleged affinities between Islam and Nazism to survive as an organization.[173] The Islamic Community, which was founded by socialist revolutionaries and had once boasted Jewish converts among its ranks, appealed to the Nazis by portraying the Ahmadi as a Jewish Bolshevist organization.

The Ahmadi's accommodationist statements and actions after 1933 demonstrate that the mission failed to live up to many of its Weimar-era promises. Most of these actions were meant to curry favor with the regime by adopting its terminology so that the organization could continue to exist and hold on to the mosque. Yet, even if not based on ideological rapprochement, such actions as publishing anti-Semitic material and dismissing a Jewish officeholder did subject them to "personal liability for the interaction with a totalitarian and racist regime" and for crimes of the era, for they facilitated the Nazi project of separating Jews from Germans.[174] Moreover, they betrayed their own principles by distinguishing between Muslims based on "racial" categories.

The Ahmadi in England presented a different message, which befit the Ahmadi aim to be on good terms with the majority society. Articles in *Islamic Review* after 1933, in contrast to the *Moslemische Revue*, criticize fascism and persecution of Jews. An article condemns fascism as extremism and dictatorship.[175] Another argues that "the renewed persecution of the Jews under the Christian governments of the twentieth century, contrasted with their enviable position under Muslim sovereigns in the past, has set all serious people thinking."[176] The author argues that "the Jews seem destined to suffer persecution" under Christians, whether medieval or modern.[177] Hitler has renewed the medieval persecution and "the Nazis are trying to rid Germany of the Jews."[178] The author allows that although one can claim "somewhat reasonably" that Nazi persecution was a response to "Jewish treachery" during World War I, it does not explain why anti-Semitism has swept the continent.[179] Abdul Majid, imam of the Woking Mosque, reacted sharply when comparisons between Muhammad and Hitler were made in the English press (and in Ahmadi publications in Berlin). He declared that "Muhammad is the very essence of the anti-thesis of Hitler" and that "the ideology of Islam is fundamentally opposed to that of Nazism. Islam stands for the universal equality of mankind, whereas the hall-mark of Nazism is racial particularism."[180]

Like other foreigners in Nazi Germany, the Ahmadi in Berlin responded in contradictory ways, for other actions they took successfully opposed Nazi racism. Marcus continued to head the German Muslim Society and remained editor of the mosque's publications for several years after he was prohibited from doing so by Nazi law. Some members of the community supported his continuing role in the organization and, astonishing in the face of the new racial statutes, the public life of the mosque. They maintained social relations with him long after they were forbidden to do so, and they supported him financially until 1939; otherwise he would have been penniless. The society and mosque resisted pressure to merge with pro-regime organizations and withstood Gestapo and local Nazi Party inquiries. Sermons at the mosque—republished in its journal—continued to call for interreligious and interracial harmony until the end of 1939. The Qur'an translation published that same year condemns religious persecution and racism and offers rejoinders to those wishing to escape culpability for following leaders such as Hitler. These actions in context and the choices made by other Muslims stand as proof of Ahmadi open-mindedness.

When it mattered most, the Ahmadi, Imam Abdullah, and the international leader of the organization, Muhammad Ali, converted their profession of interreligious harmony and condemnation of persecution of Jews into life-saving action. Even as their accommodation to Nazi ideology helped contribute to the anti-Semitic atmosphere in Berlin, they ultimately frustrated the Nazis' attempt to annihilate the Jews of Europe, if only by saving one life. They brought together a diverse group of men—one Protestant, one Catholic, and one Muslim, a "Weimar coalition" that had formed interconfessional affinities at the mosque during the 1920s—who apparently saved Hugo Marcus from the Sachsenhausen concentration camp in 1938. As Marcus revealed after the war, "The united efforts of Superintendent Joachim Ungnad and Father Georg, Crown Prince of Saxony—both men had visited our 'Islam Evenings'—and our Imam Dr. Abdullah managed to free me."[181] Joachim Ungnad (1873-1942) was a member of the Bekennende Kirche (Confessing Christians) who opposed the Nazification of the Church and the persecution of baptized Jews, although they, too, discriminated against Christians of Jewish background and had an ambivalent relationship to Nazi anti-Semitism. Father Georg was the last crown prince of Saxony (1893-1943). Both men promoted ecumenism and interreligious dialogue and opposed the Nazis; the latter is credited with protecting Jews during the war.

A historian would be hesitant to claim, like Marcus, that the three men actually saved him from the camp. Marcus, like most Jewish men arrested and incarcerated there at that time, was imprisoned as a brutal warning, slated for release on condition that he leave the country as quickly as possible. While it is improbable that the men actually "saved" Marcus from the camp, it is likely that the well-connected men visited the camp to ask about Marcus's condition, to testify to his good character, and to try to have him released. It is possible that their efforts convinced camp commanders to release him earlier than planned.

The Ahmadi created a sinecure for Marcus in Lahore, and the imam got him a visa to India, testifying to Marcus's good character and obtaining certification that he was not a danger to the state. As a result, he was granted an exit permit that enabled him to leave Germany just one week before the outbreak of World War II and thus to escape the brutal end meted out to his brothers. "Rescued" from the concentration camp by the three ministers including his imam, Marcus emigrated to Switzerland thanks to the "persistent efforts" of his homosexual comrade Dr. Max Jordan.[182]

CHAPTER 4

Who Writes Lives

Swiss Refuge, 1939–1965

The Holy Book [the Qur'an] is the true homeland that cannot be lost, that the believer carries with him. It is the fatherland that always remains open to the Muslim, even if he has lost his own.[1]

Just before World War II broke out, on the last day he was permitted to enter Switzerland, Marcus arrived by train at Basel's Badischer Bahnhof (German train station). Although located within Swiss territory, the station was considered part of Germany and was controlled by German railways.[2] Despite having to disembark in a train station bedecked with swastikas as if it were Berlin, Marcus was lucky. He was one of an estimated five thousand foreigners granted entry to Switzerland in 1939.[3] Swiss asylum was granted only reluctantly and only to political refugees. It was accorded to "very few" Jews, who were not given asylum on the basis of "racial persecution."[4] Jews were considered "undesirable foreigners" and "alien elements" whose immigration needed to be hindered; they were not seen as "vulnerable people needing protection" since they suffered from political persecution.[5] They were labeled "émigrés" rather than "refugees." For Marcus it was not a case of asylum. When he arrived in Switzerland on August 24, he possessed a visa to British India. At that point Switzerland only accepted migrants "in possession of visas for onward migration."[6] Xenophobic Swiss authorities' restrictive immigration policies were based on their perception of Switzerland as a "country of transit" rather than permanent home to refugees.[7] The long-serving head of the Federal Aliens' Police, Heinrich Rothmund (1919–1954; d. 1961), had declared one year before the war broke out that the "Jewish Question" was the threat of "foreign infiltration" of Switzerland by Jews; his self-perceived role was "to hinder the Judaization of the country."[8] For that reason Swiss authorities had accepted Germany's proposal in autumn 1938 to mark the passports of German Jews, including Marcus's, with a "J" for "Jude" (Jew).[9]

The Swiss authorities presumed Marcus would soon leave the country. The Federal Aliens' Police decreed that "residence may only be granted until November 20, 1939 with the aim of preparation for emigration from Switzerland. By this date the departure from Switzerland must have been made. Reason: Foreign infiltration (*Ueberfremdung*)." Furthermore, "*any gainful employment is forbidden*."[10] The decision was confirmed by the federal government in Bern four days after World War II had begun. Marcus, a stateless person, was allowed to enter the country on condition that he had to leave it within two and a half months. During wartime. As a Jew.

Germany's invasion of Poland on September 1 caused the British to cancel his visa. Marcus had nowhere to go. Marcus was stuck in Switzerland, dependent on the good will of Swiss authorities. He became one of the estimated twenty-five thousand Jews who took refuge in the country and survived the Holocaust.[11] An unknown number of Jews—estimated to be at least as large as the number allowed to take refuge—was refused entry to Switzerland during the war and turned back from the French or German border to face near certain death. Most Jews accepted into the country were interned in camps. They were not allowed to work and were forced to rely on private donors and especially Jewish organizations to support them. After the war they were encouraged to leave the country. Marcus was lucky to be allowed in, not to be interned, and especially not to be pursued by the Federal Aliens' Police when his visa was cancelled. Jews in similar circumstances were often made to leave the country, many with fatal consequences.[12] Like the several hundred other German Jewish refugees living in Basel at the time, however, in addition to not being allowed to work, Marcus also faced other restrictions, including not being permitted to be out past 10 p.m. and not being able to eat in the restaurants and cafes of the entire Old Town.[13] He may have been spared other indignities, for he resided in fairly isolated Oberwil, Baselland Canton—a twenty-five minute tram ride from the central Marktplatz and a further ten-minute walk from the station up a hill—where he was more likely to see apple trees than people outside his window.

Despite his entry into the country having been made conditional on his agreeing to leave it by November 20, 1939, Marcus never left; he was allowed one temporary visa after another over the next five years. Nonetheless, like other refugees during the war, he was unable to earn an income to support himself and constantly had to seek aid. To repeatedly obtain and maintain his temporary, two- to three-month residence permit, limiting him to the canton that had granted it, he had to acquire a "certification of good reputation" issued by the municipality where he lived.[14] For example, in 1942, the same year that the Swiss federal government decreed that it would turn back refugees without visas, "even when the foreigners affected by this decision will subsequently face endangerment to life and limb," the authorities of the community of Oberwil issued such a certification.[15] It testified that "Mr. Hugo Israel Marcus"—using the name the Nazis had forced him to take—had since August 24, 1939, "been a resident in the local community and holder of a *Toleranzbewilligung* [temporary residence permit granted to Jews], and that during this time he has fulfilled his civic duties and honors and has not incurred any penalties in this place and enjoys a good reputation."[16] The cantons of Basel and Baselland were more "tolerant" than other cantons, often acting in humanitarian fashion resisting the orders of the Federal Aliens' Police, and repeatedly renewed his temporary, short-term residence permit granted to Jewish refugees during the war.[17] While the German consulate in Basel had extended his German passport annually until 1942, it did not do so thereafter.[18]

Only two years after the war ended did Swiss authorities begin to grant permanent asylum (*Dauerasyl*); thus, in 1947 it granted the status to Marcus, giving him the ability to "work again as a writer without any special approval."[19] Marcus was fortunate to be permitted to stay after the war.

RELATIONS WITH JEWS AND JUDAISM, 1939–1947

Marcus had used all the networks he had to leave Germany, including his far-flung family. In the autumn of 1939, Marcus exchanged letters with his cousin Else, who had settled in New York. After Marcus had resettled in Switzerland, Else wrote him a lengthy letter concerning his mother. She had heard from her cousin Hermann that Marcus's mother had not yet emigrated to Switzerland, and she was very worried for her well-being. Marcus's enquiry about remittances made her even more worried. Marcus had apparently asked her for money for his mother. His cousin explained that it was difficult for her to get access to her money in Germany or to that of other relatives because they were no longer able to reach them. She knew the Nazi regime had blocked her funds, the real estate that she inherited. A relative, Friedel, "who still has quite a bit in Germany in *Sperrmark* [currency blocked from remittance leaving Germany] is too hard to reach. You, of course, want the payments ordered quickly. I will inquire with Friedel, who hopefully is still free, by airmail regardless. The newspaper reports are conflicting and F.'s last letter talked about the imminent possibility of internment. . . . It would be good to do this right away." At any rate, she declares, "I am happy that you have left Barbaria [Germany] behind you." Else had mentioned that she would contact an aunt who settled in Palestine who had adequate funds. Although Marcus had family in the United States and in British Palestine, there is no evidence of efforts, on his part or on theirs, to take refuge from Nazi Germany in either of those lands.[20]

Marcus was not a Zionist.[21] On the contrary: in the autumn of 1932 he was one of the founding members of the Berlin branch office of future notorious anti-Semite and Nazi supporter al-Haj Amin al-Husayni's World Islamic Congress.[22] The congress had been established in Jerusalem the previous year to oppose Jewish settlement of Palestine, "to defend Muslim interests and preserve the holy places and lands from any intervention."[23] The Berlin branch—led by Zeki Kiram, future Hitler fan—lists its aims as "strengthening the unity of Muslims, promoting their cooperation; safeguarding Islamic interests; protecting their sanctuaries and places of worship [read: Jerusalem]; educating about Islamic culture; highlighting the special merits of Islam; defending against unjustified attacks; and nourishing the Islamic sciences."[24] As a sign of his significance, Marcus is listed as the fifth member of the organization, right after the four office holders; he also received the fourth highest vote total (and second highest for a German) in the ballot for general secretary. Such a man would not willingly migrate to the Jewish state-in-the-making in Palestine.

In 1939 Marcus also contacted his cousin on his mother's side, Leonie Cahn (b. 1896, d. after 1966), and her husband, Fritz Cahn (1894–1959), who lived in Zürich.[25] Like Else in New York, Leonie also tried to find ways to ensure Marcus received the promised funds from the Ahmadi. At the end of 1940 she asked him whether the Ahmadi in Lahore could send it to a bank account of one of her friends or relatives in England, and that person could send it to Leonie, who could then pass it on to Marcus.[26] She also informed him that, "as a Jew," he had the option to ask the Jewish community of Basel for the seventeen francs (today: $64.40) weekly financial assistance they gave to every Jewish immigrant; in addition, her family promised fifty francs (today: $189) in support per month.[27] Finally, she contacted the British Lloyds Bank in Geneva, asking whether remittances would be possible from British India to Palestine, and the manager replied that he believed they would be. They continued to try ways to obtain his Ahmadi funding the following year. Marcus suggested having the Ahmadi in India send the funds to relatives in Palestine who were English subjects, including a representative of a bank in Jerusalem; the funds could then be wired to his cousin Else's account in Zürich. Meanwhile, she tried to calm him down regarding his residency permit, urging him to have patience, for "it can take weeks or months to receive written approval."[28]

Marcus's mother, Cäcilie, who was eighty-five years old at the time, finally managed to escape Nazi Germany, arriving in Switzerland three months after her son on December 30, 1939.[29] Was her son able to pull strings so that this elderly widow could both leave Germany and be allowed to settle in Switzerland? He had delayed his exit as long as he could in part to aid her but left before her, perhaps having secured the necessary documents for her before doing so. Did the Ahmadi help her get out? Was a Jewish organization able to do so? Or someone in Marcus's homosexual network, such as Jordan? She did not settle in the canton of Baselland as did Marcus, however, nor did she live with him; her destination was the canton of Zürich, where her niece Leonie resided, who could make sure she was well taken care of and serve as a go-between between Marcus and his mother. She corresponded with his mother, visited her, and read his letters aloud to her.[30]

Marcus's mother passed away in Zürich eight years later in the winter of 1947.[31] Marcus's cousin Ernst Kantorowicz—who left Germany in 1938 without his mother—reflected on the death of Cäcilie's brother, his uncle Felix Hepner, which was "calm and peaceful, and I also hope pain free and without distress." Ernst took consolation in the fact that "at least he [Hepner] was spared what befell my poor mum."[32] Marcus's mother, by contrast, was able to end her life in dignity. One assumes Marcus attended the funeral. Marcus had sent her over 250 practically illegible letters during the war years narrating his student life at Basel University; she responded with a dozen entirely illegible letters. What is significant is that despite his homosexuality, conversion to Islam, and resigning membership in the Jewish community of Berlin, his mother never rejected him. One could argue that she had no other choice: she had lost her husband in 1930 and her other three sons in 1919, 1933, and 1944. Hugo was her last surviving son.[33] All of her sons were childless.[34] Marcus's attempts to take care of her as well as her staying in touch with his friend Roman Malicki in Berlin—as did Leonie, who sent him care packages by way of friends traveling to Berlin—provide evidence of a continued relationship between mother and son.[35]

Being in Switzerland afforded Marcus other avenues for continuing spiritual pursuits he formerly practiced in Germany. In Basel he resumed connections with Jewish disciple of Stefan George, Edith Landmann (1877–1951). Landmann, one of the women closest to George, "who played the role of Eckermann to George's Goethe," gained renown as the author of two major works devoted to the master in the 1920s.[36] She sent Marcus poems: in 1944 she sent passages from George's "Aus dem traurigen Tänzen" (From the sad dances) from his masterwork *Jahr der Seele* (Year of the soul) to refresh his memory: "in three years it will be the 50th anniversary since the *Jahr der Seele* was published, with which a new world for me was opened."[37] She read his work carefully: she praised his manuscript of *Metaphysik der Gerechtigkeit* (Metaphysics of justice, which would not appear until four years later).[38] She visited him, spoke with him on the phone, told him what George would have thought of his analyses.

Landmann had lost her husband, Julius, who was a professor of political economy at the University of Basel from 1910 to 1927 and then at the University of Kiel from 1927 until his death in 1931. She had dutifully taken detailed notes of the conversations she and her husband had with George between 1912 and 1931, completing her well-known *Gespräche mit Stefan George* in 1942 (although it was not published until a decade after her death).[39] During the war Landmann reconstituted her George circle in Basel, pursuing philosophic and spiritual interests, which resulted in two additional major studies, which she discussed with Marcus as she worked on them, assisted by her son, Michael, who also had a close relationship with Marcus.[40] When Marcus was temporarily disallowed from visiting the University of Basel library in the autumn of 1944, Michael provided him the books he needed.[41]

Michael Landmann was the president of the Philosophical Society, which invited Marcus to lecture in 1946. Because he was an émigré, Marcus needed police approval to be allowed to give a public lecture. Landmann wrote a letter on his behalf, stating it would "be a pleasure" to have "one of the most devoted members of our Society" expound his ideas before the public.[42] Landmann asked the police to grant approval on the grounds that his lecture concerned a cultural and thus by no means political matter, after all, its title was "Das Prinzip der

Äquivalenz in Natur- und Geisteswelt" (The principle of equivalence in the natural world and the spiritual world).

Edith Landmann told Marcus that his ideas "could only come from a time that was different," reminding her of a passage in George's *The Seventh Ring*: "Verklärtes Lächeln ins gestirnte Blau" (Blissful smile into the starry blue), words that she found "all the more important that they . . . urge us in the nadir not to forget the zenith!"[43]

RELATIONS WITH MUSLIMS AND ISLAM, 1939–1947

Despite World War II, which made enemies of friends and prohibited their contacts, Marcus maintained relations with Muslims in Germany while reediting the introduction to the German translation of the Qur'an, serving as intermediary between the Ahmadi in England and British India. He published in Ahmadi periodicals in German and English and lectured on Islam in Switzerland.

Marcus did not appear to be in contact with any Muslims in Switzerland, however—neither in Zürich nor in Geneva, for those Muslims were from non-Ahmadi circles. Before his departure from Berlin he had come into contact with Swiss-based Muslim exiles such as Shakib Arslan, but there is no evidence that he had relations with such Muslims after his arrival in Switzerland. He was fortunate that during his long years in Basel the university boasted a renowned scholar of Sufism and Persian poetry, Fritz Meier, who at that time was writing about monism in Islam.[44] One imagines the two of them having many conversations during the first eight years of his exile, when Marcus was a nontraditional student a generation older than his professor. Forbidden to work, Marcus enrolled as a student majoring in philosophy and minoring in psychology and political science in the Philosophy-History faculty at the University of Basel from the winter semester 1942 to the summer semester 1947. His student registration lists his nationality as "stateless" and his religion as "Muslim."

Marcus raised eyebrows with his frequent use of the university library and the philosophy seminar library. In November 1944 inquiries were made to the police whether this "émigré" had permission to do so, for only students could use seminar libraries. University professor and head of the philosophy seminar Dr. Schmalenbach supported Marcus, giving testimony that he was "a highly-gifted scholarly person." At the end of November approval was confirmed, for no objections were raised.[45] But despite his eager pursuit of knowledge, attending many courses, he failed to earn a degree for the second time in his life.[46]

Marcus continued to try to obtain funds from the Ahmadi in Lahore, who believed Marcus's stay in Switzerland was temporary. They desired him in India. At the end of October 1939 he received a note from Sadr-ud-Din: "Dear Brother in Islam Hamid Marcus, Assalamo Alaikum! I received two friendly letters from you and wrote one to you. I have tried to send money to you, but that is hard to do. . . . I wrote to the government on your behalf to demand they allow you to travel to India. We need to wait. Dr. Abdullah is in Copenhagen. He would like to travel to India, but it is hard because the route is dangerous. With fraternal wishes, Sadr ud Din."[47]

One finds a flurry of letters exchanged with the Ahmadi concerning financial support for Marcus and the Qur'an introduction. In the summer of 1940, S. M. Abdullah, having finally arrived in Lahore, mentions that the Ahmadi were doing everything they could to help him, including trying to send money to him in Switzerland, possibly by way of Max Jordan in New York.[48] That autumn Abdullah explains how difficult it was: "Money transfer to Switzerland is very hard and almost impossible. Because the bank wanted to determine your nationality, I indicated 'Polish Jew by Birth' (in English). The money could not be easily sent to America [by way of Jordan]. One has to answer a lot of questions."[49] Abdullah was naive and incorrect to label Marcus as a Polish Jew, a group that the latter abhorred. Posen had been part of Imperial Germany when he was born. Why would Abdullah not refer to him as a German, or as a Muslim?

The Qur'an translation had been published in 1939, but the Ahmadi in Lahore were unhappy with the introduction. In February 1940 Sheikh Abdullah wrote to Marcus that he was glad to hear that the Ahmadi Qur'an was well received in Switzerland, but by whom we have no idea. We assume Marcus was sharing his own personal copy, but with whom? Most likely his philosophical, university, and even family circles. But there was a problem. Sadr-ud-Din, the author of the introduction, translated into German by Marcus, was convinced that the three-page section "Fremdquellen im Islam" (Foreign sources in Islam) was not written by him, and he was very angry. Had Marcus slipped in his own interpretation? Was it a German Muslim in Berlin? Or was Sadr-ud-Din enraged that someone would challenge his authority? Among Marcus's private papers is an undated typescript originally delivered as a lecture at the mosque, "Berührungspunkte zwischen den

Koran und ausserislamischen Glaubensquellen" (Points of shared understanding between the Qur'an and extra-Islamic religious sources).[50] In it Marcus lists the instances where the Qur'an uses "raw material" from Jewish, Christian, Zoroastrian, Hindu, and ancient Egyptian sources. He argues that God "repeated his earlier revelations issued at different times and revealed to different nations resulting in each nation finding in the Qur'an something familiar from its own world of ideas," leading people of different faiths to recognize the message as credible and then convert to Islam. As published in the extant introduction to the Qur'an, as "Fremdquellen im Islam" (pages 26–28), the section gives the same list of foreign sources as contained in Marcus's lecture. Arguing that while the Qur'an uses "Jewish, Christian-heretical, pagan-Arab, and Persian [Zoroastrian] spiritual material," nevertheless it "expresses its spirit of a world religion that takes beauty from the whole world in order to bring it to the whole world. When the different nations found elements in the holy book of Islam that were familiar to them it only increased the effect of the revelation among them and as a consequence Islam constructed a global brotherhood" (page 28). There is little difference between Marcus's lecture and the published version. Islam is depicted as an international religion that unifies humankind, and for that reason its message is delivered in a language that all peoples can understand. Sadr-ud-Din must have felt threatened by loss of editorial control.

Abdullah asked for Marcus's help in contacting Berlin and getting them to replace the pages, including the couple of hundred copies already sold.[51] Abdullah instructed Marcus to inform the German mosque community that the Ahmadi Qur'an should not be distributed.[52] The following month Abdullah informed Marcus he was going to send the new pages of the introduction to him soon. From Switzerland Marcus was supposed to mobilize the mosque community in Berlin to take care of the "necessary steps" (printing it and inserting it in the existing copies). In other words, Abdullah repeated, Marcus should tell them not to give out any of the old Qur'ans; everyone who bought the old version would get a new copy and should hand the old version back.[53]

The incident caused a fury among the worldwide Ahmadi community. In June Marcus received a letter from Abdullah stating that not only Sadr-ud-Din but the entire community was "very angry and frustrated" by the mistake in the introduction. Abdul Majid from Woking condemned it. The community had become very circumspect and did not want *Moslemische Revue* to be published by a "non-Muslim," which may be understood to refer to a convert to Islam—specifically,

Marcus. However, Abdullah, trusting Marcus and blaming the German community in Berlin for the "satanic verses," asked Marcus to take care of the issue.[54]

Abdullah's letters took a fatalistic turn: World War II was the result of European civilization, he writes, and the wrath of God. Only prayer can help.[55] Abdullah regretted that Marcus did not come to India when they first invited him; by that summer Abdullah thought the Indian government would not give Marcus a visa. Moreover, under the political circumstances, he realized he could not send the new pages for the introduction.[56]

Over the next two years they managed to revise it in collaboration with the mosque community in Berlin, despite the prohibition of contacts between British subjects (the Ahmadi in British India) and Germans (the mosque community in Berlin) and despite German laws forbidding relations with Jews. At the beginning of 1941 Marcus received a letter from Abdullah saying that Sadr-ud-Din was "very sorry that you are still without money. What did you write Mister [Abdul] Majid [in Woking] and what did he respond? That would be possible, if he sent you the necessary money. We'll gladly refund him. Please write him to that effect. . . . Have you heard from the Mosque? Do the [German Muslim mosque caretakers the] Gaedickes still live there and how are things going there?"[57] In March 1941 Marcus sent Abdullah the first edited version of the introduction, praying "May God protect us all in the future. The times are terrifying."[58]

By the autumn of 1941, two years after his arrival in Switzerland, Marcus still considered himself a Muslim, was lecturing about Islam, and was endeavoring to fulfill his obligations to the Ahmadi community, with whom he remained in close contact and who were still supporting him and even his relatives. His financial situation seemed assured. Consider this letter to Abdullah in September 1941: "My dear Brother in Islam, Dr. Abdullah, Assalaam Aleikum! . . . I gave a short lecture at the university on questions of Islamic religion. One still knows very little about Islam here. Even university professors did not know that Islam recognizes the prophets and the holy books of all religions, and admired that tolerance a lot." He writes: "I am incredibly thankful that Maulvi Magid [Abdul Majid in Woking] has helped my relatives in England. I was helped here too. Totally unexpected I received payment of two month's salary. My situation has much improved. I was very happy about that. I reminisce with indescribable gratefulness about my brothers in faith in Lahore, whom I hope I will finally be able to visit." He signed the letter "Your old Hamid Marcus."[59]

He continued to work closely with the Ahmadi in Lahore and Berlin to complete the new version of the Qur'an introduction. Marcus served as mediator between the mosque and the Ahmadi. Abdullah wrote him: "In the name of God! My dear Brothers in Islam, Dr. Hamid Marcus! Wonderful to have received letter of September 30, 1941. As you said, 'who writes lives.'"[60] In fact, in an early philosophical work, Marcus had written: "So long as you still take pleasure in a strong, bold word, so long as you are still able to grasp the beauty of a tender thought, then so long is your life still worthwhile."[61] This suggests that the Ahmadi read Marcus's philosophical work. The imam continues: "All of us—Maulana Mohammad Ali, Maulana Sadr ud Din and I are very happy to learn that you are able to serve Islam by your efforts and by giving presentations, despite your complicated situation. Switzerland has not had a chance to learn something important and true about Islam. Maybe the war allows a chance to do that." To pursue this aim he had Marcus's "Moslemischer Schicksalsglaube" translated into English as "Fatalism and Islam" and published it in *The Light*. He asked whether Marcus had received the two pages to the introduction of the Quran, which he had sent four months prior. He asks "How goes the mosque in Berlin? In God's name!"[62]

While communications with the Ahmadi in Lahore were warm and personable, the letters exchanged with the mosque community in Berlin were proper and businesslike, which in itself is remarkable, seeing how Marcus was considered an enemy of the state who would have been murdered had he remained. He received the following typical letter:

> Dear Mr. Dr. Marcus,
>
> We confirm the reception of your [writing]—, about which we will speak with Frau [Amine] Mosler. You will receive news soon about whether it is possible to print the Qur'an pages the way you requested. In the house and mosque here everything is absolutely fine. We are in good health too. . . . A small group of us celebrated the last festivity in the mosque. The annual guided tour of the mosque with Dr. Lederer occurred last Saturday. Around 150 people showed up. We were able to sell a series—and other writings. Please send our regards to our friends.
>
> With regards, L [Charlotte] Gaedicke.[63]

Soon after, Amine Mosler, whose own teenage son was a fanatic Nazi, sent a much friendlier letter to Marcus:

> Esteemed Herr Doctor!
>
> Unfortunately, I can respond to your letter from February 27, 1942, only today. Dr. Gaedicke also sent me your letter from February 26, 1942, and the manuscript of the planned changes. . . . Whether interest in the Qur'an is as great at present as it had been roughly two years ago, I do not dare judge. . . . Please send the final manuscript because things can change any day. Otherwise we are all well, the congregation sends its wishes, everyone thinks and speaks a lot of you and the Abdullah family. Business goes on as usual. Many many visitors to take care of. I have many letters to respond to, since all come to me, my house is the house for all. I myself, unfortunately, am often ill, my sir. My nerves, I suffer a lot from our [son] Ahmad. Keep staying under God's protection.
>
> Warm regards to you, Herr Doktor, and to the Abdullah family from your Amine Mosler.[64]

By 1942 the revision of the Qur'an introduction was finished and prepared to be redistributed. Thereafter Marcus ceased contact with the German Muslim community in Berlin, although he maintained relations for another decade with the Ahmadi in England and in what became Pakistan.

From the time the last Ahmadi imam, S. M. Abdullah, had to leave Berlin in 1939 until near war's end in 1945, senior civil servant Dr. Herbert Gaedicke (d. 1945) and his wife, Charlotte, were financially responsible for the mosque and mission house in which they lived.[65] Dr. Gaedicke joined the Nazi Party at the end of 1941.[66] With a German Nazi as caretaker, al-Husayni as preacher, and Muslim SS troops as the regular mosque users, one can see how much the composition of the community—once led by a Jew—had been altered by the war.

During the war the Muslim community was not threatened by Nazis who attempted to instrumentalize Islam and the Berlin mosque as part of their propaganda aims in pursuit of global domination, which was to be assisted by Muslims recruited to fight on their behalf against the "Judeo-Bolshevik" threat (the USSR) and England.[67] The mosque survived the war although it suffered extensive damage in April 1945 as mainly Turkic SS units used the building to withstand the Soviet advance in the neighborhood. The Soviet troops, coincidentally, were also largely made up of Turkic peoples. Allied bombing during the war not only damaged the mosque's dome and minarets—used by the Nazis as a machine gun stand—but also set off a fire that burned almost the entire stock of *Der Koran* that Marcus had worked so diligently on in Germany and in exile.[68] German Muslim Amine Mosler, the mosque caretaker at war's end, claimed that, whereas during the war six thousand Muslims had been members of the Muslim community centered at the mosque, only a few hundred remained in 1945.[69]

A few years after the war, a convert named Muhammad Aman (Herbert) Hobohm (1926–2014) of Lübeck became imam, the first German to fill that position at that mosque. He was never fully repentant about his faith in Nazism.[70] He had converted to Islam in 1939. He remembered fondly the 1942 visit to the mosque of "the Palestinians' Führer," al-Husseini, welcomed by a Muslim regiment of the German army. Too young to join the army, he cofounded a German Muslim patriotic youth organization that same year (all of whose members would die or be captured on the Russian front, save Hobohm) and served as a navy cadet during the war.[71] Of his 1939 conversion he explains: "I have lived under different systems of life and have had the opportunity of studying various ideologies, but have come to the conclusion that none is as perfect as Islam. Communism has its attractions, so have democracy and Nazism. But none has a complete code of a noble life. Only Islam has it."[72]

Hobohm estimated that by 1950 there were three hundred Muslims in Berlin, two hundred from Muslim-majority societies and one hundred German converts, the latter figure appearing to be wildly exaggerated. But the overall estimate makes clear that Berlin was no longer the center of Muslim life in Germany. It had been replaced by Munich where several thousand Soviet Turkic Muslim veterans of the Eastern Muslim SS Division coalesced under United States and West German sponsorship.[73] According to Hobohm, "at least seventy percent of the Muslims living in Berlin are at present unemployed and live under very poor circumstances."[74] This was a far cry from the "Muslim middle class" that predominated in the 1920s. Although a few businessmen were well off, "generally speaking the Berlin Muslim community is regarded as being very poor." Regarding the theme of conversion and the German character, Hobohm observed that "since I took charge of the Berlin Mission, by the Grace of God, thirty-four Germans have entered the fold of Islam." Of these, "two are medical doctors, two are craftsmen, one is an architect, five are merchants, six are housewives, and the rest are otherwise working or unemployed. With the exception of two, who are a disappointment, on the whole the others are very much attached to the mosque, and, as far as I can judge, are very sincere in their Islam." He claimed to know "from my own experience that the German, as such, is very conservative and that it will take a long time to convince him of the value of anything new, although, being like Faust, the German is perpetually on the search for knowledge." Deploying the Ahmadi conversion strategy of double consciousness that attracted Marcus, he added that "it takes some time to convince him that his conversion is not a breach of faith or loyalty towards his previous religion, for the object of adoration of both the religions [Christianity and Islam] is one and the same God." To Hobohm, this "illustrates another peculiarity of a German, for, once he is convinced, and once he has associated himself with the religion of Islam, he will faithfully stick to his decision, in a faithfulness, which, as the Hitler period proved, can go to the extent that it turns him blindly against his environment. But, although a Muslim should avoid extremes and always walk on the middle path, too much faithfulness is better than too little."[75]

RELATIONS WITH HOMOSEXUALS AND HOMOSEXUALITY, 1939–1947

During these same years Marcus maintained correspondence with Kurt Hiller in England, exchanging letters and works in progress.[76] Marcus also continued a detailed and lengthy correspondence with his friend Roman Malicki, with Max Jordan acting as their courier, although the latter would soon retire from the world in favor of the brotherhood of a remote German monastery. Marcus's mother not only knew of his longstanding friendship with Roman but maintained contact with him even after Hugo had left Germany. Marcus had given his mother the portrait Julie Wolfthorn had made of him. Before leaving Berlin for Switzerland, his mother gave the portrait to Roman.[77]

Although we do not possess Marcus's letters to Roman, we gain a sense of their relationship from Roman's lengthy letters that display Malicki's passion for Marcus and their long-lived relationship, which had begun prior to World War I: "It feels to me like I have not seen you in a long, long time—as if you should come home soon now! I feel that you have been away long enough and should come home now. I miss so much the vibrant resonance from you and a few deep questions which I would wish to reconcile myself with, I carry silently. The realization grows ever stronger that you are gone a long time!" In fact, the two would never see each other again. Roman mentions that he suffered from kidney stones and melancholia that makes it hard for him to write: "It weighs on me that you have to wait so long for my letter, because it is already February and I owe you news and thanks. Thanks for your last detailed letter as well as for the exchanged one. I certainly worry about you—how you will manage and who will help you?" At the same time, Roman reflects on their past relationship: "But in everything I sense how much worries I caused you until 1914. And later even more so!"[78]

What is most significant is what Malicki reveals about his sister. Roman came from a Roman Catholic family; his sister was a nun. His wide circle of family and friends in Berlin and Poland included Jews and Catholics, Nazi Party members, and gays. After his sister died, Roman comments, "She will not be able to pray for you anymore! To convert you was her goal, that is what her prayers were toward. Maybe she succeeded, maybe it happened after all through Islam! Every time I had to disclose your progress to her. She achieved her aim and so we will meet her on the path of good ideals."[79]

Marcus continued to rely on Jordan. When Marcus arrived in Switzerland in August 1939, Jordan paid the substantial security deposit necessary for Marcus to obtain his temporary residence permit.[80] In the autumn of 1941 Jordan assured Marcus, "My guarantee for you is of course still valid. If you encounter any difficulties, please use my name to contact Administrative and National Councilman Dr. Gschwind in Liestal, who has been oriented and will gladly be helpful. In addition, my monthly contributions will continue of course, so long as you need them. I will instruct my bank in Basel to comply."[81] Hugo Gschwind (1900–1975), a Roman Catholic like Jordan and a member of the Catholic-Conservative Party, was president of the governing council of the canton of Baselland in 1940–1941 and served in the position again in 1944–1945. That council had given Marcus permission to settle and reside in the district.

Over the next few years, Marcus continued to correspond frequently with Roman. Roman told Marcus that reading his letters makes "everything they experienced together rise again and awaken a nice feeling of gratitude." Roman thought of Marcus often and believed it was important to be faithful in hard times: "As much as the days bring painful moments, your faithfulness, your loyalty makes everything easy for me and is my consolation for everything that cannot be achieved."[82] In the summer if 1944 Roman wished Hugo a happy birthday, telling him, "Alas, even when the distance from here to you is great, you have never been closer to me, *lieber* Hugo, than today."[83]

After the war Roman's wavering and quivering voice called Marcus from the ruins of Berlin, a city whose gay scene had "lost the prominence it had previously enjoyed."[84] Roman pleaded, "—my dear Hugo—this time I veil my heart in silence. Please forgive me but the past few months I was struggling with my health." Living in a home without an oven, heater, or glazed windows, he suffered from the cold, his eyesight was ruined, he was barely able to write. He closed one letter by proclaiming, "My only goal is to not lose my eyesight before I set eyes on you again. I hug you. Your Roman." He had vertigo and could barely walk. Malnutrition caused him to be exhausted. Finally he suffered a nervous breakdown, as did many of those around him: "This war has infused my limbs with the poison of terror and has distorted my face. These years of hopelessness—not one day without fear of death or the military or imprisonment—have not passed me by as easy as I had thought initially. For days now, however, my health is better. My mood, too, is healthier and so I write to you, dear Hugo." Marcus is his light. Roman tells him: "A lot of times I conduct an imaginary dialogue with you, with your portrait [painted by Wolfthorn, which he still possessed]. In your loving, knowing face your gaze is directed at me. I sense your kindness and lenience. A lot of times I envisioned your temperament and on Sundays, at the usual lunch hour, my room is filled with your step."[85] The depiction of Sunday as the day lovers meet in secret would appear in Marcus's homoerotic fiction published after the war.

Roman describes Berlin as having been "stripped of everything beautiful, suffers from hunger, and is nothing but ruins. The best—here—for me, us, is irretrievably over." Nevertheless, he sometimes took "pleasure in the fact that red geraniums remain and sunflowers drape the heaps of rubble of bombed out buildings and grow in the wreckage and abandoned gardens. And that there are things that the Nazis cannot suffocate in blood with violence and deceit."[86] Like the love between two men.

Just as Marcus had sat for his own portrait two decades earlier, Roman explained that "at the moment the painter Thea Schleusner—an acquaintance of [the painter Julia] Wolfthorn at whose tea she met you in person—is making an expressionist portrait of me, but [there is no need for that as] I believe that my gaunt face has already been marked by the war." She "finds my type interesting, she comes over on Fridays. She is preparing studies for her new cycle, since her life's work of forty-six years went up in flames along with her studio. She is an exceptionally elegant, gentlewomanly person of your age–. To my gain. Odd–You end one of your letters writing that I should, . . .'remain a model for all who can see well.' Well, Thea Schleusner can see well and I am her model."[87]

The pastel portrait offers a haunting vision of a mournful-looking, deathly thin man with tussled, reddish-blonde hair leaning against a windowsill. What horrors has he experienced? The man faces the painter, his thin lips pressed together beneath bony cheeks and dark rings under his large eyes. His white shirt is open beneath his light blue jacket and oversized white shawl, which reaches to his knees. He holds a Jesus-like pose, the bony fingers of his left hand on his stomach, the right hand rests palm up–first two fingers touching the thumb, third and fourth fingers outstretched–on the windowsill. Light flows through the window into his open right hand, bathing him in late-morning light. The warmth of the sunlight and the liveliness of the pastel colors contrast with the apartment's dark red interior and the pale, wan, ghost-like figure of Roman. A gruesome and sad portrait of a shattered man, it is a beautiful composition, expressing salvation among the ruins.[88] It is no wonder that Schleusner called Roman "a martyr type."[89]

At the end of 1946 Roman wishes Marcus a Merry Christmas and a Happy New Year, "affectionately kissing his dear" Marcus goodbye.[90] Roman, suffering from cold and losing his sight, spends a couple of hours each day sorting the manuscripts Marcus left behind in Berlin. Jordan could only take a little of it to Marcus each time he visited Switzerland. Roman found two mysterious parcels of manuscripts that were taped and sealed and on which Marcus had written that "they may only be opened fifty years later and given to the Berlin Library or the Raczyński Library in Posen." He asked Marcus what to do with them. Their contents and whereabouts are unknown today. Roman did not hope to get the permit for emigration before the new year; he is trying to prepare for the winter. When he traveled to Berlin, Jordan would try to provide him with shoes and clothes sent by Marcus. In the summer of 1947 Roman wished Hugo a happy birthday, accepting that he had to cope with his yearning alone: "Only the desire for you has to keep still, because I feel that I must get ready to deal with it alone."[91] At some point after that Roman was given permission to leave Berlin, and he returned to Poland.[92]

DR. HAMID MARCUS, 1947–1957

After the war Marcus lived as a Muslim in Swiss exile. With his relationship to German Muslims severed in the middle of the war, he did not reestablish them after war's end. Whatever relations he had to Muslims thereafter were with Ahmadi in England and in newly independent Pakistan. In 1949 and 1950 the *Islamic Review* published his "A Bridge Between the East and the West," "Switzerland and Its Relations to Islam," "Islam in Switzerland," and "Two Friends, One Muslim, the Other Christian, Discuss the Problems Facing the World" (which had originally appeared in 1932 as "The Message of the Holy Prophet Muhammad to Europe"; see chapter 2).[93] The editors of the Ahmadi journal described Marcus as "a German Muslim who left Germany due to Nazi persecution." No explanation was given as to why a Muslim would be targeted by the regime.

In these articles Marcus writes as a devout and cheery Muslim, confident that Islam can save the world (again). In "A Bridge Between the East and the West," he thanks God for having protected his community (Muslims). His sentiment could have been expressed by a Jew: "The world was afire from one end to the other. Some of us were saved from perils in the East, while others in the West in various ways. Those who were saved and had previously formed religious communities, have now for the second time to re-form themselves into a community of fellow-sufferers and community of the saved."[94] But he is speaking of Muslims, and of himself, who have not lost their faith despite years of "immense hardship," "fighting and destruction," and who "can entrust ourselves to Islam in this new era." He relies again on Goethe—"Islam endows its followers at all times with a confident and comforting attitude"—as he resigns himself to the will of God, as he submits to God. He proclaims that he shared the same sentiment as "the greatest German poet and thinker, Goethe," who wrote, "'If Islam means submission unto God, then we all live and die in Islam.'"[95] Marcus continued to be engrossed with Goethe in the postwar period. His private papers include two additional handwritten pieces from this period: "Goethes Begegnungen mit dem Islam" (Goethe's encounters with Islam), and "Goethe und der Islam" ("Goethe and Islam," which is less legible).

Marcus ends "A Bridge Between the East and the West" on a by now familiar pacifist note, referring to Nietzsche. He claims Nietzsche wrote, "Real peace can only come from the peace of mind, while the so-called armed peace at present in evidence in nearly every country is really a state of unrest of mind."[96] Marcus had earlier lectured at the mosque in Berlin that the Qur'an is a lawbook that is a blueprint for peace and tolerance, as Muhammad "was one of the first people to make the law not only serve justice, but rather make law and justice serve the idea of peace."[97] In this article he reiterates his conviction that Islam, "which means peace"—or, more specifically, Ahmadi Islam, as expressed by Muhammad Ali of Lahore—provides that peaceful state of mind so necessary to save humanity from itself and offers the only hope for creating a true "brotherhood of all mankind." Marcus nicely summarizes his life's work as "building a bridge spanning the gap between the most famous and misunderstood thinkers of the West [read: Goethe and Germany] and the wise men of the East [read: Muhammad, Sadr-ud-Din, and Muhammad Ali]."[98]

The Ahmadi community continued to send Marcus funds each year. In 1947 he wrote a letter to Muhammad Ali, addressed to him and "his dear brothers in Pakistan," profusely thanking him for his help: "I cannot thank you enough for your generous act. . . . How wonderful is it to know that there are souls who remain faithful over a quarter century as one world collapses and another arises, according to God's will. Always one with you, I remain full of reverence, your ever grateful H. M."[99] In fact, the mosque was still sending payments to him in return.

A letter from S. M. Abdullah—based at the mosque at Woking, England, after the war—attests to this fact:

> My dear Dr. Marcus, my dear brother in Islam, Assalam Alaikum!
>
> How are you? I have word from India that the community has authorized £5 per month for you, but the difficulty lies in transferring this money. I have tried to send the money to you through the post, but unfortunately without success. . . . Now I tried to transfer the money through the bank, but to do so I need to have a declaration from you that you work for us and translate our religious books into German, etc. Please send me such a letter *in English* and I will again try to obtain permission from the bank.
>
> Your brother in Islam, S.M. Abdullah.[100]

That same year Marcus wrote at least four times to the Swiss Federal Aliens' Police (April 30, May 6, July 1, and July 15) requesting permission to translate and publish Ahmadi religious writings from English into German. Marcus had been allowed to take refuge in Switzerland but on condition that he not work. He aimed to convince the Swiss authorities to allow him to work, but to do so he had to also explain who the Ahmadi were, offering a positive depiction of them as an important piece of Berlin's culture from the time of his association. In his account, the Ahmadi mosque in Berlin "was congenially supported by all the governments" of the Weimar period, "including the Social Democrats and later the Liberals and Catholics. Also under the National Socialist regime it remained unchallenged until the imam (the minister) left Germany in 1939." He declared that he knew "nothing about what happened after that." That the work of the Berlin mosque was valued positively "is demonstrated by the fact that it was given the responsibility for the religious education of all Muslim students in all of Berlin. When the House of Foreign Students was opened in Berlin in 1926, the Ministry of Education invited the imam of the mosque to deliver the formal address in the presence of Reich Chancellor Marx (Catholic Center)." In addition, "along with the diplomats of Muslim countries, diplomats of countries with Muslim subjects, such as Holland, also appeared at the festivals of the community. The community also had friendly relations with the Protestant and Catholic clergy." For example, "the Protestant theology professor Grützmacher spoke repeatedly in the mosque and worked together with us on the *Revue*. Superintendent Ungnad, Chair of the Union of Protestants of the Old-Ministry and member of the Berlin Dominican order, as well as the former Crown Prince of Sachsen, Father Georg S.J. were regular visitors to festivals at the mosque."[101] Two weeks later he repeated his request for permission to publish the writings of the Ahmadi in German.[102]

But there was more driving him than that. He wanted to "salvage" a piece of himself and the past annihilated by Nazi Germany. On July 1 he wrote again, pleading that while his "envisaged literary assistance" for the Ahmadi would be "important" to him as "a means of financial support," he sought to distinguish his "independent literary work" from it, for it would mean the world to him—"at an advanced age and after suffering long illness—to salvage something from my life's work, that would be a contribution to literature and scholarship."[103] Two weeks later he wrote again, more desperate:

> On April 30 I requested permission to be involved with the publication of German writings of the Indian religious community the Ahmadiyya-Lahore. More essential than this work is my petition of May 6, where I requested

> general permission to publish my own literary works. Economic aspects were not relevant to this petition. I was motivated, rather, by the desire—at my advanced age and with faltering health, and after the greatest part of my life's work had fallen prey to annihilation in Germany—perhaps still to be able to salvage but one work which may be of scholarly and literary interest.[104]

Marcus achieved the results he desired. Perhaps someone in the police department felt moved by his pleas? Or were they worn down by his monthly and even biweekly missives? Marcus must have been relieved to receive a letter from the police of Baselland Canton informing him that "as of October 23, 1947 we have released you from temporary residence status. From now on the residence permit you are granted is no longer attached to any conditions, namely, you can now work as a writer without any special approval."[105] For the first time since he had entered the country eight years earlier, he was finally granted a one-year residency that he would renew annually for the next decade.[106]

In 1951 he composed "Why I Became Muslim," a manuscript that is located among his personal papers. It is a worthy response to those—then and now—who would deny that Marcus was actually a Muslim, and it helps us understand what being Muslim meant to him. In it, as had been the case since the 1920s, Marcus brings together a German-Jewish approach to Islam, an effort to make Islam local and German—explicitly praising the "greatest German," Goethe, again as the "greatest Muslim"—and devotion to the Ahmadi leader. Within his normative description of Islam he also manages to subtly mention his own homosexuality. In chapter 2 I examine the first paragraph, which has been published. Here I analyze the complete narrative, which is unpublished, for the insight it offers into this remarkable man and his personalized understanding of Islam.

Marcus begins his conversion narrative asserting that he had become acquainted with Islam while a youth in his hometown by reading the same edition of the Qur'an translation that his life model Goethe read. He claimed to have been impressed by how Islam was at once rational and sublime. Converting to Islam under the guidance of Sadr-ud-Din "deprived me of nothing, for it allowed me to preserve the world view that I had formed for myself. But in addition it gave me several of the most path-breaking human thoughts that have ever been conceived." In the subsequent unpublished passage he relies on the German-Jewish approach to Islam, describing it as a rational religion that "remains aloof from all dogmas that are incompatible with the current status of the sciences. In Islam there is thus no conflict between faith and knowledge. This is a singular advantage for a man who in his modest capacity contributes to current scientific research." In his view Islam is not "an idealistic doctrine" but a religion grounded in real life which offers "spiritual spaces" without "tying it down unnecessarily"; Islamic laws "are not binding commandments that impede freedom" but "directions and 'grooves' that first make freedom possible." What Marcus, a self-described "calm and staid man," finds so satisfying about Islam is how it "maintains the golden means between individualism [capitalism] and socialism and because it liberally and without prejudice recognizes the good wherever it encounters it." He then promotes the Ahmadi: "I am convinced that thoughts of the kind that Muhammad Ali is expressing today about the state of the world might save the world. And these thoughts are based on a wise, simultaneously pious and modern application of the teachings of the holy Prophet Muhammad."

In the rest of the narrative Marcus adds his own spin to each of the five pillars of normative Islam, "the deeper significance which has revealed itself" to him. About prayer he writes, "the five daily interruptions of our routine by a short prayer remind us of purity amidst the daily grind and recall the most noble laws of human co-existence. I have often observed that quarrels that threaten to turn ugly before prayer fell silent after prayer and had lost their significance. But I also saw that someone who was unable to make a decision in a certain practical affair after prayer suddenly knew what he had to do because prayer had enabled him to collect himself."

Concerning fasting, he notes, "when we are animated by a great thought, to our own amazement we may forget to eat and drink and we experience this like a victory of the spirit over matter. But the reverse occurs as well: when, for example, we are fasting during the month of Ramadan and keep away from food and drink, a lofty sensation of bliss overcomes us because in so doing we have come closer to the existence of a pure disembodied spirit." The existence of pure spirit "is God's manner of existence." Fasting "delivers us from the lowly world of the compulsion to take. Whoever is fasting harms no creature. In its divine needlessness fasting is no permanent condition for a worldly creature, but temporarily, it is the most noble condition conceivable. Who would not want to re-experience it from time to time!" Finally, when fasting, people learn "how the poor feel when compelled to go hungry. No knowledge is as convincing as one's own experience."

On pilgrimage, Marcus observes, "sometimes, a small trait permits a glance deep into the heart of man. But also into the heart of things; thus it has always appeared particularly moving to me that Islam requires the pilgrimage to Mecca as a binding rule. But as long as our parents are alive, we are called upon not to make the pilgrimage to Mecca but instead to support our parents. Can there be a more delicate expression of the benevolent basic attitude of Islam than this special requirement?" When he converted to Islam, he "did not know yet what significance the word 'jihad' would one day acquire for me. For it also signifies the duty to leave a country that is under godless rule, even if in so doing one has to give up one's homeland. In this sense I have been on a pilgrimage for the last twelve years."[107]

Regarding charity, he argues, "the *zakat* tax is intended as charity but so are a whole range of other measures." He finds the variety of Islamic charity to be "singular. Islam supports widows, orphans, the ill, the old, travelers on the road, and even the indebted. No philanthropy, regardless of how modern it is, has gone farther in its social welfare."

Marcus seems to have forgotten that, normatively speaking, the first pillar of Islam is the *Shahadah*, the proclamation of faith, "there is only one God and Muhammad is his Prophet." But his stance is consistent with the Ahmadi view of conversion presented to him in the Weimar era, that one must neither leave one's old beliefs and religions behind nor publicly convert. This was expressed by the man who converted him, Sadr-ud-Din: "No ceremony is required to become Muslim . . . no one needs to convert to become a Muslim. One can be a Muslim without telling anybody. Committing to Islam is merely an organizational formality."[108] Accordingly, Marcus skips the *Shahadah*, replacing it with *his* own personal first pillar, purity. And under the obligation of purity he includes themes that interested him his entire life: fatalism, pacifism, love and beauty, and brotherhood.

First, he discusses fatalism and pacifism. He asserts that "objections are commonly raised against Islam: Islam is said to be the religion of the sword and the religion of fatalism. So many objections, so many errors." He counters this by arguing, "it goes without saying that a religion that precedes each conversation with the greeting 'peace be with you!' cannot be blood-thirsty." He begins by explaining that "since the First World War, we know how peaceful citizens may be turned into warriors and how warriors ultimately produce robber hordes that solely live from plunder." In his view, "Islam has produced the opposite development. For it encountered robber hordes; first it disciplined them into an orderly army and then turned them into police troops that attacked nobody, only served defensive purposes, and provided its citizens with help and security against enemies and robbers." In his analysis, "as a result, the citizens were able to devote themselves entirely to their civil profession. The European development went from the peaceful citizen via the warrior to the robber. The Muslim development went from the robber via the warrior to the peaceful citizen." Having asserted this claim, he asks "which development is more peaceable? That famous and profoundly true word of the Holy Prophet 'Peace lies in the shadow of the sword' explicitly states that the sword is not intended to bring war, but to protect peace. Who would want to challenge this truth today? With his insight the Prophet has anticipated more than a thousand years."

He then examines love and marriage. He first defends polygamy: "The Prophet permitted his contemporaries to marry up to four women. But it was not the case that the Arab tribes had lived monogamously up till then; rather they lived in an unlimited concubinage. And the Prophet limited this unlimited 'concubinage' to the number of four wives. Today monogamy is almost everywhere present in Islam." He is able to turn the discussion from marriage to homosexuality: "But if you ask me what I think of the kind of polygamy today existent in Islam, I answer: in matters of the heart I do not favor an ironclad order, nor do I favor disorder. Rather, I favor an elastic order which also provides due space for exceptional cases. Islam constitutes this elastic order and is—this is its inestimable advantage—that religion that allows exceptions as well." Here he is referring to himself, the homosexual, as "an exceptional case," and to his understanding that Islam, as taught and lived by the Ahmadi, tolerated his innate difference. He returns to the defense of polygamy: "In my professional life I have encountered numerous cases where a married man was tied to two women through the bonds of duty as well as of the heart and where the only honorable solution that would have satisfied all parts would have been the double marriage. But this is unknown in Europe. Only Islam features it." But here again he inserts himself: "I, however, especially love Islam for the fact that it also keeps open advice and legal channels for exceptional cases and exceptional human beings."

Fatalism is a topic that concerns him, and he returns to it: "I have previously provided an extensive demonstration of the fact that so-called Islamic fatalism does not render one inactive but rather allows one to remain carefree about one's life, to remain calm and brave. Islam does not mean that one blindly accepts one's fate; rather, it means acquiescence to God's moral laws, i.e. to properly employ those laws."[109] This discussion allows him to again present Goethe as the ideal

Muslim: "[Islam] teaches to derive peace of mind and reassurance from this predetermination, so that for the Muslim death loses its barriers, nay, fashions itself into a beautiful prospect. No one was as deeply penetrated by these effects of Islam as the greatest German: Goethe. He says: 'if Islam means submission to God, then we all live and die as Muslims.'"

From fatalism he turns to beauty: "Islam does not only offer wholesome truths but also extraordinary beauties. For it is not merely sober reason but also encompasses profound customs, symbols, legends, and sayings." As example, "whoever enters a mosque nowhere encounters the image of a saint; instead, he finds only an empty niche [*mihrab*] on smooth walls. This niche points in the direction of Mecca. And mosques all over the world point in the direction of Mecca. In the same way all believers incline toward Mecca when praying. And the dead in the cemeteries as well are buried in the direction of Mecca." He asks his reader to "imagine how at the hour of prayer all the faithful all over the world kneel in prayer in the direction of Mecca: in the same direction as the mosques and the dead." This exploration calls to mind his conceptualization that just as the world is based upon the principle of *Einheit der Vielheit* (unity of multiplicity), beauty is also a composite made up of the repetition of individual elements, which together are perceived to form a beautiful whole. Beauty is not only found in nature but also manifests itself in what is true, what is good, and the social, which for him is Islam.[110]

He also finds it beautiful "that the Muslim is allowed to perform his daily devotions at home with the family but that he is compelled to participate in the Friday prayer at the mosque of his part of town. And on the high holy days he repairs to the great community of those who gather in the national mosques." But once a lifetime, "if in any way possible, the Muslim seeks out the greatest living community of peoples that exists—the worship before the sanctuary, the Ka'aba." He turns from expressing the beauty in the social to brotherhood. His narrative "should serve as a symbol for the power to create and organize the community of the Islamic world brotherhood. And with this I come to the final point which I would like to call the development of the I via the Thou to the We. Christianity connects the individual with his neighbor, with the Thou. Islam connects him via the Thou with the community."

Marcus maintained his correspondence with his community, the Ahmadi, who continued to support him into the 1950s, despite their own problems after British South Asia was partitioned into India and Pakistan in 1947, when the headquarters of the Ahmadi in Lahore became part of the latter nation-state.[111] Marcus continued to complain of his financial woes. In 1952 Sadr-ud-Din, who had become the leader of the movement the previous year and would serve in that position until his death nearly thirty years later, wrote a passionate letter:

> My dearest Hameed Marcus, Assalmo Alaikum! May God envelope you in His Mercy and may kind Providence look after you. I am in receipt of your painful letter, and feel highly distressed because of its sorrowful contents. Your stipend is still alive. Dr. Abdullah will be asked to pay you all the arrears. I hope God will relieve you of your troubles. I am loyal to you, my dearest Hameed Marcus. I shall never forget you, indeed you have all along lived on in my heard [*sic*]. You can recall I asked you to come to Lahore and pass the remainder of your life with me. My word still stands true. When I received your letter, I felt like flying to your bedside and waiting on you personally. Such are my thoughts and such are my feelings concerning you.[112]

A follow-up letter repeated that his stipend was "still alive" and that he would receive it "as long as you are alive."[113] Marcus translated his own thank you letter into passable English and sent it to Pakistan: "I received the generous and saving help which you and my brothers in Pakistan did granted [*sic*] to me," it begins. "There are not words enough to thank you for your generous deed and for both your letters full of comforts." He hopes "with all my heart once to be able to prove my gratitude in deeds." He finds it "a comfort to know" that for over a quarter century "during which a whole world collapsed" they stayed faithful to him. Ever the utopian, he believes a new world is being built "according to Allah's will" and remains "always with you in all that is blessed with veneration. Your most grateful."[114]

S. M. Abdullah passed away in 1956. Marcus sent his condolences to Abdullah's wife, Mahmudal Abdullah. She responded in German: "My dear brother Dr. Marcus, Asslamo Aleikum. I thank you heartily for your sympathetic letter you sent upon the passing of my husband." She mentions that "my husband was always very glad when he had received a letter from you, and he had always highly valued your friendship." She signed it "your sister, Mahmudal Abdullah."[115] Up until that time the Ahmadi mosque at Woking remained an influential center of Islam in the United Kingdom. But in the context of the exponential growth in the nation's Muslim population, the Woking Mosque became merely a local mosque, one among many serving the needs of the large postcolonial immigrant population. While the mosque in Berlin has remained in Ahmadi hands to this day, the mosque at Woking was soon taken over by Sunni Muslim immigrants from Pakistan who were not Ahmadi. The mosque's current website offers only disdain for the Ahmadi, who are severely persecuted in Pakistan:

> The Mosque was under Ahmediya [*sic*] administration from the early 19th century. We strongly disagree with the beliefs of the Ahmediya [*sic*] along with most of the Muslim world and scholars. . . . The Mosque changed administration in the 70's when the Mosque was being misused and not functioning as a place of worship. All praise to Allah SWT since the 70's the Mosque has been under the classical understanding of Islam Sunni/Hanafi/Sufi and the Mosque was revived back to serving the community as a place of worship and the centre of Islam in Britain.[116]

"I HAVE ALWAYS BEEN A JEW": MARCUS RECLAIMS HIS JEWISHNESS IN THE 1950S

As much as he considered himself a Muslim during these years, Marcus also maintained relations with Jewish relatives and sought reparations for having been victimized as a Jew in Germany. Democracy in the Federal Republic of Germany led to the first acknowledgments of the scope of the Shoah in the 1950s. In the early part of that decade, after not considering himself a Jew for over twenty years following his rejection of Judaism, Marcus reclaimed his Jewish status. But he did so as victim, refugee, and survivor, and he realized the material consequences of these designations. He applied to Germany for reparations on behalf of his mother and for himself, and he would begin to receive annual payments after recognition of being persecuted for being a Jew. But as lengthy correspondence with the Swiss bureaucracy, German restitution office, and international Jewish refugee aid organizations demonstrates, Marcus had to first convince Swiss authorities to recognize him as "fully Jewish." He had to explain why he had converted to Islam and withdrawn his membership in the Jewish community. Like other survivors, he claimed he was always a Jew and never abandoned Judaism; he only converted due to political pressure and for the sake of others. This explanation allows us to consider how men of Jewish background such as Marcus reconciled their vision of *Bildung* as the Enlightenment ideal and their role as its most vocal advocates with their experience under National Socialism and the catastrophe of the Shoah.[117]

To be awarded reparations Marcus had to declare his Jewishness, prove he was maltreated by the Nazis because he was a Jew, explain his conversion to Islam, and demonstrate financial need. He first applied for reparations from the German government in 1953.[118] In the summer of 1954 he applied, successfully, on behalf of his mother, as her only living heir, to be paid back the 272 Reichsmark (today: $1,880) "emigration tax" paid to the Jewish community of Berlin and 4,250 Reichsmark (today: $29,400) *Judenvermögensabgabe* (tax on Jewish assets) she had to surrender to the regime when she left Nazi Germany.[119] Two years later, writing from his cousin's home in Zürich, he composed a five-page summary of his life. He narrates how, after the Nazi takeover, one brother had been hounded until he committed suicide while the other, like Marcus, had been deprived "on racial grounds" of the ability to work in his profession due to the Nuremberg Laws. Marcus had been compelled to resign as president of the German Muslim Society. The worst persecution followed: "On November 9, 1938 I was sent to concentration camp Oranienburg-Sachsenhausen during the general persecution of Jews." Fortunately, "the united efforts of Superintendent Ungnad, former crown prince of Sachsen Father George—both men had visited our 'Islam Evenings'—and our Imam Dr. Abdullah managed to free me after about a month" (although Marcus's concentration camp records state that he was scheduled to be discharged after ten days). However, "on the day of release, those who were being released were strongly urged in three speeches to leave Germany post-haste, because otherwise they would disappear forever in a concentration camp. Also at the Tax Office I was officially advised to leave Germany as fast as possible if I still wanted to save my freedom." After that, however, "I delayed my exit from the country until August 23, 1939, out of consideration for my then already 85-year-old mother, whom I wanted to take with me." Marcus does not mention that he remained in Nazi Germany to complete the Qur'an translation, commentary, and introduction.

When his mother "could finally follow [me to Switzerland] on December 31, 1939, our furniture and books [at Fürtherstrasse 11a, where they had resided together] were put out into the courtyard. I do not know what happened to them afterwards." When they left Germany "my mother and I abandoned our assets to my brother Dr. Alfred Marcus, to protect him and his wife, as much as possible, from need. But my brother was deported to Theresienstadt on May 17, 1943, and his assets were seized. He died in that place." His last will and testament from 1917 "named his spouse his sole heir, after whose death her only niece would have the law of succession." Thereafter, "I lived for seventeen years at Ms. Kaiser-Graf's in Oberwil, Baselland from August 23, 1939 until her very sad death in October 1956." During this time "I have published two books and numerous articles in philosophical journals, that are scientifically recognized. But they have earned me no revenue. . . . Printing and production have become much more expensive so that the authors come away empty handed."[120]

There was more Marcus needed to do to receive reparations. He wrote an extraordinary letter to the Federal Aliens' Police at the beginning of 1957, declaring "I hereby request that the Federal Aliens' Police allow my civil status under the category 'religion' to henceforth be 'Jewish.' I have always been a Jew, and can verify that I have never renounced my affiliation with Judaism." To explain his conversion to Islam he deploys the Ahmadi concept of double consciousness: "However, in the interests of the Berlin mosque, whose syndic I was for sixteen years, the society permitted me to accept the Muslim religion in addition to my Judaism, especially since there are no principle differences in doctrine between the two confessions. That which was done, however, in the summer of 1936 took place under the pressure of the most grave responsibility."[121]

He also had to explain why he considered himself a Muslim after leaving Germany. He places responsibility with the Ahmadi: "By request of our superiors, the Ahmadiyya-Lahore, I then also called myself a Muslim in Switzerland after it had been decided that for the time being I could not travel to India." He planned "to open a Muslim cultural center in Lausanne, where I should find temporary assignment." There were also plans "to have the 'Muslim Review' published in Switzerland at first, where I was supposed to be the editor,—provided that Swiss officials permitted all this. Nothing came of these plans, however, as the English blocked funds sent to India."[122]

Finally, he asks for reparations: "I believe I cannot relinquish the assistance of the Jewish community to free others as much as possible of being burdened by me, which greatly distresses me. I may beg for this assistance without qualms when considering that [because I am a German Jew, when I was still in Germany] I also had to endure everything that Jews in Germany had to endure [before I fled to Switzerland]." As proof, he provided photocopies of "the elucidation to the Jews' Assets Inventory from 1938/9," his "police notice of departure from my last day in Berlin dated August 23, 1939, in which I clearly call myself Jewish and Muslim," and his "registration in Oberwil where I was designated as Hugo *Israel* Marcus and categorized as an Israelite [Jew], in accordance with my German passport." He expresses "the hope that the Federal Aliens' Police will grant my request."[123]

His claims are not consistent. His police notice of departure labels him a Jew alone, not a Muslim. He had registered at the University of Basel as a Muslim in 1942. Yet that same year the confirmation of his having a good reputation had designated him as "the Jew, Hugo Israel Marcus," Israel being the name by which the Nazis forced all Jews in Germany to call themselves.[124] Some of his official documentation had already referred to him as a Jew. Perhaps he was making sure none mentioned his being a Muslim. A month later, Marcus had given his religion (*Konf.*) as Jewish (*isr.*, which stands for *israelitisch*, i.e., Jewish) when he filled out other government paperwork.[125]

Marcus had also received assistance from his Jewish relatives in Switzerland.[126] He had resided with Leonie and Fritz Cahn for a short period in 1956 after his landlady in Oberwil passed away, and they had stayed in touch with him over the final ten years of his life.[127] He had warm relations with Fritz and Leonie, as demonstrated by their correspondance.[128] Marcus's uncle Felix Hepner had given Marcus books on Islamic history. Hepner had kept in contact with Roman in Poland, urging him to visit Marcus.[129] The Jewish community in Germany continued to recognize him as a Jew. In 1960 Armin Wegner had informed him that "Only now did I read in an old issue of the *Allgemeinen Wochenzeitung der Juden* (General weekly newspaper of the Jews) in Germany that you turned eighty."[130]

Marcus had also contacted the Ahmadi for their assistance in providing reference letters that he could send to the restitution authorities in Berlin. In summer 1957 Marcus had written to a Dr. Ahmad, signing his letter "Yours faithfully, very old Hugo Hamid Marcus" and addressing it "Assalamo Alaikum!" It reads, in part, "During the most hard time you have been always courageous on my side with many signs of your friendship. Now, by chance, here is a fact, that you might give me another help, by signing the included declaration and mail it to me by return."[131] Dr. Ahmad, Lahore, Pakistan, faithfully did as he requested and declared "that Dr. Hugo (Hamid) Marcus, Oberwik [*sic*] Schweiz of Berlin, until 1939, has given considerable support to my scientific working in German language during 1935/6 at Berlin. He also translated several lectures of mine to be held in German language and to be printed. Dr. Marcus also gave help to a number of compatriots of mine. The payment was depending to the inflation of this time."[132] Sadr-ud-Din, then head of the Ahmadi, responded to his request as follows: "My Dear

Hamid Marcus, Assalam Aleikum! I am in receipt of your letter, for which I must thank you and thank God who is sustaining you. I have much pleasure in certifying that you, Hugo Marcus, worked for our mosque in Berlin from January 1923 to August 1939, for a salary of 100 Reichsmark per month, and that you, Hugo Marcus received 600 Reichsmark for your assistance in the translation of the Holy Quran." Calculated in terms of U.S. dollars, during these years (excluding 1923 and 1924, which had outrageous inflation) Marcus's salary rose from the $300s (1925–1932) to nearly $700 per month (1934–1939) for his labors, and he received $4,150 for his contribution to the Qur'an edition. Sadr-ud-Din concludes his letter: "I and the members of the Ahmadia Anjuman have ever been grateful to you for your valuable services. I hope you are getting on well. I cherish affectionate regard for you."[133]

Marcus began to receive reparations in 1953. Finding this was too little to live on, he wrote a letter to liberal politician and first president of the Federal Republic of Germany, Theodor Heuss (1884–1963; in office 1949–1959), asking for further compensation for the wrongs he suffered at the hands of the Nazis.[134] He expected the president to have a sympathetic ear: the men were similar in age, both had studied at Berlin's university, and both had written for liberal newspapers. Marcus mentions his income from being a writer, legal counsel at the Berlin Mosque, and tutor, although he was often not paid for his literary work or for his tutoring. He notes that he had written and published seven books, at least one of which, *Die ornamentale Schönheit der Landschaft und der Natur als Beitrag zu einer allgemeinen Ästhetik der Landschaft und der Natur*, was successful. He mentions being a permanent staff member of *Die Gegenwart*, being responsible for *Moslemische Revue*, and publishing articles in a number of liberal newspapers.[135] After mentioning his work, he gives a brief narrative of his life, including how "Because of National Socialism, as one with Jewish background, I lost the option to continue working as a writer; my students were deprived of me. I also had to finally give up my position at the Berlin Mosque, which had been meant to be life long. . . . With that my humble existence, so painstakingly constructed, collapsed." Thereafter,

> my emigration became unavoidable after I was interned in concentration camp Oranienburg-Sachsenhausen on November 9, 1939 [*sic*]. I was freed from there through the united efforts of Messrs. Superintendent Ungrad, Father Georg, Prince of Saxony, and the imam of the mosque Dr. Abdullah, for which I still owe deep gratitude to the three men. I was not able to reach India, where

> I intended to emigrate, because in the meanwhile the war had broken out and England rescinded my visa.

After arriving in Switzerland on August 23, 1939, "I lived for sixteen years in Oberwil in Basel, supported by refugee aid in the amount of seventy Francs [today: $271] along with thirty Francs [today: $117] each from two private sources." At the beginning he thus received less than what he had earned from working for the Ahmadi. He states that later his aid doubled, as "the contribution I received from refugee aid was raised to 100 Francs and the two private donors gave fifty Francs each." He explained that his landlady in Oberwil passed away in October 1956, after which he moved to Basel, receiving seventy francs per month (today: $144) from der Bund (the federal government of Switzerland) and an equal amount from the canton of Baselland. Marcus was assisted in obtaining these funds by his cousin Leonie's husband, Fritz Cahn.[136] After the death of the landlady, the Oberwil, Baselland administration and the state refugee organization in Bern were of the view that Marcus should live in a nursing home. Cahn wrote to the Oberwil administrators, noting that doing so would greatly increase his costs of upkeep, so he sought to persuade them to cover the costs. He stated that the refugee organization, acting on the advice of the federal police, would request the canton of Basel to chip in toward these costs, as was done on behalf of most of the immigrants in the canton. He pleaded for them to agree to that request. Assuming that they would agree, he assured them that, until then, they were prepared to let Marcus stay with his family in Zürich. The seventy-six-year-old asked the president of Germany for financial assistance in addition to what he received from refugee aid, the federal government of Switzerland, the canton of Baselland, and two private donors, one being the Cahn family and the other either Jordan or the Ahmadi.

To help his case, he attached character testimony from well-known writer and human rights activist Armin Wegner.[137] Wegner had served with the German army in the Ottoman Empire during World War I. As an assistant to Field Marshall Colmar von der Goltz, Wegner was an eyewitness to the Armenian genocide. He managed to smuggle out photographs he had illegally taken of the slaughter. After the war he became an activist in pacifist circles: he published *Der Weg ohne Heimkehr* (Journey of no return) about the annihilation of the Armenians; composed an open letter to President Woodrow Wilson in 1919, published in the German press, imploring the American leader to help the Armenian survivors obtain an independent state; and traveled Germany giving public lectures in which he described in horrifying detail the extermination of the Armenians, illustrated by his graphic photos.[138] In 1933, in a private letter to his Jewish wife, who had already fled to England, Wegner noted the similarity between the Young Turks, who had annihilated the Armenians, and the Nazis, who were attacking Jews.[139] As he had sent an open letter to Wilson over a decade earlier, this time Wegner promptly composed an open letter to Adolf Hitler, which he sent to Nazi Party headquarters in Munich in the spring of 1933.[140] In the letter he notes, "A hundred years after Goethe's death, long after Lessing, we are returning to the greatest affliction of all—to the bigotry of superstition."[141] This earned him the wrath of the Nazis, who incarcerated him in various concentration camps and tortured him; eventually he was released and fled the country. Wegner spent the war in Italy, first in Padua, then, like Jewish convert to Islam Essad Bey, in Positano, with his Jewish wife.

Immediately after the war ended in 1945 Wegner began to correspond again with Marcus.[142] By the beginning of 1957 Marcus had asked Wegner to serve as a character witness.[143] He was wise to do so: in 1956 Wegner received the Highest Order of Merit by the Federal Republic of Germany for having openly spoken out against Nazi persecution of Jews. In his letters to Marcus, Wegner criticizes contemporary German broadcasting stations for their reluctance to transmit true information about the Holocaust and the fate of Jews and complains about the cowardice of German newspapers as well, which do not dare to print the truth.[144] Wegner worried about Marcus and his poor health, proposing that he move into a home for the aged in Zürich, where the Jewish actress Else Flatau-Pinkus lived; she was the widow of Zionist journalist and banker Lazar Felix Pinkus (b. 1881, Breslau; d. 1947, Zürich). Wegner also suggested Marcus contact his friend Dr. Hermann Levin Goldschmidt (b. 1914, Berlin; d. 1998, Zürich), a Jewish philosopher who had migrated to Switzerland in 1938.[145] Wegner visited Marcus at least twice in Switzerland and was in contact with his relatives there.[146]

In his testimony, Wegner declares he has known Marcus since 1910. He asserts that they were particularly close from 1918 until 1933, when Wegner fled Germany after being persecuted by the Nazi regime. He mentions how his last memories of Marcus in Germany "are of the quite distressing kind." Due to the "dictatorship in Germany he was not only completely sidelined from his professional activities, but he was also thrown into deep depression. His already delicate health was harmed by his own distressing experiences and that of his friends such that he had to repeatedly go to the hospital. He was afraid he would have a heart attack."[147]

Marcus and Wegner had traveled in the same circles of journalists and writers, pacifists, expressionists, gay rights activists, orientalists, and Muslims in Berlin. In a private letter, Wegner reminisces about how he and Marcus used to be good friends when they were still living in Berlin.[148] He shares memories of their close friendship when Marcus still used to live with his father and Wegner visited him secretly.[149] He also mentions that Wegner and Marcus came to know each other during their time as students, thus half a decade earlier than he writes in his letter of support.[150] Wegner expressed his ambivalence about returning to Germany, feeling guilty to have survived the war while many others died.[151] In contrast with his affection for Marcus, Wegner expressed only disdain for fellow exile in Positano Essad Bey. He viewed him as "a typical literary swindler" and a "Jewish-Viennese journalist," an "unhappy, apostate Jew."[152]

Marcus received aid from all quarters. At the beginning of 1958 the Christlicher Friedensdienst (Christian Movement for Peace, Refugee Relief Section) began providing financial support to Marcus, covering just over one-fifth, or seventy francs, of his maintenance, which amounted to 340 francs per month, the rest provided by "the Canton of Baselland, a friend, and a relative of Mr. Marcus."[153] The Christian Movement declared it would support him until he begins receiving reparations from Germany, but should reparations not be forthcoming the charity would continue to support him as agreed.[154] It also helped pay part of his medical costs.

According to Swiss authorities, Marcus began to receive reparations from Germany (referred to as "a pension") in the amount of 468 Deutsche Mark per month beginning in March 1959.[155] He also received a cash settlement (financial compensation). Upon receiving this, he paid back the Christian refugee organization the entire amount it had given him over the years.[156] In fact, the Berlin restitution authority paid Marcus a monthly income that, calculated in terms of today's U.S. dollar, began at $918 in 1953 and continually rose over the years to reach $1,190 per month in 1965, substantially more than he received from Swiss and private sources.[157]

Like his friends among the Ahmadi in England and India, Marcus's gay friends in Germany remained devoted to him until the end. Jordan may have retired to a Benedictine abbey in southern Germany in 1947, but he had written to the Swiss Federal Aliens' Police at that time declaring that he remained "fully responsible for the financial maintenance and all claims arising from Mr. Marcus's stay in Switzerland."[158] In 1957 Marcus asked Jordan for additional financial assistance, but Jordan refused.[159] Marcus conceded that Jordan had every reason to reject higher payments but that émigrés like him needed greater living allowances.[160]

A passport-sized photo of Marcus taken in spring 1964 shows a vigorous senior, his face marked with age spots, a paisley ascot wrapped tightly around his neck under a thick black overcoat.[161] He still has a thick head of hair and a thin mustache, now gray. His alert eyes look directly at the photographer.

CHAPTER 5

Hans Alienus

Yearning, Gay Writer, 1948–1965

Remaining to the end of his long life in Swiss exile, rather than return to a Federal Republic of Germany that persecuted homosexuals under Paragraph 175, as had Wilhelmine, Weimar, and Nazi Germany, Marcus participated in a thriving homosexual circle in Zürich and published philosophical works that used examples from Islam and the gay rights struggle to prove their points, and gay fiction and nonfiction that incorporated Islamic elements.[1] As his continued promotion of Goethe demonstrates, Marcus shared Friedrich Meinecke's (1862–1954) call in *Die deutsche Katastrophe* to heal Germany (in this case, the German-speaking world) through the creation of "Goethe communities" promulgating the great poet's ideals, or at least his interpretation of them.[2]

One of the reasons Marcus did not return to Germany may have been that, just as Marcus was more openly expressing his homosexuality, if under a pen name, Germany continued to persecute gay men. In 1929 a Reichstag committee had voted to eliminate Paragraph 175, but the committee's draft was never voted on in Parliament. The law remained in place as Weimar fell. The Nazis imposed a more draconian version in 1935, where proof of penetration, difficult to obtain, was no longer necessary for conviction; instead, mutual masturbation, penile contact, and snuggling by two nude males were considered enough evidence.[3] Paragraph 175a mandated "imprisonment up to ten years for exploitation of subordinate relationships and the molestation of youth under the age of twenty one. The subordinate partner and the molested youth are also liable to prosecution."[4] Homosexuals were subject to castration, imprisonment at concentration camps, sadistic treatment by camp guards, brutal medical experimentation, and execution. Between five thousand and fifteen thousand homosexuals were murdered in the camps.[5]

After World War II, the Federal Republic of Germany legally upheld the validity of the Nazi versions of Paragraph 175 (175 and 175a). In the aftermath of defeat, in the context of U.S. occupation and the rise to prominence of church leaders and conservative politicians, who perceived crises of marriage, masculinity, morality, and sexuality, "reconstruction of a domesticated heterosexuality coincided with a renewed commitment to the criminalization of homosexuality."[6] Dagmar Herzog makes two important arguments to explain this. West Germany, ruled by the Christian Democrats, reacted to the sexual libertinism, excess, and inducements to antibourgeois sexual promiscuity of the Nazis, who encouraged pre- and extramarital sexual activity and pleasure (for those deemed politically and racially pure), by turning away from the licentiousness of the Nazi era in favor of sexual conservatism and propriety, prudishness, and chastity. At the same time, they adopted Nazi logic about homosexuality. Paragraph 175's proponents accepted "the notion that men had a potentially bisexual disposition, and that young men in particular were vulnerable to conversion via seduction," which they "explicitly named as *the* reason for retaining" it.[7] In contrast to the ideal of the father who raised democratic sons and protected them from harm, gays were depicted as morally depraved and threatening to youth, the family, and the nation.[8] Because gays were "viewed as simple criminals whose convictions and punishments had been just," they were initially denied compensation for persecution by the Nazis.[9] In Frankfurt in 1950, "during a massive police and court action which brought 700 investigations and 140 prosecutions," defendants faced "the same man as judge, Kurt Romini, who had also been their prosecutor during the Third Reich," and who "remembered these men from a few years earlier."[10] The result was multiple prison sentences and at least half a dozen suicides. The Federal Supreme Court of West Germany ruled in 1951 that Paragraphs 175 and 175a were valid since they contained no elements of Nazi ideology.[11]

Although there were law courts, judges, newspapers, and individuals who challenged the validity of Paragraph 175, "the support given by the churches to antidecriminalization efforts had a decisive impact."[12] It was nearly unanimously seen as compatible with the Basic Law. During the 1950s and 1960s, nearly 100,000 men were registered in police files for suspected homosexual acts, and every year there were 2,500–3,500 convictions. In 1955 the introduction of the Law for the

Protection of Minors in West Germany led to the banning of homosexual journals; two years later the Federal Constitutional Court again upheld the constitutionality of 175 and 175a, the federal reparations law excluded homosexuals from obtaining settlements as victims of the Nazis, and "a wave of persecution of homosexuals" began.[13] Basing its assessment on majority opinion, the view of the churches, and prior legal decisions, the Court declared "homosexual activity unequivocally violates moral law."[14] It was not until the end of 1957 that gays were permitted to apply for compensation for having been persecuted by the Nazis, but only a handful did so, fearing making themselves vulnerable to further prosecution.[15] In 1962 a commission including medical and legal experts recommended "that male homosexuality remain a crime." Contradicting the work of Magnus Hirschfeld, the commission argued that homosexuality was not an "inborn disposition" but that homosexuals were men who "through seduction, habituation, or sexual supersatiation have become addicted to vice or who have turned to same-sex intercourse for purely profit-seeking motives."[16] Homosexuality, the commission argued, was communicable, contagious, and aberrant; the law was necessary to keep it from spreading. It concluded that "wherever same-sex immorality has run rampant and grown to great proportions, the degeneration of the people and the deterioration of its moral strength has been the consequence." As late as 1963 castration was still approved in West Germany for cases of "perversion," as the 1935 Law for the Prevention of Hereditarily Diseased Offspring was still in effect.[17]

By contrast, as of 1942 it was legal for men age twenty and over to have sexual relations with other men in Switzerland.[18] This is not to claim that Switzerland was safe. A climate of fear existed, as there were murders of gays and police raids and roundups of homosexuals in Zürich during these years. Nevertheless, Marcus expressed no desire to return to Germany. As an exile he continued to promote gay rights.

In *Rechtswelt und Ästhetik* (Law and aesthetics), published in Germany in 1952, Marcus notes that art can sometimes be on the side of what the law forbids.[19] Illegal acts, he adds, can also have positive effects on feelings. In this context Marcus mentions how Heinrich Triepel, in his *Vom Stil des Rechts* (The style of law, 1947) argued that legal conceptions do not change over the course of time; rather, they are defended by new rationales. As an example for this assertion, Marcus takes up Paragraph 175. The persecution of homosexuals in Germany was justified by different reasons over the centuries but never abolished. He argues that "legal views and individual laws, whose explanations become obsolete, do not fade away, but rather immediately acquire new rationales that take into account the changed age." Paragraph 175 "was justified in the Middle Ages because it was believed the acts it punished caused plagues of vermin and locusts." Later, "in decidedly religious times they pointed to the disapproval of the Bible, which speaks of this [homosexual] tendency as a punishment by God for sins of another type previously committed." With the dawn of modern, liberal times "the law was rationalized on the basis of public opinion." Under National Socialism "the law was justified as the acts it outlawed were seen as a danger to the race. Today in Russia the law is legitimized on the grounds that in overly intimate friendship between men exists the potential seed of counterrevolutionary actions." For Marcus, "the example proves well how laws, notwithstanding their various rationales, maintain themselves unchanged across the ages."[20] Marcus was still fighting the gay rights struggle in his old age. And still as a Muslim.

In the same work, referring to Goethe, Marcus asserts that both aesthetics and jurisprudence concentrate on the external of things. For Marcus the Islamic custom of reconciliation with enemies on Eid al-Fitr exemplifies a juridical act that at the same time performs a public and thus aesthetic spectacle.[21] Concerning the relationship of law and art to the public, he finds "especially instructive are those cultural situations where the law has not been separated from religion. The best example we find in Islam, where the greatest holiday of the year, Eid al-Fitr exercises the function of public justice of the peace. During this festival one reconciles with one's enemies. And all hug one another publicly. This act is also theater, a stage play of an aesthetic spectacle." But "this stage play includes a contract which has legal force. It is silent language, sign language, and has sealed and heralded importance, no different than a publicly executed signature."[22] Marcus connected gay rights, Islam, and Goethe in his life and writing to the end.

GOETHE AGAIN, AS A HOMOSEXUAL

Marcus was not the first to explore Goethe's approach to love between men. Marcus was deeply influenced by his friend Hirschfeld, who frequently cites Goethe in his monumental *Die Homosexualität des Mannes und des Weibes* (The homosexuality of men and women, 1913), "the most comprehensive study of homosexuality in the first half of the twentieth century," a section of which is entitled "The Restoration of the Good Name of Homosexual Men and Women: Pioneers in the

Struggle for Freedom from Goethe to Krafft-Ebing."[23] Hirschfeld explores eight themes in the work and life of Goethe: sexual substitutes; the superiority of the male nude to the female nude; "Greek love" or pederasty; friendship as homosexuality; the intermediate, yearning figure; his understanding and tolerance for outspoken gays; homosexuality as an innate human characteristic and inborn drive; and the superiority of eroticism to sexual gratification.

On the occasion of Goethe's two hundredth birthday in 1949, Marcus published an article in *Der Kreis*, "Goethe und die Freundesliebe" (Goethe and love of friends, i.e., homosexuality) which also focuses on how Goethe approached these eight themes.[24] The term Marcus uses to connote homosexuality, "love of friends" (*Freundesliebe*) was coined by novelist Johann Paul Friedrich Richter (1763–1825, nom de plum, Jean Paul) and became popular among early-twentieth-century German homosexuals.[25] Marcus begins with Goethe's motto: "I decided, in order not to envy others, to love boundlessly." The article is an in-depth examination of Goethe's relation to homosexuality, focusing especially on the erotic attraction of youth, an issue of special concern to the sixty-nine-year-old Marcus. He examines the poet's private life (*Letters from Switzerland* and "letter to Jacobi") and his writings (coming-of-age story Bildungsroman *Wilhelm Meister's Journeyman Years*, "Mignon," *Faust*, "The Elf King," and "To the Moon") to compare how the German master felt toward men, women, and same-sex tendencies, mentioning his mentor Stefan George and acquaintance Kurt Hiller, with whom he maintained an active correspondence to the end of his life.

What is astounding about the piece is Marcus's promotion of Magnus Hirschfeld's no-longer-popular medical explanations of homosexuality, which were out of sync with the postwar science of sexology, which had turned from biological to psychological, sociological, and psychoanalytic theories.[26] One of Marcus's main arguments is that "the twice pronounced secret conflict in Goethe's feelings is parallel to a dual pronounced harmonizing of this conflict through the crossing between the sexes. Goethe thus anticipated the scientific theory of sexual intermediaries [*Zwischenstufentheorie*]."[27] In other words, Goethe's eighteenth-century literary works anticipated the twentieth-century theory of "intermediate sexual stages" developed by Hirschfeld, whose basic idea "is that all human characteristics, be they physical or mental (characteristics of the sex organs, other physical characteristics, sex drive, and psychological characteristics) appear in feminine or masculine form. Masculine and feminine parts of human characteristics appear ... in infinite mixing ratios, and all ... are operative in each person."

According to this theory, "there can never be a 'fully male' man with exclusively masculine characteristics, just as the 'fully female' woman with exclusively feminine characteristics is also a fiction."[28] While for some people the male characteristics are more pronounced, for others the female are, as no one is simply male *or* female. Each person is characterized through a unique male-female mixture of characteristics, "as sexual intermediary between the extremes 'fully male' and 'fully female.'"[29] For Hirschfeld, this theory has a political and emancipatory dimension: if every person is in fact an "intermediate stage," then it makes no sense to exclude or persecute "homosexuals" and "transvestites." For Hirschfeld, people are born the way they are. It is wrong to criminalize people for acting "immorally" when they are in fact acting according to their nature, which is not an illness to be cured, for it cannot be changed.[30] Hirschfeld concludes that "genuine homosexuality is always an inborn condition" and that "homosexuality is neither a disease nor a degeneration, but rather is a part of the natural order, a sexual variant." As homosexuality is inborn, "same-sex love was a congenital condition, which could neither be acquired through environmental factors or suggestion, nor extinguished through medical treatment or psychological conditioning."[31] It should be accepted without moral judgment, and this is why Hirschfeld includes Nietzsche's quote, "That which is natural cannot be immoral," as epigraph to his *Sappho und Sokrates: Oder wie erklärt sich die Liebe der Männer und Frauen zu Personen des eigenen Geshlects?* (Sappho and Socrates: How can the love of men and women for persons of the same sex be explained?).[32]

Charlotte Wolff argues that "Hirschfeld tapped at the door of modern science but could not get it to open, which was one of the reasons why his theory on sexual intermediaries had feet of clay." He "remained unaware of its fallacy, though he had to admit that physically normal people can be homo- or bisexual." He also did not realize "that physical characteristics of the opposite sex are, as a rule, not found in either. His idea of 'feminine' qualities in men and 'masculine' ones in women rested on a conventional concept imposed by a male-dominated society," whereas "sexual variations, not only homo- and bisexuality, occur in people of all shapes and forms, independent of hormonal difference."[33] More recent scholarship has been more forgiving. Mancini argues Hirschfeld's theory of sexual intermediaries "exposed the epistemological and empirical limits of the fixed dual-gender system and advanced the notion of the fluidity of gender in its stead. By destabilizing the artificially constructed categories of male and female, Hirschfeld's theory accounted for and scientifically legitimated myriad expressions or gradations of intersexed identities."[34] His theory "'queered' culturally constructed gender ideals of masculinity or femininity," paving the way for the transgender movement, and lay "the critical foundation for contemporary gender studies," which promotes "the non-identity of sex and gender."[35]

Having already referred to both models of homosexuality—George's masculinist and Hirschfeld's medicalist—in "Goethe und die Freundesliebe" Marcus explores Goethe's use of sexual substitutes and the related theme of the superiority of the male body to the female. In his *Letters from Switzerland* Goethe narrates how, when the then twenty-six-year-old reached Geneva, he befriended a wealthy art collector—the eighteenth-century art world "comfortable for the many men interested sexually in other men who frequented it"[36]—who "finally shows him, as the crowning glory of his collection, the image of a naked life-sized Danae who receives the golden shower in her lap."[37] Goethe was amazed "at the splendor of the limbs, the magnificence of the posture, the tenderness of the gesture," but he was surprised to find that the erotic figurine did not arouse in him "that kind of rapture, that joy, that inexpressible delight that he had expected. Instead, he remains 'cold.'" He thought perhaps it was because he had not yet seen a nude person. As Goethe related, he persuaded his male traveling companion Ferdinand to bathe in the lake while he watched. He observed, "What a glorious shape my friend has! How duly proportioned all his limbs are! what fullness of form! what splendor of youth! What a gain to have enriched my imagination with this perfect model of manhood! . . . I can see him as Adonis chasing the boar, or as Narcissus contemplating himself in the mirror of the spring!" Adonis and Narcissus "are doomed to an early death in Greek mythology," reflected in the passionate deathbed kisses in *The Sorrows of Young Werther* and *Wilhelm Meister's Journeyman Years*.[38]

One might ask why, when desiring to see a real woman in the nude, Werther first asks his male friend to undress for him. Marcus asks instead how he was able to see a woman in the same natural state as he had beheld his friend. Marcus claims Goethe pays a servant and an old woman who lead him into a room where he is allowed to witness a pretty young woman undress. Goethe actually paid a prostitute. Marcus relates that Goethe observes the strange effect on himself: as she began to undress, the nude female "appeared strange to me and almost, I am tempted to say, made a frightening impression on me." Marcus relates that Goethe concludes the experiment asking anxiously, "What do we see in women? Why do women please us?"[39] Just as Hirschfeld had already detailed Goethe's use of sexual substitutes, and boys' love for girls replacing their love of boys, Marcus notes that Goethe framed the nude male, his friend Ferdinand, between two experiences with women. Marcus asks whether Goethe conjured the bath of his traveling companion only as "an intermediate link necessary to establish a mediation between the image of a woman and the reality of a woman."[40]

To answer this question, Marcus turns to a passage in *Wilhelm Meister's Journeyman Years*, which has been described by a modern scholar as "the most unabashed description of homoerotic desire," where we again see the naked male friend appearing first and then the girl.[41] Marcus asks: "Was this, too, just about a mere idea predominating in Goethe's mind, the conception of friendship as the natural precursor of love? Or is this sequence in reality a basic trait of Goethe's mental state?" In the novel, when Wilhelm goes to the lake to bathe, he suddenly beholds "a most beautiful boy his age undressed for bathing standing up to his knees in the summerlike warm water. Wilhelm gazes at the boy with inexpressible sensations, with the highest aesthetic delight, and becomes his friend on the spot." They agree to meet again in the evening when Wilhelm will be returning home. During the remainder of the journey he can think of nothing other than the boy and the evening rendezvous. However, at journey's end, at his relatives' home, "a young girl approaches him. [Sexually] awakened by the boy [at the lake], Wilhelm feels increasingly attracted to her. . . . He is soon entirely ensnared by her charms and drunk on the most tender feelings for her." On the journey home he only thinks of her. When they reach the lake, they learn that the beautiful boy has drowned. Wilhelm gazes upon the dead boy to say farewell. Actually, "for Wilhelm Meister, strictly speaking, the friend had already drowned, through the girl, before he lost him to the lake." Yet, as Marcus concludes, "the brightest glow of the entire chapter rests on the moment when one boy beholds another standing nude in the water, as a bright image. And it cannot be ignored that the Wilhelm Meister experience portrayed here is of the same type as the one from the *Letters from Switzerland*." Marcus notes both use the vehicle of "a lake and an unclothed beautiful friend bathing, subsequently the girl as ornament."[42]

It is remarkable that Marcus remains silent about the explicit homoerotic aspects of the tender, passionate story. In Goethe's narrative, Wilhelm was instantly attracted to the boy who invited him down to the river, where, leaning against one another, the older boy taught the younger how to fish: "He kindly showed me what to do, how to bait my line, and I succeeded a few times running in jerking the smallest of these delicate creatures." Unable to resist the temptation, his new friend undressed and ran into the water. Seeing him, Wilhelm relates the "very strange" mood that came over him:[43]

> Grasshoppers danced around me, ants scurried about, colorful beetles hung in the branches, and gold-glittering dragonflies (sun virgins), for so he had called them, hovered and fluttered, phantomlike, at my feet, just as the boy, pulling a large crab from a tangle of roots, held it up gaily for me to see, then skillfully concealed it again in its old place, ready for the catch. It was so hot and sultry all around that one longed to be out of the sun and in the shade, then out of the cool of the shade and down into the cooler water.[44]

For Wilhelm, "it was easy for him to lure me down. He did not have to repeat his invitation often, for I found it irresistible and felt, despite some fear of my parents, as well as wariness toward the unknown element, extraordinary excitement."[45] Wilhelm undressed and cautiously went into the water. The other boy "let me linger there, moved away in the buoyant element, then swam back, and as he climbed out and stood up to dry off in the light of the sun, I thought my eyes were dazzled by a triple sun: so beautiful was the human form, of which I had never had any notion." The boy looked at him "with the same attention. Quickly dressed, we still faced each other without veils. Our hearts were drawn to one another, and with fiery kisses we swore eternal friendship."[46] Wilhelm encounters the boy in his nude splendor again, after he had drowned. He engages in necrophiliac pleasure with the nude body: "The unfortunates lay stretched out on straw, naked, gleaming white bodies, brilliant even in the dim lamp light. I threw myself upon . . . my friend. I would not be able to describe my state. I wept bitterly and flooded his broad chest with countless tears. I had heard something about rubbing being helpful in such a case, so I rubbed my tears in, and deceived myself with the warmth I generated."[47] In his confusion, he "thought of blowing breath into him, but the rows of pearly teeth were firmly clamped shut, and the lips, on which our parting kiss still seemed to linger, refused the slightest sign of response." They had to tear him away, "weeping, sobbing."[48]

Marcus's interest remains with the nonexplicit aspects of the boys' love and with the object of a man's affection. From the tale he concludes, "what some sow, others reap. With Goethe, the friend sows what the girls may later reap." He turns to explore the view that the male body is more beautiful than the female nude, explaining that an aging Goethe made a remark (in 1830): "'In actual fact, Greek pederasty is based on the fact that, measured purely aesthetically, the man is after all far more beautiful, more excellent, more perfect than the woman.... Pederasty is as old as humanity, and therefore it may be said that it is rooted in nature, although at the same time it is against nature.'" Marcus finds this to be remarkable, a "free, original, unprejudiced point of view in opposition to the entire world; after all, as long as humankind exists, it was always the female sex that has been called the more beautiful one." But to Marcus "it is also evident that these words reveal the existence of a deeper ambivalence between his aesthetic and emotional way of apprehending.... And since the aesthetic usually marks the beginning [and] the erotic develops out of this beginning, to the introspective Goethe, the erotic may have appeared nothing less than the fall of the aesthetic." Marcus further explains with the formula: "first friendship, then love."[49]

Marcus might have examined Goethe's *Italian Journey*, but he turns instead, as did Hirschfeld, to the theme of "Greek love," or pederasty, in Goethe's poetry. He first explores "The Elf King" (1782). The subject of this haunting poem, memorized by secondary students in Germany to this day, is a man's rape and the murder of a boy:

Who rides by night in the wind so wild?
It is the father, with his child.
The boy is safe in his father's arm,
He holds him tight, he keeps him warm.

My son, what is it, why cover your face?
Father, you see him, there in that place,
The elfin king with his cloak and crown?
It is only the mist rising up, my son.

'Dear little child, will you come play with me?
Beautiful games I'll play with thee;
Bright are the flowers we'll find on the shore,
My mother has golden robes fullscore.'

Father, O father, and did you not hear
What the elfin king breathed into my ear?
Lie quiet, my child, now never you mind:
Dry leaves it was that click in the wind.

'Come along now, you're a fine little lad,
My daughters will serve you, see you are glad;
My daughters dance all night in a ring,
They'll cradle and dance you and lullaby sing.'

Father, now look, in the gloom, do you see
The elfin daughters beckon to me?
My son, my son, I see it and say:
Those old willows, they look so gray.

'I love you, beguiled by your beauty I am,
If you are unwilling I'll force you to come!'
Father, his fingers grip me, O
The elfin king has hurt me so!

Now struck with horror the father rides fast,
His gasping child in his arm to the last,
Home through thick and thin he sped:
Locked in his arm, the child was dead.[50]

Marcus asks whether it is "not astonishing that these verses amaze us so little? Certainly, they too completely transcend the erotic sphere despite the open acknowledgement 'I love you!' But what does 'The Elf King' actually hope from this disastrous love for the poor child?" He concludes that "besides Goethe, no other poet created a figure like the elf king in his fatal lust for a boy." Marcus mentions *Faust*, where the reader also finds the expression of pederastic feelings for young boys, asking "what does Goethe's Mephisto get out of gaining power over Faust through many years of servitude, one man over the other?" He argues we cannot understand their relationship without considering how same-sex desire is key. He observes that in the conclusion of *Faust*, "the devil catches sight of a few adolescents that are so graceful that he barely manages to resist their boyish charm . . . through same-sex love heaven may aspire to allure and draw over even the devil."[51]

Marcus argues that Goethe finds same-sex desire at the root of friendship. True friendship is homosexuality. To prove this he analyzes the poem "To the Moon"

(1777), also mentioned by Hirschfeld.[52] The poem includes an image of a man resting on the chest of his male friend:

Flooding with a brilliant mist
Valley, bush and tree,
You release me. Oh for once
Heart and soul I'm free!

Easy on the region round
Goes your wider gaze,
Like a friend's indulgent eye
Measuring my days.

Every echo from the past,
Glum or gaudy mood,
Haunts me—weighing bliss and pain
In the solitude.

River, flow and flow away;
Pleasure's dead to me:
Gone the laughing kisses, gone
Lips and loyalty.

All in my possession once!
Such a treasure yet
Any man would pitch in pain
Rather than forget.

Water, rush among the pass,
Never lag at ease;
Rush, and rustle to my song
Changing melodies,

How in dark December you
Roll amok in flood;

Curling in the gala May,
Under branch and bud.

Happy man, that rancor-free
Shows the world his door;
One companion by—and both
In a glow before

Something never guessed by men
Or rejected quite:
Which, in mazes of the breast,
Wanders in the night.

Marcus finds that "the lunar sensation of friendship unfolds like an enchanted flower. Emotional closeness between two human beings embedded in their embrace, an embrace embedded in the countryside, the countryside embedded in the grand all-encompassing feeling of the celestial bodies." He finds this beautiful feeling is demonstrated in "the most beautiful poems on friendship," in Nietzsche, George, and Hiller.[53]

By "friendship" he means homosexuality. George had written in 1888 of his sexual awakening:

What brings now this transformation? Surely not just
My roaming in the abandoned alcoves
Where, next to many a strange device,
I discover the mirror of glistening metal
Before which I first learned to consider
The secret of my own body, and that of others.
And it would be wicked sacrilege to believe any longer
That the blonde child, the youngest pupil there,
Who often seeks me out with his large eyes,
Could so utterly shake my soul.[54]

A decade later, in the poem, "The Victory of Summer," the beloved is male, and that relationship's true nature is spelled out in explicit terms:

> Are you still reminded of the beautiful image of him
> He who boldly grabbed the roses on cliff's edge
> He who forgot the day in hot pursuit
> He who supped the full nectar from umbels?"[55]

Referring to Goethe's "To the Moon," Marcus opposes modern critics who "want to convince us that in reality the poem is not addressed to a male friend at all but to his female lover, solely for reasons of discretion did the friend of the text take the place of the woman." But as Marcus notes, "The young Goethe also had 'intimate conversations in the moonlight'" with other young men. What Marcus finds remarkable is "that Goethe would not have been able to resist conceding to a man, without further ado, the room he had given to his lover. The prospect of holding a male friend to his bosom was certainly not against his instinct. It does not at all spoil his joy in his creation." Turning to his own feelings, Marcus reflects how "all of us have to admit to ourselves . . . it is something earth-shattering . . . if we conceive of the person to whom right now our entire feeling and thinking belong as having a different sex." He points to the example of the philosopher Paul Jakob Deussen, who admitted that he had to imagine Plato's youths as girls to be able to enjoy Plato's dialogues. Goethe, in contrast, did "not need to imagine the friend who delighted him as a woman, nor did he even resist transforming the beloved woman into a friend and to capture her in male shape: everywhere he was the great lover of continuity, of transitions, and intermediate stages [*Zwischenstufen*]," which compels Marcus to examine the theme of the yearning figure.[56]

Marcus claims literature is indebted to Goethe, for whom "the male and the female are not separated by an unbridgeable chasm." He discusses Goethe's Mignon, the world-famous companion of the blind old harp player in *Wilhelm Meister's Apprenticeship* and *Wilhelm Meister's Journeyman Years* (1795).[57] Mignon's charm "is due to the fact that she is a girl transformed into a boy. Consequently, here too, just as in 'To the Moon,' [there is] a sexual transformation, even if of another kind and one almost arrested in its execution." From this Marcus concludes that "the twice-mentioned secret conflict of Goethe's emotional life is paralleled with a twice-mentioned harmonization of this conflict by way of a transition between the sexes. With this, Goethe has anticipated [Hirschfeld's] scientific theory of intermediate stages."[58]

Mignon has been appropriated by gays as a queer figure from Goethe's era to the present. Her famous poem, which begins, "Know you the land where lemon blossoms blow, / And through dark leaves the golden oranges glow," as it expresses longing to see her native Italy again, is already a homosexual reference.[59] More significant is her androgynous appearance and nature. When Wilhelm first encounters Mignon, "He looked at the figure with amazement, uncertain whether it was a boy or a girl."[60] He finds "her whole appearance and the mystery that surrounded" the twelve- or thirteen-year-old "strange girl" to be so striking that "he could not take his eyes off her."[61] He repeatedly refers to her as a "strange character" whose "person and character" utterly fascinated him.[62] After he took her to be his live-in servant, she desired to dress in the same colors Wilhelm dressed and had a tailor make her "a new jacket and sailor pants, such as she had seen on boys in the town."[63] She is referred to by one character as an "androgynous creature"; a surgeon takes her for a boy.[64] When another character complains that she does not wear women's clothes, Mignon passionately retorts, "I am a boy, I do not want to be a girl."[65] Only near the end of the novel does she begin to dress in women's clothes, which seems to transform her.[66]

In Goethe's era, "Mignon" had the meaning of "a male homosexual prostitute or favorite" and was used for the courtiers of French king Henri III.[67] Nevertheless, Mignon displayed intense sexual desire for her master, Wilhelm, as she "clasped him so firmly in her arms and kissed him so passionately" at every opportunity.[68] She even yearned to make love with him. Mignon literally dies from heartbreak when she witnesses Wilhelm and a woman kissing and pledging eternal union.[69] At her funeral, the abbot declared that "nothing was clear or apparent about her except her love" for her master.[70] As Tobin relates, "although wasting away with heterosexual desire for Wilhelm, she is characterized by a complicated enough gender identity and sexual orientation" that she was given a prominent position in a contemporary novel of homoerotic desire. Indeed, "the general understanding of Mignon as 'yearning' incarnate makes her an ideal figure for appropriation by those who yearned without hope for others of the same sex."[71] This is best illustrated by her song, which begins "Only the one who yearns, / Knows what I suffer!"[72] Her poem's first stanza is "Bid me not speak, let me be silent / My secret I am bound to keep."[73]

Marcus also discusses Goethe's understanding and tolerance of the gay sentiment and activities of outspoken gays in the context of his view that homosexuality was a natural inclination. From Rome, Goethe writes to the grand duke aiming to familiarize him "with 'a peculiar phenomenon' which he has nowhere encountered as widely displayed as in this place. It is, he continues, 'the love of men among each other. Provided that it is rarely carried to the highest degree of sensuousness, but lingers in the intermediate realms of affection and inclination, I can say that here I have been able to behold with my own eyes its most beautiful features, which we only know from Greek tradition, and to observe as an attentive natural scientist its mental and moral aspects." Reflecting his age, Goethe declares, "It is a subject that scarcely allows discussion, let alone written treatment: therefore let us save it for future conversations."[74]

However, as Marcus notes, "Goethe not only talked about it, he also wrote about it, and even in public."[75] Marcus analyzes Goethe's discussion of the sexual proclivities of the founder of the discipline of art history and Hellenist Johann Joachim Winckelmann, well known for his admiration of male beauty and his homoerotic sensibility; despite his sexual relations with other men, Winckelmann denied being a pederast "but asserted his need to study pederastic desires to get into the classical mindset."[76] Marcus notes Goethe's praise of Winckelmann's "proclivity for young men." Goethe describes how "Winckelmann felt he had been born to a Greek-style friendship, [and] not only capable but also to the highest degree in need of it; he perceived his own self solely in the guise of friendship."[77] Goethe states frankly: "'We often encounter Winckelmann in a relationship with beautiful youths, and never does he appear more lively and more amiable than in such moments.'" According to Marcus's analysis, "It is probably not possible to understand and sympathetically approve of another's emotional life more profoundly than Goethe has done" with Winckelmann. At the same time, "Goethe legitimizes and legalizes the forbidden inclination; by deriving it from Greek culture, back then universally admired, he makes us completely forget about the prohibition. Now it is sacrosanct and even presentable." To "convey Goethe's innermost conviction in regards to homosexuality, we might let him meditate as follows: 'Let others wonder whether it is a good thing that such beautiful and good feelings grow in what the common mind considers the wrong place, i.e., when they apply to the friend instead of the beloved woman. And let these others be apprehensive whether such noble feelings might not devalue themselves because of their wrong aim.'" Marcus notes that Goethe held the opposite view: "whenever a relationship awakens such high and noble feelings as love between friends at its peak, then the relationship is fully justified and deserving of praise rather than mere recognition." Goethe "does not stop with praise; where one feels as described here, one should participate. It would be a duty, it would be beautiful, nay, it would also be a great happiness to carry one more sensation of this powerful, wing-sweeping kind in one's own bosom." Goethe writes effusively: "'The passionate fulfillment of loving duties, the bliss of inseparability, the devotion of one to the other, the acknowledged commitment for the entire life, the necessary accompaniment to death—all these arouse our amazement in the case of the alliance of two youths, yes, one feels ashamed when poets, history writers, philosophers, orators of the old word shower us with fables, events, feelings, inclinations of this kind and content.'" Marcus interprets this to mean that Goethe is "almost jealous not to be able to participate in the kinds of lofty states he is here outlining in his own words. . . . And that is why it is, in a grandiose sense, shameful to him to have to stand aside, he who has become no different than in the days of his youth when he had decided 'to be selfless in friendship and love' and to locate in this the actual principle of his nobility." With Goethe, repeatedly, "eternal youth bursts the solemn privy councilor style of his old age, which seems to have patterned itself on the official style—eternal youth and nature itself. To the latter he ascribes *the occasional compulsion to be unnatural for its own ends* as essential."[78] In Nietzsche's words, "that which is natural cannot be immoral."

Marcus turns from Goethe's works to Goethe's life and his promotion of eroticism over sexual gratification. In his autobiographical *Dichtung und Wahrheit* (Poetry and truth), the student Goethe describes how his "multiple eccentricities" caused problems at home with his parents. He had been so fond of a harp-playing boy that he invited him home, a manifestation of "that peculiarity that all my life cost me so much." He describes how he "likes to see young creatures gather around me and befriend me. . . . One unpleasant experience after another failed to bring me back *from this inborn drive*, which at present, in the event of the most explicit conviction, still threatens to lead me (the sixty five year old!) astray."[79] Marcus finds that, with surprising frankness, Goethe "confesses traits representing the type of Blüher's 'male heroes,'" exhibiting homoerotic friendship and pedagogical eros—a homoeroticism that was aesthetic rather than physical.[80] Hans Blüher, author of the two-volume *Die Rolle der Erotik in der männlichen Gesellschaft* (The role of eroticism in masculine society, 1918) and historian of the Wandervogel German youth movement, explained in a 1913 article, "Die drei Grundformen der Homosexualität," the three types of homosexuals in the movement: suppressed homosexuals, effeminate inverts (Hirschfeld's third sex), and the virile male heroes (Blüher's healthy but spiritual homosexuals), the latter group being the most prominent in the organization. More than that, Blüher expresses that male homosexuality is the basis of the perfect political state and culture, which harnesses male erotic energy without dissipating it. Marcus continues, "As far as the case of the young harp-player is concerned, there are clues that the youth exhibited certain girlish traits; as a result, his image was later transformed into the harp-playing girl with the boyish traits, Mignon. This would mean that the *female* Mignon was modeled on a *male* mignon, just as she in turn became the archetype of the modern concept of the male Mignon as the youth with the girls' traits." In other words, "by way of an invented masculine girl, a real, feminine youth would have become constitutive of the concept of a certain kind of feminine young man of today. Experiences like the one with the young harp-player may be described as pseudo-erotic."[81]

Marcus notes that Goethe introduces a pseudoerotic experience of an entirely different kind in the person of the philosopher Friedrich Jacobi (1743–1819), known for his "effusive declarations of same-sex love."[82] As a scholar has noted, "the eighteenth-century cult of friendship recurrently blurs the distinctions that modern society draws between gays and straights. . . . Members of the same sex were able to say and write things to each other under the rubric of 'sentimental friendship' that sound incredibly queer today."[83] Goethe's relationships with various men were described as those between husbands and wives, such as in an 1777 letter that his servant Phillip Seidel wrote to a friend, stating, "We have a relationship with each other like man and woman. As I love him, so he loves me, as I serve him, so he expresses authority over me."[84] To Marcus, "Goethe himself was still fully 'fermenting and seething,' for Fritz Jacobi was 'the first' to whom he 'granted a glimpse into this chaos of the soul . . . whose nature similarly labored in the profoundest depth, cordially accepted my confidence, reciprocated it, and tried to initiate me into his mind. —Such a pure kinship of the spirit was new to me and aroused a passionate yearning for further communication. . . . The moonlight trembled above the broad Rhine, and we, standing on the window, basked in the abundance of mutual devotion which, at that wonderful time of development, gushed so plentifully!'" Marcus notes that the atmosphere between Goethe and Jacobi is closely related to the one in "To the Moon" and suggests that this encounter might have played a major role in the creation of the moon elegy. Marcus explores another passage from one of Goethe's letters to Jacobi, "just about between dreaming and waking": "'You have felt that it was bliss for me to be the object of your love. —O that is wonderful that each feels he has received more from the other than he has given! O love, love!'" Goethe describes the relationship with such phrases as having "enjoyed the rapturous feeling of a connection by way of the innermost soul [*Gemüt*]," and "the most blissful sensation of eternal union."[85]

Tobin asks why, when a male and female character in an eighteenth-century novel "hugged, kissed, expressed their love for each other, and declared that they wanted to live together for ever and ever," we do not assume they were "just friends," but when a same-sex pair do the same, we assume they are indeed "just friends"? Heterosexual presumptions hinder our "thinking of male-female relationships in a non-physical way, while homophobia prevents them from viewing same-sex friendships as physical."[86] Susan Gustafson takes Tobin's argument a step further by claiming Goethe's "highly developed self-conscious articulation of same-sex identity, desire, and community" is not only found in his work but even "structures his entire thought." She argues that Goethe (like Winckelmann before him) used his art to construct a desiring self "who desires other men and who identifies himself with other men who desire men."[87] W. Daniel Wilson, however, criticizes Tobin and others for imposing a modern queer reading on such accounts instead of seeking to understand eighteenth-century Germany culture on its own terms before heterosexuality and homosexuality became interpretative categories.[88] Rather than determining whether Goethe was "really gay," what is significant for us is the way Marcus—rightly or wrongly, as with his interpretation of Goethe's "conversion to Islam"—depicts Goethe's "homosexuality" as a sentiment, an aesthetic taste, that was not manifested physically.

Promoting eroticism as superior to sex, Marcus never analyzes *West-East Divan*, an example of "the orientalization of intense, erotic male bonding, and the homosexualization of the non-European male."[89] Goethe even noted that one of the themes of this work is "the tender feeling for the beauty of the growing boy."[90] One wishes Marcus had analyzed "Saki Nameh: Book of the Cupbearer," where the wine drinking, male Muslim tavern-goer, overcome with "lover drunkenness," and the "charming boy" cupbearer who serves him, his "darling of darlings," express their love for one another in words and action.[91] In the words of the cupbearer,

> But my love is yet more dear
> When a mem'ry kiss I win.
> Words go by and disappear.
> Yet your gift remains within.[92]

As Goethe notes in his commentary to his work, "Neither intemperate propensity for half-illicit wine drinking nor delicacy of feeling for the beauty of an adolescent could be omitted from the Divan. But the latter had to be treated in all purity, in accordance with our morals."[93] He then quotes examples from medieval Persian poet Saadi's (1184–1291) *Gulistan* (Rose garden, 1258), including an incident where "an extremely handsome, graceful boy" "wholly enticed" him; as the poet relates, "my heart burst open toward you like a rose beginning to bloom." When they separate, he concludes, "In parting, those who love are each like an apple; one cheek pressing on the other turns red from desire and life; the second one, pale from sorrow and sickness."[94] He also quotes another Saadi tale that stands as a perfect articulation of the type of friendship for which Marcus's fictional characters long: "When I was young I maintained a sincere and durable friendship with a young man like myself. To my eyes, his face belonged to the heavenly realm that magnetized our prayers. Being with him was the greatest gain in all my life's activities." The author expressed how "no earthly mortal, perhaps only an angel in heaven, could equal him in beauty of form, sincerity, and uprightness." Having enjoyed such a friendship, he "took an oath, and it would seem wrong to me if after his death I were to bestow my love upon someone else." When his friend died suddenly, he "kept him company sitting and lying on his tomb, holding vigil for many days, and composed a good many songs of grief on his loss and our separation."[95]

Hirschfeld, writing of Saadi, quotes Arthur Schopenhauer: "If we turn to Asia, we see that every country of this part of the world, and certainly from the earliest times up to the present, is filled with the vice, and taking no special pains to conceal it: Hindu and Chinese no less than the Islamic peoples, whose poets we likewise find much more preoccupied with boy-love than with women-love; such as, for example, in Gulistan, in his book, *Of Love*, Saadi speaks exclusively about it."[96] Hirschfeld also lectured and published on the text "Love in the East," focusing on the Islamic world.[97] Kurt Hiller, in his crise de conscience *§175: Die Schmach des Jahrhunderts!*, notes that "in Islamic countries . . . the state tolerates sexual intercourse between males."[98] Also Hiller's "Appeal on Behalf of an Oppressed Human Variety," written for the Second International Congress for Sexual Reform (Copenhagen, 1928) and delivered on his behalf by Hirschfeld, notes that "love between man and youth was no more excluded from the heroic and golden ages of Ancient Greece, than it was from the most illustrious period of Islamic culture."[99] Marcus mentions Ferdinand Karsch-Haack (1853–1936), for whom homosexuality in Islamic lands was a major theme.[100] Yet in this piece,

Marcus, who had converted to Islam, does not reflect upon homosocial Islamic male bonding, the practice of gazing at beautiful youth celebrated in Islamic literature, or homosexuality and sexual activity between Muslim men or in the Near East. This is a strange omission as Germans had been linking non-Europeans and especially "Orientals" with sexual permissiveness, including pederasty and sodomy, since at least the seventeenth century. Indeed, they situated homosexuality in the Orient and traveled to the Orient or had relations with people from the region visiting Europe precisely because engaging in such practices there or with people from there was seen as less taboo.

Marcus had multidecade relations with younger Muslim South Asian men of the Berlin mosque community after he was hired to introduce them to German language and German culture. Such relations between the older teacher, Marcus, and younger male pupils presented precisely the opportunity for the idealized, intergenerational, erotic pedagogical/pederastic Greek love. After all, Marcus could fulfill the role of the active, "older, socially more prominent, wealthier, and hopefully wiser lover," and the Ahmadi, the passive, "younger beloved hoping to learn and profit from his partner."[101] If not in his analyses of Goethe, Marcus pursued this topic in an unpublished mosque lecture and more concretely in a brief, unpublished, homoerotic exploration of his relationship with his imam, in his philosophical work from the turn of the twentieth century, and in his fiction begun at least as early as the 1930s.[102]

Reader responses to Marcus's Goethe piece were varied, with some critical, others approving. He felt compelled to pen a letter to the editor, defending himself, in which he explains his own life philosophy, view of erotic literature, and experience being gay.[103] He uses most of the letter to criticize those who wanted to read more explicit sex in the pages of *Der Kreis*, "who desire our short stories to begin where stories usually end. You demand the fulfillment of pipe dreams. And right is on your side if such depictions express not only sensuousness (with its after-taste, which is always bitter and often disdainful) but also human nature and human value as well." Furthermore, "the drawers of the editor are not, as you seem to assume, filled with piles of manuscripts that conjure pipe dreams in congenial words. And with incomprehensible doggedness and for inscrutable reasons, the editor always makes a mistake and, instead of these, pulls out nothing but lofty, serious, and incomprehensible, that is to say, verbose and boring manuscripts," such as his own. "In truth, he does not publish those frank and yet tactful stories because unfortunately, they are not in his desk." Moreover, "the author himself does not choose his topic, *but is chosen by it.*"[104] Marcus's innate nature compels him to write about love between men. Reflecting Hiller's view, he wants anyone of any inclination who reads the stories to conclude that "there is something beautiful after all, something supremely pure, nay powerful and divinely ordained in this inclination!" for "besides the sex drive there is a second all-powerful drive, the drive for nourishment." That is why "the words from the Our Father: 'Give us this day our daily bread!' A prayer for Absinth and cocktails, however, would be blasphemy. Eros, too, is as essential as the daily bread, and more so. But there is a difference between Eros as sacred necessity and Eros as pocket change and a means to flavor boring hours." In a previous issue of the journal, a Dr. Fischer of Zürich, "animated by the most genuine humanity, with an uncommon talent and the most noble intentions, champions our cause without reserve as sacred, as a cause that is humanly thoroughly legitimate. On our behalf, he does not even shy away from being attacked and persecuted." He asks his readers if it is "right that we abandon ourselves exclusively to frivolous and cheap entertainment behind the front while human beings of this sort sacrifice themselves in our defense?" Should they not rather "make sure that men like Dr. Fischer will be proven right when they talk of a holy cause? But this means that we make sure to prevent the lofty registers of our inclination from shriveling. As for the lower ones, nature itself will see to it that they will remain alive."[105] Marcus's jihad is to write of "eros," not "animal sex."

Marcus proclaims Goethe a pole star for gays (just as he is for German Muslims). In the article, what he reported about Goethe's attitude toward friendship—that is, homosexuality—Marcus "discovered independently in Goethe at a young age, at a time when passionate friendships could not be talked about anywhere."[106] Here he chides a younger generation searching for shallow entertainment and immediate gratification, who may not understand what men of Marcus's generation faced. Goethe's words

> cannot always pretend to be diverting. . . . But these words have shone a light from his youth on all phases of his life and provided something unforgettable, since they touch on the highest meaning friendship may achieve. And he now felt that these words, although not always diverting to read, might shine forth for so many of our comrades as well and help preserve the faith in our emotional world (*Gefühlswelt*), a faith that constantly begins to totter because of so many happenings of daily life.[107]

Goethe's words are "pole stars" that "provide direction and orientation." Nevertheless,

> Goethe was clever enough, despite his "confessions," to refrain from disclosing an ultimate secret. . . . The many clues which we have gratefully received from various quarters, really seem to suggest that on occasion, Goethe would have been capable of taking an intimate interest in youths—if he had permitted himself to do so. And this certainly goes with the Olympian who (alongside different experiences!) could not do without a Ganymede. But it is also in line with the emotional universalism of Goethe who desired to possess "everything completely," i.e., everything that could be experienced.[108]

The reference to Ganymede might be explained by the fact that like "Prometheus" and *Faust* (written between 1773 and 1775), the poem is an example of how "Goethe consistently directs male desire for the feminine through other men."[109] In the eighteenth century, "Ganymede" was understood as "a signifier of male-male sex."[110] Thus, the poem concerns "a male imitation of femininity in the form of passive male sexuality toward other men."[111] The narrator is a boy, speaking to an older man:

> How in the morning gleam
> All around you glow at me,
> Springtime, beloved!
> With joy of love a thousandfold
> Rushes to my heart
> Of your eternal warmth
> A holy feeling,
> Infinite beauty!
> That in this arm I might
> Hold you.
>
> Ah, upon your breast
> I stretch out, swoon,
> And to your flowers, your grass
> Rush to my heart.
> You slake the burning

Thirst in my breast,
Delicate morning wind,
Withal the nightingale lovingly
Calls from the misty vale to me.

I am coming, coming,
Where, ah where?
Up, a striving upward.
The clouds are floating
Down, the clouds
Bow to love that is yearning.
Take me, take me,
Clouds, in your lap,
Upward,
Embraced, embracing!
Upward to your breast,
All-loving father![112]

In his *Italian Journey*, Goethe mentions having seen an antique chalk drawing of Ganymede, mentioned by Winckelmann, showing Ganymede "offering Jupiter a cup of wine and receiving a kiss in return." Goethe confides, "Yesterday I saw it for myself and I must confess that I do not know of anything more beautiful than the figure of Ganymede, especially the head and the back."[113]

MARCUS'S HOMOEROTIC FICTION

In the face of societal hostility and legal persecution, the journal *Der Kreis* and its affiliated club and social activities allowed gays to create a "counter public" in which "desires and perspectives could be affirmed, social and personal personas fashioned and refashioned, and arguments against legal and social discrimination developed."[114] Emotionally and practically speaking, *Der Kreis* offered readers escape from isolation and loneliness, linking gays locally and internationally while offering them the pleasure of seeing images of men depicted as sex objects, validating readers' desires.[115] A typical monthly issue contained photos of nearly nude males (full frontal being prohibited) who were usually white European, but some "travel" editions featured African, Middle Eastern, and Asian men placed against "native fauna" (such as nude African men in a tree). There were also homoerotic fiction; updates on the progress toward full civil rights for gay men mainly in Europe and reports of persecution of gay men across the continent; translations of the work of Walt Whitman, André Gide, Goethe, and other homosexuals or men considered fellow travelers; or writings that did not specify the gender of the object of affection through history; and paintings and sculptures of male nudes from ancient to modern times. There were advertisements for clubs in Zürich, where the readers of the journal gathered, and reports on their spring, fall, and Christmas costume balls. In later years there was an insert enabling men to find partners.

The editor of *Der Kreis* from 1943 to 1967 was Karl "Rolf" Meier (1897–1974), a Swiss stage actor and director who had lived in Berlin and experienced its gay subculture and probably first met Marcus in the 1920s. Writing to Hiller, who had returned to Germany in 1955, settling in Hamburg, which boasted 1950s Germany's "most impressive gay scene," Meier describes Marcus's writing as "a little stuck in the 1930s, in its manner of expression, atmosphere, lack of plot, etc."[116] He may have had in mind some of the homoerotic novels published in the 1920s, including Klaus Mann's *Der fromme Tanz* (The devout dance, 1925), John Henry Mackay's *Der Puppenjunge* (The hustler: The story of a nameless love from Friedrichstrasse, 1926), and Stefan Zweig's *Die Verwirrung der Gefühle* (The confusion of feelings, 1929). All are "queer *Bildungsroman*" that chart the transplanted provincial protagonist's journey from hometown and bourgeois family relations to Berlin and homoerotic entanglements.[117] They view homoerotic love as "an exercise in spiritual edification through self-denial" rather than physical satisfaction. In Mann's tale, the well-bred protagonist, descendant of a provincial, patrician family, considers suicide but runs away instead to Berlin where he "makes friends with all sorts of bohemians, good-natured prostitutes, sympathetic flotsam," earning his living "by reciting poetry, dressed up as a sailor, in a cabaret," and then meets another young man whom he worships, quitting his job and following him from city to city.[118] In Mackay's story, middle class, mature Graf falls in love with the poor adolescent male prostitute Gunter, creating a romanticized image of the young man, paying for his time without asking for sex, preferring to "burden him with probing emotional questions," which is the same blueprint for many of Marcus's stories.[119] In Zweig's novel, a professor declares his "exalted spiritual love" for his student, Roland; the professor surrounds himself with young men but does not fulfill his homoerotic desires; the two kiss only once, when they part ways.[120] These novels, especially the latter, promote homoerotic desire as something pure and romantic, never to be sullied by sexual gratification: the "intellect/soul" or "spiritual and chaste pedagogical eros" is preferred to "body" and "carnality."[121] Zweig's professor "shuns a life that would allow him to embrace homoerotic sexual gratification to idealize and, to a certain extent, pursue a spiritual bond with the objects of his desire." While "as a homoerotic subject" he "also desires carnally, he chooses a life that allows him to keep his status and pursue an extremely idealized form of his love for young men by educating them and to allow them to function as his muses."[122] The novels reflect the masculinist views of Adolf Brand and his journal *Der Eigene* (The self-owner, 1896–1932), or Hans Blüher, who favored homoerotic bonding without surrendering to homosexual passions, as opposed to Hirschfeld, who promoted pleasure and fulfillment for "third sex" people.[123]

Meier's comment that Marcus's fiction was out of date is revealing. As much as the homophile movement as represented by *Der Kreis* was criticized—especially by activists in the post-1969 gay rights movement, for its "elite aesthetics" and "sexual sobriety," for downplaying explicit sexuality to promote gay respectability, for hypocrisy in condemning actual gay practices in pursuit of assimilation, and for its "sense of introspection, longing, and existential quandry"—for the editor of its leading international publication to call Marcus's writing prude and old-fashioned must really be saying something.[124] Meier defends Marcus, adding that there is more to eros than wild, dionysian nights; only artists and poets can capture the creative and beatified aspects of gay love.[125] Marcus was following his model, Goethe. The attribution of writing outmoded stories is appropriate, however, for Marcus was not new to gay fiction: as he notes in a 1951 letter to the editor of *Der Kreis*, he had been penning homoerotic novellas and novels "for decades"; it would be more correct to say more than half a century, as his first work appeared in 1900.[126] In the same period, he expressed the links and similarities between German philosophy and Islam, and he composed stories marked by "unusual fantasies and the affirmation of our (homosexual) existence," according to Meier. There are only a few echoes of Islam in these writings. But the fact that the protagonist often has a doppelganger calls to mind the many dimensions of Marcus's personality.

As much as to Goethe's writing, exhibiting homoerotic friendship and pedagogical eros, Marcus's fiction bears similarities to other short stories published in *Der Kreis*. It was a "magazine with a mission"—to defend the human rights of a minority—committed to discreet sexuality, and no public profile, and its editors were committed to what it considered "clean" and "tasteful" explorations of homoeroticism.[127] To fit editor Rolf Meier's desire that the journal portray "the ideal gay man," fulfilling social and ethical duties (being inconspicuous, keeping homosexuality a private matter, being discrete in public and in publications[128]—to adhere to obscenity laws so that the journal would not be closed down by authorities and its authors and subscribers arrested), authors were permitted only "a lot of hand-holding, deep sighs filled with unrequited passion, fluttery sidelong glances, and not an erection to be seen or mentioned anywhere."[129] In other words, "Concrete sexuality remained taboo; in its place came the strived-for 'male male Eros,' the veneration of masculinity."[130] The short stories written by Marcus fit this description and focus on man-boy love—the idealized bodily, spiritual, and intellectual relations between older men and beautiful youth.[131]

Nearly half a century after publishing *Das Frühlingsglück*, in 1948 Marcus penned the novel *Ein paar Schuhe* (A pair of shoes).[132] *Ein paar Schuhe* is a homoerotic story that takes place in post-World War I Berlin and concerns the relationship between an unnamed boy prostitute and university student Heinrich (Marcus?), who denies his homosexual desires until he comes to terms with them through imagined pederasty. When Heinrich first encounters the barefoot youth, he describes him as "a fellow member of the holy army of youth!," reminiscent of Marcus's homoerotic pacifist piece, "Die Kirche zu den heiligen Brüsten der Jünglinge."[133]

Heinrich's epiphany occurs when the boy unexpectedly visits him at his boardinghouse.[134] The scene calls to mind Wilhelm observing another boy undress in Goethe's *Wilhelm Meister's Journeyman Years*. Even though Heinrich had bought him a pair of shoes, the prostitute is again barefoot. The youth asks him for clothes to match the beautiful shoes, which would help him find a job. Saying, "'I have nothing except these rags. You can see for yourself,' the youth suddenly unbuttons his worn-out shirt, and in great, silvery rhythms, as each of his breaths dies slowly, suffusing the entire room, the light of his bare, broad chest flows through the room."[135] The young man's bare chest brings to Heinrich's mind the bare chest of the Cupid of Caravaggio, "hanging in the museum, a colorful, distant echo of the Renaissance." The young man puts his hand on his belt, and is soon "a naked statue of a young Phobus" standing in the middle of his room.[136] Ephebes were the adolescent boys engaged in erotic relationships with adult men in ancient Greece.[137] He makes an offer to Heinrich:

> "If you want to give me some of your clothes, I will put them on. But I will dress slowly, and you can watch!"
>
> Heinrich suddenly understood. He asks his guest, "so you mean that is what I want?"
>
> "You did buy me the shoes."
>
> "And?" asks Heinrich. "If I understand correctly, do you mean that I bought you the shoes, because I took a certain amount of forbidden delight in you? . . ."
>
> "I would not say it so directly. I only believe that whoever does such a deed, like what you did with the shoes, can feel for some other person, as you suggest. And why should I not be this person?"[138]

Despite the youth's overture, Heinrich does not yet know what his feelings are: "Whatever potentialities there are in me, I myself am not yet in a position to recognize. I still rack my brains about this. Is it not the case that a person does not even know himself? Do you know yourself? Because of this I cannot answer your question. . . ." Upon reflection, he denies having any desire for him: "But I know this much: I honestly observe my own feelings. And now I find that I bought you the shoes, because I thought here is a young man like me, and he is shoeless. And does he not also belong to the holy army of the young? We are the same age, the same generation, comrades of the same . . . world. This is our relationship." He claims he can locate no personal feelings for the youth, he is only motivated by empathy for the poor boy. He, too, could very well be shoeless.[139]

The young man laughs with disbelief, as perhaps do the readers. Heinrich, worried the boardinghouse owner might come in and discover the other boy in his naked glory in the middle of his room, rushes to block the door. The youth quickly dresses. Heinrich offers him some clothes and promises to try to find him a suitable job. After the visitor leaves, it becomes completely quiet in the room, until the Sunday church bells begin to peel. They cause a stirring within, and he recognizes his homosexuality. He feels like "an apple tree flower opening longingly in the wind," realizing "the guest is right. There are potentialities in me which I had never seen, but he had shown them to me. I am indebted to him for this." Then the story takes a Goethean twist, calling to mind "Ganymede." Heinrich realizes "I now have a son. He is just as old as I am. Why should one not be able to have a son who is the same age as oneself?"[140]

In the melancholy short story "Licht fällt ins Fenster" ("Light shines through the window"), Marcus explores the themes of the alienation and loneliness of a gay man who cannot find a lover in the metropolis.[141] More significant is "Stärker als der Tod" ("Stronger than death"), another episode in Heinrich's unrequited search for love, another brooding tale of devoted friendship, suppressed male desire, loss, death, and loneliness, which is illustrated with Titian's near nude, "Der heilige Sebastian" (the holy Sebastian).[142] The setting again is post–World War I Berlin, this time a smoke-filled jazz bar, where Heinrich chats with another young man. Heinrich tells him he was involved in a relationship where his friend "did not know about our friendship, which was one-way, it was my secret."[143] Astonished, the other man asks him if he had never told him he loves him, and Heinrich confirms he neither told him he loves him nor that he is good looking: "That is what young men say to young women. Instead, I would say, 'the wide world is beautiful. . . . And I thank the world, that you are also in it.'" He had not said to him that he has feelings for him, preferring "'I have turned into a garden, in which all of my seasons blossom at the same time.'"[144] He asks, like the reader does, whether Heinrich was "too autumnal, serious, scowling, and sad." He describes his deceased boyfriend as "one visited by the god Eros, a man who inspired love, longing, and desire wherever he went. . . . But he was sad, and unfulfilled. He had a strong will, and would always end a relationship just before it came to a head. He did not want a relationship to be exhausted. So wherever he went, the young man went with him, to take care of him, to cheer him up, to heal him."[145]

The expression of the man's love for the other makes Heinrich realize his error: "Why, I now reproach myself, was I so narrow-minded as to believe in the mind and its might alone!" Why, he asks, "was I so blind, waiting in libraries and galleries to meet someone who revered the same paintings!" Instead, "I should have decked myself out and hit the streets, visiting the lovers' corners and circles of friends as lovers, who are wiser than sages, because they know that it is not with the mind, but with the heart, that one wins love!"[146] Was Marcus at his advanced age expressing regret for the way he had lived his love life? Heinrich asks the other man to help teach him this way to love.

Marcus turned up the heat a few notches in his most successful short story, "In Geschäften nach Paris" (A business trip to Paris), with Paris a stand-in for Berlin. The story combines homoerotic Mediterranean, ancient Greek, and Islamic conceits.[147] The older, lonely narrator is a john who describes his tryst with a young male prostitute, Jean, whom he routinely pays to worship like a god. The plot is all the more remarkable for a Muslim author, to whom sex between men is already forbidden. At the end of the day, having visited just about all of his customers and before leaving the city, the narrator takes the metro to the center. This is no accident, for the main train station was "a central location for gay cruising in nearly every city."[148] Exiting the station, he observes that the streets are as empty as on Good Friday. He thinks it is as if the young Jean has died and all were mourning him. Then out of the darkness "something bright flashes." He realizes it is Jean, "and that he is here for me. An incomprehensible feeling that this young man has come here for me, and that he is waiting for me." The narrator deliberately delays the planned rendezvous by hiding out in the tunnel belowground, "waiting with palpitating heart," making his lover wait, pacing back and forth above. The narrator is grateful "that he waits for me, that someone waits for me." Jean notices him, walks over, smiling.[149]

They greet briefly and walk side by side toward Jean's apartment, located in a gloomy building on a quiet side street. Silently they go up the unlit steps. Leading him up the dark stairs, touching him gently or putting his arm on his shoulder is a demonstration "of the gentle trust they hold for one another." The narrator looks through the window and sees enchanted views of strange courtyards and rooftop gardens shimmering in the pink lights of the nighttime city, and feels "as if he is in a foreign southern land" (i.e., the Orient), stretching from Switzerland, Italy, and Greece to the Middle East.[150]

Jean appears to the narrator as an angel, and the steps to his apartment the biblical ladder that stretches to heaven:[151] "He disappears above me, where the stairwell is completely dark. Going ahead of me, he is always a little above me, like an angel showing me the way, whom I must follow. He becomes an angel, and the staircase Jacob's Ladder. The feeling that he is an angel increasingly overwhelms me the more his light outfit and his glowing cheeks shine in the darkness and float above me." When Jean opens his apartment door, the narrator compares it to a door to a tomb. All is dark, and he surrenders to the young male prostitute: "I am completely in the hands of my angel. He could be my guardian angel. Because he is strong." He finds himself in Jean's tiny, lonely room, which he "loves and likes to caress," as it is an extension of the youth's garb, so he calls it "Jean's Coat," an allusion to the biblical story of Joseph and his coat of many colors. Jean takes off his coat, and everything else: "He stands naked before me, brightly luminous as if bathed in a white phosphorus light emitting from him. He is a pillar of light that unlocks a final wisdom." This line calls to mind the "naked, gleaming white bodies, brilliant even in the dim lamp light" in Goethe's *Wilhelm Meister's Journeyman Years.* In his nakedness, Jean's unnamed angel, "whose underarms emit a fragrance like forest resin, like a balsam of scented candles and alpine roses," becomes an ancient Greek god: "I wanted him to concede to cease being an angel and to transform himself into a god. Now I stand before him fully clothed, wretched like the twentieth century, like a pauper of an eccentric age standing before a Greek Hermes. I place him on a chair that will serve as the pedestal for his god likeness. I prostrate myself before him, lay my head at his feet." He cries "tears that he should not see. In such a way I deify him step by step for myself because I am arrogant enough only to want to embrace a young god, whom I expect will soon descend to me."[152] The passage is similar to poems Stefan George wrote to commemorate and glorify the teenage Maximin, for whom he felt the most powerful, spiritual love. George is the secular priest worshipping Maximin, the god, before whom he kneels down and prays:

> To him you are a child to him a friend.
> I see in you the God
> Whom I recognized with a shudder
> Whom I worship.[153]

It is also similar to the homoerotic poem devoted to the Greek youth Marcus included in *Meditations*, "Teacher and Pupil," which begins, "My boy stood in the waves."

The narrator in "A Business Trip to Paris" notices that the young man is also crying, "because I was allowed to see him, as no one else had yet seen him." His tears gave away the fact that he felt completely exposed, which made him also feel ashamed. The author compares him to a virgin, and himself to the one who takes his virginity away. Since the young man acted like a shy, exposed virgin, they "celebrated the festival of his reawakened virginity, the reawakened virginity which has been given away, to tell the truth, so many times."[154] Here Marcus uses the Qur'anic figure of the *houri*, the male and female virgins who are awarded in paradise, virgins who never lose their virginity. The difference is that the young man has not given himself away many times but rather has sold himself many times. He is a prostitute, not a *houri*. Nevertheless, the narrator denies this and considers, "you give yourself to me because you see that I need you. You let me drink from your lips because you fear that otherwise I will die of thirst, which you do not want to happen. You are mindful that it is an act worthy of a god to quench the thirsty. But when I go, I will have the burning need to give you something, because I have become wealthy from all that I have received. I will find out for what it is that *you* thirst."[155] Marcus, having edited a Qur'an translation, was aware that a dozen Qur'anic verses speak of God quenching thirst; he deploys the theme in this story.

The narrator, recognizing that "love is another type of hunger," and that they both hunger—one for the other's beauty, the other one for money, as in the short story "A Pair of Shoes"—resolves to arrange the prostitute a position in the local branch of the family business, which "carries the good name of my grandfather and father," risking his bourgeois existence.[156] Did this story reflect Marcus's experience with prostitutes in Berlin when he was being groomed to take over the family business prior to World War I?

Marcus may have set the narrator's encounter with Jean in Paris, but he invokes the male prostitution scene in Weimar Berlin. Jean calls to mind descriptions of male prostitutes in Berlin in the late 1920s. According to Christopher Isherwood, such young men were

> greedy but not calculating, temperamentally unable to take thought for the morrow.... Although it would have been in their own interests to have their clients fall in love with them, they did nothing to encourage this. If you mooned over them they became bored and soon began to avoid you. Beyond keeping their hair carefully combed, they showed few signs of vanity. They didn't seem able to picture themselves as objects of desire. Their attitude was almost indifferent: "take me or leave me."[157]

Isherwood famously declared "Berlin meant boys."[158] By "boys" he was referring to the ubiquity of boy prostitutes in Berlin in the last years of Weimar. Anywhere from twenty thousand to fifty thousand young men—primarily orphans, unskilled workers, and members of the working class with limited education as well as members of the middle class brought low by inflation—worked as prostitutes.[159] The prostitutes were visible in the center of the city, serving a more well-heeled clientele in the West End as well as in the dive bars of east Berlin.[160] Whereas the "effeminate" prostitutes in the West End "were better turned out, earned higher fees, and exhibited greater 'professionalism,' the poorer youth who worked the humble bars and outdoor spaces of central and east Berlin engaged more often in 'occasional' prostitution—due primarily to unemployment—and were themselves frequently heterosexual."[161] Another observer described them as "unemployed young workers, idle swastika soldiers, burnt-out reform-school youth, ship's boys, sailors, boys from the provinces, and those who wanted or had to run away from home."[162] Stefan Zweig remembered how "made-up boys with artificial waistlines promenaded along the Kurfüstendamm—and not professionals alone: every high school student wanted to make some money, and in the darkened bars one could see high public officials and high financiers courting drunken sailors without shame."[163]

On the occasion of Marcus's seventy-fifth birthday in 1955, Roman Malicki sent him a passport-sized photograph of Marcus taken when he was approximately twenty years old. Although he does not smile, he looks just past the photographer, his round features, full cheeks, bushy, dark hair, and dark eyebrows give the impression of a healthy, vigorous young man. Roman sent the photo to Marcus to remind him of their salad days spent together in Posen and Berlin. It is testament to Roman's lifelong commitment to his friend.[164] It is also the last time Marcus heard from Roman.

To honor the lifetime activist and aged writer on the same birthday, *Der Kreis* published an excerpt from another of his novels, *Die einander bei Händen und bei Sternen halten* (Those who hold each other by the hands and stars), whose main themes are gay suicide, the love of an older boy for a younger boy, and the superiority of homosexual friendship to heterosexual love.[165] The protagonist is again Heinrich, who experiences the deeply shocking suicide of his school benchmate, Kaltenegg, whom he secretly loved. The story consists of excerpts from Heinrich's diary. His parents decide to send him to the countryside to live with another family for the summer vacation. When he arrives in the village he feels as if his depression lifts, and he is warmly welcomed. Waldemar, the elder son of the family, a complete stranger, is sent in exchange to live with Heinrich's parents. Waldemar's younger brother Ulrich, who is younger than Heinrich, remains at the country home, where the tension of the story arises.

Concerning Ulrich, Heinrich finds that "the longer one looks at him, the more delicacy one is astonished to discover in his face, and in the way he moves his long, fine hands."[166] Ulrich and Heinrich are first alone in the single room the two brothers share, as the former helps the latter try on his brother's hiking outfit: "It was embarrassing and yet strangely sweet. Embarrassing to undress before him. Because I am not used to that. At home I sleep alone. Embarrassing also, that he unfastened and fastened the buttons."[167] The hiking outfit fits perfectly, and wearing it Heinrich feels enveloped by the presence of the absent Waldemar. Ulrich had also undressed without any shame. He was almost naked: "I was able to catch an eyeful of everything that his beautiful, supple, still budding body had to offer." Alluding to his own homosexuality, he thinks, "But as for me, I had to always remember that if he only knew what it meant to me, he certainly would not reveal himself to me anymore."[168]

This serves as an occasion for Marcus, through Ulrich, to ruminate on the meaning of true love. Ulrich has no idea what a gift he is giving the older boy. Although he freely offers the penultimate "gift," Ulrich could never offer the greatest "gift." They could never truly go beyond being strangers, could never truly "know" each other: "How strange it is that one receives as a limitless gift, what one never dared hope for, because there is no room for hope that the final barrier of strangeness will fall even once. It is in fact this eternal strangeness between us that allows us to come so near as to be able to lie here together in the same bedroom."[169] Young men and women cannot even obtain two-thirds intimacy, Heinrich muses, because giving it all away through sexual intercourse is a real possibility. Yet where going all the way is never even a possibility for a man of Marcus's generation, one gives everything else away unselfconsciously, and near intimacy is easily obtained. As with his nonfiction writing and his understanding of Goethe's view of "homosexuality," Marcus wishes the reader to infer that eros and love between men—i.e., pure, unconsummated homosexual desire—is superior to love between men and women because it can never be requited.

Heinrich senses "a sweet perfume penetrating my entire body. It appeared to me as if the entire room and I were suffused with the scent of jasmine, that emanated not from the garden window, but from Ulrich."[170] Ulrich says goodnight, turns out the light, and all is quiet in the dark room. Heinrich, having already sensed being intimately embraced by Waldemar when he tried on his clothes, now finds being in Waldemar's bed, whose sheets and blankets had "tenderly touched" and embraced the other, gives him the same feeling of intimate connection to the other boy. Lying in the bed he feels "the most intimate stirring of (the other boy's) body, soul, and breath within me." Almost becoming Waldemar, he thinks of Ulrich as his own brother. Yet his thoughts are on his doppelganger: "All of Waldemar's aura was still present in his pillows, entering every pore of my body. I was penetrated by his rays like Saint Sebastian under a hail of arrows."[171] He might have referred here to Goethe's "Ganymede." Instead, it is another fitting allusion, to Titian's Sebastian, depicted since the Renaissance as a nearly nude young man, a homosexual icon, and which Marcus may have viewed when it was exhibited in Zürich in 1949, an illustration of which accompanies Marcus's "Stärker als der Tod."[172]

Marcus was influenced by a novella by his acquaintance and contemporary Thomas Mann, *Death in Venice* (1912), in which Sebastian also appears. *Death in Venice* bears many of the traits of the homosexual subculture of Goethe's era: art history; Greek antiquity and culture, particularly the propensity for male-male love; and orientalism (a region stretching from the Muslim world to Italy, where one found classical civilization and sexuality perpetuated).[173] In this novella the Orient is a place where Europeans gain freedom to express homosexual tendencies on a journey of self discovery. The protagonist is repressed, dour, and abstinent, gray-haired fifty-something writer Gustave von Aschenbach, who had lived a life of reason and self-control and had written a biography of Frederick the Great—as would George Circle member and Marcus cousin Ernst Kantorowicz[174]—a ruler known for his homosexual tendencies. Gustave first fantasizes about a journey to the Orient, a modern Goethe, a desire to travel "coming upon him with such suddenness and passion as to resemble a seizure, almost a hallucination. Desire projected itself visually." He fantasized about a sensuous landscape, "a tropical marshland, beneath a reeking sky, steaming, monstrous, rank—a kind of primeval wilderness-world of islands, morasses, and alluvial channels. Hairy palm-trunks rose near and far out of lush brakes of fern, out of bottoms of crass vegetation, fat, swollen, thick with incredible bloom." Trees "mis-shapen as a dream, that dropped their naked roots straight through the air into the ground or into water that was stagnant and shadowy and glass-green, where mammoth milk-white blossoms floated, and strange high-shouldered birds with curious bills stood gazing sidewise without sound or stir. Among the knotted joints of a bamboo thicket the eyes of a crouching tiger gleamed" causing him to feel "his heart throb with terror, yet with a longing inexplicable."[175]

Grave and serious like the protagonists in Marcus's fiction, Aschenbach travels to exotic, indolent, disease-ridden, rotting, forbidden, sultry-aired Venice, with its churches like oriental temples and homes with Moorish (i.e., Islamic) lattices, a city at once exciting and enervating, "half fairy-tale, half snare," so "weirdly lulling and lascivious," a city threatened by plague originating in the hot moist swamps of India, peopled by incomprehensible, lying, corrupt natives and vacationing Europeans.[176] He travels there to satisfy his desire for "three or four weeks of lotus-eating at some one of the gay world's playgrounds in the lovely south."[177]

Aschenbach compares his beloved fourteen-year-old Tadzio—who calls to mind Hanno Buddenbrook—to classical Greek forms. He likens his own relation with Tadzio, who conjures within him the forgotten homosexual pangs of his youth, ever since laden and suppressed, to that between the mature Socrates and youthful Phaedrus. Socrates instructs Phaedrus "upon the nature of desire": When "he beholds a godlike face or a form which is a good image of beauty," he is to gaze and "worship the beautiful one" while "scarcely" daring "to look upon him," sacrificing "as to an idol or a god," which is precisely what the protagonist does in Marcus's "Business Trip to Paris."[178] Watching the boy play with a ball, Aschenbach compares him to Hyacinth, lover of rivals Apollo and Zephyr, who was killed by a discus thrown by Apollo.[179] He also equates the boy's smile to that of Narcissus.[180]

Sebastian as homosexual icon appears early in the story. A critic of Aschenbach's work noted he favored a hero displaying "virginal manliness, which clenches its teeth and stands in modest defiance of the swords and spears that pierce its side." Aschenbach found the analysis "beautiful, it was *spirituel*, it was exact," but objected to "the suggestion of too great passivity." He believed that "forbearance in the face of fate, beauty constant under torture, are not merely passive. They are a positive achievement, an explicit triumph," and "Sebastian is the most beautiful symbol, if not of art as a whole, yet certainly of the art we speak of here."[181] The life and work of Aschenbach are an expression of the idea that "almost everything conspicuously great is great in despite: has come into being in defiance of affliction and pain, poverty, destitution, bodily weakness, vice, passion, and a thousand other obstructions."[182] He is a master at dreaming high thoughts, postponing fulfillment, having a self-command that hides the "embers of smouldering fire" within.[183] These are also themes articulated by Marcus's character Heinrich. Aschenbach falls in love with Tadzio, a lad of "perfect beauty" whose "face recalled the noblest moment of Greek sculpture," an "expression of pure and godlike serenity."[184] In Aschenbach's eyes, the boy of "godlike beauty," "a masterpiece from nature's own hand," has a head "poised like a flower, in incomparable loveliness. It was the head of Eros."[185] Watching the boy swim, like Goethe watching Ferdinand or Goethe's Wilhelm watching a boy, von Aschenbach realizes, "The sight of this living figure, virginally pure and austere . . . beautiful as a tender young god, emerging from the depths of sea and sky—conjured up mythologies, it was like a primeval legend, handed down from the beginning of time, of the birth of form, of the origin of the gods."[186]

Hiller criticized the author for treating Aschenbach's homosexual desire for Tadzio as "a symptom of degeneration," described "nearly the same as cholera."[187] Aschenbach dies worshipping the boy, never having fulfilled his physical desires, never consummating the love he feels, overcome by passion for the boy's beauty, yet always remaining distant, intoxicated with desire, permitting only detachment, rejecting knowing the beloved in favor of worshipping his beauty, like Socrates.[188] As Tobin argues, referring repeatedly to Aschenbach as "the observer" demonstrates how Mann envisioned homosexuality as visual, "an aesthetic and nonphysical phenomenon," which is what we observe in Marcus's fiction and his interpretation of Goethe.[189]

While the protagonist Aschenbach "promotes a Hellenizing, masculinist, antiliberal, antimedical understanding of sexuality," the narrator offers "liberal presumptions of homosexual identity as a characteristic of a fixed, biological, pathological, and gender-inverted minority."[190] Mann rejected the "moralistic, pathological, medicinal and humanitarian outlook" in favor of a "symbolic, spiritual, and cultural" view that homoeroticism is aesthetic, that men's desire for men is visual, a desire that cannot be realized, "an aesthetic and nonphysical phenomenon," a desire "primarily satisfied through visual observation."[191] The reader is offered a synthesis of Aschenbach's "antiliberal, masculinist critique of identity" and the narrator's "liberal understanding of the third sex as a minority."[192] The dialectical resolution is the suggestion that "(homo)sexual identity is the product of Western culture, typical for Western culture, and produces art that is central to Western society."[193] Homosexuality does not always have to be traced to ancient Greece; it is a product of the modern West. For Marcus, we can replace "Western" with "German," and for Marcus, the central artist is Goethe rather than someone from the Renaissance or ancient eras.

Heinrich's Tadzio is Ulrich. Heinrich is tormented by the absent presence of Waldemar and the nearness of Ulrich. Heinrich's thoughts and the dark stillness are broken when Ulrich says he can not sleep and he wants to join the older boy in bed: "Taking on ghostly, light form, like a resurrected boy Lazarus, he rises from the other bed as from a sarcophagus and stands in his nightshirt next to me." Then he gets into bed, and they lay so close that "when we speak, I can drink his fresh and pure breath, which inebriates me." Sometimes entwining his younger body around him, Ulrich declares Heinrich is the friend for whom he always longed. But Heinrich is more circumspect "because I cannot trust myself. Because he is innocent and suspects nothing." Ulrich finally falls asleep, and Heinrich slips quietly over to the other bed, where he can be embraced vicariously by the other boy's aura.[194]

Safe a short distance away in the other bed, Heinrich muses that during the conversation they shared in bed together, "both spoke with a strange enthusiasm, as if two souls rose to an unknown heaven." Although he had to keep silent what was stirring within him, Heinrich finds it delicious irony that while on the outside he appears as though all is quiet and in conformity with societal expectations, he keeps the secret, his desire for the other boy, that within him bursts a mighty force, a gushing stream, the passion of a martyr. Again comparing himself to Saint Sebastian and his body to a church, he finds it a "delicious awareness that a spring lies in the deep along with the crypt in whom lies a saintly martyr" below the apse and altar. The relationship between them "remained, as it had begun, and how it also should remain."[195] It was never consummated.

A perfect expression of unconsummated desire is suggested in the way Mann describes Hanno Buddenbrook's piano playing: "It swelled, it broadened, it slowly, slowly rose: suddenly, in the forte, he introduced the discord C sharp, which led back to the original key." Then "he dwelt on the dissonance until it became fortissimo. But he denied himself and his audience the resolution; he kept it back. What would it be, this resolution, this enchanting, satisfying absorption into the B major chord? A joy beyond compare, a gratification of overpowering sweetness! Peace! Bliss! The kingdom of Heaven: only not yet—not yet!" Instead, "a moment more of striving, hesitation, suspense, that must become well-nigh intolerable to heighten the ultimate moment of joy.—Once more—a last, a final tasting of this striving and yearning, this craving of the entire being, this last forcing of the will to deny oneself the fulfillment and the conclusion, in the knowledge that joy, when it comes, lasts only for the moment."[196]

For Hanno as for Mann, for Heinrich as for Marcus, and for Marcus's Goethe, to have and to keep the penultimate forms of intimacy "meant that I had to constantly forego wanting to obtain the ultimate." This was what made Heinrich lose weight and appear "hungry." It was "hunger for the last stage of intimacy, which remained unsatisfied, which had to remain unrequited." This yearning, "this hunger is the same hunger that makes the bird sing and the poet write poetry. Satisfied birds do not sing, and sated poets write no more verse."[197]

Conclusion

A Goethe Mosque for Berlin

On the outskirts of Basel, Switzerland, a sculpture in gray stone, partially covered in green moss, depicts a mother and daughter. Their faces are worn away by years of snow and sun. The mother is lying on her back. She crosses her left hand over her right at her belly, and her right bare foot sits atop her left. Her daughter lies to her right, her knees doubled up upon the ground, her upper body astride her mother's chest. Her left arm grips her mother's right shoulder, and she reaches her right arm to the crown of her mother's head. Neck to neck, both turn their heads to the right in a sublime expression of surrender.

The statue lies near a stone marked "Grave of the Lonely," which is next to a grove of aspen trees. There the ashes of the cremated who have no heirs are spread in the communal grave at Friedhof am Hornli (Cemetery at Hornli). Am Hornli is the largest cemetery in Switzerland, with approximately forty thousand individual and family graves. Among the best known are historian of art and culture Jacob Burckhardt (1818–1897), Protestant theologian Karl Barth (1886–1968), and philosopher Karl Jaspers (1883–1969), who had signed the 1925 petition to rescind Paragraph 175. How many have been buried in the communal grave is unknown. This book has explored the life of one of them.

MARCUS'S FINAL YEARS

Marcus's main form of identity in Swiss exile was his Third Reich passport, which he was compelled to use as an identity card.[1] He had managed to escape Nazi Germany, but he had to retain the document, stamped with a large red "J" for "Jude"

(Jew), filled with nearly a dozen swastikas, including two framing his photo, as it was his only form of official identity. The photo shows a gaunt Marcus, his thin face framed by an outdated elegance—a fancy, upturned, patterned tie, a starched white collar, and a black suitcoat—betraying his look of terror. Finally, twenty-five years after receiving it, very near the end of his life, he was able to rid himself of it by exchanging it for a Swiss foreigner's pass.

Although Marcus was granted permanent asylum in 1947 and was given a ten-year fixed-term permanent residency permit (*Niederlassungsbewilligung*) in 1957, he was never granted Swiss citizenship.[2] He possessed an *Ausländer Ausweis* (foreigner's identity card), which he had to keep renewing. As a sickly and frail eighty-four-year-old, he applied for (and received) a *Pass für Ausländer* (foreigner's passport).[3] Did he apply for it because he wanted to be rid once and for all of his swastika-marred World War II–era passport? Did he want to regain the ability to travel whenever and wherever he wished, robbed from him a quarter of a century earlier? But did he realize it was unlikely he would ever leave Switzerland? Did he just want to possess a document that would confirm the name and identity he chose for himself? In his application for the passport, he declared he had left his homeland for "racial/political reasons." Likewise, he claimed he did not return for "political reasons." Was he objecting to the treatment of gays? He expressed a desire to travel abroad in summer 1964. But if the eighty-four-year-old was not planning to travel to Germany, where was he headed? Was it to his birthplace, formerly part of imperial Germany, which was now located in Poland, to visit the grave of Roman? Or was it the Raczyński Library in Poznań, to which he had asked Roman to deliver two sealed packages of manuscripts?

Ironically, the new passport retained one crucial stain from the Nazi era: it gives his name as Mr. Hugo Israel Marcus, the Jewish name the Nazis had forced him to adopt.[4] When Marcus had submitted the application, he had typed his first name as "Hugo" alone. But a diligent official, relying on the Nazi-era documents provided as proof of identity, corrected the application and penciled in "Israel" in pink next to "Hugo." Free at last of the Nazi passport, Marcus's new Swiss passport still identified him as a Jew. He never used it.

Marcus continued to write homoerotic fiction and nonfiction for *Der Kreis* and was in contact with its affiliated gay activists until the end of his long life. In 1965, on the thirtieth anniversary of Hirschfeld's death, an eighty-five-year-old Marcus offered this rousing declaration: "Magnus Hirschfeld died of a stroke on May 14, 1935 in exile in Nice—driven there by an ignominious injustice. The most beautiful task remains to continue his great work of liberation internationally and (more) effectively than he was able to achieve at that time."[5] Marcus was describing himself. He, too, was unjustly driven into exile and had promoted Hirschfeld's aims internationally. And he, too, would die in exile.

While hospitalized that autumn, Marcus received a letter from the editor of *Der Kreis*, Rolf Meier, providing him with Kurt Hiller's address and an update on when his latest contributions, including "Journal intime," would be published.[6] Meier wanted Marcus to review Hiller's latest book and sent him a draft of *Archangelos*—"a collection of poems written in the years from 1934 to 1947"[7]—because Marcus's writing was "still clear and composed."[8] Marcus had the manuscript in his possession when he died.

From letters exchanged between Hiller in Hamburg and Meier in Zürich, it would appear that Marcus had a very solitary existence the last decade of his life. The two had only sporadic contact with the latter, living at a retirement home in Basel. Meier attempted to have more frequent contact with Marcus through a middleman, but without success. Marcus permitted contact only when he wanted.[9] It is conventional wisdom that Marcus and Hiller were close until Marcus's conversion, when they broke off relations, only coming into contact again in the 1960s. However, they exchanged letters and unpublished manuscripts during the war and immediately after, as discussed in chapter 4. Armin Wegner was worried about Marcus, having visited him in Basel. He tried to organize home help for Marcus, proposing that he could also financially support him if Marcus decided to go to a sanatorium.[10]

In fact, Marcus and his cousin Leonie kept in close contact, and she made sure he was well attended to. In September 1965 Leonie wrote to the hospital in Basel where Marcus was staying.[11] She had been informed that Marcus's health had improved. She wrote to ask what would happen to him when he no longer needed hospital care. Previously he had been staying at a small hotel, but its owner was in poor health and would be unable to take care of Marcus when he was discharged. The building was apparently not suitable—it had no elevator, the stairs were difficult, there was no bell in his room (should he need to call for assistance), and there was no one there to help him. The home was poorly heated. He could not return there. She asked them to recommend a nursing home and informed them she would travel from Zürich to Basel in October and would like to meet with them then to discuss Marcus's care. As it turns out, Marcus stayed with her at her home in Zürich for a month that autumn.[12] She also made sure he was taken care of by the local Jewish charity organization; she visited him in his new care home in November and spoke with him on the phone.[13] She did everything she could for him, to make sure he was comfortable where he was, and to find him other accommodations when needed. She acted like a caring mother, telling him to be sure he covers his legs with a blanket when he rides in a taxi.[14]

After returning to his retirement home after a hospitalization at the end of 1965, Marcus became even more isolated from his homosexual friends. Meier reported to Hiller that "from my middleman in Basel I learned that Hans Alienus is not so ill as we feared, but is old and somewhat helpless, yet stubborn—he did not want to receive the comrades who really are helpful, but the middleman will return with a small present before the holiday."[15] At the end of 1965 Marcus was sent to the geriatric hospital of the Adullam Foundation, next to the university in whose Philosophy Department he spent much of his first years in exile (1942–1947).[16] In April 1966, after Marcus wrote him a brief letter, Meier sent him a book to read.[17]

Less than a week after that letter, Meier informed Hiller, "Sad news: Hans Alienus/Hugo Marcus passed away on Sunday, April 17th in Basel."[18] Marcus was not buried in Basel's Jewish cemetery, and not in Zürich's alongside his mother, which his cousin Leonie could presumably have arranged. At that time there was no Muslim cemetery in Basel.[19] "Based on his express desire," Meier relates, Marcus's passing "was not mentioned in the daily newspapers. According to the instructions given in his will he also did not want any eulogies or funeral sermon, and did not want his ashes to be preserved."[20] But "the city of Basel cannot honor this last desire because after some time the city buries all ashes from the deceased who die alone, together with the urns, in the forest cemetery in the large communal Grave of the Lonely, which of course Alienus could not have known." Marcus was similar to his friend, Hirschfeld, in that both wished to be cremated—contrary to Jewish tradition—and did not want any eulogies or a religious ceremony led by a rabbi. Contrary to his wishes, Hirschfeld's funeral did feature a rabbi, although the sexologist was cremated.[21] Marcus was also cremated, contrary to Muslim tradition. As Manfred Backhausen notes, "one can only guess why Dr. Marcus was not buried according to Islamic rite. He appears not to have desired belonging to any Islamic community in Switzerland—his own community, the Lahore-Ahmadi-Movement was not represented there."[22]

Meier perceived it as "a very solitary death. The comrade in Basel, who called upon him once and spoke with him on my behalf also did not know of his death, and he [Marcus] also did not have the manager of the retirement home report it to him. Thus he had willfully closed himself off to all who wanted to come closer to him, and has passed in great isolation." Meier had wanted to quickly let Hiller know. Marcus "had asked that two gentlemen in Germany be informed of his death; the manager (of the retirement home) has not revealed their names. I still have a number of manuscripts from him— . . . homoeroticism hardly perceptible."[23] Meier could not let go of the isolated death of his comrade, Hans Alienus, who "was quite helpless, but had, as my source in Basel said, kindly rejected every offer of help. I do not believe that he was completely poverty stricken, because residency in a retirement home is not cheap in Switzerland. My source will soon come to Zürich and I will try and learn more." He regrets his own behavior: "What a shame that I did not speak to him more when he was alive. After his last letter I could not have supposed that the end was so near, because he still asked for appropriate literature."[24] Meier was surprised to learn of Marcus's religious convictions from Hiller: "I had not known that Alienus had converted to Islam, but (knowing this) now clarifies for me something about his attitude. Hence it also makes it clear why he had wanted his departure (from this world) to be silent."[25]

Soon after Meier penned the obituary of "Hans Alienus" for *Der Kreis*:

> Our coworker of many years, who had earlier contributed subtle articles to our journal, has passed away. He was a member of the Stefan George circle, which shaped his behavior, and greatly influenced his creative oeuvre. He was always occupied with the master-apprentice relationship in his short stories and pieces from his novels, and he never tired of portraying it in new ways. This inner belonging shaped his style of speech and made it appear slightly alienated from the present. But everything that he wrote had a high nobility of attitude, far removed from superficiality and vulgarity.
>
> When he was young he converted to Islam and this also resulted in his solitary death, which for him, like for all Muslims, possesses no terror, rather only the logical consequence of temporal being. He lived a long life, intellectually vibrant to the end. We will never forget him among our ranks.[26]

In a condolence letter sent to Marcus's cousin Leonie, Stefan George disciple Edith Landmann's son, Michael, refers to Marcus as "an unforgettable friend, who fought for his cause to the end."[27]

A brief notice on the occasion of a birthday six years earlier in the German-Jewish community newspaper offers a different description of the same man:

> On July 6 the writer Hugo Marcus, who has lived in Basel since emigrating from Germany, will celebrate his 80th birthday. Marcus, who developed his own philosophy of nature, and created the concept of "monopluralism," became known through the publication of numerous philosophical writings and books. After settling in Switzerland he wrote, "The Ornamental Beauty of the Landscape," and "The Metaphysics of Justice." The study, "The Foundations of Reality as Regulators of Language" was only recently published by Bonner Press.[28]

Rather than pay respect to Hans Alienus, a Muslim author of homosexual fiction, this birthday notice celebrates a writer and philosopher of Jewish origins named Hugo Marcus.

Until his dying day Marcus kept many volumes of *Der Kreis* published between 1948 and 1966, two volumes of *Moslemische Revue*—one that contained his long discourse on Islam and fatalism including Goethe's interpretation of Islamic fatalism, published despite the "racial laws" in Germany, and the journal's final issue, from December 1939, that included a book review published by "Dr. H.," which may have been Marcus[29]—*Die Nürnberger Gesetze* (The Nuremberg Laws), Spinoza's *Ethics*, letters from Roman, and a copy of his homoerotic novella, *Das Frühlingsglück*.

A GOETHE MOSQUE FOR BERLIN

The year Marcus died, the Social Democrats governed the Federal Republic of Germany (in coalition) for the first time since serving in the coalition government of 1928–1930, when Paragraph 175 was almost rescinded. The Social Democrat justice minister called for its repeal, and in 1969 Paragraph 175 was amended, decriminalizing homosexual acts between adult males (set at 21 years). Following German reunification in 1990, Paragraph 175 was finally abolished in 1994, 123 years after it was made law.[30] The "disgrace of the century" was history. Men were finally given the right over themselves, on par with other citizens.

Especially since the reunification of Germany, Berlin has become renowned for being an open, multicultural metropolis, boasting a reborn Jewish community and especially large gay population. Berlin's Jewish communities, from liberal to orthodox, encompassing Russian immigrants and German converts, have grown in numbers and visibility, just as the Jewish past has been memorialized by the state through such landmarks as the Jewish Museum in Kreuzberg (opened in 2001), which welcomed its tenth million visitor in 2015, and the Memorial to the Murdered Jews of Europe (its 2005 opening ceremony broadcast live on national German television), located next to the city's central landmark, the Brandenburg Gate.[31] Across the street from the Holocaust memorial, the same foundation also completed the Memorial to the Homosexuals Persecuted Under the National Socialist Regime (opened in 2008) in Tiergarten park.[32] Berlin, which hosts an annual ten-day Queer Days festival, the largest (and longest) gay and lesbian festival in Europe, also boasts the Schwules (Gay) Museum (established in 1985, its spacious new building opened in Tiergarten in 2013), "one of the world's largest and most significant institutions for archiving, researching and communicating the history and culture of LGBTQ communities."[33] These memorials and museums were opened or expanded during the era of long-serving openly gay Social Democratic mayor Klaus Wowereit (in office 2001–2014), who famously declared "I am gay, and that is a good thing." As a further illustration of how times have changed, Switzerland presented the docudrama *Der Kreis* as its nominee for Best Foreign Language Film at the Academy Awards in 2014. And in the summer of 2017 Germany voided the convictions of fifty thousand men prosecuted under Paragraph 175 after World War II.[34]

In German-speaking Europe such a visible presence and celebration of both groups—and state memorialization and condemnation of anti-Semitic and homophobic violence as well as determined attempts to replace persecution with justice—is a relatively recent phenomenon. Concerning Vienna, Matti Bunzl argues that, since the 1990s, Jews and queers "emerged as prominent components" of the city's "urban topography," and "even more remarkably, the state, formerly the principal agent in the violent abjection of Jews and homosexuals, became the strongest champion of Jewish and queer participation" in the city's cultural landscape.[35] What is true for Vienna is equally valid for Berlin. Today Jews and queers are more visible than at any other point in Berlin's (and Vienna's and Zürich's) history. As Jews and gays have been incorporated into the imagined national community and their presence celebrated as evidence of overcoming of past exclusion and violence, Muslims are the group now targeted for rejection from the body politic.[36]

Diverse communities of Muslims, mainly Turkish migrants, who first arrived en masse beginning over a decade after the end of World War II, and their descendants, especially concentrated in such neighborhoods as Kreuzberg and Neukölln, make up as many as 10 percent of Berlin residents today. The Şehitlik Cami (Martyrdom Mosque, completed in 2005) in Neukölln, a near replica of a sixteenth-century Ottoman mosque, with space for 1,500 worshippers, is the most impressive of Muslim houses of worship in the city.[37] The mosque is evidence of the recent growth of the foreign-origin Muslim population.

Tens of thousands of Germans have also converted to Islam in the past five decades since the mass arrival of Muslim immigrants. As Esra Özyürek has found, today in Berlin, "some German converts try to open up a legitimate space for Islam by disassociating it from Turks and Arabs," as Marcus had in the 1920s and 1930s, by promoting the view "that Islam can be experienced as a German religion."[38] Some argue "that being German is not only compatible with but also can even lead to a better way of being Muslim, and some advance the idea that becoming Muslim can be an especially proper way of being German." Based in a room within a church in Moabit, Berlin's newest mosque community may have appealed to Hugo Marcus had he lived to see it. Opened in summer 2017, the Ibn Rushd-Goethe Mosque is billed as Germany's "first liberal mosque."[39] According to one of the cofounders, Seyran Ateş, the mosque was named after the German poet since Goethe "was a great admirer" of Islam, engaged with the Qur'an and Sufism in "West-östlichen Diwan," and was "a bridge builder between East and West."[40] As cofounder Mimoun Azizi explains, Goethe "admired Islamic mysticism, philosophy and theology, read the *ghazals* of the Persian poet Hafiz as intensively as he studied the Qur'an . . . rid Voltaire's tragedy, 'Muhammad' of prejudice as he translated it into German . . . saw Muhammad as a warm, loving, innocent soul . . . studied Arabic . . . and wrote, 'If Islam means submission unto God, then we all live and die in Islam.' "[41] The community places great emphasis on gender equality, as men and women pray together at Friday prayer led by male and female imams, soon to include Ateş.[42] The mosque, "a model project also for Europe," cofounded by the author of *Islam Needs a Sexual Revolution*, is also open to open homosexuals, including a gay imam who founded a liberal mosque in Marseille.[43] He is expected to also preside over prayers.[44] The mosque community's preamble explicitly welcomes people "of all sexual orientations and identities."[45] The founders boast that it is the first inclusive mosque in Germany. It is the second, when one considers the history of the Ahmadi mosque community and its queer convert, Hugo Marcus.

Notes

INTRODUCTION: GOETHE AS POLE STAR

1. Nachlass Hugo Marcus, "Lebenslauf," end of 1956. Hirschfeld founded the organization in 1897 and led it until 1929. For Marcus's relationship with Hirschfeld, see Hans Alienus (pseudonym for Hugo Marcus), "Erinnerung an Magnus Hirschfeld," 6. There is a Hirschfeld Memorial in Charlottenburg, Berlin; in 1982 scholars and activists established the Magnus Hirschfeld Society; and in 2011 the federal German government established the Magnus Hirschfeld Foundation in Berlin to pursue his aims including fighting against discrimination against homosexuals in German society. See the homepage of the Magnus Hirschfeld Gesellschaft, http://magnus-hirschfeld.de/, and the homepage of the Bundesstiftung Magnus Hirschfeld, http:/mh-stiftung.de. On Hirschfeld, see Wolff, *Magnus Hirschfeld*; Herzer, *Magnus Hirschfeld*; Herrn, *100 Years of the Gay Rights Movement in Germany*; Dose, *Magnus Hirschfeld: Deutscher–Jude–Weltbürger*; Herzog, *Sex After Fascism*, 19–25; Mancini, *Magnus Hirschfeld and the Quest for Sexual Freedom*; and Dose, *Magnus Hirschfeld: The Origins of the Gay Liberation Movement.*
2. Hiller, *§ 175*, 1. See esp. "Recht und sexuelle Minderheiten," 105–18. Hiller led the Wissenschaftlich-humanitäres Komitee from 1929 until its closure in 1933. On Marcus's relationship with Hiller, see Hiller, *Leben gegen die Zeit*, 1:74, 107, 408. Hiller, who wrote a two-volume autobiography, is also well known; there is a vibrant Kurt Hiller Society in his native Hamburg and a Kurt-Hiller-Park in Schöneberg, Berlin. See the homepage of the Kurt Hiller Gesellschaft, http://www.hiller-gesellschaft.de/.
3. Leck, *Georg Simmel and Avant-Garde Sociology*, 13.
4. Leck, *Georg Simmel and Avant-Garde Sociology*, 15–16.
5. Tobin, *Peripheral Desires*, 182.
6. Norton, *Secret Germany*; Ruehl, "Aesthetic Fundamentalism in Weimar Poetry"; and Lane and Ruehl, Introduction to *A Poet's Reich.*
7. The more well-known Jewish converts to Islam in this period—Lev Nussimbaum / Essad Bey and Leopold Weiss / Muhammad Asad—did not join the Ahmadi mosque community but the Islamische Gemeinde zu Berlin.
8. *Die Allgemeine Bildung in Vergangenheit, Gegenwart und Zukunft*; *Meditationen*; *Musikästhetische Probleme auf vergleichend-ästhetischer Grundlage*; *Die Philosophie des Monopluralismus*; *Die*

ornamentale Schönheit der Landschaft; and *Vom Zeichnerischen, Malerischen, Plastischen und Architektonischen*.

9. Bisno, "Stefan George's Homoerotic *Erlösungsreligion*, 1891–1907," 46.
10. Marcus, *Meditationen*, 107, 199–200.
11. Marcus, *Meditationen*, 79.
12. Hiller, *Leben gegen die Zeit*, 1:107; and Leck, Georg *Simmel and Avant-Garde Sociology*, 171.
13. The family was compensated much later in "completely deflated Posen Marks." Nachlass Hugo Marcus, Hugo Marcus, Basel, Switzerland, to President Theodor Heuss, Bonn, Federal Republic of Germany, October 27, 1958.
14. Perhaps he had made his first contact with the mosque community when he was sent by one of the liberal dailies for which he wrote; perhaps he was introduced by one of his gay writer acquaintances who had already made contact, such as Hermann Hesse (b. 1877, Calw, Germany; d. 1962, Montagnola, Switzerland) or Thomas Mann (b. 1875, Lübeck; d. 1955, Zürich); or perhaps some combination of homosexual friends and professional duties—contacts in the gay community who were also writing for liberal newspapers, such as Dr. Max Jordan (1896–1977)—had put him in touch.
15. "Islam in Germany: Great German Scholar Won, First Eid Celebrated," 1. Marcus was not actually a "Dr." Although he studied at Friedrich Wilhelm University in Berlin, he did not earn a doctorate. Despite this fact, Ahmadi would address Marcus as "Dr." from their first contacts with him in the 1920s to their last exchanges three decades later. Labeling Marcus "Dr." speaks to the Ahmadi desire to promote a positive image of the organization and of Islam, promoting the bourgeois notion that the best-educated and, hence, most intelligent echelon of German society was converting.
16. The 1925 petition to repeal Paragraph 175 can be found online at http://www.schwulencity.de/Sexus_Paragraph_267.html. On the history of the petition, see Moeller, "The Regulation of Male Homosexuality"; and Moeller, "Private Acts, Public Anxieties."
17. It is not possible to determine how many lectures he gave at the mosque. Over three dozen lectures on Islam are found among his personal papers, several of which were published as articles in *Moslemische Revue*.
18. Marcus, "The Message of the Holy Prophet Muhammad to Europe," 223.
19. Marcus, "The Message of the Holy Prophet Muhammad to Europe," 284.
20. Marcus, "The Message of the Holy Prophet Muhammad to Europe," 285.
21. Marcus, "The Message of the Holy Prophet Muhammad to Europe," 286. Arguing along these lines in a lecture given in the mosque in the 1930s, Marcus criticizes the mechanization of society and culture, asserting a role for religious people in putting it back on the right path. He distinguishes between two opposites: "the religious person," which Marcus considers himself, and the "technical person." The former "serves his God," whereas the latter wants "to be part of God," in other words, has lost sight of the fact that people are servants of God and not God themselves, despite their technological progress. Nachlass Hugo Marcus, "Der religiöse Mensch und der technische Mensch."
22. Gay, *Weimar Culture*, 7.
23. On Goethe's views of Islam, see esp. Mommsen, *Goethe und die arabische Welt*; and Mommsen, *Goethe and the Poets of Arabia*.
24. Germain, "The First Muslim Missions on a European Scale," 105; and Motadel, "Islamische Bürgerlichkeit-Das soziokulturelle milieu."

25. Weitz, *Weimar Germany*, 2, 39.
26. Hesse, "Die Sehnsucht unser Zeit nach einer Weltanschauung," 366.
27. Hesse, "Die Sehnsucht unser Zeit nach einer Weltanschauung," 366.
28. Fritzsche, "The Economy of Experience in Weimar Germany," 369.
29. Fritzsche, "Landscape of Danger, Landscape of Design," 44–45.
30. Canning, "Introduction," 3. Canning is referring in particular to Föllmer, Graf and Leo, "Einleitung," 10–11, 21.
31. Graf and Föllmer, "The Culture of Crisis in the Weimar Republic."
32. Kaes, Jay, and Dimendberg, Preface to *The Weimar Republic Sourcebook*.
33. Baer, "Muslim Encounters with Nazism and the Holocaust." For Marcus's account of the events of 1935 and 1938, see Nachlass Hugo Marcus, "Lebenslauf," end of 1956.
34. See Baer, "Muslim Encounters with Nazism and the Holocaust." For Nazi relations with Islam and Muslims during World War II, see Motadel, *Islam and Nazi Germany's War.*
35. On Taqi al-Din al-Hilali, one of Nazi Radio Berlin's main Arabic service speakers, see Lauzière, "The Evolution of the Salafiyya"; Ryad, "A *Salafi* Student"; and Lauzière, *The Making of Salafism*, especially chap. 4, 130–62.
36. On the mufti's collaboration with Hitler, espousal of Nazi anti-Semitism, and support of the genocide of the Jews of Europe and the Middle East, see Höpp, *Mufti-Papiere*; Bauknecht, *Muslime in Deutschland*, 117–26; Wildangel, *Zwischen Achse und Mandatsmacht*, 331–32, 336–43; and Achcar, *The Arabs and the Holocaust*, 150–58. As Philip Mattar has observed, most accounts of al-Husayni either vilify or glorify him, which tells us more about the politics of the biographers than about the Palestinian leader. Mattar, *The Mufti of Jerusalem*, xiii–xiv.
37. To see how it has impacted the historiography of the Jewish past in Islamic history in general and that of Egypt, Iraq, and Morocco in particular, see Cohen, *Under Crescent and Cross*, chap. 1; Beinin, *The Dispersion of Egyptian Jewry*; Bashkin, *New Babylonians*; and Boum, *Memories of Absence*.
38. As an example, see Wiesenthal, *Grossmufti*. See Höpp, "The Suppressed Discourse," 213–16.
39. Novick, *The Holocaust in American Life*, 158.
40. Aderet, "Yad Vashem Names Egyptian First Arab Righteous Among the Nations"; and the Yad Vashem website, https://www.yadvashem.org/righteous/stories/helmy-szturmann.html. See also Steinke, *Der Muslim und die Jüdin*.
41. Rudoren, "Netanyahu Denounced." As Israeli historian Moshe Zimmerman notes, Netanyahu's depicting Hitler as merely wanting to expel the Jews until the mufti told him to "burn them" instead "moves the responsibility of the Holocaust, for the destruction of the Jews, to the mufti and the Arab world," which is "intended to stain the Arabs of today because of the Arabs of the past." Many other historians and politicians in Israel condemned Netanyahu for these remarks.
42. Herf, *Nazi Propaganda for the Arab World*. For a similar view, see Gensicke, *The Mufti of Jerusalem and the Nazis*; and Mallmann and Cüppers, *Halbmond und Hakenkreuz*, translated into English with the redundant and extreme title *Nazi Palestine: The Plans for the Extermination of the Jews in Palestine*. But see Krämer, "Anti-Semitism in the Muslim World"; Wien, "Coming to Terms with the Past"; Nordbruch, "'Cultural Fusion' of Thought and Ambitions?"; and McKale, Review of Jeffrey Herf, Nazi Propaganda for the Arab World.

More nuanced studies that focus on French North Africa, such as Scheck, "Nazi Propaganda Toward French Muslim Prisoners of War," demonstrate that Nazi propaganda was largely ineffective in inciting Muslims to commit violence against Jews.

43. See Rubin and Schwanitz, *Nazis, Islamists, and the Making of the Modern Middle East*; and Boggioni, "Anti-Muslim Long Island Blogger."
44. Moreover, "in the majority of instances, fascination with fascist ideas (and elements of fascist politics, not all of them symbolic) did not stretch to include racism and anti-Semitism." Krämer, "Anti-Semitism in the Muslim World," 260. See also Wildangel, *Zwischen Achse und Mandatsmacht*, 143–57, 181–89; Gershoni and Jankowski, *Confronting Fascism in Egypt*, 281–82; Gershoni and Nordbruch, *Sympathie und Schrecken*; Nordbruch, *Nazism in Syria and Lebanon*, 135–36; Bashkin, *New Babylonians*, chap. 5; Gershoni, "Confronting Nazism in Egypt"; Gershoni, "Egyptian Liberalism in an Age of 'Crisis of Orientation'"; Gershoni, "'Der verfolgte Jude'"; Wildangel, "'Der größte Feind der Menschheit'"; Wien, *Iraqi Arab Nationalism*; and Bashkin, *The Other Iraq*.
45. Gerhard Höpp complains, "There is a discourse about Arab perpetrators, but none about Arab victims," see "The Suppressed Discourse," 170. See also Wien, "The Culpability of Exile: Arabs in Nazi Germany," 332.
46. For an exception, see Bauknecht, *Muslime in Deutschland*, 58–99.
47. For an analysis of Muslim encounters with Nazism in the Balkans, the Soviet Union, and other regions, see Motadel, *Islam and Nazi Germany's War*.
48. For this era, see Höpp, "Zwischen Moschee und Demonstration"; Höpp, "Zwischen Entente und Mittelmächten"; Höpp, "Zwischen Universität und Straße"; Nordbruch, "Arab Students in Weimar Germany"; Cwiklinski, *Die Wolga an der Spree*; Cwiklinski, "Between National and Religious Solidarities"; Guttstadt, *Turkey, the Jews, and the Holocaust*; and Baer, "Turk and Jew in Berlin."
49. An intriguing example of what is possible is found in Ghosh, *In an Antique Land*. On the study of Jews in India, see Egorova, *Jews and India*, 1–8. For an analysis of Jewish–Muslim relations in contemporary South Asia and how they are impacted by anti-Semitism, Islamophobia, and global politics, see Egorova, *Jews and Muslims in South Asia*.
50. By "Muslims in the Holocaust" I do not mean the figurative *Muselmänner* of Auschwitz, the Jews who had lost all will to live and were on the verge of annihilation, but actual Muslims. On the former term see Levi, *If This Is a Man*, 103; Agamben, *Remnants of Auschwitz*, 41–86; and Anidjar, *The Jew, the Arab*. On the latter term, see Höpp, "In the Shadow of the Moon." The consequences of Muslims being mistaken for Jews are explored in Motadel, "Veiled Survivors"; and Baer, "Mistaken for Jews."
51. See Satloff, *Among the Righteous*, chaps. 5–7; and Gershman, *Besa*; Katz, "Did the Paris Mosque Save Jews?" See also Kenbib, "Mohammed V, Protector of Moroccan Jews"; Stora, "Messali Hadj, the Refusal to Collaborate"; Kazdaghli, "The Tunisian Jews in the German Occupation"; and Steinfeldt, "Muslim Righteous Among the Nations."
52. Most studies focus on the mass migration of "guest workers" from Muslim-majority lands after World War II. See Herbert, *Geschichte der Ausländerpolitik in Deutschland*; Ercan Argun, *Turkey in Germany*; Göktürk, Gramling, and Kaes, *Germany in Transit*; Kosnick, *Migrant Media*; Yurdakul, *From Guest Workers into Muslims*; and Chin, *The Guest Worker Question in Postwar Germany*. Popular studies such as Johnson, *A Mosque in Munich*, and

Meining, *Eine Moschee in Deutschland* ignore the interwar period and the Ahmadi, focus on World War II and after, linking Nazis and the Muslim Brotherhood.

53. For a recent example, see Goldstein, Introduction to *Beyond Religious Borders.*
54. See Meri, Introduction to *Jewish-Muslim Relations*; Meri, *The Routledge Handbook of Muslim-Jewish Relations*; Cooperman and Zohar, *Jews and Muslims in the Islamic World*; Lassner, *Jews, Christians, and the Abode of Islam*; Montville, *History as Prelude*; Gottreich and Schroeter, *Jewish Culture and Society in North Africa*; Mazower, *Salonica, City of Ghosts*; Peters, *The Children of Abraham*; Gottreich, *The Mellah of Marrakesh*; Menocal, *The Ornament of the World*; Brann and Sutcliffe, *Renewing the Past, Reconfiguring Jewish Culture*; Levy, *Jews, Turks, Ottomans*; Meri, *The Cult of Saints Among Jews and Muslims in Medieval Syria*; Scheindlin, *Wine, Women and Death*; Scheindlin, *The Gazelle*; Wasserstrom, *Between Muslim and Jew*; Cohen, *Under Crescent and Cross*; Brann, *The Compunctious Poet*; Lewis, *The Jews of Islam*; Goitein, *A Mediterranean Society*; and Goitein, *Jews and Arabs.*
55. Meddeb and Stora, General Introduction to *A History of Jewish-Muslim Relations*, 16.
56. Boyarin, *Border Lines*, 1–2.
57. Freidenreich and Goldstein, *Beyond Religious Borders.* Despite its title, the volume does not contain a single essay concerning religious converts.
58. This includes the Ahmadi translation and commentary in German and Asad's *The Message of the Quran.*
59. See Baer, *The Dönme.*
60. Höpp, "Mohammed Essad Bey"; Reiss, *The Orientalist*; Asad, *The Road to Mecca*; Chaghatai, *Muhammad Asad*; Andrabi, *Muhammad Asad*; Kramer, "The Road from Mecca"; Windhager, *Leopold Weiss alias Muhammad Asad*; Nawwab, "A Matter of Love"; Hofmann, "Muhammad Asad"; Asad, "Muhammad Asad Between Religion and Politics"; and *A Road to Mecca.*
61. For another example, see Baer, "Turk and Jew in Berlin."
62. Endelman, *Radical Assimilation in English Jewish History, 1656–1945.*
63. Endelman, *Leaving the Jewish Fold*, 5, 11.
64. Endelman, *Leaving the Jewish Fold*, 5.
65. Hertz, *How Jews Became Germans*, 218.
66. Heschel, *Abraham Geiger and the Jewish Jesus*; Heschel, "Abraham Geiger and the Emergence of Jewish Philoislamism;" and Heschel, "German Jewish Scholarship on Islam"; Kramer, *The Jewish Discovery of Islam*; and Kalmar and Penslar, *Orientalism and the Jews.*
67. Miller, "The Contribution of Jewish Orientalists," 828.
68. Efron, "Orientalism and the Jewish Historical Gaze," 81; and Efron, *Germany Jewry and the Allure of the Sephardic*, 194.
69. Heschel, "German Jewish Scholarship on Islam," 106.
70. Efron, "Orientalism and the Jewish Historical Gaze," 85–87; and Cohen, "The 'Golden Age' of Jewish-Muslim Relations," 28.
71. Heschel, "German Jewish Scholarship on Islam," 95. See also Lassner, "Abraham Geiger," 106; Efron, "Orientalism and the Jewish Historical Gaze," 89; and Marchand, *German Orientalism in the Age of Empire*, 323–33.
72. Efron, *German Jewry and the Allure of the Sephardic*, 223.
73. Heschel, "German Jewish Scholarship on Islam," 91.

74. Heschel, "German Jewish Scholarship on Islam," 94.
75. Efron, "Orientalism and the Jewish Historical Gaze," 83.
76. Miller, "The Contribution of Jewish Orientalists," 829.
77. Efron, *German Jewry and the Allure of the Sephardic*, 207.
78. Graetz, *History of the Jews*, 4:271.
79. Graetz, *History of the Jews*, 4:271.
80. Graetz, *History of the Jews*, 4:364, 593.
81. Graetz, *History of the Jews*, 5:72, also quoted in Efron, "Orientalism and the Jewish Historical Gaze," 85–86.
82. Graetz, *History of the Jews*, 3:41, also quoted in Stillman, "History," 54. Mark Cohen credits Lewis, "The Pro-Islamic Jews," for recognizing that Graetz used the medieval model of Islamic tolerance of Jews to criticize his own modern society. Cohen, "The 'Golden Age' of Jewish-Muslim Relations," 28. For a detailed study of how nineteenth-century German Jewish intellectuals perceived medieval Sephardim as cultural mediators offering a model for successful integration, see Schapkow, *Role Model and Countermodel*.
83. Quoted in Heschel, "German Jewish Scholarship on Islam," 100.
84. Quoted in Efron, "Orientalism and the Jewish Historical Gaze," 89.
85. Quoted in Heschel, "German Jewish Scholarship on Islam," 101.
86. Efron, *German Jewry and the Allure of the Sephardic*, 223–24.
87. See Johnston-Bloom, "Jews, Muslims and *Bildung*," 50–51.
88. Heschel, "German Jewish Scholarship on Islam," 96. One also finds a liberal Jewish reading of Islam expressed by the orientalist Max Freiherr von Oppenheim (1860–1946). See Gossman, *The Passion of Max von Oppenheim*.
89. Reiss, *The Orientalist*, 145, 169, 193.
90. Reiss, *The Orientalist*, 199.
91. Reiss, *The Orientalist*, 195, 196. He had apparently made an attempt to convert to Islam in Constantinople two years earlier. Reiss, *The Orientalist*, 199.
92. Reiss, *The Orientalist*, 224, 227, 228.
93. Reiss, *The Orientalist*, photo preceding page 197.
94. Reiss, *The Orientalist*, 200, 203, 212.
95. Reiss, *The Orientalist*, 217.
96. Nawwab, "A Matter of Love," 161; and Hofmann, *Religion on the Rise*; and *A Road to Mecca*.
97. Dubrovic, *Veruntreute Geschichte*, 48.
98. Hofmann, "Muhammad Asad," 234–35.
99. Asad, *The Road to Mecca*, 49, 136, 185, 349.
100. Rubin, "Muhammad Asad's Conversion to Islam," 20.
101. Gioja, "Reasons for my Acceptance of Islam."
102. Talal Asad, Muhammad Asad's son, criticizes those who would see Asad as a bridge builder, for "he was concerned less with building bridges and more with immersing himself critically in the tradition of Islam that became his tradition, and with encouraging members of his community (Muslims) to adopt an approach that he considered to be its essence." Asad, "Muhammad Asad Between Religion and Politics."
103. For a brief account of de Haan's life, see Berkowitz, "Rejecting Zion, Embracing the Orient." De Haan helped Asad, then known as Leopold Weiss, gain his position as

Palestine correspondant for the *Frankfurter Zeitung*. Berkowitz, "Rejecting Zion, Embracing the Orient," 114.

104. Kalmar and Penslar, "Orientalism and the Jews," xviii.
105. I have found only one photo of Marcus in "Oriental" garb, wearing a fez; he scowls at the camera with arms folded.
106. Mosse, *German Jews Beyond Judaism*, 2.
107. Sutcliffe, "Religion and the Birth of Jewish Radical Politics," 34.
108. Löwy, *Redemption and Utopia*.
109. Biale, *Not in the Heavens*, 24-25.
110. Biale, *Not in the Heavens*, 25.
111. Sutcliffe, "Religion and the Birth of Radical Politics," 34.
112. Sorkin, *The Transformation of German Jewry, 1780–1840*; and Beller, *Antisemitism*, 32-33.
113. See the collection of essays in Berghahn and Hermand, *Goethe in German-Jewish Culture*.
114. Brenner, *The Renaissance of Jewish Culture in Weimar Germany*; Hermand, "German Jews Beyond Judaism," 240-44; Volkov, "German Jewish History," 225-27.
115. Herrn, *100 Years of the Gay Rights Movement in Germany*, 26.
116. For a dramatization, see the docudrama *Der Kreis*. For further insight into this era, see Bauer, *Queer 1950s*.
117. Tobin, *Peripheral Desires*, 83.
118. Tobin, *Peripheral Desires*, 84.
119. Tobin, *Peripheral Desires*, 231, 233.
120. See, esp., Tobin, *Peripheral Desires*; and Tobin, *Warm Brothers*.
121. Tobin, *Warm Brothers*, 5, 23, 35.
122. El-Tayeb, "'Gays who cannot properly be gay'," 80.
123. El-Tayeb, *European Others*, 167-68.
124. Manfred Backhausen was the first to provide a sketch of his life and work. See "Der deutsche Muslim Dr. Hamid Hugo Marcus," in Backhausen, *Die Lahore-Ahmadiyya-Bewegung in Europa*, 110-19. Because the author was unable to examine Marcus's private papers, unfortunately his account contains factual errors. A more extensive engagement with Marcus's work appears in Jonker, *The Ahmadiyya Quest for Religious Progress*. However, Gerdien Jonker avoids discussing Marcus's homosexuality, which limits the value of her interpretation of his life and the Ahmadi mission. A briefer sketch that also contains errors appears in the catalogue of exhibits *Goodbye to Berlin?*, 125-26, which is the reference given for a one-paragraph version of his life, also replete with factual errors, "Marcus, Hugo," in *Mann für Mann*. Most accurate is Nipp, "Hugo Marcus." The article emphasizes his being Muslim, referring to his religion as Islam, and is accompanied by the single photograph of him wearing Muslim dress (a fez). Marcus wrote a brief bibliographic essay which has long been out of print. Marcus, *Einer sucht den Freund*.

1. FIGHTING FOR GAY RIGHTS IN BERLIN, 1900–1925

1. Quoted in Tobin, *Warm Brothers*, 194.
2. Hirschfeld, *Sappho und Sokrates*, 35, quoted in Herzer, *Magnus Hirschfeld*, 97. Rosa Winkel (pink triangle, 1975) is the first gay publisher in West Berlin. Hirschfeld wrote this

pamphlet, "a manifesto, a call to arms against the prevailing prejudice against homosexuals," which contains "the most important arguments for amending the criminal code" in the wake of the Oscar Wilde trial in London in 1895. That cause célèbre motivated him to pen this pamphlet and found the Wissenschaftlich-humanitäres Komitee (WhK) a year later. Herrn, *100 Years of the Gay Rights Movement in Germany*, 8–9.

3. From the hotel's website: http://www.quisisana.com/en/index.
4. Small portrait of a young Hugo Marcus, A. Alberino, Capri, July 1901. Bildnis Hugo Marcus, Portr. Slg/Lit. kl/Marcus, Hugo, Nr. 1, Staatsbibliothek zu Berlin-Preussischer Kulturbesitz, Handschriftenabteilung. (Back) Hugo Marcus, Juli 1901, Studio Fotografico, A.Alberino.
5. Tobin, *Warm Brothers*, 57.
6. Tobin, *Warm Brothers*, 97.
7. Goethe, *Italian Journey*, 129.
8. *Goethes Werke: Herausgegeben im Auftrage der Großherzogin Sophie von Sachsen*, 1.5.2: 381, quoted in Tobin, *Warm Brothers*, 97. Goethe's modern English translator of *Italian Journey*, W. H. Auden, was himself a sex tourist who took pleasure in the young male prostitutes in Weimar Berlin. Beachy, *Gay Berlin*, ix–x, 188–200. Auden would marry Klaus Mann's sister, Erika, who was, in today's terms, bisexual.
9. Beachy, *Gay Berlin*, 219.
10. Hiller, "Appeal on Behalf of an Oppressed Human Variety," written for the Second International Congress for Sexual Reform (Copenhagen, 1928), delivered on his behalf by Magnus Hirschfeld.
11. Nachlass Hugo Marcus, "Aus fernen Tagen," 1.
12. Nachlass Hugo Marcus, "Aus fernen Tagen," 2.
13. Nachlass Hugo Marcus, "Aus fernen Tagen," 4.
14. Nachlass Hugo Marcus, "Aus fernen Tagen," 2.
15. Nachlass Hugo Marcus, "Aus fernen Tagen," 3.
16. Nachlass Hugo Marcus, "Aus fernen Tagen," 4.
17. Nachlass Hugo Marcus, "Aus fernen Tagen," 5.
18. Herzer, *Magnus Hirschfeld*, 74–75.
19. Hans Alienus (pseudonym for Hugo Marcus), "Erinnerung an Magnus Hirschfeld," 6. Homosexuality was "defined as the secret that always threatened to be revealed. No one, on the other hand, could reveal it like the Socialists." Spector, *Violent Sensations*, 137.
20. Marcus, "Aus fernen Tagen," 5.
21. Marcus, "Aus fernen Tagen," 7.
22. Nachlass Hugo Marcus, "Lebenslauf," end of 1956.
23. For a comprehensive history of the gay rights movement in Germany, see Herrn, *100 Years of the Gay Rights Movement in Germany*; for a more recent survey covering the period to the end of World War II, see Whisnant, *Queer Identities and Politics in Germany*.
24. Marcus, *Das Frühlingsglück*. The novella is 119 pages long. Long out of print, I read the copy included with his private papers, Nachlass Hugo Marcus.
25. Marcus, *Das Frühlingsglück*, 27.
26. Marcus, *Das Frühlingsglück*, 14, 16.

27. Marcus, *Das Frühlingsglück*, 29–30.
28. Marcus, *Das Frühlingsglück*, 35.
29. Marcus, *Das Frühlingsglück*, 56, 62.
30. Marcus, *Das Frühlingsglück*, 63.
31. Marcus, *Das Frühlingsglück*, 81.
32. Marcus, *Das Frühlingsglück*, 100.
33. Marcus, *Das Frühlingsglück*, 104.
34. Marcus, *Das Frühlingsglück*, 109.
35. Marcus, *Das Frühlingsglück*, 110.
36. Marcus, *Das Frühlingsglück*, 111.
37. Marcus, *Das Frühlingsglück*, 116.
38. Marcus, *Das Frühlingsglück*, 116–17.
39. Marcus, *Das Frühlingsglück*,, 117.
40. Tobin, *Peripheral Desires*, 44.
41. Goethe, *Wilhelm Meister's Apprenticeship*, 175.
42. Tobin, *Peripheral Desires*, 45.
43. Motto: Zwar lebt' ich ohne Sorg' und Mühe / Doch fühlt ich tiefen Schmerz genug. Goethe, *Wilhelm Meister's Apprenticeship*, 316. Another allusion in the book to Goethe's novel is a black-haired Italian boy, who calls to mind Goethe's Mignon. See Marcus, *Das Frühlingsglück*, 81–82.
44. Marcus, *Das Frühlingsglück*, 106.
45. Marcus, *Das Frühlingsglück*, 108.
46. Potempa, "Wir Poeten und Artisten," 709.
47. Potempa, "Wir Poeten und Artisten," 710.
48. The letters between Marcus and Mann are available at the Thomas Mann Archives, ETH Zürich, Dr. Hans Marco (Hugo Marcus), Berlin, to Thomas Mann, Munich, April 18, 1902.
49. Potempa, "Wir Poeten und Artisten," 709.
50. Potempa, "Wir Poeten und Artisten," 710.
51. Thomas Mann, Munich, to Dr. Hans Marco, Berlin, May 11, 1902; Potempa, "Wir Poeten und Artisten," 710; and Mann, *Buddenbrooks*, 585–86.
52. Potempa, "Wir Poeten und Artisten," 711.
53. Mann, *Buddenbrooks*, 827.
54. Mann, *Buddenbrooks*, 826. Emphasis in Mann's letter, not in the original text.
55. Potempa, "Wir Poeten und Artisten," 712.
56. Potempa, "Wir Poeten und Artisten," 712–13.
57. Potempa, "Wir Poeten und Artisten," 713.
58. Potempa, "Wir Poeten und Artisten," 714.
59. Marcus, *Die Allgemeine Bildung*, 6, quoted in Potempa, "Wir Poeten und Artisten," 714.
60. Marcus, *Meditationen*, 82–83, quoted in Potempa, "Wir Poeten und Artisten," 714.
61. Marcus, *Meditationen*, 165, quoted in Potempa, "Wir Poeten und Artisten," 714–15. On Höchstetter, see Marti, "Sophie Höchstetter."
62. Potempa, "Wir Poeten und Artisten," 715. Mann wrote Marcus again six months later, asking him to do him a favor by sending him his own response back, if he still possessed

it, so that Mann could borrow it. Thomas Mann, Munich, to Hugo Marcus, Berlin, January 1, 1904, quoted in Potempa, "Wir Poeten und Artisten," 716. He explained that working on some piece of writing reminded him of their correspondence, and he wished to reread his own letter, of which he had made no copy. Marcus promptly responded, pleased that Mann had remembered their correspondence. Hugo Marcus, Berlin, to Thomas Mann, Munich, January 4, 1904. He returned the letter, signing his own letter this time with his true name (717). The piece of writing that Mann was working on was his next literary piece, a book review entitled, "Gabriele Reuter," in the Berlin journal *Der Tag*, which appeared in two parts in February 1904, and indeed "the writer Thomas Mann was born." For in it he reflected less on the subject at hand, the life and work of Reuter, than on himself and his own artistic position (717–18). His thoughts were first formulated in his letter to Marcus, as were the important motifs which appear again in the Reuter piece, "like a thread, taken up again and spun" including the "talent of artists," "the posh individuals who benefit no one" (718). He even reuses a number of sentences from the original letter to Marcus, such as, "We poets and artists are already seen as a very dubious tribe" and "those among us who can not compensate society for their total uselessness by the delight of their talents, would do well to perish as soon as possible, instead of astonishing the public by means of extravagant demands," although Mann takes the edge off these cutting words by having the artist say them to himself, rather than directing them toward another, as in the original (718–19). Two and a half weeks later Mann sent his own letter back to Marcus. Thomas Mann, Munich, to Hugo Marcus, Berlin, January 21, 1904.

63. Marcus, *Meditationen*, 199–200.
64. Herrn, *100 Years of the Gay Rights Movement in Germany*, 4–6.
65. Dose, *Magnus Hirschfeld: Deutscher—Jude—Weltbürger*, 52. For an introduction to the history of Paragraph 175 in Germany, see *Die Geschichte des §175*; and Schäfer, "*Widernatürliche Unzucht*". For the text of the petition, see Hiller, *§ 175*, "Anhang: Die Petition," 119–29.
66. Marcus, *Meditationen*, 67.
67. The quotes are found in both Mancini, *Magnus Hirschfeld and the Quest for Sexual Freedom*, 27–28; and Mancini, "Boys in the City," 95.
68. Mancini, "Boys in the City," 95–96.
69. Mann, *The Turning Point*, 86–87. Also quoted in Beachy, *Gay Berlin*, ix.
70. Beachy, *Gay Berlin*, 189–91.
71. Beachy, *Gay Berlin*, 188, 196.
72. Mann, *The Turning Point*, 86.
73. Norton, *Secret Germany*, 122.
74. Mann, *The Turning Point*, 210.
75. Mann, *The Turning Point*, 210.
76. Gay, *Weimar Culture*, 47.
77. Quoted in Ruehl, "Aesthetic Fundamentalism in Weimar Poetry," 241.
78. "Fastidious young men": Mann, *The Turning Point*, 210; and "cultivate their inner life": Gay, *Weimar Culture*, 4.
79. In response to criticisms of the number of Jews in his circle, George quipped, "I could have another ten Jews in my circle like the Jews that I already have; it would not harm

me at all." Landmann, *Gespräche mit Stefan George*, 146. The conversation occurred between December 25, 1925, and February 6, 1926, and March 7–15, 1926, Basel. George did not refrain from anti-Semitic stereotypes. When the talk of the day was about the Zionists rebuilding Jerusalem, he said, "If that were the case, I would gladly donate money for it, if only to rile the Bible Thumpers, who do not want to allow it. But [it will not happen because] Sir Oppenheim has said: [he will not pay for it because] it is too expensive!" Landmann, *Gespräche mit Stefan George*, 200, conversation dated January 3-February 1929, Kiel. Like Marcus, Kantorowicz was also expected to take over the family business, in his case a liquor distillery, but like his older cousin, Ernst also studied philosophy at the university in Berlin before studying medieval history at Heidelberg where he fell under the sway of George. On Kantorowicz's work and his ambivalent response to the Nazi seizure of power, see Ruehl, "Imperium transcendat hominem." Kantorowicz is far better known for his postwar *The King's Two Bodies* than for his prewar panegyric to a king whom he portrayed as the heroic embodiment of the German nation, emphasizing his homoerotic, romantic, Mediterranean sides. On Kantorowicz's relationship to Marcus, see Nachlass Hugo Marcus, letter from Ernst Kantorowicz, Berkeley, California, to Cäcilie Markus [*sic*], Zürich, September 26, 1946. Kantorowicz addresses Marcus's mother as "aunt," and refers to himself as her nephew.

80. Norton, *Secret Germany*, 659. On May 10, 1933, the day of bonfires of "un-German" authors across Germany, George declared, "I absolutely do not deny being the forefather of the new national movement and also do not push aside my spiritual collaboration. What I could do for it I have done. The youth that gathers around me today is of the same opinion as I am." Quoted in Norton, *Secret Germany*, 729. Many of his followers concurred that George's "secret Reich" was realized in the "Third Reich." Yet upholding George's views led follower Claus von Stauffenberg to try to remove Hitler from power in a July 20, 1944, bomb plot. See Karlauf, "Stauffenberg."
81. Mann, *The Turning Point*, 210.
82. Gay, *Weimar Culture*, 48.
83. Keilson-Lauritz, "Stefan George's Concept of Love and the Gay Emancipation Movement," 207, quoted in Bisno, "Stefan George's Homoerotic *Erlösungsreligion*, 1891-1907," 37.
84. Herzer, *Magnus Hirschfeld*, 117.
85. Beachy, *Gay Berlin*, xi.
86. Beachy, *Gay Berlin*, 112.
87. Wolff, *Magnus Hirschfeld*, 116.
88. Wolff, *Magnus Hirschfeld*, 118.
89. Wolff, *Magnus Hirschfeld*, 119.
90. Marcus, *Meditationen*, 107.
91. Marcus, *Meditationen*, 79.
92. On Hiller's path to pacifism, see Münzer, "A Twisted Road to Pacifism." Hirschfeld had been a member of the Social Democratic Party (SPD) most likely since his university days. His battle for sexual reform based on scientific research was part and parcel of a social democratic reform policy and contribution to the end goal of democratic socialism. Herzer, *Magnus Hirschfeld*, 56. He had a close relationship with the founder of the

party, August Bebel (d. 1913), since the early 1890s. This is not to deny the antihomosexual sentiment that existed among SPD members or the SPD press, such as the party's press organ, *Vorwärts*, and its role in the 1902 Krupp scandal. Herzer, *Magnus Hirschfeld*, 74-75. Already in 1907 opponents of the workers' and homosexual movements saw a conspiracy of gays and socialists undermining social order. The SPD used the same tactic (damaging the reputation of their opponent) when they also outed Hitler's confidant and head of the Sturmabteilung (the paramilitary wing of the Nazi Party), Ernst Röhm, in 1931-1932 in an attempt to damage public perceptions of the Nazis. Herrn, *100 Years of the Gay Rights Movement in Germany*, 22-25. On November 10, 1918, the day after the proclamation of the republic and the day before the armistice, Magnus Hirschfeld celebrated the red flag of the revolution with a stirring speech praising the socialist republic in the public square in front of the Reichstag on behalf of a pacifist organization. Wolff, *Magnus Hirschfeld*, 167–68. Other than a brief nationalistic spasm from 1914-1915 befitting his assimilated Jewish background and public role defending the right of homosexuals to serve in the military and die for the fatherland, Hirschfeld changed his tone to pacifism in 1916. See Wolff, *Magnus Hirschfeld*, 157–71. For an exploration of Hirschfeld's evolving views regarding the war, see also Groβe, "Patriotismus und Kosmopolitismus."

93. Beachy, *Gay Berlin*, 149.
94. Mann, *The Turning Point*, 76.
95. Gay, *Weimar Culture*, 78–79.
96. Marcus, "Aus einem stillen Buche," 106.
97. Landmann, *Gespräche mit Stefan George*, 87. The conversation occurred between July 10 and the middle of August 1919, Matten.
98. Mann, *The Turning Point*, 76.
99. Beachy, *Gay Berlin*, 155.
100. Beachy, *Gay Berlin*, 156–57.
101. Hirschfeld, *Racism*, 239, 254–55.
102. Herzer, *Magnus Hirschfeld*, 43.
103. Herzer, *Magnus Hirschfeld*, 54–55.
104. Nachlass Hugo Marcus, Abgangs-Zeugnis der Königliche Friedrich-Wilhems-Universität zu Berlin, Berlin, November 27, 1906. While his leaving certificate provides a list of his course of study at the university, the university has no record of his completing a dissertation or being awarded a doctorate. Email communication, Dagmar Seemel, Universitätsarchiv der Humboldt-Universität, October 20, 2016.
105. Hirschfeld resigned after the vote. Under Hiller's leadership the WhK rejected the proposed reform. See Marhoefer, *Sex and the Weimar Republic*, 113, 129.
106. Hiller, *Leben gegen die Zeit*, 1:74.
107. Hiller, *Leben gegen die Zeit*, 1:408. In an issue of *Der Feuerreiter: Blätter für Dichtung und Kritik* (1922-1923), a short-lived avant-garde journal (1921-1924), Marcus published a review of Hiller's *Der Aufbruch zum Paradies* where he praised Hiller's knowledge as well as his writing style.
108. Leck, *Georg Simmel and Avant-Garde Sociology*, 29.
109. Leck, *Georg Simmel and Avant-Garde Sociology*, 38.

110. Leck, *Georg Simmel and Avant-Garde Sociology*, 37.
111. Leck, *Georg Simmel and Avant-Garde Sociology*, 13.
112. Leck, *Georg Simmel and Avant-Garde Sociology*, 25.
113. Leck, *Georg Simmel and Avant-Garde Sociology*, 15–16.
114. Leck, *Georg Simmel and Avant-Garde Sociology*, 27.
115. Leck, *Georg Simmel and Avant-Garde Sociology*, 70–71.
116. Leck, *Georg Simmel and Avant-Garde Sociology*, 120–21.
117. Leck, *Georg Simmel and Avant-Garde Sociology*, 208.
118. Leck, *Georg Simmel and Avant-Garde Sociology*, 186.
119. Leck, *Georg Simmel and Avant-Garde Sociology*, 216.
120. Nachlass Hugo Marcus, Abgangs-Zeugnis der Königlichen Friedrich-Wilhelms-Universität zu Berlin, Berlin, den November 27, 1906.
121. Leck, *Georg Simmel and Avant-Garde Sociology*, 216–18. See also Taylor, *Left-Wing Nietzscheans*.
122. Leck, *Georg Simmel and Avant-Garde Sociology*, 223.
123. Leck, *Georg Simmel and Avant-Garde Sociology*, 227–28.
124. Leck, *Georg Simmel and Avant-Garde Sociology*, 229.
125. Leck, *Georg Simmel and Avant-Garde Sociology*, 132.
126. Leck, *Georg Simmel and Avant-Garde Sociology*, 150.
127. Leck, *Georg Simmel and Avant-Garde Sociology*, 16–17.
128. Hans Alienus, "Erinnerung an Magnus Hirschfeld," 6.
129. Spector, "Where Personal Fate Turns to Public Affair," 16.
130. See Bauer, "Suicidal Subjects."
131. Bauer, "Suicidal Subjects," 244. He wrote this in 1914.
132. Hans Alienus, "Erinnerung an Magnus Hirschfeld," 6. On the affair, see Wolff, *Magnus Hirschfeld*, 68–85; Mancini, *Magnus Hirschfeld and the Quest for Sexual Freedom*, 96–102; and Domeier, *The Eulenburg Affair*.
133. Hans Alienus, "Erinnerung an Magnus Hirschfeld," 6.
134. Domeier, *The Eulenburg Affair*, 113–14.
135. Beachy, *Gay Berlin*, 131; compare with Wolff, *Magnus Hirschfeld*, 72–73.
136. Domeier, *The Eulenburg Affair*, 120, 125.
137. Domeier, *The Eulenburg Affair*, 126, 134, 139–40.
138. Domeier, *The Eulenburg Affair*, 135, 169.
139. Dose, *Magnus Hirschfeld*, 57.
140. Herzer, *Magnus Hirschfeld*, 115.
141. Herrn, *100 Years of the Gay Rights Movement in Germany*, 12.
142. Wolff, *Magnus Hirschfeld*, 80.
143. Hans Alienus, "Erinnerung an Magnus Hirschfeld," 6.
144. Wolff, *Magnus Hirschfeld*, 431–32.
145. Beachy, *Gay Berlin*, 64–65.
146. Hiller, *Leben gegen die Zeit*, 2:27–28, quoted in Beachy, *Gay Berlin*, 65.
147. Hiller, *Leben gegen die Zeit*, 2:50–52, 113–14, quoted in Marhoefer, *Sex and the Weimar Republic*, 112–13.
148. Mann, *The Turning Point*, 87.

149. Hiller, *Leben gegen die Zeit*, 2:191.
150. Hiller, *Leben gegen die Zeit*, 2:171.
151. Hiller, *Leben gegen die Zeit*, 1:107.
152. Leck, *Georg Simmel and Avant-Garde Sociology*, 238–39.
153. Leck, *Georg Simmel and Avant-Garde Sociology*, 239. Although the Deutsche Kommunistische Partei (KP, the German Communist Party) was more radical than the SPD, which did not favor like the KP the complete cancellation of the penalties for abortion and homosexuality, only the abolition of milder punishments. Herzer, *Magnus Hirschfeld*, 86–87.
154. Leck, *Georg Simmel and Avant-Garde Sociology*, 242.
155. Leck, *Georg Simmel and Avant-Garde Sociology*, 243.
156. Leck, *Georg Simmel and Avant-Garde Sociology*, 244.
157. In his *Metaphysik der Gerechtigkeit*, Marcus connects heroism, justice, and eroticism:

    A historic by way teaches us that, indeed, hope existed that would always incite heroism to highest deeds. At any time, after all, the who-knows-how-high or some other way unhappy loving one wished for glory. Specifically, this used to happen in the dark feeling that no object of love could refuse one who is famous, that glory would open any heart's gates and would substitute for missing personal charms with no effort. Surely an illusion, but one of the kind that, if circumstances permit, inexorably establishes itself, as history and particularly intellectual history teaches us. But how is glory obtained, if not through great personal deed? And so the acceptance of his love would be the reward that would have to come naturally to the doer of great deeds, if we lived in a civilian-heroic world. The offspring of one such love however—this way we can conclude the point of this image—would inherit their Geist from their father, extraordinarily proven by deeds, and their appearance from their mother, presumably gifted with looks. With Plato we find rudiments of a social order, in which the doer of great deeds received a public right to a great romance each. Thus, justice connects heroism and eroticism here, a connection that has always existed in man's subconsciousness (41).

158. Marcus paid for and signed the burial forms for his brother. Nachlass Hugo Marcus, Kuratorium für das Bestattungswesen der Stadt Berlin, 1 Empfangsbescheinigung vom May 23, 1919.
159. Alienus, "Die Kirche zu den heiligen Brüsten der Jünglinge."
160. Alienus, "Die Kirche zu den heiligen Brüsten der Jünglinge," 7.
161. Alienus, "Die Kirche zu den heiligen Brüsten der Jünglinge," 8.
162. Alienus, "Die Kirche zu den heiligen Brüsten der Jünglinge," 8.
163. Gay, *Weimar Culture*, 48. See Crouthamel, "'We Need Real Men.'"
164. "Politischer Rat geistiger Arbeiter," 218–19, quoted in Leck, *Georg Simmel*, 242.
165. Leck, *Georg Simmel*, 243.
166. Hiller, "Philosophie des Ziels," quoted in Leck, *Georg Simmel*, 246.
167. Hiller, "Philosophie des Ziels," quoted in Leck, *Georg Simmel*, 246. The usual translation of *Geistigkeit* is "intellectuality."
168. Hiller, "Philosophie des Ziels," quoted in Leck, *Georg Simmel*, 247.

169. *Das Junge Deutschland, Monatsschrift für Literatur und Theater.*
170. Marcus, "Mein toter Freund erzählt sich selbst seine Knabenzeit."
171. Marcus, "Mein toter Freund erzählt sich selbst seine Knabenzeit," 222.
172. Nachlass Hugo Marcus, Abgangs-Zeugnis der Königlichen Friedrich-Wilhelms-Universität zu Berlin, Berlin, den November 27, 1906.
173. Marcus, *Einer sucht den Freund*, 5–7.
174. Marcus, *Einer sucht den Freund*, 19–20.
175. Marcus, *Einer sucht den Freund*, 20.
176. Marcus, *Einer sucht den Freund*, 21.
177. Marcus, *Einer sucht den Freund*, 18–19, 26–27, 33.
178. Marcus, *Einer sucht den Freund*, 23–24.
179. Marcus, *Einer sucht den Freund*, 24.
180. Marcus, *Einer sucht den Freund*, 28.
181. Lane, "The Platonic Politics of the George Circle," 134.
182. Marcus, *Einer sucht den Freund*, 53.
183. Marcus, *Einer sucht den Freund*, 54.
184. Marcus, *Einer sucht den Freund*, 55.
185. Marcus, *Einer sucht den Freund*, 58.
186. Marcus, *Einer sucht den Freund*, 58–59.
187. Dose, *Magnus Hirschfeld*, 52.
188. 1897 letter of Max Spohr, quoted in Herzer, *Magnus Hirschfeld*, 100.
189. Monthly Bulletin of the WhK, *Jahrgang* VI, 5 (May 1907), quoted in Wolff, *Magnus Hirschfeld*, 449.
190. Beachy, *Gay Berlin*, 87.
191. Hirschfeld, *Die Homosexualität des Mannes und des Weibes*, 441–42, quoted in Beachy, *Gay Berlin*, 179–80.
192. Dose, *Magnus Hirschfeld*, 55.
193. Hiller, *§175*, 121–22.
194. *Bericht über das erste Tätigkeitsjahr (1. Juli 1919 bis 30. Juni 1920) des Instituts für Sexualwissenschaft*, 1, quoted in Herzer, *Magnus Hirschfeld*, 198.
195. Dose, *Magnus Hirschfeld*, 67.
196. Beachy, *Gay Berlin*, 163, 178.
197. Dose, *Magnus Hirschfeld*, 70.
198. The list comes from the *Bericht über das erste Tätigkeitsjahr (1. Juli 1919 bis 30. Juni 1920) des Instituts für Sexualwissenschaft*, quoted in Herzer, *Magnus Hirschfeld*, 199–203.
199. Wolff, *Magnus Hirschfeld*, 432.
200. Dose, *Magnus Hirschfeld*, 79.
201. Isherwood, *Christopher and His Kind*, 17.
202. Isherwood, *Christopher and His Kind*, 16.
203. Isherwood, *Christopher and His Kind*, 18.
204. Isherwood, *Christopher and His Kind*, 19.
205. Quote from Isherwood, *Christopher and His Kind*, 18. On *Anders als die Anderen*, see Herzer, *Magnus Hirschfeld*, 138–39.
206. Wolff, *Magnus Hirschfeld*, 178; and Herzer, *Magnus Hirschfeld*, 143–44.

207. Wolff, *Magnus Hirschfeld*, 191.
208. Beachy, *Gay Berlin*, 167.
209. Backhausen, *Die Lahore-Ahmadiyya-Bewegung in Europa*, 110–12, 298n83. The SEXUS series is not to be confused with the journal *Sexus*, published only once, by the IS in 1933. Wolff, *Magnus Hirschfeld*, 210, 373.
210. Alienus, "Erinnerung an Magnus Hirschfeld," 6.
211. Alienus, "Erinnerung an Magnus Hirschfeld," 7.
212. Nachlass Hugo Marcus, Roman Malicki to Hugo Marcus, summer 1922.
213. Hiller, *§ 175*, 1, 6. See esp. "Recht und sexuelle Minderheiten," 105–18.
214. Hiller, *§ 175*, 118. Hiller was taking up the argument of an earlier homosexual activist, Karl Heinrich Ulrichs (1825–1895), who had compared the persecution of Jews with the persecution of homosexuals, seeing in the liberation of the Jewish minority a model for the hoped-for liberation of the homosexual minority. See Tobin, *Peripheral Desires*, 86–92. Tobin argues that although Hirschfeld did not explicitly compare homosexuals and Jews, which by that point had become more common in anti-Semitic attacks, his understanding of homosexual identity was indebted to Ulrichs, who did compare the two groups explicitly. Tobin, *Peripheral Desires*, 97.
215. Hirschfeld, *Die Homosexualität des Mannes und des Weibes*, 894, quoted in Beachy, *Gay Berlin*, 82.
216. The petition appeared in *Jahrbuch für sexuelle Zwischenstufen* 1 (1899), 239–41, which is translated in Wolff, *Magnus Hirschfeld*, 445–49. This quote appears in Wolff, *Magnus Hirschfeld*, 447.
217. *Jahrbuch für sexuelle Zwischenstufen* 1 (1899), quoted in Wolff, *Magnus Hirschfeld*, 447.
218. *Jahrbuch für sexuelle Zwischenstufen* 1 (1899), quoted in Wolff, *Magnus Hirschfeld*, 448.
219. SEXUS: Monographien aus dem Institut für Sexualwissenschaft in Berlin, 3. The text and list of signatories can be found online at http://www.schwulencity.de/hirschfeld_was_muss_volk_wissen_1901.html#eingabe.
220. Höchstetter, *Lord Byrons Jugendtraum*.
221. Dose, *Magnus Hirschfeld*, 30. Mann would have his signature removed, for, as Tobin argues, he favored an antiliberal, antimedical, masculinist perspective on homosexuality. Tobin, *Peripheral Desires*, 185, 190.
222. Alienus, "Erinnerung an Magnus Hirschfeld," 6.
223. Beachy, *Gay Berlin*, 220–21.
224. Alienus, "Erinnerung an Magnus Hirschfeld," 7. Hirschfeld was so impressed by the tour and the painting that he sent Marcus a dense, eight-page, hand-written thank you note that very afternoon. The letter's whereabouts is unknown; it is not in Marcus's private papers. The catalog misspells the subject's name as "Dr. Hugo Markus." The exhibit was held between September 19 and November 8 at the Landesaustellungsgebäude at Lehrter Bahnhof. See *Juryfreie Kunstschau Berlin 1925: Malerei, Plastik, Gartenkunst*, 79.
225. Carstensen, *Leben und Werk der Malerin und Graphikerin Julie Wolfthorn*, 130–31, 331. For a description of the portrait, see 330.
226. Mancini, *Magnus Hirschfeld and the Quest for Sexual Freedom*, 25.
227. Nachlass Hugo Marcus, Abgangs-Zeugnis der Königlichen Friedrich-Wilhelms-Universität zu Berlin, Berlin, den November 27, 1906.

228. According to the secretary of the Ahmadi, "He came into contact with Islam through our Muslim Mission at Berlin, and after a critical enquiry, declared his acceptance of the Truth of Islam in May 1925." Marcus, Preface, "Muhammad's Personality," 1. But the date 1932 is given in the catalog to his private papers: Nachlass Hugo Marcus, "Warum ich Moslem wurde," Bescheinigung über den Beitritt zum Islam, November 30, 1932. I did not locate any such certificate of conversion, nor do I believe they exist, for the Ahmadi did not issue them (see below). Marcus officially left the Jewish community in 1936. Nachlass Hugo Marcus, Austritt aus der Synagogengemeinde Berlin, Bescheinigung vom May 18, 1936. And as will be discussed below, Marcus had not actually earned the title "Dr."
229. Dose, *Magnus Hirschfeld*, 25.
230. Mancini, *Magnus Hirschfeld and the Quest for Sexual Freedom*, 26–28.
231. Mancini, *Magnus Hirschfeld and the Quest for Sexual Freedom*, xiii.
232. Dose, *Magnus Hirschfeld*, 34. For a photo of Hirschfeld before a Christmas tree and Santa at his home in 1917, see 35.
233. Dose, *Magnus Hirschfeld*, 33–34.
234. Wolff, *Magnus Hirschfeld*, 182.
235. Festschrift on the occasion of Hirschfeld's 60th birthday, in 1928, edited by Hiller, published by the WhK, quoted in Wolff, *Magnus Hirschfeld*, 256.
236. Marcus, *Meditationen*, 91.
237. Marcus, *Die Philosophie des Monopluralismus*.
238. Marcus, *Die Philosophie des Monopluralismus*, 6.
239. Marcus, *Die ornamentale Schönheit der Landschaft*.
240. Marcus, *Die ornamentale Schönheit der Landschaft*, 4–5.

2. QUEER CONVERT: PROTESTANT ISLAM IN WEIMAR GERMANY, 1925–1933

1. Marcus, "Die Religion und der Mensch der Zukunft" (Fortsetzung), 97.
2. Hesse, "Die Sehnsucht," 4–5, as "The Longing of Our Time for a Worldview," 366–67.
3. Quoted in Fritzsche, "The Economy of Experience in Weimar Germany," 370. See also Manjapra, *Age of Entanglement: German and Indian Intellectuals Across Empire*; and Manjapra, *M. N. Roy: Marxism and Colonial Cosmopolitanism*.
4. Höpp, *Muslime in der Mark*, chap. 2; Germain, "The First Muslim Missions on a European Scale," 102; Ansari, *The Making of the East London Mosque, 1910–1951*; and Motadel, "The Making of Muslim Communities in Western Europe, 1914–1939," 17–23. The mosque at the Wünsdorf prisoner of war camp may have been founded during the war, but it was not established by Muslims.
5. Abdullah, *Geschichte des Islams in Deutschland*; Höpp, *Muslime in der Mark*, 9–18; Schäfer-Borrmann, *Vom "Waffenbruder"*; Emre, *300 Jahre Türken an der Spree*; and Böer, Haerkötter, and Kappert, *Türken in Berlin, 1871–1945*.
6. Beachy, *Gay Berlin*, 9.
7. While small numbers of Muslims—especially Turkish doctoral students, laborers, and craftsmen—lived elsewhere in Germany, Berlin is unique because it was home to the

overwhelming majority of Muslim residents in Germany and their institutions. See Sagaster, *Achmed Talib.*

8. Motadel, "Islamische Bürgerlichkeit," 104.
9. Green, "Spacetime and the Muslim Journey West," 418–43. See also Green, "Journeymen, Middlemen"; and Jonker, "A Laboratory of Modernity."
10. Nachlass Hugo Marcus, "In der Moschee zu Berlin," 1.
11. "Kurze Geschichte der Lahore-Ahmadiyya-Bewegung," in Backhausen, *Die Lahore-Ahmadiyya-Bewegung in Europa*, 9–17; "Wer war Mirza Ghulam Ahmad?," in Backhausen, *Die Lahore-Ahmadiyya-Bewegung in Europa*, 18–24; Reetz, *Islam in the Public Sphere*, 76–77, 97–98, 100–101, 139–42; and Friedmann, *Prophecy Continuous*, esp. 105–18.
12. Shah Jahan Mosque, http://www.shahjahanmosque.org.uk/; Backhausen, *Die Lahore-Ahmadiyya-Bewegung in Europa*, 25–39; and Ansari, "The Woking Mosque."
13. The Ahmadiyya Muslim Community retains a belief that Ahmad is the promised messiah and mahdi as well as a prophet. See the organization's homepage, http://www.ahmadiyya.us/about-ahmadiyya-muslim-community. This branch established a mission in the United States in 1920, the first Muslim American organization, and a journal to propagate its view, the *Muslim Sunrise*. It is led by an infallible caliph, to whom all members owe absolute obedience. It is not the subject of this book. The second, based in Lahore, maintains that Ahmad is the promised messiah and mahdi but a *mujaddid* (renewer of Islam) rather than a prophet and rejects the idea of a caliphate. See the group's homepage, http://www.aaiil.org/. This is the group referred to in this book with the term "Ahmadi."
14. Ali, "Correspondence," 2–3. See also Ahmad, "A Brief History of the Berlin Muslim Mission, 1922–1988"; and Ahmad, "Brief History of the Woking Muslim Mission."
15. Anmeldung zur Eintragung der Islamischen Gemeinde zu Berlin, e.V., an das Preussische Amtsgericht Berlin, November 4, 1922, Akten vom Amtsgericht Charlottenburg betreffend die Islamische Gemeinde zu Berlin, e.V., Landesarchiv Berlin, Rep. 42, Acc. 2147 [hereafter, Akten Islamische Gemeinde], in Bibliothek Zentrum Moderner Orient, Berlin, Nachlass Professor Dr. Gerhard Höpp [hereafter Nachlass Höpp], 07.05.002.
16. Siddiqi, "Bluff, Doubt and Fear"; Liebau, "The Kheiri Brothers and the Question of World Order after World War I"; and Ansari, "Making Transnational Connections." See also Ansari, "Maulana Barkatullah Bhopali's Transnationalism."
17. Backhausen, *Die Lahore-Ahmadiyya-Bewegung in Europa*, 51–57.
18. Hassan (Walter) Hoffmann, Islamische Gemeinde zu Berlin, an das Amtsgericht, Berlin Mitte, Berlin, April 17, 1929, Akten Islamische Gemeinde, Nachlass Höpp, 07.05.002; Prof. Sattar Kheiri, Berlin, an Amtsgericht Berlin Mitte, Geschäftsstelle, Abteilung 94, August 7, 1930, Akten Islamische Gemeinde, Nachlass Höpp, 07.05.002; and Statuten der Islamischen Gemeinde zu Berlin, e.V. 1922, Berlin, February 21, 1934, Akten Islamische Gemeinde, Nachlass Höpp, 07.05.002.
19. Höpp, "Zwischen Moschee und Demonstration," pt. 1, 142–46; and Kuck, "Anti-Colonialism in a Post-Imperial Environment."
20. Rifat, *Der Verrat der Ahmadis an Heimat und Religion*, 7. He also penned *Vollständiger Zusammenbruch der Ahmadia-Sekte.* See Höpp, "Zwischen alle Fronten."
21. Washburn and Reinhart, Introduction to *Converting Cultures*, xiii; Viswanathan, *Outside the Fold*; and van der Veer, *Imperial Encounters.*

22. See Shah Jahan Mosque, http://www.shahjahanmosque.org.uk/; and Backhausen, *Die Lahore-Ahmadiyya-Bewegung in Europa*, 25–39. See also Ansari, *"The Infidel Within"*; and Greaves, *Islam in Victorian Britain*.
23. Ali, "Correspondence"; and Ahmad, "Brief History of the Woking Muslim Mission."
24. *Der Koran Arabisch-Deutsch*, xi.
25. Höpp, "Islam in Berlin und Brandenburg," 16–20. The only purpose-built mosque in Germany at that time was constructed during the war for the use of Allied prisoners of war interned at the "Crescent" camp at Wünsdorf, an hour and a half by train from Berlin. Paid for by the German General Staff, as War Ministry and Foreign Ministry sources concede, the well-publicized construction of the mosque was nothing more than wartime propaganda and instrumentalization of Islam and Muslims, although it was used for a decade after the war by Berlin Muslims. Kahleyss, *Muslime in Brandenburg*; Höpp, *Muslime in der Mark*, chap. 4 and 8; and Cwiklinski, "Between National and Religious Solidarities," 65–66.
26. Bauknecht, *Muslime in Deutschland*, 61.
27. Protokoll und Satzungen, March 22, 1930, Satzungen, "Deutsch-Muslimische Gesellschaft Berlin," Landesarchiv Berlin, B Rep. 42, Nr. 27515, "Deutsch-Muslimische Gesellschaft, Berline.V." [hereafter, "Deutsch-Muslimische Gesellschaft"].
28. Protokoll und Satzungen, March 22, 1930; September 19, 1931; September 24, 1932; September 22, 1934; September 19, 1936; August 14, 1937; and October 1, 1938.
29. Ahmad, *Eid Sermons at the Shah Jehan Mosque*, xxix.
30. Kamal-ud-Din, "Note: The Berlin Mosque."
31. As reported in Ahmad, "A Brief History of the Berlin Muslim Mission." This seems an exaggeration. In these years one comes across the same nine converts in mosque publications and organizations: Hugo Hamid Marcus, Sheikh Omar Schubert, Mustapha Konieczny, Hikmet Beyer, Fritz Amin Boosfeld, Chalid Albert Seiler-Chan, Faruq Fischer, Huda Johanna Schneider, and Baron Omar Rolf von Ehrenfels. The exact numbers of Muslims and converts cannot be determined since Islam was not (and is not yet today) a recognized religion in Germany given community status.
32. Stromberg, "The Role of Language in Religious Conversion"; and Hindmarsh, "Religious Conversion as Narrative and Autobiography."
33. Sadr-ud-Din, "Das Glaubensbekenntnis des Islams," 91. The article was republished verbatim in every subsequent issue from 1924 to 1926. It later appeared as F. K. Khan Durrani, "Was ist Islam?," such as in *Moslemische Revue* 4, no. 1 (January 1929): 41–45.
34. Hindmarsh, "Religious Conversion as Narrative and Autobiography."
35. Hirschfeld went global with the battle for sexual liberation by founding the World League for Sexual Reform Based on Sexual-Science (1928–1932), established with numerous other social democratic and communist scholars. Their aim was to promote sexual expression and sexual freedom for all men and women, which not only included striking down antisodomy laws but also encouraging access to birth control and decriminalization of abortion. Von Ehrenfels spoke on the topic, "Kann Prostitution Bekämpft Werden?" (Can prostitution be combated?) at the London Congress of the World League for Sexual Reform presided over by Hirschfeld in 1929. Ehrenfels's talk is included on the program reproduced in Wolff, *Magnus Hirschfeld*, 453.
36. Reiss, *The Orientalist*, 306.

37. Reiss, *The Orientalist*, photo between pages 196 and 197.
38. Khulusi, *Islam Our Choice*, 234–235. See also Germain, "The First Muslim Missions on a European Scale," 99; and Backhausen, *Die Lahore-Ahmadiyya-Bewegung in Europa*, 85.
39. Motadel, "Islamische Bürgerlichkeit," 106.
40. For examples of Muslim students in Berlin serving as mediators of conversion, see "Drei Europäerinnen bekennen sich zum Islam."
41. Widdig, "Cultural Capital in Decline."
42. Motadel, "Islamische Bürgerlichkeit," 111; and Höpp, "Islam in Berlin und Brandenburg," 19.
43. Clayer and Germain, Introduction to *Islam in Inter-War Europe*, 15.
44. Germain, "The First Muslim Missions on a European Scale," 105; for example, on Mohammed Ali van Beetem, see Ryad, "Among the Believers in the Land of the Colonizer." In many ways, van Beetem was the Dutch equal of Marcus; van Beetem headed the Dutch Islamic Society. Marcus's short biography of Muhammad was translated into Dutch and published in Indonesia by the Ahmadi, and van Beetem owned a copy. Marcus, *De Boodschap van den heiligen Profeet Moehammad aan Europa.*
45. Ansari, "Making Transnational Connections," 48.
46. Editor's note, Hugo Marcus, "Muhammad's Personality." The Ahmadi boasted of converting this "scion of a high German family, a Ph.D. of Berlin University, a scholar of distinction and author of [a] good many books." "Islam in Germany: Great German Scholar Won," 1.
47. The 1937 visit to the mosque of the Aga Khan was written up in the *Berliner Illustrirte Zeitung*. "Aus Unserer Arbeit," 70. The circulation figure of 1.85 million is from 1930. Weitz, *Weimar Germany*, 211. For a Berlin society write-up of the mosque and its imam, see "Ein Gespräch mit Professor Abdullah am Fehrbelliner Platz," *Rumpelstilzchen* 9, no. 14 (December 13, 1928), quoted in Höpp, "Islam in Berlin und Brandenburg," 20. For other accounts in the contemporary German press, see Bauknecht, *Muslime in Deutschland*, 65–69.
48. Such as Geneva-based Lebanese pan-Islamist Shakib Arslan (1869–1946) in 1931. See "Empfang in der Deutsch-Muslimischen Gesellschaft," *Der Tag*, January 16, 1931, 1, Beiblatt, Nachlass Höpp, 07.05.035.
49. Nachlass Hugo Marcus, Hugo Marcus, Oberwil, Basel, Brief an Eidgenössenische Fremdenpolizei, Bern, July 1, 1947. While the SPD favored homosexual rights and the elimination of Paragraph 175, the BVP supported continued persecution of homosexuals. It would appear ironic that Marcus, but not his mosque community, should have good relations with them. On the other hand, consider the results of a 1926 survey carried out among fifty thousand members of the bourgeois homosexual organization Human Rights League. Roughly thirty-one thousand declared having a political affiliation, sixteen thousand to the Left (Socialist and Communist parties), twelve thousand to the Right (German Nationalist Party, German People's Party, and the Nazi Party), and three thousand to the Catholic Centre Party. Cited in Beachy, *Gay Berlin*, 236.
50. Nachlass Hugo Marcus, Bestätigung vom August 21, 1939, Der Imam der Moschee Berlin-Wilmersdorf, S. M. Abdullah.
51. Marcus, "Muhammad's Personality," 1.

52. Marcus, "Islam und Protestantismus."
53. Marcus, "Islam und Protestantismus," 17.
54. Marcus, "Islam und Protestantismus," 19.
55. Marcus, "Muhammad's Personality," 1–2, 6. "But Mohammad is not only a prophet, for one of his most important tasks consists in bringing back to life the revelation of his predecessors in its original purity, in perfecting it and revising it in the spirit of his age and people. It means that Mohammad is also a Reformer" (1).
56. Marcus, "Islam und Protestantismus," 21.
57. Marcus, "Spinoza und der Islam."
58. Marcus, "Spinoza und der Islam," 9.
59. Marcus, "Spinoza und der Islam," 10. Goethe had written in *Italian Journey*: "I am now so remote from the world that it gives me a curious feeling to read a newspaper. 'The fashion of this world passes away' and my only desire is to follow Spinoza's teaching and concern myself with what is everlasting so as to win eternity for my soul." Goethe, *Italian Journey*, 377.
60. Marcus writes:

    If the Jew Spinoza had absorbed the Islamic world view and heritage, via Spinoza this Islamic heritage entered the German spirit and helped determine the German destiny. Because among the great proponents of Spinoza was Bismarck. Spinoza was probably the only philosopher he read. And Spinoza's teaching of self-preservation, self-fulfillment and the noble self-love of the I was surely not without influence on Bismarck the politician. The establishment of the German empire crowned his aim to make the monarchy, and later the German federation, as strong "in itself" as possible. But the higher self-love taught by Spinoza that Bismarck realized in the German Reich is indeed a basic pillar of Muslim thinking. We all know that the Muslim can approach the Divine only through self-fulfillment of all his attributes. But we draw the historical conclusion: Via Spinoza and Bismarck Islam has itself helped build the German Second Reich in 1870. (Marcus, "Spinoza und der Islam," 10–11)

61. Marcus, "Der Islam und die Philosophie Europas," 84–88.
62. Marcus, "Islam and the Philosophy of Europe," 295.
63. Marcus, "Islam and the Philosophy of Europe," 301. In a later piece Marcus would argue that "the greatest German philosopher after Kant," Johann Gottlieb Fichte, based his philosophy on the sentence, "I am I." Since Fichte "did not mean the narrow and private individual I, but rather the divine all-I," it is equivalent to what is expressed in the Qur'an as "God is God." Marcus claims Fichte's "I am I" or "God is God" is the same as Kant's conclusion in the *Critique of Pure Reason* that God exists without proof, as sure as "I am I." And in this, "Kant and the Qur'an are in agreement." Nachlass Hugo Marcus, "Was ist uns der Koran?," 20–21.
64. Marcus, "Islam and the Philosophy of Europe," 298.
65. Aschheim, *The Nietzsche Legacy in Germany, 1890–1990*, 7–8, 308.
66. Aschheim, *The Nietzsche Legacy in Germany*, 72, 41–42; and Nachlass Hugo Marcus, Bestätigung 1902–1903, Königliche Friedrich-Wilhelms-Universität Berlin. On Nietzsche's influence in the Stefan George circle, see Aschheim, *The Nietzsche Legacy in Germany*, 71–84.

67. Beachy, *Gay Berlin*, 106.
68. Tobin, *Peripheral Desires*, 53–54, 57.
69. Tobin, *Peripheral Desires*, 183.
70. Marcus, "Nietzsche und der Islam," 80.
71. Marcus, "Nietzsche und der Islam," 81. The deployment of the idiom was so widespread that even some Jews at that time argued Eastern European Jews were Dionysian and Western European Jews Apollonian; their synthesis would bring about a Jewish Renaissance in Germany. Aschheim, *The Nietzsche Legacy in Germany*, 97.
72. Marcus, "Nietzsche und der Islam," 81–82.
73. Marcus, "Die Religion und der Mensch der Zukunft," 69.
74. Marcus, "Die Religion und der Mensch der Zukunft" (Fortsetzung), 96.
75. Marcus, "Die Religion und der Mensch der Zukunft," 69.
76. Kashyap, "Sir Mohammad Iqbal and Friedrich Nietzsche," 178. Muhammad Iqbal wrote that Nietzsche's "voice is a peal of thunder. Those who desire sweet songs should fly from him. He has thrust a sword into the heart of the West, his hands are red with the blood of Christianity. He has built his house of idols on the foundations of Islam, his heart is a believer though his brain denies." Muhammad Iqbal, *Payam-e-Mashriq*, in Kashyap, "Sir Mohammad Iqbal and Friedrich Nietzsche," 179. Iqbal labeled Nietzsche "a faithless Muslim," quoted in Marcus, "Nietzsche und der Islam," 79. Nearly a century later, another European Muslim also sought to correlate Nietzsche's philosophical writings and Islam. See Jackson, *Nietzsche and Islam*.
77. Aschheim, *The Nietzsche Legacy in Germany*, 201–2.
78. Marcus, "Nietzsche und der Islam," 82.
79. Some German Jews at the time also claimed the idea of the *Übermensch* to be a basis of Jewish faith as well or used the concept to link Greek thought and Judaism. Aschheim, *The Nietzsche Legacy in Germany*, 99–100.
80. Aschheim, *The Nietzsche Legacy in Germany*, 215.
81. McNeal, "Roy Jackson, Nietzsche and Islam."
82. Marcus, "Muhammad's Personality," 6.
83. Marcus, "Nietzsche und der Islam," 83. "In truth, democracy and aristocracy are not at all two contrasts that exclude each other. The so-called liberal doctrine and its mixture of democratic and aristocratic components reveal this. Liberalism fights against all prejudices and barriers and demands equal opportunities for all. But it does not insist on the equality of abilities; rather, it desires the most superior abilities to triumph. The goal is an aristocracy of achievement, made possible by democracy. When accompanied by social measures, this aristocracy is the greatest basis of progress. But how was it possible for a contrast between democracy and aristocracy to arise? Hereditary aristocracy is the problem. What is needed is the reintroduction of the aristocracy of achievement, an inwardly genuine, individual aristocracy against the aristocracy of class" (84). Thus, "the main principle for the envisioned government is 'All human beings are equal.' This is the teaching of the perfect aristocratic democracy, and Islam has set itself the task to realize it. And indeed, in the right mixture of aristocratic, democratic, liberal and social measures consists the well-being of each society" (86).
84. Marcus, "The Message of the Holy Prophet," 273, 274.

85. Marcus, "Die Religion und der Mensch der Zukunft," 68.
86. Marcus, "Die Religion und der Mensch der Zukunft," 69.
87. Two other Weimar German converts also publicized Goethe's views on Islam and interpreted them as if the poet had virtually converted. See von Ehrenfels, "Goethe und der deutsche Islam"; and Fischer, "Ist der Islam 'unmodern'?," 71. See also Grützmacher, "Goethes Würdigung des Islam." For more recent examples, see the various articles in *Islamische Zeitung*, Thema: Goethe (www.islamische-zeitung.de), 05.07.2001, including Gross, "In Islam leben und sterben wir alle," and Al-Murabit, "Goethe als Muslim," www.islamische-zeitung.de; see also Abu-r-Rida', *Bruder Johann Ibn Goethe*.
88. Von Arnim, "Goethe als Leitfigur eines deutschen Islam?"
89. Mommsen, *Goethe und die arabische Welt*, 157; and Mommsen, *Goethe and the Poets of Arabia*, 70.
90. Noten und Abhandlungen zum *West-östlichen Diwan*, I 7, 153, quoted in Mommsen, "Goethe's Relationship to Islam," 12; Mommsen, *Goethe und die arabische Welt*, 157; and Mommsen, *Goethe and the Poets of Arabia*, 70.
91. Mommsen, *Goethe und die arabische Welt*, 157, 194; and Mommsen, *Goethe and the Poets of Arabia*, 88.
92. Quoted in Mommsen, "Goethe and the Arab World," 88; Mommsen, "Goethe's Relationship to Islam," 12; and Mommsen, *Goethe und die arabische Welt*, 157.
93. Bidney, Introduction to *West-East Divan*, xxix.
94. "Who knows himself and others well," Poem 242, *West-East Divan*, 167. This poem was not published by Goethe. See Mommsen, "Goethe and the Arab World," 92.
95. "Come, darling come! My cap needs winding well!" Poem 161, *West-East Divan*, 95. See also Mommsen, "Goethe and the Arab World," 86.
96. Goethe, *Wilhelm Meister's Apprenticeship*, 31.
97. "Admittance," Poem 234, *West-East-Divan*, 154. See Mommsen, "Goethe and the Arab World," 83.
98. "I find it foolish, and quite odd," Poem 128, *West-East Divan*, 78. In Mommsen, "Zu *Goethe und der Islam*," Mommsen argues that the two Goethe quotes in particular—"that the author (of the *West-East Divan*) does not deny being a Muslim," and "in Islam we all live and die"—have been misinterpreted to mean that Goethe was a confessing Muslim because they have been taken out of their textual context. The first is picked out of a passage that is intended to mean that Goethe writes as a traveler, who behaves in a foreign land like a traveler should—"when in Shiraz do as the Persians"—a statement made to provoke and raise the curiosity of Germans prior to the book's publication. The second quote is connected to his universal critique of dogmatism and intolerance. He did not mean Islam as institutionalized religion, rather, submission to the will of God. Rather than speak about membership in a religious community, Goethe called on his acquaintances to accept human subservience to fate determined by a higher power—the same is true for all people, regardless of confession, thus intolerance and religious zeal are pointless, as no confession is superior.
99. Goethe, "Notes and Essays for a Better Understanding of the *West-East Divan*," 191.
100. "Muhammad's Song" was published in the opening pages of the second issue of *Moslemische Revue* in 1924, along with these quotes from Goethe's 1827 conversations with

Johan Peter Eckermann (1792–1854) concerning Islam: "As the basis of their religious training, they indoctrinate their young people first of all in the conviction that nothing could happen to a person that had not been determined long beforehand by a God who guides the universe; with that, they are prepared and at peace for their entire lives and need hardly anything more"; and "You see that his doctrine lacks nothing, and that we, with all our systems, have come no further, and that no one can reach any further." "Mahomets Gesang"; and Omar, "Goethe über die Moslems."

101. Mommsen argues his "truly positive" view was formed by the correspondence of what his tolerant Enlightenment teachers taught him and his own beliefs and thoughts; together they produced "a very deeply grounded sympathy" and that "deep sympathy resulted in such frank remarks." Mommsen, *Goethe und die arabische Welt*, 166; and Mommsen, *Goethe and the Poets of Arabia*, 73. He repeated in his work his dictum that "everyone has a religion of his own, his own way of worshipping God." Mommsen, *Goethe und die arabische Welt*, 168; Mommsen, *Goethe and the Poets of Arabia*, 74. And he spent his life developing his "own religion" incorporating various facets, from Christianity, pietism, mysticism, Neoplatonism, kabbalism, pantheism, and Islam, from which he identified especially with the belief in predestination and personal submission to fate. In short, "Goethe concentrated his attention on certain aspects of Islam because they were in accordance with his own thoughts and feelings." Mommsen, *Goethe and the Poets of Arabia*, 201. Rather than convert to Islam, Goethe simply expressed how Islam and his *Weltanschauung* corresponded. For Goethe, manifest religions—Christianity, Islam, etc.—differ in rites and doctrines yet contain the same original, universal truth. In his view, the primordial "world-piety" is best expressed by "Islam," not the religion but the word's literal meaning, "submission to God." Submission is the "innate," human approach to the divine. Kermani, *Between Quran & Kafka*, 86.

102. Mommsen, *Goethe und die arabische Welt*, (critique of misogyny) 362–405; (prohibition of wine and inebriation) 405–36; (antagonism toward poets and poetry) 436–75; and Mommsen, *Goethe and the Poets of Arabia*, (critique of misogyny) 174–97; (prohibition of wine and inebriation) 197–213; (antagonism toward poets and poetry) 213–34. See esp. in *Notes and Essays* the chapters "Arabs," "Muhammad," "Caliphs," and "Mahmud of Ghazna"; and in the *Diwan*, the "Book of Hafiz" and its poem, "Fetwa."

103. Mommsen, *Goethe und die arabische Welt*, 12. For example, by calling Muhammad the "author" of the Qur'an, Goethe denies that the Qur'an had always existed and was not created. Mommsen, *Goethe und die arabische Welt*, 446; and Mommsen, *Goethe and the Poets of Arabia*, 218. Marcus also considered Muhammad as the author of the Qur'an: "Mohammad produced the Qur'an. He dictated it to his friends. Entirely alone he completed that code. . . . Mohammad is therefore the first and only prophet who has himself composed a book of law. He is the first author, first literateur [*sic*] among the Prophets." Marcus, "Muhammad's Personality," 2. Goethe could not accept the Islamic division of history between "the age of ignorance," before Islam, and "the age of Islam" because for Goethe what mattered most was culture; if it blossomed, as in pre-Islamic times as manifested in its poetry, he claimed, it cannot be considered to have been at a low point. Mommsen, *Goethe und die arabische Welt*, 437–39. For Goethe, Arab culture was greater before Islam than after.

104. For an introduction to the debate concerning the relation between Goethe and orientalism, mainly focusing on his *West-östlicher Diwan*, see Said, *Orientalism*, xxiv–v, 19; Kontje, *German Orientalisms*; Wilson, "Enlightenment Encounters the Islamic and Arabic Worlds"; and May, "Goethe, Islam, and the Orient."
105. *Der Koran Arabisch-Deutsch*, 757; and "Sweetest child, a pearly row," Poem 246, *West-East Divan*, 169.
106. "Wer schildert sie, die vielen wunderschönen Plätze, Paradiese in Paradiesen, wo man sich gern ergehen, gern ansiedeln möchte? Scherz und Ernst verschlingen sich hier so lieblich ineinander, und ein verklärendes Alltägliches verlieht uns Flügel, zum Höheren und Höchsten zu gelangen. Was sollte uns hindern, Mohammeds Wunderpferd zu besteigen uns durch alle Himmel zu schwingen? Warum sollten wir nicht ehrfurchtsvoll jene heilige Nacht feiern, wo der Koran vollständig dem Propheten von eben her gebracht ward?" *Der Koran Arabisch-Deutsch*, 864.
107. Nachlass Hugo Marcus, "Warum ich Moslem wurde" (1951). Earlier Marcus had explained that "whoever converts from another confession to Islam will not be expected to 'foreswear his former values.' Rather, the Qur'an says to him: 'your former values are reconfirmed; value them. And add as many new ones as you are able.' . . . The content of his message is not a conflict of values, a war of annihilation between the values of one against another, and the victory of one value over the others, but rather, the enrichening of values, the fulfillment of values, the universitality of values!" Marcus, "Was ist uns der Koran?," 20.
108. Marcus, "Warum ich Moslem wurde," 2.
109. Van Kuylenburg, "Why I Became a Muslim"; Fisher, "Why Islam Appeals to Me"; Nicholson, "Some Reasons for Accepting Islam"; von Ehrenfels, "The *How?* and *Why?* of Conversion to Islam"; and Robert, "Warum ich aus der römisch-katholichen Kirche austrat."
110. Schütz, "Wie ich Moslem wurde"; and Saunders, "Why I Embraced Islam," 403.
111. Hermansen, "Roads to Mecca," 57, 60, 62.
112. Hildegard Rahet Scharf of Berlin was also introduced to Islam by a Muslim student in Berlin to whom she was giving German lessons. Scharf, Schneider, and Gohl, "Drei Europäerinnen bekennen sich zum Islam," 53–54. Saffiah Irma Gohl of Munich also narrates being introduced to Islam by an Egyptian student, which led to her conversion (56–59).
113. Hermansen, "Roads to Mecca," 62, citing Asad, *Road to Mecca*, 48.
114. Marcus, "Warum ich Moslem wurde."
115. Nachlass Hugo Marcus, "Was ist der Islam?," 4. Elsewhere he includes Confucius. See Marcus, "Was ist uns der Koran?," 12.
116. Nachlass Hugo Marcus, Marcus, Brief an Eidgenössische Fremdenpolizei (Swiss Federal Aliens' Police), Bern, Switzerland, January 23, 1957.
117. Compare with other conversion narratives cited in notes 109 and 110.
118. Hans Alienus, "Erinnerung an Magnus Hirschfeld," 7; and Carstensen, *Leben und Werk der Malerin und Graphikerin Julie Wolfthorn*, 130–31, 331.
119. Nachlass Hugo Marcus, "Goethes Begegnungen mit dem Islam."
120. Nachlass Hugo Marcus, "Goethes Begegnungen mit dem Islam," 1.
121. Nachlass Hugo Marcus, "Goethes Begegnungen mit dem Islam," 3.

122. Nachlass Hugo Marcus, "Goethes Begegnungen mit dem Islam," 4.
123. "A Song to Mahomet," in Goethe, *Selected Poems*, 23–27.
124. Nachlass Hugo Marcus, "Goethes Begegnungen mit dem Islam," 5–6.
125. Klopstock published the last cantos of *The Messiah* in 1773; the first had been published twenty-five years earlier. He met Goethe in 1775.
126. Nachlass Hugo Marcus, "Goethes Begegnungen mit dem Islam," 6–7.
127. Nachlass Hugo Marcus, "Goethes Begegnungen mit dem Islam," 7–8.
128. Nachlass Hugo Marcus, "Goethes Begegnungen mit dem Islam," 8–9.
129. Nachlass Hugo Marcus, "Goethes Begegnungen mit dem Islam," 9–10.
130. Nachlass Hugo Marcus, "Goethes Begegnungen mit dem Islam," 10.
131. Mommsen, *Goethe und die arabische Welt*, 222; and Mommsen, *Goethe and the Poets of Arabia*, 102.
132. Mommsen, *Goethe und die arabische Welt*, 221; and Mommsen, *Goethe and the Poets of Arabia*, 101.
133. Actually the problem for Goethe, as he relates in his autobiography, *Dichtung und Wahrheit* (*Poetry and Truth*), was that Muhammad was not only a prophet but military leader and statesman, and Goethe's conviction was that "the career of every religious prophet, who wants to convert the world to his belief by force endangers his integrity." Mommsen, *Goethe und die arabische Welt*, 202.
134. Nachlass Hugo Marcus, "Goethes Begegnungen mit dem Islam," 14–15.
135. Nachlass Hugo Marcus, "Goethes Begegnungen mit dem Islam," 15c. Marcus inserted pages 15a, 15b, and 15c between pages 15 and 16.
136. Mommsen, *Goethe und die arabische Welt*, 194; and Mommsen, *Goethe and the Poets of Arabia*, 88.
137. Katherina Mommsen, email communication with author, September 1, 2013.
138. Mommsen, *Goethe and the Poets of Arabia*, 97.
139. Marcus, "Was ist uns der Koran?," 2.
140. On the link made between the Orient and sodomy in British and German literature, see Matar, *Turks, Moors, and Englishmen in the Age of Discovery*; Vitkus, *Turning Turk*; and Wilson, *Goethe Männer Knaben*.
141. "No one who has not been here can have any conception of what an education Rome is. One is, so to speak, reborn and one's former ideas seem like a child's swaddling clothes. Here the most ordinary person becomes somebody, for his mind is enormously enlarged even if his character remains unchanged.... The rebirth which is transforming me from within continues. Though I expected really to learn something here, I never thought I should have to start at the bottom of the school and have to unlearn or completely relearn so much. But now I have realized this and accepted it, I find that the more I give up my old habits of thought, the happier I am... May Heaven grant that, on my return, the moral effect of having lived in a larger world will be noticeable, for I am convinced that my moral sense is undergoing as great a transformation as my aesthetic." Goethe, *Italian Journey*, 150–51.
142. Alienus, "Goethe und die Freundesliebe." On *Der Kreis* see Kennedy, *The Ideal Gay Man*; Steinle, "*Der Kreis*"; Portmann, "Konzepte männlicher Homosexualität in der Schweiz 1932–1967"; Vena, "Etre homosexuel en Suisse"; and Rupp, "The Persistence of Transnational Organizing."

143. Tobin, *Warm Brothers*, 44–45; see also Beachy, *Gay Berlin*, 103.
144. Marcus, *Die Philosophie des Monopluralismus*, 67.
145. Beachy, *Gay Berlin*, 107, citing the study of Derks, *Die Schande der heiligen Päderastie.*
146. Alienus, "Goethe und die Freundesliebe," 7.
147. Mancini, *Magnus Hirschfeld and the Quest for Sexual Freedom*, 28.
148. Hans Alienus, "Brief eines 'Mitschuldigen,'" 2.
149. Hans Alienus, "Brief eines 'Mitschuldigen,'" 3. The article is discussed in more detail in chapter 5.
150. Bambach, "Weimar Philosophy and the Crisis of Historical Thinking," 133.
151. Fritzsche, "The Economy of Experience in Weimar Germany," 367–68.
152. Kheiri, "Der Untergang und die Rettung," 2, cited in Höpp, "Zwischen Moschee und Demonstration," 138.
153. Iqbal studied Goethe and Nietzsche and earned a doctorate at Ludwig Maximilian University in Munich in 1908. Like Marcus, Iqbal viewed Islam from the point of view of German philosophy. Kashyap, "Sir Mohammad Iqbal and Friedrich Nietzsche," 175.
154. Weitz, *Weimar Germany*, 106.
155. Marchand, "Eastern Wisdom in an Era of Western Despair."
156. Marcus, "Was ist uns der Koran?," 14.
157. On Wilhelm, whose German hero was Goethe, see Marchand, *German Orientalism in the Age of Empire*, 463–73.
158. Marchand, "Eastern Wisdom in an Era of Western Despair," 352.
159. T. J. Lears coined the phrase to refer to the Boston Brahmins. Lears, quoted in Marchand, *German Orientalism in the Age of Empire*, 472.
160. Reiss, *The Orientalist*, 192.
161. Marchand, "Eastern Wisdom in an Era of Western Despair," 353.
162. Marchand, "Eastern Wisdom in an Era of Western Despair," 349; and Marchand, *German Orientalism in the Age of Empire*, 482.
163. Fritzsche, "The Economy of Experience in Weimar Germany," 360.

3. A JEWISH MUSLIM IN NAZI BERLIN, 1933–1939

1. Quoted in Isherwood, *Goodbye to Berlin*, 182.
2. See the first Ahmadi publication in Germany, *Moslemische Revue* 1, no. 1 (April 1924), including "Der Zweck der Zeitschrift"; Sadr-ud-Din, "Die internationale Religion"; and Sadr-ud-Din, "Moses, Jesus, und Mohammed sind Brüder."
3. Sadr-ud-Din, "Eine Botschaft an die Juden."
4. Sadr-ud-Din, "Die internationale Religion," 7.
5. Sadr-ud-Din, "Die Christen und die Juden."
6. Hobohm, "Islam in Germany."
7. Nachlass Hugo Marcus, "über Lessing" (1929).
8. Nachlass Hugo Marcus, "über Lessing," 1.
9. In another mosque lecture Marcus declared,

   Muhammad was the first to raise [tolerance] to a religious duty. Tolerance is consideration. Consideration of foreign values, the value of others. Tolerance that there are foreign values. To recognize that what I do not value is not valueless. To value the values that are not our own. Muhammad made it a duty for Muslims to have complete tolerance for foreign religions and their practices. By this was meant the values of others. He was the first to feel that we must bear reverence for the feelings of others, even if we do not see the object of the reverence as they do. (Marcus, "Was ist uns der Koran?," 17)

10. Marcus, "über Lessing," 2.
11. Marcus, "über Lessing," 3.
12. Marcus, "über Lessing," 4.
13. Marcus, "über Lessing," 5.
14. Marcus, "über Lessing," 8.
15. Marcus, "über Lessing," 9.
16. Gerwarth, *The Vanquished*, 4–5, 7.
17. Quoted in Gerwarth, *The Vanquished*, 5.
18. Gerwarth, *The Vanquished*, 13; emphasis original.
19. Gerwarth, *The Vanquished*, 254.
20. Nachlass Hugo Marcus, "über Lessing," 10.
21. Nachlass Hugo Marcus, "über Lessing," 11.
22. "Die Eröffnung der Moschee."
23. "Monatliche Zusammenkünfte in der Moschee."
24. Klemperer, *I Will Bear Witness, 1933–1941*, 11.
25. Klemperer, *I Will Bear Witness, 1933–1941*, 52, 54, 129, 272.
26. Klemperer, *I Will Bear Witness, 1933–1941*, 69.
27. Klemperer, *I Will Bear Witness, 1933–1941*, 119.
28. Herzer, *Magnus Hirschfeld*, 45.
29. Herzer, *Magnus Hirschfeld*, 47.
30. Herzer, *Magnus Hirschfeld*, 48.
31. Herzer, *Magnus Hirschfeld*, 51.
32. Herzog, *Sex After Fascism*, 20.
33. Herzog, *Sex After Fascism*, 23.
34. Herzog, *Sex After Fascism*, 5.
35. Beachy, *Gay Berlin*, 243–44.
36. Beachy, *Gay Berlin*, 89; and Giles, "The Institutionalization of Homosexual Panic in the Third Reich," 240-42. On the unparalleled scale of Nazi use of castration as punishment of those accused of homosexuality, see Giles, "'The Most Unkindest Cut of All'." On Himmler's inconsistent implementation of policies regarding persecuting gays within SS ranks, sometimes caused by the fear that attacking homosexuality would give recognition to its existence among the elite Nazi echelon, see Giles, "The Denial of Homosexuality."
37. Hiller, *§ 175*, 118.
38. Magnus Hirschfeld, *Mein Testament* Heft II, 77, quoted in Dose, *Magnus Hirschfeld: Deutscher—Jude—Weltbürger*, 44.
39. Quoted in Wolff, *Magnus Hirschfeld*, 379. See also Herzer, *Magnus Hirschfeld*, 230–33; Dose, *Magnus Hirschfeld: Deutscher—Jude—Weltbürger*, 89–90.

40. Quoted in Beachy, *Gay Berlin*, 169. Perhaps another reason the institute was attacked within months of the Nazi rise to power was that, in the words of a Jewish gynecologist who worked at the foundation, "We knew too much. . . . Our knowledge of such intimate secrets regarding members of the Nazi Party and other documentary material . . . was the cause of the complete and utter destruction" of it. Ludwig Levy-Lenz, quoted in Beachy, *Gay Berlin*, 243.
41. Dose, *Magnus Hirschfeld: Deutscher—Jude—Weltbürger*, 44.
42. Nachlass Hugo Marcus, "Lebenslauf," written in Zürich at Mr. Fritz Cahn's, end of 1956.
43. Alfred was deported from Berlin to the Theresienstadt ghetto on May 19, 1943, and died January 29, 1944. *Das Gedenkbuch des Bundesarchivs für die Opfer der nationalsozialistischen Judenverfolgung in Deutschland (1933–1945)*, http://www.bundesarchiv.de/gedenkbuch/.
44. Nachlass Hugo Marcus, "Lebenslauf," written in Zürich at Mr. Fritz Cahn's, end of 1956.
45. Bauknecht, *Muslime in Deutschland*, 83.
46. Fischer, "Ist der Islam 'unmodern'?"
47. Fischer, "Ist der Islam 'unmodern'?," 67; see also Bauknecht, *Muslime in Deutschland*, 87.
48. Fischer, "Ist der Islam 'unmodern'?," 67.
49. Ali, "Der Beitrag des Islams zur Zivilisation," 45; see also Bauknecht, *Muslime in Deutschland*, 88.
50. Protokoll, September 22, 1934, "Deutsch-Muslimische Gesellschaft."
51. He joined the Nazi Party on May 1, 1932. On his position on the board, see Landesarchiv Berlin, A Pr. Br. Rep. 030-04, Nr. 1350; for his membership in the Nazi Party, see A3340, MFOK Series (Master File, Ortsgruppenkartei, Nationalsozialistische Deutsche Arbeiterpartei), Roll No. A068, Frame 770, National Archives Collection of Foreign Records Seized (RG 242), NARA, Washington, D.C.; Protokoll, March 22, 1930, and September 22, 1934, "Deutsch-Muslimische Gesellschaft." In the 1934 election Marcus received thirteen votes at the meeting to Beyer's twelve; write-in-ballots from converts Huda Schneider and von Ehrenfels gave him a more comfortable margin of victory.
52. Brief, Deutsches Generalkonsulat, Kalkutta, an das Auswärtige Amt, Berlin, May 14, 1935; and Brief, Geheimes Staatspolizeiamt Berlin, an das Auswärtige Amt, Berlin, June 26, 1935, both Parch AAB, R 78242, Nachlass Höpp, 07.05.032.
53. "Die Moschee aus der Vogelschau: Dr. Abdullah vom Fehrbelliner Platz," *Rumpelstilzchen* 38 (May 31, 1934), Nachlass Höpp, 07.05.028.
54. Protokoll, July 20, 1935, "Deutsch-Muslimische Gesellschaft."
55. Nachlass Hugo Marcus, "Lebenslauf," end of 1956.
56. Protokoll, September 21, 1935, "Deutsch-Muslimische Gesellschaft."
57. Protokoll, September 21, 1935. Azeez had served as assistant imam in 1933. The other was Iraqi Yussuf Aboud al-Ibrahim.
58. Klemperer, *I Will Bear Witness*, 186.
59. ZSg. 101/7/169/Nr. 250, March 6, 1936, in *NS-Presseanweisungen der Vorkriegszeit: Edition und Dokumentation*, 249.
60. Nachlass Hugo Marcus, Austritt aus der Synagogengemeinde Berlin, Bescheinigung vom May 18, 1936, Das Amtsgericht Berlin-Charlottenburg. The document lists his address as Fürtherstrasse 11a and his profession as writer.
61. Protokoll, September 19, 1936, "Deutsch-Muslimische Gesellschaft."

62. Klemperer, *I Will Bear Witness*, 161.
63. The Nazi Beyer, by contrast, received fifteen votes. Dr. Klopp vom Hofe was elected chairman with twenty votes.
64. Amin (Fritz) Boosfeld (b. 1888) had converted to Islam in 1932. "Nachruf auf Amin Boosfeld."
65. A 1933 wedding photo of Beyer posing on the steps of the mosque with his new wife, Fatima, a fellow convert, appeared in *Moslemische Revue* 10, no. 1 (January 1934): iii.
66. "Nachruf auf Amin Boosfeld," 72.
67. Protokoll, September 19, 1936, "Deutsch-Muslimische Gesellschaft."
68. Protokoll der konstituierenden Generalversammlung der Islamischen Gemeinde zu Berlin, February 21, 1934, in Humboldhaus Berlin, Akten Islamische Gemeinde, Nachlass Höpp, 07.05.002.
69. Nationalsozialistische Deutsche Arbeiterpartei, Reichsleitung, Amt für Schulung, Abteilung Verbände, Berlin, an Polizeipräsidenten in Berlin, Abteilung V, Vereine, November 24, 1936, Landesarchiv Berlin, A Pr. Br. Rep. 030-04, Nr. 1350.
70. Sonderbeauftragten zur überwachung der geistig und kulturell tätigen Juden im deutschen Reichsgebiet, December 15, 1936, Landesarchiv Berlin, A Pr. Br. Rep. 030-04, Nr. 1350.
71. Nationalsozialistische Deutsche Arbeiterpartei, Reichsleitung, Abteilung Verbände an den Herrn Polizeipräsidenten in Berlin, Abteilung V, Vereine, April 13, 1937, Landesarchiv Berlin, A Pr. Br. Rep. 030-04, Nr. 1350; Backhausen, *Die Lahore-Ahmadiyya-Bewegung in Europa*, 123; and Bauknecht, *Muslime in Deutschland*, 96–97.
72. Goebbels, "Around the Gedächtniskirche"; and Hecht, *Deutsche Juden und Antisemitismus in der Weimarer Republik*.
73. Backhausen, *Die Lahore-Ahmadiyya-Bewegung in Europa*, 100.
74. Marcus, "Moslemischer Schicksalsglaube."
75. Backhausen, *Die Lahore-Ahmadiyya-Bewegung in Europa*, 124–27.
76. "Maulana Sadr-ud-Din verläßt Berlin." Sadr-ud-Din would succeed Muhammad Ali as the amir (leader) of the Ahmadi movement upon the death of the latter in 1951 and serve in that position until his own death thirty years later.
77. Nachlass Hugo Marcus, "Ansprache" (1937), 250.
78. Ruehl, "Aesthetic Fundamentalism in Weimar Poetry," 250.
79. Gay, *Weimar Culture*, 48.
80. Nachlass Hugo Marcus, "Ansprache" (1937).
81. Marcus, "In der Moschee zu Berlin."
82. Marcus, "In der Moschee zu Berlin," 1.
83. Marcus, "In der Moschee zu Berlin," 2.
84. Marcus, "In der Moschee zu Berlin," 2.
85. Marcus, "In der Moschee zu Berlin," 3.
86. Marcus, "Was ist uns der Koran?," 13–14.
87. Marcus, "Was ist uns der Koran?," 15.
88. Marcus, "Was ist uns der Koran?," 22–23.
89. Marcus, "Was ist uns der Koran?," 23. Marcus disdained love, relationships, and sex between men and women. See Marcus, "Was ist uns der Koran?," 23.

90. Marcus, "In der Moschee zu Berlin," 3.
91. Marcus, "In der Moschee zu Berlin," 3.
92. Marcus, "In der Moschee zu Berlin," 3.
93. Originally known as the Lahore Mission College, Forman Christian College was founded in 1864 by Dr. Charles W. Forman, a Presbyterian missionary from the United States. See the university's website, https://www.fccollege.edu.pk/about/.
94. Ahmad, "A Brief History of the Berlin Muslim Mission."
95. Hauptstelle Kulturpolitisches Archiv an die Deutsche Arbeitsfront, Amt Deutsches Volksbildungswerk, Abt. II/Vortrag, Berlin, September 27, 1938, Bundesarchiv, NJ 15, Nr. 27, Nachlass Höpp, 07.05.033. Other Muslims in Germany at the time published works promoting Nazi ideology, especially the view that Judaism and Bolshevism were the common enemies of Nazism and Islam. See Sabry, *Islam, Judentum, Bolschewismus*; and Motadel, *Islam and Nazi Germany's War*, 69.
96. Hauptstelle Kulturpolitisches Archiv an das Sicherheitshauptamt, Berlin, September 27, 1938, Bundesarchiv, NJ 15, Nr. 35, Nachlass Höpp, 07.05.033.
97. Hauptstelle Kulturpolitisches Archiv an das Sicherheitshauptamt, Berlin, October 10, 1938, Nachlass Höpp, 07.05.033.
98. Hauptstelle Kulturpolitisches Archiv an die Deutsche Arbeitsfront, Amt Deutsches Volksbildungswerk, Abt. II/Vortrag, Berlin, March 31, 1939, Bundesarchiv, NJ 15, Nr. 28, Nachlass Höpp, 07.05.033; and Film 15205, Brief der Geheimen Staatspolizei an den Reichsminister für die kirchlichen Angelegenheiten, February 11, 1939, Bundesarchiv Berlin, Nachlass Höpp, 07.05.039.
99. Protokoll, July 21, 1923, Akten Islamische Gemeinde, Nachlass Höpp, 07.05.002.
100. Ryad, "From an Officer in the Ottoman Army."
101. Brief, Der Chef der Sicherheitspolizei und des SD, Berlin, an das Auswärtige Amt, z.Hd.d. Hernn Gesandten Luther, Berlin, December 10, 1940, Politisches Archiv des Auswärtigen Amts, R 101196, Nachlass Höpp, 01.21.013; Ryad, *Wathiq Tijarat al-Silah al-Almani fi Shibh al-jazira al-Arabiyya*; and Baer, "Mistaken for Jews."
102. Brief, Dr. Zeki Kiram, Sanaa, Yemen, an Führer und Reichskanzler Herrn Adolf Hitler, Berlin, May 19, 1936, Politisches Archiv des Auswärtigen Amts, R 101196, Nachlass Höpp, 01.21.013.
103. Kiram, "Ein Moslem über das neue Deutschland: Hitler ist der berufene Mann," 60; and Bauknecht, *Muslime in Deutschland*, 88–89. Kiram later attempted to have two book manuscripts published, *Der Prophet Mohamed und die Juden* (The Prophet Muhammad and the Jews, 1940), and *Nordischer Gottglaube, Islam und Geist der Zeit* (Nordic belief in God, Islam, and the zeitgeist, 1942), but they were rejected by Nazi censors. Motadel, *Islam and Nazi Germany's War*, 70.
104. Morsch and Ley, *Sachsenhausen Concentration Camp, 1936–1945*, 52, 55; and Marcus's concentration camp records, 1367/1/15, Bl. 080, Russian State Military Archive, Moscow; D1 A/1015, Bl. 080, formerly R 203/M 10, Bl. 147, Stiftung Brandenburgische Gedenkstätten, Gedenkstätte und Museum Sachsenhausen.
105. Morsch and Ley, *Sachsenhausen Concentration Camp*, 50.
106. Marcus's concentration camp records.
107. Marcus's concentration camp records.

108. Nachlass Hugo Marcus, "Lebenslauf," end of 1956.
109. See Sternweiler, "Er hatte doppelt so schwer zu leiden . . . Homosexuelle Juden," 175–76; and Müller, "'Wohl dem, der hier nur eine Nummer ist': Die Isolierung der Homosexuellen." On Nazi persecution of gays in Berlin, see Pretzel and Roßbach, *Wegen der zu erwartenden hohen Strafe*.
110. Jews had owned businesses on the largest avenue, Hohenzollerndamm, near the mosque, and a Jewish family had lived on the same street as the mosque. The nearest synagogue was located at Prinzregentenstrasse 69, although the Berlin West skyline would have been marked by smoke and flames. See *Jüdisches Adressbuch für Gross-Berlin 1931*, 20–21, 316, https://digital.zlb.de/viewer/readingmode/34039536_1931_1932/1/.
111. Albania was to be occupied by Fascist Italy in April 1939 and by Nazi Germany thereafter. Nachlass Hugo Marcus, Erteilung eines Einreisevisums für das Königreich Albanien, November 26, 1938.
112. Nachlass Hugo Marcus, S. M. Abdullah to British Passport Officer, Berlin, December 1, 1938.
113. Klemperer, *I Will Bear Witness*, 292.
114. Klemperer, *I Will Bear Witness*, 293; see also Evans, *The Third Reich in Power*, 604.
115. Quoted in Höpp, "Islam in Berlin und Brandenburg," 21.
116. Anmeldung zur Eintragung der Islamischen Gemeinde zu Berlin, Nachlass Höpp, 07.05.039.
117. Höpp, "Muslime unterm Hakenkreuz."
118. Taheri, *Deutsche Agenten bei iranische Stämmen, 1942–1944*.
119. Islam-Institut (Mahad al-Islam) zu Berlin an Polizeipräsident, Abteilung V, March 21, 1939, Satzungen, "Islam Institut," Landesarchiv Berlin, A Pr. Br. Rep. 030-04, Nr. 2314.
120. Nationalsozialistische Deutsche Arbeiterpartei, Aussenpolitisches Amt an Herrn Polizeipräsidenten in Berlin, August 8, 1939, A Pr. Br. Rep. 030-04, Nr. 2314, "Islam-Institut."
121. Vorstandsmitglieder, October 30, 1940, A Pr. Br. Rep. 030-04, Nr. 2314, "Islam-Institut"; Protokoll, July 21, 1923, Akten Islamische Gemeinde, Nachlass Höpp, 07.05.002. Rahman was executive director from 1934 to 1936, general secretary in 1936 and 1937, and chairman in 1941 and 1942 (Protokoll, Generalversammlung der Islamischen Gemeinde zu Berlin e.V., January 18, 1936; and Habibur Rahman, Islamische Gemeinde zu Berlin, an Amtsgericht Berlin, June 3, 1942, both Landesarchiv Berlin, Rep. 42, Acc. 2147, "Islamische Gemeinde zu Berlin, e.V.," in Bibliothek Zentrum Moderner Orient, Berlin, Nachlass Professor Dr. Gerhard Höpp, 07.05.002). See also Bauknecht, *Muslime in Deutschland*, 110–111.
122. Despite pro-Nazi actions and pronouncements, during World War II, both Habibur Rahman and Zeki Kiram were accused by other Arabs in Europe of being British agents.
123. Nachlass Hugo Marcus, Kennkarte Deutsches Reich, ausgestellt: Berlin, March 16, 1939.
124. The pass is found today in the Swiss Federal Archives in Bern.
125. The decree was promulgated in October 1937. Evans, *The Third Reich in Power*, 575. More than three hundred baptized Christians of Jewish background in Berlin were murdered in death camps. Frisius, Kälberer, Krogel, and Lachenicht, *Evangelisch getauft—als Juden verfolgt*.

126. Nachlass Hugo Marcus, S. M. Abdullah to British Passport Officer, Berlin, March 16, 1939.
127. Freimark, "Promotion Hedwig Klein."
128. Klemperer, *I Will Bear Witness*, 299, 307.
129. Evans, *The Third Reich in Power*, 594–95.
130. Evans, *The Third Reich in Power*, 596.
131. Nachlass Hugo Marcus, Sadr-ud-Din, Head of the Ahmadia Anjuman, Lahore, India, to Hugo Marcus, Basel, Switzerland, August 20, 1957. The Ahmadi gave Marcus financial support into the 1950s.
132. Kaplan, "When the Ordinary Became Extraordinary," 66; and Evans, *The Third Reich in Power*, 565. In the spring of 1941, Klemperer could still assert his commitment to Germanness. Klemperer, *I Will Bear Witness*, 343, 385.
133. Nachlass Hugo Marcus, Danksagung vom September 30, 1919, Kriegsministerium Berlin; and Verleihung der Roten Kreuz-Medaille 3. Klasse, der Kommissar und Militär-Inspektor der freiwilligen Krankenpflege, Berlin, April 10, 1920.
134. Nachlass Hugo Marcus, Verleihung "Ehrenkreuz für Kriegsteilnehmer" Berlin, April 9, 1936. He left the Jewish community in May. Nachlass Hugo Marcus, Austritt aus der Synagogengemeinde Berlin, Bescheinigung vom May 18, 1936.
135. The highest levels of support for the Nazis in Berlin in the elections of September 1930 and July and November 1932 "came from the upper- and upper-middle-class districts." Hamilton, *Who Voted for Hitler?*, 82, 90. Wilmersdorf, by all measures the wealthiest district in the city, had the fourth-highest Nazi vote total in July 1932, 35.1 percent (82). This was above the figure for Berlin total, which was 28.6 percent (78). When one corrects this figure by subtracting Jewish voters (13.5 percent the population of the district), one determines that 40.6 percent of the non-Jewish population voted for the Nazis, the second highest total in the city (84–85).
136. Evans, *The Third Reich in Power*, 595.
137. Klemperer, *I Will Bear Witness*, 339, 351. Klemperer describes what befell him in Dresden in the spring and summer of 1940.
138. Backhausen, *Die Lahore-Ahmadiyya-Bewegung in Europa*, 112.
139. Beachy, *Gay Berlin*, 194, 203.
140. His address is confirmed by the entry in a 1943 Berlin address book, "Malecki, Roman, Konfektionär Charlb Kantstr 30 T." "T." stands for telephone connection ("Fernsprechanschluß"). The address book is available here: http://digital.zlb.de/viewer/image/10089470_1943/1870. Appropriately, the Chinese restaurant located in the building today is named "Good Friends."
141. Schweizerisches Bundesarchiv BAR, Dossier E4264#1988/2#33540*, Marcus, Hugo, 06.07.1880, Aktenzeichen: P070214, Deutsches Reich Reisepass.
142. Nachlass Hugo Marcus, Sadr-ud-Din, Lahore, Ahmadiyya Buildings, to Hugo Marcus, Berlin, n.d, 1939.
143. Nachlass Hugo Marcus, Sadr-ud-Din, Lahore, to Marcus, Berlin, April 17, 1939, translated from Hindi and sent December 14, 1939, after Marcus had already left Berlin.
144. Nachlass Hugo Marcus, Secretary, Ahmadiyya Anjuman Ishaat-e-Islam, Lahore, India, to Herr Hamid Marcus, c/o Dr. S. M. Abdullah, Der Imam der Moschee, Berlin-Wilmersdorf, Germany, April 19, 1939.

145. Nachlass Hugo Marcus, J. G. Simms, Under-Secretary of the Government of India, Home Department, Simla, to British Passport Control Officer, Berlin, May 12, 1939.
146. *Der Koran Arabisch-Deutsch*, x.
147. Backhausen, *Die Lahore-Ahmadiyya-Bewegung in Europa*, 128–31, 146–51. Marcus was not credited by name in the 1964 or 2005 editions either (77).
148. *Der Koran Arabisch-Deutsch*, commentary on Qur'an 5:14, p. 188.
149. *Der Koran Arabisch-Deutsch*, 192.
150. *Der Koran Arabisch-Deutsch*, 53.
151. *Der Koran Arabisch-Deutsch*, 57.
152. *Der Koran Arabisch-Deutsch*, commentary on Qur'an 2:205–6, p. 61.
153. *Der Koran Arabisch-Deutsch*, 105.
154. *Der Koran Arabisch-Deutsch*, 502.
155. *Der Koran Arabisch-Deutsch*, 77.
156. *Der Koran Arabisch-Deutsch*, commentary on Sura 22:40, p. 557.
157. *Der Koran Arabisch-Deutsch*, commentary on Sura 5:2, p. 184; and *Der Koran Arabisch-Deutsch*, commentary on Sura 7:38, p. 260.
158. Nachlass Hugo Marcus, Letter from Imam of the mosque S. M. Abdullah to Hugo Marcus, August 21, 1939. It is unknown why Abdullah referred to Marcus as the mosque's syndic. Marcus had no legal or business training. It is odd that he would be referred to by a term denoting his being the mosque's legal counsel or business agent.
159. Nachlass Hugo Marcus, Bestätigung vom August 21, 1939, Der Imam der Moschee Berlin-Wilmersdorf.
160. Marcus's previous one had expired on July 14. On August 16 he obtained a new one, set to expire on August 24, which was indeed the day he arrived in Basel. Schweizerisches Bundesarchiv BAR, Dossier E4264#1988/2#33540*, Marcus, Hugo, 06.07.1880, Aktenzeichen: P070214, Deutsches Reich Reisepass.
161. Freimark, "Promotion Hedwig Klein."
162. Nachlass Hugo Marcus, Hugo Marcus, Zürich, Brief an Eidgenössische Fremdenpolizei, Bern, Switzerland, January 23, 1957; and Nachlass Hugo Marcus, S. M. Abdullah, The Ahmadiyya Anjuman Ishaat-e-Islam, Lahore, India, to Hugo Marcus, Oberwil, Baselland, Switzerland, June 3, 1940.
163. On von Ehrenfels's internment, see Nachlass Hugo Marcus, S. M. Abdullah, The Ahmadiyya Anjuman Ishaat-e-Islam, Lahore, India, to Hugo Marcus, Oberwil, Baselland, Switzerland, December 1, 1940.
164. Chronik der Erzabtei Beuron: Advent 1977–Advent 1978, 4–5; Nachlass Hugo Marcus, "Lebenslauf," end of 1956; and Nachlass Hugo Marcus, Max Jordan, Washington, D.C., to Hugo Marcus, Basel, Switzerland, September 1, 1941.
165. He returned to British India, where he served as general secretary of the Ahmadi in Lahore from 1940 to the end of the war, and from 1946 as imam at the Woking Mission. He revised the English translation of the Qur'an in 1952 before passing away in England in 1956.
166. Landesarchiv Berlin, B Rep. 42 Nr. 27515, "Deutsch Muslimische Gesellschaft, Berlin e.V," S. M. Abdullah an Amtsgericht Berlin, October 27, 1939.
167. Nachlass Hugo Marcus, Brief von Sadr-ud-Din, Lahore, to Hugo Marcus, October 24, 1939.

168. "Id-ul-Fitr in Berlin."
169. "Id-ul-Fitr in Berlin," 76; and Bauknecht, *Muslime in Deutschland*, 89–90.
170. "Introduction," *American Historical Review* 118, no. 1 (February 2013): 45.
171. For another idiosyncratic Jewish character whose life provides insight into larger historiographical issues, see Stein, "Protected Persons?"
172. Nordbruch, "The Arab World and National Socialism," 3.
173. On Nazi efforts to recruit Arab Muslims to serve their aims, see Nordbruch, *Nazism in Syria and Lebanon*; Wildangel, *Zwischen Achse und Mandatsmacht*; and Schröder, *Deutschland und der Mittlere Osten im Zweiten Weltkrieg*. For efforts to recruit other Muslims from southeastern Europe and the Soviet Union to fight in the Wehrmacht and SS, see Motadel, "The 'Muslim Question' in Hitler's Balkans"; Motadel, "Islam and Germany's War in the Soviet Borderlands, 1941–1945"; Lepre, *Himmler's Bosnian Division*; Heine, "Die Imam-Kurse der deutschen Wehrmacht im Jahre 1944"; the speech of al-Husayni before the imams of the Bosnian SS division on October 4, 1944, in Höpp, *Mufti-Papiere*, 219; letters from al-Husayni to Heinrich Himmler, in Höpp, *Mufti-Papiere*, 212, 213, 229; and Abdullah, *Geschichte des Islams in Deutschland*, 34–42.
174. On the question of the culpability of foreigners in Nazi Germany, see Wien, "The Culpability of Exile," quote from 1.
175. See, for example, Kidwai, "The Post-War Problems and Their Solution."
176. Abdullah, "Jews Under Crescent and Cross," 388.
177. Abdullah, "Jews Under Crescent and Cross," 389.
178. Abdullah, "Jews Under Crescent and Cross," 390.
179. Abdullah, "Jews Under Crescent and Cross." The author compares the tolerance of Islam with the intolerance of Christianity, but betrays anti-Jewish sentiment nonetheless. He repeats the theme of Jewish treachery, here during the life of Muhammad, and blames a Jewish woman for poisoning the Prophet, allegedly the ultimate cause of his death. The author ends the article by condemning Jews, for "if the persecuted Jews of to-day, instead of showing gratitude to the Muslims for giving them home and shelter when they were chastised by the iron rod of persecution by the Christians, actually try to stifle the Arab demands in Palestine, we can only wonder at their sense of gratitude" (397).
180. "Letter," July 14, 1940, Imam of the Mosque to the Editor of the *New Statesman and Nation*, London, reprinted in *Islamic Review* 29 (February 1941), 42–43.
181. Nachlass Hugo Marcus, "Lebenslauf," end of 1956; Evans, *The Third Reich in Power*, 220–30; and Klemperer, *I Will Bear Witness*, 431. On the German Christian churches and Nazism, see Barnett, *For the Soul of the People*; Bergen, *Twisted Cross*; Ericksen and Heschel, *Betrayal*; Koonz, *The Nazi Conscience*; Hockenos, *A Church Divided*; Heschel, *The Aryan Jesus*; and Ericksen, *Complicity in the Holocaust*.
182. Nachlass Hugo Marcus, "Lebenslauf," n.d. [ca. 1958].

4. WHO WRITES LIVES: SWISS REFUGE, 1939–1965

1. Marcus, "Was ist uns der Koran?," 26.
2. The same was true with Basel's French train station. The Badischer Bahnhof is still considered German territory today.

3. Lienert, "Swiss Immigration Policies 1933–1939," 43.
4. Lienert, "Swiss Immigration Policies 1933–1939," 41, 43.
5. Sibold, "Menschen ohne Schutz," 21.
6. Lienert, "Swiss Immigration Policies 1933–1939," 47.
7. Fivaz-Silbermann, "Ignorance, Realpolitik and Human Rights," 89.
8. Roschewski, "Heinrich Rothmund in seinen persönlichen Akten," 120.
9. Lienert, "Swiss Immigration Policies 1933–1939," 47–48.
10. Nachlass Hugo Marcus, Unterlagen Aufenthaltsbewilligung Eidgenössische Fremdenpolizei und Polizeikommando Baselland, Polizeikommando Baselland, Aufenthaltsbewilligung Quittung, September 6, 1939; Eidgenössische Fremdenpolizei Bern, September 5, 1939, Zustimmensverfügung mit Frist zu Ausreise aus der Schweiz bis zum November 20, 1939.
11. Kaufmann, "Jüdisches Leben in der Schweiz nach 1945." The refugees—one-fifth to one-quarter arriving between 1933 and 1939 and the rest during the war, despite official policies—more than doubled the size of Switzerland's already existing Jewish population.
12. Lienert, "Swiss Immigration Policies 1933–1939," 43. For example, German Jewish refugee Kurt Preuss's removal was insistently demanded by the Foreign Aliens' Police, and as a result he was handed over to the German authorities and then murdered in a concentration camp. See Heim, "Fremdenpolizei-Akte 29496."
13. Sibold, "Menschen ohne Schutz," 22.
14. Nachlass Hugo Marcus, Gemeinde Oberwil Baselland, Leumunds-Zeugnis vom November 10, 1942.
15. Bundesratsbeschluss, August 4, 1942, Swiss Federal Archives Berne, E1004.1 1/424, cited in Fivaz-Silbermann, "Ignorance, Realpolitik and Human Rights," 91. The translation is my own. Switzerland changed its official policy two years later—when it was already too late (94).
16. Nachlass Hugo Marcus, Unterlagen Aufenthaltsbewilligung Eidgenössische Fremdenpolizei und Polizeikommando Baselland, Gemeinde Oberwil, Baselland, Leumunds-Zeugnis, November 10, 1942.
17. Lienert, "Swiss Immigration Policies 1933–1939," 44.
18. Schweizerisches Bundesarchiv BAR, Dossier E4264#1988/2#33540*, Marcus, Hugo, 06.07.1880, Aktenzeichen: P070214, Deutsches Reich Reisepass.
19. Nachlass Hugo Marcus, Unterlagen Aufenthaltsbewilligung Eidgenössische Fremdenpolizei und Polizeikommando Baselland, letter from Polizeikommando Baselland, Liestal, to Dr. Hugo Markus [*sic*], Bruderholzweg (today: Bruderholzstrasse) 7, Oberwil, October 27, 1947. Marcus was granted permanent asylum (*Dauerasyl*) on October 20, 1947. Staatsarchiv Basel-Stadt, PD-Reg 3a, 52516, Marcus, Hugo (1944–1966), Akten der Fremdenpolizei des Kantons Basel-Stadt, Meyer, Der Chef der Polizeiabteilung, Eidgenössisches Justiz- und Polizeidepartment, Polizeiabteilung, Bern, August 8, 1950, an Herrn Dr. H. Eckert, Basler Hilfsstelle für Flüchtlinge, Rheinsprung 1, Basel.
20. Nachlass Hugo Marcus, Else Th. Marcus, M.D., St. George, Staten Island, N.Y., to Hugo Marcus, September 23, 1939.

21. Hirschfeld, who also did not consider emigrating to Palestine, was much more equivocal about the Zionist enterprise. Writing in 1933–1934, he wrote:

> It certainly has not succeeded in making an end of race-hatreds, for it has evoked a new one, between Arabs and Jews. . . . Zionism and the assimilation of the Jews in the lands where they have been settled for centuries are not mutually exclusive solutions of the Jewish problem. One may favour both. Not all Jews want to settle in Palestine, nor is there room for them all in that little land. But if the Arab difficulties can be overcome, and if the Zionist Jews can peacefully establish themselves in the region with which they have so many traditional and religious ties, the wish-dream of a great many worthy persons will have been happily fulfilled. (Hirschfeld, *Racism*, 235–36)

22. Amtsgericht Charlottenburg, Islamischer Weltkongress, Zweigstelle Berlin, Landesarchiv Berlin, Rep. 42, Acc. 2147. The organization was founded on October 31, 1932, by Marcus and five other men from the Ahmadi mosque community—listed as Dr. Hamid H. Marcus, Dr. Sheikh Muhammad Abdullah, Mirza Azeez ur-Rahman, Omar Schubert, Chalid Al Seiler, and Mustapha Konieczny—together with fourteen men from other Muslim organizations in the city, including Zeki Kiram and Alimjan Idris.
23. Appendix 7: Charter of the General Islamic Congress, in Kramer, *Islam Assembled: The Advent of the Muslim Congresses*, 192.
24. Amtsgericht Charlottenburg, Islamischer Weltkongress, Zweigstelle Berlin, Landesarchiv Berlin, Rep. 42, Acc. 2147.
25. Nachlass Hugo Marcus, Hugo Marcus, Oberwil, Baselland, to Fritz Cahn, November 30, 1939. In this letter, composed ten days after he should have left the country, Marcus discusses literature!
26. Nachlass Hugo Marcus, Leonie Cahn, Zürich, to Hugo Marcus, Basel, December 27, 1940.
27. I calculated the value in today's U.S. dollar by first converting values in Reichsmarks to U.S. dollars by using historical exchange rates: https://www.measuringworth.com/exchangeglobal/. Then I calculated the present purchasing power of the past U.S. dollars: https://www.measuringworth.com/ppowerus/. I use this same method throughout the book.
28. Nachlass Hugo Marcus, Leonie Cahn, Zürich, to Hugo Marcus, Basel, January 10, 1941; and Leonie Cahn, Zürich, to Hugo Marcus, Basel, January 14, 1941.
29. Nachlass Hugo Marcus, Antrag Entschädigungszahlung, Entschädigungsamt Berlin, August 25, 1954.
30. Nachlass Hugo Marcus, Leonie Cahn, Zürich, to Hugo Marcus, Basel, November 12, 1946; and Leonie Cahn to Cäcilie Marcus, January 16, 1947.
31. Nachlass Hugo Marcus, Antrag Entschädigungszahlung, Affidavit given by Marcus on September 5, 1957, at the Notary of Basel.
32. Nachlass Hugo Marcus, Brief von Ernst Kantorowicz, Berkeley, California, an Cäcilie Markus [*sic*], Zürich, September 26, 1946.
33. Otto Marcus died in Berlin in 1919; Joseph Marcus died in Berlin on February 3, 1930; Dr. Richard Marcus died in Leipzig on May 2, 1933; and Dr. Alfred Marcus died at Theresienstadt concentration camp on January 29, 1944.

34. Hugo's brother Alfred's widow, Gertrud, survived Theresienstadt concentration camp and emigrated to New York after the war. Nachlass Hugo Marcus, Antrag Entschädigungszahlung, Affidavit given by Marcus on September 5, 1957, at the Notary of Basel. Gertrud Meyer was born in Berlin on May 7, 1878, and died August 20, 1953, in Roetland State Hospital, Orangeburg, New York. See also Nachlass Hugo Marcus, Brief von Ernst Kantorowicz, Berkeley, California, an Cäcilie Markus [*sic*], Zürich, September 26, 1946.
35. Nachlass Hugo Marcus, Leonie Cahn, Zürich, to Hugo Marcus, Basel, November 22, 1946.
36. George, *Georgika: Das Wesen des Dichters George* (1920); and George, *Die Transcendenz des Erkennens* (1923). The quote is from Oelmann, "The George Circle," 34. On Judith Landmann, see Oelmann, *Frauen um Stefan George*.
37. George, *Das Jahr der Seele* (1897). Nachlass Hugo Marcus, Brief von Edith Landmann, undated 1944. The poem is as follows:

    Es lacht in dem steigenden jahr dir
    Der duft aus dem garten noch leis
    Flicht in dem flatternden haar dir
    Eppic und Ehrenpreis

    Die wehende saat ist wie gold noch
    Vielleich nicht so hoch mehr und reich
    Rosen begrüssen dich hold noch
    Ward auch ihr glanz etwas bleich

    Verschweigen wir was uns verwehrt ist
    Geloben wir glücklich zu sein
    Wenn uns nicht mehr auch beschert ist
    Als noch ein rundgang zu sein.

38. Nachlass Hugo Marcus, Brief von Edith Landmann, Basel, Stapfelberg 4, April 16, 1943.
39. See also Landmann, *Erinnerungen an Stefan George*.
40. The two works are *Die Lehre vom Schönen* (1952), and *Stefan George und die Griechen: Idee einer neuen Ethik*, redaktion Michael Landmann (1971).
41. Nachlass Hugo Marcus, letters from Michael Landmann, October 12, 1944, November 16, 1944, December 10, 1944, and February 2, 1945.
42. Staatsarchiv Basel-Stadt, PD-Reg 3a, 52516, Marcus, Hugo (1944–1966), Akten der Fremdenpolizei des Kantons Basel-Stadt, Michael Landmann, Präsident, Philosophische Gesellschaft Basel, Stiftsgasse 5, Basel, April 24, 1946, an den Vorsteher des Kontrollbüreaus Herrn (Fritz) Jenny, Basel, Spiegelhof.
43. Nachlass Hugo Marcus, Brief von Edith Landmann, March 10, 1947.
44. In *Eranos-Jahrbuch* 14 (1946), Zürich 1947, 149–227, translated as "The Problem of Nature in the Esoteric Monism of Islam." See Schubert, "Meier, Fritz."
45. Staatsarchiv Basel-Stadt, PD-Reg 3a, 52516, Marcus, Hugo (1944–1966), Akten der Fremdenpolizei des Kantons Basel-Stadt, an das Polizeikommando Abt. Fremdenpolizei,

Liestal, November 27, 1944, von Kontrollbureau, Kantonale Fremdenpolizei, der Adjunkt Bickel.

46. Email correspondence, Susanne Grulich Zier, University Archivist, University of Basel; and email correspondence, Hermann Wichers, Head of User Services, Staatsarchiv Basel-Stadt, both October 2016. His university leaving certificate reads, "Mr. Hugo Markus [*sic*] . . . matriculated as a student of philosophy at the university on November 10, 1942, and according to his course book he attended courses until winter semester 1946/7." Nachlass Hugo Marcus, Abgangs-Zeugnis Universität Basel, Basel, May 9, 1947.
47. Nachlass Hugo Marcus, Sadr-ud-Din, Lahore, to Hugo Marcus, Basel, October 24, 1939.
48. Nachlass Hugo Marcus, Dr. S. M. Abdullah (imam), Ahmadiyya Buildings, Lahore, to Hugo Marcus, Basel, July 9, 1940.
49. Nachlass Hugo Marcus, Dr. S. M. Abdullah (imam), Ahmadiyya Buildings, Lahore, to Hugo Marcus, Basel, September 21, 1940.
50. Nachlass Hugo Marcus, "Berührungspunkte zwischen den Koran und ausserislamischen Glaubensquellen."
51. Nachlass Hugo Marcus, S. M. Abdullah, Lahore, to Marcus, Basel, February 12, 1940.
52. Nachlass Hugo Marcus, S. M. Abdullah, Lahore, to Marcus, Basel, February 26, 1940.
53. Nachlass Hugo Marcus, S. M. Abdullah, Lahore, to Marcus, Basel, March 20, 1940.
54. Nachlass Hugo Marcus, S. M. Abdullah, Lahore, to Hugo Marcus, Basel, May 13, 1940.
55. Nachlass Hugo Marcus, S. M. Abdullah, Lahore, to Marcus, Basel, June 29, 1940.
56. Nachlass Hugo Marcus, S. M. Abdullah, Lahore, to Marcus, Basel, June 30, 1940.
57. Nachlass Hugo Marcus, Dr. S. M. Abdullah (imam), Ahmadiyya Buildings, Lahore, to Hugo Marcus, Basel, January 30, 1941.
58. Nachlass Hugo Marcus, Dr. S. M. Abdullah (imam), Ahmadiyya Buildings, Lahore, to Hugo Marcus, Basel, June 3, 1941.
59. Nachlass Hugo Marcus, Hugo Marcus, Oberwil, to M. A. Abdullah, Lahore, September 30, 1941.
60. Nachlass Hugo Marcus, Hugo Marcus, Oberwil, to M. A. Abdullah, Lahore, September 30, 1941.
61. Marcus, *Meditationen*, 169.
62. Nachlass Hugo Marcus, Dr. S. M. Abdullah (imam), Ahmadiyya Buildings, Lahore, to Hugo Marcus, Basel, November 26, 1941.
63. Nachlass Hugo Marcus, L. Gaedicke, Berlin, to Hugo Marcus, Basel, March 11, 1942.
64. Nachlass Hugo Marcus, Amine Mosler, Berlin-Friedenau, Hauptstrasse 83, to Hugo Marcus, Basel, April 19, 1942.
65. Gaedicke, who had earned a doctorate in political science, served as a statistician in the Reich Ministry of Statistics, which was a division of the Reich Interior Ministry. Backhausen, *Die Lahore-Ahmadiyya-Bewegung in Europa*, 131–37.
66. National Archives and Records Administration, Washington, D.C., National Archives Collection of Foreign Records Seized (Record Group 242), A3340, MFOK Series (Master File, Ortsgruppenkartei, Nationalsozialistische Deutsche Arbeiterpartei), Roll number F027, Frame 0131. Gaedicke applied for membership on November 17, 1941, and became a member January 1, 1942. Gaedicke's home address is listed as Berlin, Wilmersdorf, Brienerstr. 7, which is the address of the mosque.

67. This topic is explored extensively in Motadel, *Islam and Nazi Germany's War.*
68. Backhausen, *Die Lahore-Ahmadiyya-Bewegung in Europa*, 78. The German translation was not republished until 1965, and in Pakistan.
69. Ahmad, "A Brief History of the Berlin Muslim Mission, 1922–1988."
70. In a 2006 interview Hobohm mentioned that Nazi ideologue Alfred Rosenberg spoke highly of Islam, and that it was difficult at that time to fulfill the requirements of his new religion, such as eating only halal meat. After all, "the Jewish businesses were all closed." When asked whether Muslims felt any solidarity with the Jews who had to close their businesses, he responded: "No there was not any [solidarity] because the Muslims and also I were exposed to the propaganda that the Jews were the enemies of the Arabs, and therefore the enemies of the Muslims and Islam." Sonderausgabe: Exclusivinterview mit Mohammed Aman Hobohm, So Gesehen TV (Germany), December 24, 2009, recorded in 2006, http:/islam.de/24332.
71. Backhausen, *Die Lahore-Ahmadiyya-Bewegung in Europa*, 128–31, 146–51.
72. *Islam Our Choice* (1961), 162.
73. Johnson, *A Mosque in Munich*, 47. Efforts of the Soviet Turkic Muslim veterans to build a mosque began in 1958, but within five years the ex-soldiers had lost control of the project when their Nazi-era academic sponsor, Gerhard von Mende, passed away (174–75). The mosque, whose construction was mainly financed by Libya, was finally opened in 1973 (185). See also Meining, *Eine Moschee in Deutschland.* For information on von Mende and Turkic Muslims in the SS, see Motadel, *Islam and Nazi Germany's War*, 232–44.
74. Hobohm, "Islam in Germany," 16.
75. Hobohm, "Islam in Germany," 17.
76. For example, on October 21, 1954, Hiller sent Marcus a packet of typewritten, unpublished poems he had composed in exile between 1938 and 1950. Nachlass Hugo Marcus, Ungedruckte Gedichte von Kurt Hiller 1938–1947 [*sic*].
77. Nachlass Hugo Marcus, Roman Malicki, Berlin, to Hugo Marcus, Basel, December 12, 1939.
78. Nachlass Hugo Marcus, Roman Malicki, Berlin, to Hugo Marcus, Basel, February 2, 1940.
79. Nachlass Hugo Marcus, Roman Malicki, Berlin, to Hugo Marcus, Basel, February 2, 1940.
80. Schweizerisches Bundesarchiv BAR, Dossier E4264#1988/2#33540*, Marcus, Hugo, 06.07.1880, Aktenzeichen: P070214, Kantonales Armensekretariat Basel-Landschaft, Liestal, Fürsorgestelle für Auslandschweizer, an das Eidg. Justiz- und Polizeidepartement, Polizeiabteilung, Bern, Dezember 11, 1956.
81. Nachlass Hugo Marcus, Max Jordan (Pater Placidus), Washington, D.C., to Marcus, Basel, September 1, 1941. On Gschwind, see Hugo Gschwind, Dr.rer.pol., Therwil, Präsident des Regierungsrats Kanton Basel, 1940/1941 and 1944/1945; Regierungsgebäude Liestal; http://www.baselland.ch/rr-praes_1832-htm.273718.0.html and https://personenlexikon.bl.ch/Hugo_Gschwind.
82. Nachlass Hugo Marcus, Roman Malicki, Walramsdorf (today: Stęszewko), rural district Posen, to Hugo Marcus, Baselland, August 20, 1943.
83. Nachlass Hugo Marcus, Roman Malicki, Berlin Charlottenburg Kantstrasse 30, to Hugo Marcus, Baselland, July 2, 1944.
84. Whisnant, *Male Homosexuality in West Germany*, 3.

85. Nachlass Hugo Marcus, Roman Malicki, Berlin, to Hugo Marcus, Baselland, end of September 1946.
86. Nachlass Hugo Marcus, Roman Malicki, Berlin, to Hugo Marcus, Baselland, end of September 1946.
87. Nachlass Hugo Marcus, Roman Malicki, Berlin, to Hugo Marcus, Baselland, end of September 1946. Schleusner was a well-known painter, writer, and poet.
88. Following her death in Berlin in 1964, Schleusner's paintings were bequeathed to the Villa Oppenheim in Charlottenburg, Berlin, where Roman also lived. The portrait of Malicki is not listed on the inventory. Email communication, Elke von der Lieth, Kommunale Galerie Berlin, Villa Oppenheim, August 2016. The portrait is owned by the painter, Schleusner expert, and collector Ernst Fermen, who resides in Mönchengladbach, Germany. I thank him for sharing an image of the portrait with me.
89. Nachlass Hugo Marcus, Roman Malicki, Berlin, to Hugo Marcus, Baselland, December 10, 1946.
90. Nachlass Hugo Marcus, Roman Malicki, Berlin, to Hugo Marcus, Baselland, December 10, 1946.
91. Nachlass Hugo Marcus, Roman Malicki, Berlin, to Hugo Marcus, Baselland, June 23, 1947.
92. I found no trace of Roman being buried in the district in which he resided in Berlin. On the webpage of the Landesarchiv Berlin, I searched the Sterberegister (Register of Deaths) of Charlottenburg, Berlin, from 1955 (the last year there is a letter from Malicki) to 1980, but there is no mention of him. He most likely died and is buried in Poland.
93. Reproduced in Backhausen, *Die Lahore-Ahmadiyya-Bewegung in Europa*, 113–15.
94. Marcus, "A Bridge Between the East and the West," 44.
95. Marcus, "A Bridge Between the East and the West," 45.
96. Marcus, "A Bridge Between the East and the West," 45.
97. Marcus, "Was ist uns der Koran?," 3.
98. Marcus, "A Bridge Between the East and the West," 45.
99. Nachlass Hugo Marcus, Hugo Marcus, Baselland, to Maulana Muhammad Ali, Lahore, undated, after 1947.
100. Nachlass Hugo Marcus, S. M. Abdullah, The Mosque, Woking, to Hugo Marcus, Baselland, April 24, 1947.
101. Nachlass Hugo Marcus, Hugo Marcus, Oberwil, Baselland, to the Eidgenössenische Fremdenpolizei, Bern, July 1, 1947.
102. Nachlass Hugo Marcus, Hugo Marcus, Oberwil, Baselland, to the Eidgenössenische Fremdenpolizei, Bern, July 15, 1947.
103. Nachlass Hugo Marcus, Unterlagen Aufenthaltsbewilligung Eidgenössische Fremdenpolizei und Polizeikommando Baselland, letter from Marcus, Oberwil, Baselland, bei Frau Kaiser, to the Eidgenössische Fremdenpolizei, Bern, July 1, 1947.
104. Nachlass Hugo Marcus, Unterlagen Aufenthaltsbewilligung Eidgenössische Fremdenpolizei und Polizeikommando Baselland, Letter from Marcus, Oberwil, Baselland, bei Frau Kaiser, to the Eidgenössische Fremdenpolizei, Bern, July 15, 1947.
105. Nachlass Hugo Marcus, Unterlagen Aufenthaltsbewilligung Eidgenössische Fremdenpolizei und Polizeikommando Baselland, letter from Polizeikommando Baselland, Liestal, to Dr. Hugo Markus, Bruderholzweg 7, Oberwil, October 27, 1947.

106. Nachlass Hugo Marcus, Unterlagen Aufenthaltsbewilligung Eidgenössische Fremdenpolizei und Polizeikommando Baselland, Polizeikommando Baselland, from October 23, 1947, to June 30, 1948; Polizeikommando Baselland from July 1, 1952, to June 30, 1953; Polizeikommando Baselland from July 3, 1953, to extend to June 30, 1954; Polizeikommando Baselland, from June 23, 1954, to extend to June 30, 1955; Hugo Marcus, petition to the Fremdenpolizei des Kantons Baselland, June 15, 1956, to extend his residency, June 25, 1956, until June 30, 1957; and Polizeikommando Baselland, Niederlassungsbewilligung Quittung vom June 25, 1958.
107. Similarly, writing in exile, Hirschfeld placed Nietzsche's "To be able to speak the truth, you should choose exile," on the frontispiece of *Racism*, his work written in exile and published posthumously. Yet "jihad" is not the correct term. The proper word is "hejira," which Marcus used correctly elsewhere: "When a Muslim finds himself living in an environment that does not allow him to remain god-fearing, he should fight against it. This is holy war [jihad], a war of self-defense against evil. But if such a battle will be lost, he should leave that territory and find one where he can be god-fearing without hindrance [hejira]." Marcus, "Was ist uns der Koran?," 24.
108. Sadr-ud-Din, "Das Glaubensbekenntnis des Islams," *Moslemische Revue* 1, no. 2 (July 1924): 91. The article was republished verbatim in every subsequent issue from 1924 to 1926. It later appeared as F. K. Khan Durrani, "Was ist Islam?," such as in *Moslemische Revue* 4, no. 1 (January 1929): 41–45.
109. Hugo Marcus, "Moslemischer Schicksalsglaube." There he writes "Life is short, death is certain, and in the face of everything one has to say, the shortness of time stimulates the utmost activity. . . . One does not worry about oneself anymore. . . . In the face of danger, the real fatalist becomes unbending, strong, courageous, and full of activity" (7, 10).
110. Marcus, *Die ornamentale Schönheit der Landschaft*, 4–5.
111. Due to persecution by Pakistan, the Ahmadiyya Muslim Community, which maintains a caliph, relocated its world headquarters to London in 1984.
112. Nachlass Hugo Marcus, Sadr-ud-Din, Lahore, to Hamid Marcus, Oberwil, Baselland, January 2, 1952.
113. Nachlass Hugo Marcus, Sadr-ud-Din, Lahore, Ahmadiyya Buildings (West Pakistan), to Hugo Marcus, Oberwil, Baselland, January 31, 1952.
114. Nachlass Hugo Marcus, Translation into English of earlier thank you letter to Muhammad Maulana Ali, February 20, 1952.
115. Nachlass Hugo Marcus, Mahmudal Abdullah, Mosque, Woking, to Hugo Marcus, Oberwil, Baselland, June 24, 1956.
116. The Woking Mosque's website is found at https://www.shahjahanmosque.org.uk/history-mosque-part-3, accessed May 1, 2017.
117. For a discussion of debates about the "Jewishness" of Marcus's contemporaries who converted to Catholicism during World War II—including the former chief rabbi of Rome, Israel Zolli; Aaron Lustiger, who became French Catholic Cardinal Jean-Marie Lustiger; and Oswald Rufeisen, who migrated to Israel as the Carmelite monk Brother Daniel—and the light their cases shed on answers to the question of "who is a Jew" and Christian-Jewish relations in the context of the Holocaust and the establishment of the Jewish state of Israel, see Goldman, *Jewish-Christian Difference and Modern Jewish Identity*.

118. Nachlass Hugo Marcus, June 15, 1954, writing from Basel.
119. Nachlass Hugo Marcus, Antrag Entschädigungszahlung, Entschädigungsamt Berlin, August 25, 1954, relating to application of Marcus from June 27, 1954; Bescheid-Nr. 130 547, August 25, 1954, Entschädigungsamt Berlin, Zahlung von DM 904,40.
120. Nachlass Hugo Marcus, "Lebenslauf," written by Marcus in Zürich at Mr. Fritz Cahn's, end of 1956.
121. Nachlass Hugo Marcus, Hugo Marcus, Zürich, Brief an Eidgenössische Fremdenpolizei (Swiss Federal Aliens' Police), Bern, Switzerland, January 23, 1957.
122. Hugo Marcus, Zürich, Brief an Eidgenössische Fremdenpolizei (Swiss Federal Aliens' Police), Bern, Switzerland, January 23, 1957. By this Marcus means that the Ahmadi were not able to send funds to Switzerland to establish the cultural center and journal.
123. Nachlass Hugo Marcus, Hugo Marcus, Zürich, Brief an Eidgenössische Fremdenpolizei (Swiss Federal Aliens' Police), Bern, Switzerland, January 23, 1957.
124. Nachlass Hugo Marcus, Marcus, Gemeinde Oberwil Baselland, Leumunds-Zeugnis vom November 10, 1942.
125. Staatsarchiv Basel-Stadt, PD-Reg 3a, 52516, Marcus, Hugo (1944–1966), Akten der Fremdenpolizei des Kantons Basel-Stadt, Anmeldeformular für Ausländer, February 28, 1957.
126. Armin Wegner heard about Marcus's improved state of health through Marcus's cousin Leonie Cahn, who visited him on her way back from Israel. Nachlass Hugo Marcus, Armin Wegner, Positano, to Hugo Marcus, Basel, October 18, 1955.
127. Nachlass Hugo Marcus, Armin Wegner, Rome, Monte Verde, Viale Quattro Venti 104, to Hugo Marcus, Basel, February 2, 1957.
128. See, for example, Nachlass Hugo Marcus, Fritz Cahn, Zürich, to Marcus, Holbeinstr. 85, Basel, August 21, 1957; and Postcard, Fritz Cahn, San Francisco, to Marcus, July 17, 1957.
129. Nachlass Hugo Marcus, Felix Hepner, Zürich, to Roman Malicki, Berlin, June 3, 1956.
130. Nachlass Hugo Marcus, Armin T. Wegner, Stromboli, Italy, to Hugo Marcus, Basel, September 20, 1960.
131. Nachlass Hugo Marcus, Hugo Marcus, Zürich, to Sadr-ud-Din, Head of the Ahmadia Anjuman, Ahmadia Buildings, Lahore, August 10, 1957.
132. Nachlass Hugo Marcus, Antrag Entschädigungszahlung.
133. Nachlass Hugo Marcus, Sadr-ud-Din, Head of the Ahmadia Anjuman, Ahmadia Buildings, Lahore, to Hugo Marcus, Zürich, August 20, 1957.
134. Nachlass Hugo Marcus, Hugo Marcus, Basel, to President Theodor Heuss, October 27, 1958.
135. The journals in which he published included *Die neue Rundschau, das literarische Echo, Reklams Universum*, and *die Neue Generation*. The academic journals in which his articles appeared included *das Archiv für Philosophie, Zeitschrift für Philosophie und philosophische Kritik, Zeitschrift für angewandte Psychologie, Zeitschrift für Aesthetik und Kunstwissenschaften, Philosophie und Leben*, and *Euphorion*. After 1945 his articles appeared in *Zeitschrift für Naturphilosophie, das Archiv für Rechts- und Sozialphilosophie, Philosophische Rundschau*, and *Philosophische Literaturanzeiger*.
136. Nachlass Hugo Marcus, Fritz Cahn, Zürich 6, Haldeneggsteig 7, to the Gemeindeverwaltung Oberwil, Baselland, December 4, 1956.

137. Nachlass Hugo Marcus, Zeugnis (Testimony), Dr. Jur. Armin T. Wegner, German Embassy, Rome, April 15, 1958.
138. Wegner published his letter to Wilson in the *Berliner Tageblatt*, for which Marcus also wrote; his slide show lecture was published as *Die Austreibung des armenischen Volkes in die Wüste: Ein Lichtbildvortrag.* Two years later he wrote the introduction for the publication of the transcript of the Talat Pasha trial in Berlin, in which the Armenian assassin of the architect of the Armenian genocide was acquitted of murder: *Der Prozess Talaat Pascha*, ed. Armin Wegner (Berlin: Deutsche Verlagsgesellschaft für Politik und Geschichte, 1921). On Wegner's efforts to galvanize the German public about the horror of the Armenian genocide, see Ihrig, *Justifying Genocide*, 196–204.
139. Ihrig, *Justifying Genocide*, 359–60.
140. See Gerlach, "Document: Armin T. Wegner's Letter."
141. Gerlach, "Document: Armin T. Wegner's Letter," 406.
142. Nachlass Hugo Marcus, Armin Wegner, Positano, Italy, to Hugo Marcus, Baselland, August 22, 1945.
143. Nachlass Hugo Marcus, Armin Wegner, Rome, Monte Verde, Viale Quattro Venti 104, to Hugo Marcus, Basel, February 2, 1957.
144. Nachlass Hugo Marcus, Armin Wegner, Positano, to Hugo Marcus, Basel, November 2, 1955.
145. Nachlass Hugo Marcus, Armin Wegner, Positano, to Hugo Marcus, Basel, undated, postmarked December 28, 1955.
146. Nachlass Hugo Marcus, Armin Wegner, Stromboli, Torre dei Sette Venti, Isole Eolie, to Hugo Marcus, Basel, September 20, 1960; and Armin Wegner, Rome, to Hugo Marcus, Basel, December 26, 1961.
147. Nachlass Hugo Marcus, Zeugnis (Testimony), Dr. Jur. Armin T. Wegner, German Embassy, Rome, April 15, 1958. Marcus also obtained a declaration from Elisabeth Ilgenstein, who affirmed that Marcus had worked from 1913 for many years for *Die Gegenwart*, published by Dr. Heinrich Ilgenstein. The declaration is dated August 28, 1958. Marcus also included a statement from novelist Baroness Carola von Crailsheim (1895–1982), a "friend" of Sophie Höchstetter, saying that Marcus served as her tutor from 1919 to 1921 in Berlin, offering her six lessons a week in philosophy, which she regarded as "the foundation for my literary development." Nachlass Hugo Marcus, Antrag Entschädigungszahlung, Affidavit from Baroness Carola von Crailsheim, of Munich, March 17, 1958.
148. Nachlass Hugo Marcus, Armin Wegner, Positano, Italy, to Hugo Marcus, October 18, 1955.
149. Nachlass Hugo Marcus, Armin Wegner, Stromboli, Torre dei Sette Venti, Isole Eolie, to Hugo Marcus, Basel, September 20, 1960.
150. Nachlass Hugo Marcus, Armin Wegner, Rome, to Hugo Marcus, Basel, December 10, 1962.
151. Nachlass Hugo Marcus, Armin Wegner, Rome, to Hugo Marcus, Basel, February 1, 1963. In his letter of support, Wegner notes,

    Along with his purely literary activities Hugo Marcus developed diverse organizational, editorial, and educational activities for the Muslim students in Berlin in connection with the mosque located in West Berlin. Among other activities he edited a journal for these Muslim students and the mosque for many years. Through his extensive study of Islamic theosophy he had the opportunity to develop multiple relationships with Muslim scholars who studied in Berlin. One can say without exaggeration that Hugo Marcus really was a German emissary in the circles of these foreigners. He offered many of these students grammatical and artistic tutoring. I personally took part in diverse meetings of these foreign students and young scholars which Hugo Marcus had organized and I remember some of them, especially a student from Turkey who later became Professor at Ankara University.

152. Reiss, *The Orientalist*, 336.
153. Staatsarchiv Basel-Stadt, PD-Reg 3a, 52516, Marcus, Hugo (1944–1966), Akten der Fremdenpolizei des Kantons Basel-Stadt, Binggeli, Der Chef der Polizeiabteilung, Eidgenössisches Justiz- und Polizeidepartment, Polizeiabteilung, Bern, March 12, 1958, an Kantonales Armensekretariat, Basel-Landschaft, Liestal Baselland.
154. Staatsarchiv Basel-Stadt, PD-Reg 3a, 52516, Marcus, Hugo (1944–1966), Akten der Fremdenpolizei des Kantons Basel-Stadt, Bestätigung betr. Herrn Hugo Marcus, Basel, Frau Gertrud Kurz, Christlicher Friedensdienst Abt. Flüchtlingshilfe, Dittlingerweg 4 Bern, April 8, 1957.
155. Staatsarchiv Basel-Stadt, PD-Reg 3a, 52516, Marcus, Hugo (1944–1966), Akten der Fremdenpolizei des Kantons Basel-Stadt, Kontrollbureau, Kantonale Fremdenpolizei, Der Adjunkt Schärer, April 21, 1959, an die Polizeiabteilung des Eidg. Justiz- und Polizeidepartments, Bern.
156. Marcus had received help from the Basler Hilfsstelle für Flüchtlinge, which was dissolved in July 1956 when the Christlicher Friedensdienst took over its assistance to refugees. Schweizerisches Bundesarchiv BAR, Dossier E4264#1988/2#33540*, Marcus, Hugo, 06.07.1880, Aktenzeichen: P070214, Gertrud Kurz, Christlicher Friedensdienst, Abteilung Flüchtlingshilfe, Bern, an das Kantonale Armensekretariat Baselland, Liestal, January 25, 1957. Regarding assistance from this Christian organization and Marcus paying back the sums, see Schweizerisches Bundesarchiv BAR, Dossier E4264#1988/2#33540*, Marcus, Hugo, 06.07.1880, Aktenzeichen: P070214, Gertrud Kurz, Christlicher Friedensdienst, Abteilung Flüchtlingshilfe, Bern, an Flüchtlingssektion der Polizeiabteilung z. Hd. Von Herrn Binggeli, Bern und Kantonales Armensekretariat Basel-Landschaft z. Hd. Von Herrn Dr. Ballmer, Liestal, February 27, 1958; Der Chef der Polizeiabteilung, i.A. sig. Binggeli, an Herrn Hugo Marcus, Privatheim Holbeinstrasse 85, Basel, March 26, 1959; and Der Chef der Polizeiabteilung i.A. sig. Binggeli, Bern, April 28, 1959, an Kantonale Fremdenpolizei Kontrollbureau Basel.
157. Marcus was paid 429 Deutsche Mark (DM) per month from November 1, 1953, to December 31, 1955, and from January 1, 1956, 468 DM per month. Nachlass Hugo Marcus, Antrag Entschädigungszahlung, Entschädigungsamt Berlin, December 10, 1958, betr. Entschädigungsanträge. In addition, he was given 5,148 DM for the period prior to January 1, 1953. In total he received 33,618 DM by January 31, 1959. As of January 1, 1960, this was raised to 488 DM per month. Nachlass Hugo Marcus, Entschädigungsamt, Berlin, to Hugo Marcus, Basel, November 2, 1959. The amount was raised

again to over 500 DM per month in May 1962, and then to 550 DM, rising again as of December 18, 1963, to 586 per month; finally, as of February 28, 1965 he began to receive 627 DM per month.

158. Schweizerisches Bundesarchiv BAR, Dossier E4264#1988/2#33540*, Marcus, Hugo, 06.07.1880, Aktenzeichen: P070214, Kantonales Armensekretariat Basel-Landschaft, Liestal, Fürsorgestelle für Auslandschweizer, an das Eidg. Justiz- und Polizeidepartement, Polizeiabteilung, Bern, Dezember 11, 1956.
159. Nachlass Hugo Marcus, Father Placidus Jordan to Dr. Marcus, Zürich, January 3, 1957.
160. Nachlass Hugo Marcus, Hugo Marcus, Zürich, Haldeneggsteig 7, to Jordan, January 12, 1957.
161. Schweizerisches Bundesarchiv BAR, Dossier E4264#1988/2#33540*, Marcus, Hugo, 06.07.1880, Aktenzeichen: P070214, photo included with Marcus's application for a foreigner's pass.

5. HANS ALIENUS: YEARNING, GAY WRITER, 1948–1965

1. On persecution of homosexuals under Paragraph 175, see Moeller, "Private Acts, Public Anxieties"; Pretzel, *Homosexuellenpolitik in der frühen Bundesrepublik*; and Whisnant, *Male Homosexuality in West Germany*. On Marcus's published works during this time, see Marcus, *Rechtswelt und Ästhetik*, 6–7, 35–36; *and* Marcus, *Die Fundamente der Wirklichkeit als Regulatoren der Sprache*, 26–27.
2. Meinecke, *Die Deutsche Katastrophe: Betrachtungen und Erinnerungen* (1946), translated into English as *The German Catastrophe: Reflections and Recollections* (1950). For his part, after the war Hiller again promoted socialism and pacifism as well as "Logocracy," conceived as "a Platonic government of intellectuals that would govern the population until it was mutually and spiritually prepared" for democracy. Whisnant, *Male Homosexuality in West Germany*, 77.
3. Beachy, *Gay Berlin*, 220–22.
4. Herrn, *100 Years of the Gay Rights Movement in Germany*, 24.
5. Beachy, *Gay Berlin*, 243–44.
6. Herzog, *Sex After Fascism*, 88.
7. Herzog, *Sex After Fascism*, 94.
8. Whisnant, *Male Homosexuality in West Germany*, 56. On the conversion of German men from autocrats and soldiers to democrats, see van Rahden, "Fatherhood, Rechristianization, and the Quest for Democracy"; Biess, "Survivors of Totalitarianism"; and Biess, *Homecomings*.
9. Whisnant, *Male Homosexuality in West Germany*, 46.
10. Herzog, *Sex After Fascism*, 90.
11. Herrn, *100 Years of the Gay Rights Movement in Germany*, 32.
12. Herrn, *100 Years of the Gay Rights Movement in Germany*, 94.
13. Herrn, *100 Years of the Gay Rights Movement in Germany*, 34–35. The court had reasoned that "limits on personal expression are imposed by laws on public morals."
14. Whisnant, *Male Homosexuality in West Germany*, 110.

15. Whisnant, *Male Homosexuality in West Germany*, 47.
16. Herrn, *100 Years of the Gay Rights Movement in Germany*, 130.
17. Herrn, *100 Years of the Gay Rights Movement in Germany*, 39. The German Democratic Republic (GDR) established in the Soviet-occupied zone has a different history regarding Paragraph 175. It reverted to the version in effect before the Nazi rise to power (26). The GDR was not without its homophobia: homosexuality was viewed as a remnant of the capitalist system that must be combated, but a 1952 the draft of a new criminal code called for a repeal of Paragraph 175. Nevertheless, following the revolt in 1953, Minister of Justice Max Fechner, accused of aiding and abetting the revolt, was convicted of homosexual acts (33). That same year, following a government committee recommendation to decriminalize sex acts between men, police and judges in the GDR no longer prosecuted or imprisoned adult men engaged in consensual homosexual activity. In 1968 the GDR abolished Paragraph 175, although it introduced a new law criminalizing same-sex activity between adults (aged eighteen and over) and minors (aged under eighteen). Herzog, *Sex After Fascism*, 197–98. In 1987 East Germany granted homosexuals equal civil rights.
18. Kennedy, *The Ideal Gay Man*, 73.
19. Hugo Marcus, *Rechtswelt und Ästhetik*.
20. Hugo Marcus, *Rechtswelt und Ästhetik*, 35–36.
21. Hugo Marcus, *Rechtswelt und Ästhetik*, 6.
22. Hugo Marcus, *Rechtswelt und Ästhetik*, 6–7.
23. Bullough, Introduction to *The Homosexuality of Men and Women*, 17. Richard von Krafft-Ebing was Hirschfeld's forerunner, "the father of modern sexology." Wolff, *Magnus Hirschfeld*, 61.
24. Alienus, "Goethe und die Freundesliebe."
25. Tobin, *Warm Brothers*, 44–45.
26. Whisnant, *Male Homosexuality in West Germany*, 101.
27. Alienus, "Goethe und die Freundesliebe," 9. For a brief description of this theory, see Dose, *Magnus Hirschfeld*, 97–108.
28. Dose, *Magnus Hirschfeld*, 97–98. See also Hirschfeld, *The Homosexuality of Men and Women*, 417–21.
29. Herzer, *Magnus Hirschfeld*, 104–5.
30. Dose, *Magnus Hirschfeld*, 102–3.
31. Hirschfeld, *The Homosexuality of Men and Women*, 455.
32. Mancini, *Magnus Hirschfeld and the Quest for Sexual Freedom*, 52.
33. Wolff, *Magnus Hirschfeld*, 129–30.
34. Mancini, *Magnus Hirschfeld and the Quest for Sexual Freedom*, 10. A similar point was made earlier by Herzer, *Magnus Hirschfeld*, 106.
35. Mancini, *Magnus Hirschfeld and the Quest for Sexual Freedom*, ix–x, 144.
36. Tobin, *Warm Brothers*, 18.
37. Alienus, "Goethe und die Freundesliebe," 5.
38. Tobin, *Warm Brothers*, 106–7.
39. Alienus, "Goethe und die Freundesliebe," 6.
40. Alienus, "Goethe und die Freundesliebe," 6.

41. Tobin, *Warm Brothers*, 7. Hirschfeld also mention's Goethe's use of sexual substitutes in *Elective Affinities*, and boys' love for girls replacing their love of boys in *Wilhelm Meister's Journeyman Years*. Hirschfeld, *The Homosexuality of Men and Women*, 125.
42. Alienus, "Goethe und die Freundesliebe," 7.
43. Goethe, *Wilhelm Meister's Journeyman Years*, 286.
44. Goethe, *Wilhelm Meister's Journeyman Years*, 286.
45. Goethe, *Wilhelm Meister's Journeyman Years*, 286.
46. Goethe, *Wilhelm Meister's Journeyman Years*, 287.
47. Goethe, *Wilhelm Meister's Journeyman Years*, 288.
48. Goethe, *Wilhelm Meister's Journeyman Years*, 289.
49. Alienus, "Goethe und die Freundesliebe," 7.
50. Goethe, *Selected Poems*, 87.
51. Alienus, "Goethe und die Freundesliebe," 8.
52. Translated in Goethe, *Selected Poems*, 63–65. Hirschfeld also notes Goethe's enthusiastic expression of the meaning of friendship: "Happy are they who without being hated / Can close themselves off from the world, / Who hold friends close to their heart, / And enjoy themselves with them, / Ignorant about human striving / And ignored by everyone, / To go through the labyrinth of the heart, / Changed overnight." Hirschfeld, *The Homosexuality of Men and Women*, 229.
53. Alienus, "Goethe und die Freundesliebe," 8.
54. Quoted in Norton, *Secret Germany*, 34.
55. Norton, *Secret Germany*, 208. "Umbel" (*Dolde*) refers to a class of plant in which the stalks arise from the bulb. *Seim* (nectar) is similar to *Same* (semen).
56. Alienus, "Goethe und die Freundesliebe," 8.
57. Translated in Goethe, *Selected Poems*, 133.
58. Alienus, "Goethe und die Freundesliebe," 9.
59. Goethe, *Wilhelm Meister's Apprenticeship*, 82, 320.
60. Goethe, *Wilhelm Meister's Apprenticeship*, 50.
61. Goethe, *Wilhelm Meister's Apprenticeship*, 54. Many other characters also refer to her as "the strange girl" (287).
62. Goethe, *Wilhelm Meister's Apprenticeship*, 61.
63. Goethe, *Wilhelm Meister's Apprenticeship*, 65.
64. Goethe, *Wilhelm Meister's Apprenticeship*, 113, 140.
65. Goethe, *Wilhelm Meister's Apprenticeship*, 122.
66. Goethe, *Wilhelm Meister's Apprenticeship*, 315–16.
67. Tobin, *Warm Brothers*, 42.
68. Goethe, *Wilhelm Meister's Apprenticeship*, 156.
69. Goethe, *Wilhelm Meister's Apprenticeship*, 333.
70. Goethe, *Wilhelm Meister's Apprenticeship*, 353.
71. Tobin, *Warm Brothers*, 42. See, in particular, Goethe, *Wilhelm Meister's Apprenticeship*, 320–21, where three times her latent desire for him is described as "yearning."
72. Goethe, *Wilhelm Meister's Apprenticeship*, 142–43.
73. Goethe, *Wilhelm Meister's Apprenticeship*, 216.
74. Alienus, "Goethe und die Freundesliebe," 9.
75. Alienus, "Goethe und die Freundesliebe," 9.

76. Tobin, *Warm Brothers*, 18.
77. Alienus, "Goethe und die Freundesliebe," 10. See also Hirschfeld, *The Homosexuality of Men and Women*, 1055.
78. Alienus, "Goethe und die Freundesliebe," 10. Emphasis added.
79. Alienus, "Goethe und die Freundesliebe," 11. Emphasis added.
80. Alienus, "Goethe und die Freundesliebe," 11. Blüher's concepts are explored in Mancini, *Magnus Hirschfeld and the Quest for Sexual Freedom*, 50, 103–4.
81. Alienus, "Goethe und die Freundesliebe," 11.
82. Tobin, *Warm Brothers*, 31.
83. Tobin, *Warm Brothers*, 36.
84. Quoted in Tobin, *Warm Brothers*, 96.
85. Alienus, "Goethe und die Freundesliebe," 12. The letter was written at midnight between the thirteenth and fourteenth of August 1774.
86. Tobin, *Warm Brothers*, 38.
87. Gustafson, *Men Desiring Men*, 35–36.
88. Wilson, "But Is It Gay?," 783.
89. Tobin, *Warm Brothers*, 44.
90. *Goethes Werke: Hamburger Ausgabe in 14 Bänden*, 2:202, cited in Tobin, *Warm Brothers*, 44.
91. *West-East Divan, The Poems, with "Notes and Essays"*, ver. 194–217, pp. 123–29.
92. *West-East Divan, The Poems, with "Notes and Essays"*, ver. 213, p. 133.
93. Goethe, "Notes and Essays for a Better Understanding," 240.
94. Goethe, "Notes and Essays for a Better Understanding," 241–42.
95. Goethe, "Notes and Essays for a Better Understanding," 242.
96. Hirschfeld, *The Homosexuality of Men and Women*, 380.
97. This is a mid-sixteenth-century Tunisian text, a frank manual of love and sex that gives insight into the sexual life of Arabs, translated into German as *Liebe im Orient: Der duftende Garten des Scheik Nefzaui*. Hirschfeld compares the book to the *Kama Sutra*, declaring it is much freer and more open in its discussion of sex than its Indian counterpart. The authors of the introduction declare Arabs are much freer in their sexual life, Islam having never made love and love lust into sins (vi). Muhammad himself, while young, married a widow, a woman at her sexual prime. At his death he left widows, including the young Aisha.
98. Hiller, *§ 175*, 113. "In den Ländern des Islam . . . wird der mannmännliche Verkehr vom Staate geduldet."
99. Hiller, "Appeal on Behalf of an Oppressed Human Variety." The speech can be found at http://paganpressbooks.com/jpl/HILLER.HTM.
100. Schmidtke, "Eine doppelte Konstruktion der Wirklichkeit."
101. Tobin, *Peripheral Desires*, 76.
102. On his relationship with his imam, see Marcus, "Was ist uns der Koran?"; and "In der Moschee zu Berlin."
103. Alienus, "Brief eines 'Mitschuldigen.'"
104. Alienus, "Brief eines 'Mitschuldigen,'" 2.
105. Alienus, "Brief eines 'Mitschuldigen,'" 3.
106. Alienus, "Brief eines 'Mitschuldigen,'" 3.
107. Alienus, "Brief eines 'Mitschuldigen,'" 3.

108. Alienus, "Brief eines 'Mitschuldigen,'" 4.
109. Tobin, *Warm Brothers*, 133.
110. Tobin, *Warm Brothers*, 137.
111. Tobin, *Warm Brothers*, 137.
112. Goethe, *Selected Poems*, 32–33.
113. Goethe, *Italian Journey*, 140–41.
114. Whisnant, *Male Homosexuality in West Germany*, 92.
115. Whisnant, *Male Homosexuality in West Germany*, 93–94.
116. Letter from Rolf Meier to Kurt Hiller, March 22, 1960. Quoted in Backhausen, *Die Lahore-Ahmadiyya-Bewegung in Europa*, 115. On Hamburg as Germany's "most impressive gay scene," see Whisnant, *Male Homosexuality in West Germany*, 118.
117. Mancini, "Boys in the City," 99.
118. Mann, *The Turning Point*, 114.
119. Mancini, "Boys in the City," 102.
120. Mancini, "Boys in the City," 105.
121. Mancini, "Boys in the City," 105–6.
122. Mancini, "Boys in the City," 106.
123. On Brand, see Hubert Kennedy, "Brand, Adolf (1874–1945)," GLBTQ (2005), http://www.glbtq.com.
124. Evans, "Seeing Subjectivity," 450. Whisnant argues that despite these accurate criticisms, the success of the 1970s gay liberation struggle built upon the homophile movement's promotion of legal reforms, commemoration of gay persecution by the Nazis, the creation of an international association of homosexuals, and defining gays as a minority group in need of legal protection. Whisnant, *Male Homosexuality in West Germany*, 207–8.
125. Rolf (Meier), response to "Das Ewige und der Freund," 26.
126. Alienus, "Das Ewige und der Freund." The reason he wrote the letter was because, unlike his other writings, which were successful in attracting more general audiences, he claims, he could not expect the same result with these homoerotic stories, so he was hoping to find interested subscribers of the journal who would help him get them published, or at least find interested readers. He was able to publish this as a sixty-six-page autobiographical account ten years later entitled, *Einer sucht den Freund*. Marcus published two novellas: *Das Frühlingsglück* (Spring bliss, 1900) and a thirty-four-page piece, *Das Tor dröhnt zu* (The gate slams shut, 1915).
127. It could not publish frontal nudes, yet it was repeatedly confiscated around the world for publishing "obscenity." Kennedy, *The Ideal Gay Man*, 158–59.
128. In 1966 the Zürich police informed the editor of *Der Kreis* that they had never demanded its subscription list because the journal had always observed "the legal age of consent of 20 years when receiving new members and guests," had kept "male prostitutes away from their meetings," and had abstained "from all public propaganda." Letter quoted in Kennedy, *The Ideal Gay Man*, 147.
129. American writer Samuel Steward, quoted in Kennedy, *The Ideal Gay Man*, 43. Rather than dismiss these writers as "accommodationist" and "overly cautious," we can appreciate how "despite postwar crackdowns on homosexual men in many countries and lingering wartime enmities, organizations and individuals joined hands across national

borders. . . . They worked to repeal laws against homosexuality, to equalize the age of consent for same-sex and other-sex interactions, to persuade publics of the normality of same-sex desires, and to win full civil equality and human rights for homosexual men and women." Rupp, "The Persistence of Transnational Organizing," 1037.

130. Löw, "Der 'Kreis' und sein idealer Schwuler," 157, quoted in Kennedy, *The Ideal Gay Man*, 166.
131. See Kennedy, *The Ideal Gay Man*, 165–80; 183–203.
132. "Ein Paar Schuhe," 7–10, 22. Marcus had already introduced its main character and theme over a quarter of a century earlier. In a story published in *Das junge Deutschland*, a character named Heinrich gives away all of his money to a beggar and tries not to feel noble for doing so. Marcus, "Aus einem stillen Buche." In another piece published in *Der Feuerreiter* a few years later, the characters Eduard and Heinrich debate the meaning of "goodness." Heinrich persuades Eduard to struggle for what is good even when it is an unreachable goal. Marcus, "Dialog vom Sinn der Güte." The distinction between good and beautiful deeds is also explicated in Alienus, "Ein paar Schuhe."
133. Alienus, "Ein Paar Schuhe," 7.
134. Alienus, "Ein Paar Schuhe," 7.
135. Alienus, "Ein Paar Schuhe," 7.
136. Alienus, "Ein Paar Schuhe," 10.
137. Beachy, *Gay Berlin*, 103.
138. Alienus, "Ein Paar Schuhe," 10.
139. Alienus, "Ein Paar Schuhe," 10.
140. Alienus, "Ein Paar Schuhe," 10.
141. Alienus, "Licht fällt ins Fenster."
142. Alienus, "Stärker als der Tod."
143. Alienus, "Stärker als der Tod," 4.
144. Alienus, "Stärker als der Tod," 5.
145. Alienus, "Stärker als der Tod," 6.
146. Alienus, "Stärker als der Tod," 6.
147. Alienus, "In Geschäften nach Paris."
148. Whisnant, *Male Homosexuality in West Germany*, 127.
149. Alienus, "In Geschäften nach Paris," 9.
150. Alienus, "In Geschäften nach Paris," 10.
151. The ladder allowed angels to ascend and descend, where God appeared to Jacob in his dream in Genesis 28:10–19.
152. Alienus, "In Geschäften nach Paris," 10.
153. Quoted in Norton, *Secret Germany*, 339.
154. Alienus, "In Geschäften nach Paris," 10–11.
155. Alienus, "In Geschäften nach Paris," 11.
156. Alienus, "In Geschäften nach Paris," 11.
157. Isherwood, *Christopher and His Kind*, 30.
158. Isherwood, *Christopher and His Kind*, 2–4, also cited in Beachy, *Gay Berlin*, 187.
159. Beachy, *Gay Berlin*, 194, 200, 202.
160. Beachy, *Gay Berlin*, 206.

161. Beachy, *Gay Berlin*, 207.
162. Beachy, *Gay Berlin*, 206.
163. Zweig, *Die Welt von Gestern* (1953), 287, quoted in Gay, *Weimar Culture*, 129.
164. Nachlass Hugo Marcus, Roman Malicki, Berlin, to Hugo Marcus, Basel, undated, 1955.
165. "Zum 75. Geburtstage von Hans Alienus."
166. "Zum 75. Geburtstage von Hans Alienus," 14.
167. "Zum 75. Geburtstage von Hans Alienus," 15.
168. "Zum 75. Geburtstage von Hans Alienus," 15.
169. "Zum 75. Geburtstage von Hans Alienus," 15.
170. "Zum 75. Geburtstage von Hans Alienus," 16.
171. "Zum 75. Geburtstage von Hans Alienus," 16.
172. Alienus, "Stärker als der Tod," 7.
173. There are hints of these themes in Mann's first novel published in 1901, *Buddenbrooks*, where one character describes his own Italian journey to Venice, Rome, and Vesuvius, and the Villa Borghese where Goethe had written part of his Faust. Mann, *Buddenbrooks*, 30.
174. Kantorowicz, *Kaiser Friedrich der Zweite.*
175. Mann, *Death in Venice*, 9–10.
176. Mann, *Death in Venice*, 63.
177. Mann, *Death in Venice*, 12.
178. Mann, *Death in Venice*, 52–53.
179. Mann, *Death in Venice*, 56.
180. Mann, *Death in Venice*, 58.
181. Mann, *Death in Venice*, 15.
182. Mann, *Death in Venice*. Mann's *Doktor Faustus: Das Leben des deutschen Tonsetzers Adrian Leverkühn, erzählt von einem Freunde* (1947), like Goethe's *Faust*, has homosexual undertones. The English translation is *Mann, Doctor Faustus: The Life of the German Composer Adrian Leverkühn, as Told by a Friend* (1948).
183. Mann, *Death in Venice*, 14–15.
184. Mann, *Death in Venice*, 30–31.
185. Mann, *Death in Venice*, 34–35, 36–37.
186. Mann, *Death in Venice*, 39.
187. Hiller, "Wo bleibt der homoerotische Roman?" *Jahrbuch für sexuelle Zwischenstufen* 14 (1914): 338–41, quoted in Beachy, *Gay Berlin*, 109–10.
188. Mann, *Death in Venice*, 81.
189. Tobin, *Peripheral Desires*, 189, 193.
190. Tobin, *Peripheral Desires*, 185.
191. Tobin, *Peripheral Desires*, 186–87, 189.
192. Tobin, *Peripheral Desires*, 205.
193. Tobin, *Peripheral Desires*, 206.
194. "Zum 75. Geburtstage von Hans Alienus," 16.
195. "Zum 75. Geburtstage von Hans Alienus, "Die einander bei Händen und bei Sternen halten," 17.
196. Mann, *Buddenbrooks*, 580.

197. "Zum 75. Geburtstage von Hans Alienus, "Die einander bei Händen und bei Sternen halten," 17.

CONCLUSION: A GOETHE MOSQUE FOR BERLIN

1. Schweizerisches Bundesarchiv BAR/Swiss Federal Archive, Bern, Dossier E4264#1988/2#33540*, Marcus, Hugo, 06.07.1880, Aktenzeichen: P070214, application for a foreigner's pass, May 13, 1964.
2. Application for a foreigner's pass, May 13, 1964.
3. Staatsarchiv Basel-Stadt, PD-Reg 3a, 52516, Marcus, Hugo (1944–1966), Akten der Fremdenpolizei des Kantons Basel-Stadt, Hugo Marcus an Kontrollbureau der Kantonales Fremdenpolizei, Polizei Departement, Basel, Spiegelhof, April 22, 1964.
4. Staatsarchiv Basel-Stadt, PD-Reg 3a, 52516, Marcus, Hugo (1944–1966), Akten der Fremdenpolizei des Kantons Basel-Stadt, Eidgenössische Polizeiabteilung, Bern, May 27, 1964, an Kantonale Fremdenpolizei, Basel.
5. Alienus, "Erinnerung an Magnus Hirschfeld," 7.
6. Letter from Rolf Meier to Hugo Marcus, October 4, 1965, reproduced in Backhausen, *Die Lahore-Ahmadiyya-Bewegung in Europa*, 116. Backhausen obtained the citations from the letters from Zürich-based independent researcher Beat Frischknecht, who examined the originals.
7. Kennedy, "Hiller, Kurt."
8. Letter from Rolf Meier to Hugo Marcus, October 4, 1965; and see letter from Rolf Meier to Kurt Hiller, October 18, 1965, reproduced in Backhausen, *Die Lahore-Ahmadiyya-Bewegung in Europa*, 116.
9. Backhausen, *Die Lahore-Ahmadiyya-Bewegung in Europa*, 114.
10. Nachlass Hugo Marcus, Armin Wegner, Rome, to Hugo Marcus, Basel, December 2, 1965.
11. Nachlass Hugo Marcus, Leonie Cahn, Zürich, to Bürgerspital Basel Leitung, September 26, 1965.
12. Nachlass Hugo Marcus, Leonie Cahn, Zürich, to Hugo Marcus, Basel, October 25, 1965.
13. Nachlass Hugo Marcus, Leonie Cahn, Zürich, to Hugo Marcus, Basel, no date (1965); and Leonie Cahn to Hugo Marcus, November 16, 1965.
14. Nachlass Hugo Marcus, Leonie Cahn, Zürich, to Hugo Marcus, Basel, November 10, 1965.
15. Letter from Rolf Meier to Kurt Hiller, December 16, 1965, reproduced in Backhausen, *Die Lahore-Ahmadiyya-Bewegung in Europa*, 117.
16. Adullam is the name of King David's cave of retreat: "David therefore departed from there and escaped to the cave of Adullam. So when his brothers and all his father's house heard it, they went down there to him. And everyone who was in distress, everyone who was in debt, and everyone who was discontented gathered to him." (1 Samuel 22:1–2). The Adullam Foundation was established in 1919 by the evangelist Jakob Vetter-Baumann as a "Home for the Poor," and to this day serves "all patients, independent of background, religion and outlook." The Adullam Foundation website is http://www.adullam.ch/auftrag-struktur-stiftung.html.

17. Letter from Rolf Meier to Kurt Hiller, April 21, 1966, reproduced in Backhausen, *Die Lahore-Ahmadiyya-Bewegung in Europa*, 117.
18. Letter from Rolf Meier to Kurt Hiller, April 26, 1966, reproduced in Backhausen, *Die Lahore-Ahmadiyya-Bewegung in Europa*, 117–18.
19. The Muslim section of Friedhof am Hornli was not opened until 2000.
20. Letter from Rolf Meier to Kurt Hiller, April 26, 1966, reproduced in Backhausen, *Die Lahore-Ahmadiyya-Bewegung in Europa*, 117–18.
21. Dose, *Magnus Hirschfeld*, 94–96.
22. Backhausen, *Die Lahore-Ahmadiyya-Bewegung in Europa*, 118.
23. Letter from Rolf Meier to Kurt Hiller, April 26, 1966, reproduced in Backhausen, *Die Lahore-Ahmadiyya-Bewegung in Europa*, 117–18.
24. Letter from Rolf Meier to Kurt Hiller, April 28, 1966, reproduced in Backhausen, *Die Lahore-Ahmadiyya-Bewegung in Europa*, 118.
25. Letter from Rolf Meier to Kurt Hiller, May 5, 1966, reproduced in Backhausen, *Die Lahore-Ahmadiyya-Bewegung in Europa*, 118.
26. "Hans Alienus," *Der Kreis—Le Cercle—The Circle* 34, no. 5 Jahrgang (1966): 5.
27. Nachlass Hugo Marcus, Brief von Michael Landmann, St. Gallen, Winkelriedstr, an Leonie Cahn, Zürich, Haldeneggsteig 7, July 12, 1966.
28. "Hugo Marcus 80 Jahre alt," *Allgemeine Wochenzeitung der Juden in Deutschland*, no. XV/16 (July 15, 1960): 6.
29. Marcus, "Moslemischer Schicksalsglaube"; and Dr. H., "Buchbesprechung."
30. Herrn, *100 Years of the Gay Rights Movement*, 57–58; Whisnant, *Male Homosexuality in West Germany*, 166–203; and Beachy, *Gay Berlin*, 245–47.
31. The Jewish Museum Berlin website is https://www.jmberlin.de/en. The website for the Memorial to the Murdered Jews of Europe is https://www.stiftung-denkmal.de/en/memorials/the-memorial-to-the-murdered-jews-of-europe.html.
32. A description can be found at the website for the Memorial to the Homosexuals Persecuted Under the National Socialist Regime, https://www.stiftung-denkmal.de/en/memorials/memorial-to-the-homosexuals-persecuted-under-the-national-socialist-regime.html.
33. The website for the Schwules Museum is http://www.schwulesmuseum.de/en/the-museum/.
34. Shimer, "Germany Wipes Slate Clean."
35. Bunzl, *Jews and Queers*, x.
36. Bunzl, *Jews and Queers*, 218–23.
37. The website of the Şehitlik Mosque is http://www.sehitlik-camii.de/.
38. Özyürek, *Being German, Becoming Muslim*, 2.
39. "Benannt nach Goethe."
40. Ateş, *Selam, Frau Imamin*, 266.
41. Ateş, *Selam, Frau Imamin*, 280.
42. Ateş, *Selam, Frau Imamin*, 198–211, 259–64.
43. Ateş, *Der Islam braucht eine sexuelle Revolution*.
44. "Berlin soll liberale Moscheegemeinde bekommen."
45. Ateş, *Selam, Frau Imamin*, 297.

Bibliography

LIST OF ARCHIVES AND LIBRARIES

Bibliothek Zentrum Moderner Orient, Berlin, general collection and Nachlass Professor Dr. Gerhard Höpp (Centre for Modern Oriental Studies, Gerhard Höpp Estate)

Landesarchiv Berlin (Berlin State Archives)

National Archives and Records Administration, Washington, D.C., National Archives Collection of Foreign Records Seized (Record Group 242), A3340, MFOK Series (Master File, Ortsgruppenkartei, Nationalsozialistische Deutsche Arbeiterpartei).

ONE National Gay & Lesbian Archives at the USC libraries, Los Angeles

Schweizerisches Bundesarchiv, Bern (Swiss Federal Archive)

Schwules Museum, Berlin (Gay Museum)

Staatsarchiv Basel-Stadt (Basel City Archive)

Staatsbibliothek zu Berlin, general collection, and Preussischer Kulturbesitz, Handschriftenabteilung (Berlin State Library, including Manuscript Collection)

Stiftung Brandenburgische Gedenkstätten, Gedenkstätte und Museum Sachsenhausen (Sachsenhausen Concentration Camp Memorial and Museum)

Thomas Mann Archives, ETH Zürich

Zentralbibliothek Zürich, general collection, and Handschriftenabteilung, Nachlass Hugo Marcus (im Nachlass Walter Corti) (Zürich Central Library, Manuscript Collection, Hugo Marcus Estate)

ARCHIVAL SOURCES

Hugo Marcus's Personal Documents

ZENTRALBIBLIOTHEK ZÜRICH, NACHLASS HUGO MARCUS, PERSÖNLICHES

Bestätigung 1902–1903, Königliche Friedrich-Wilhelms-Universität Berlin.

Abgangs-Zeugnis der Königlichen Friedrich-Wilhelms-Universität zu Berlin, Berlin, den November 27, 1906.

Kuratorium für das Bestattungswesen der Stadt Berlin, 1 Empfangsbescheinigung vom May 23, 1919.

Danksagung vom March 30, 1919, Kriegsministerium Berlin.

Verleihung der Roten Kreuz-Medaille 3. Klasse, der Kommissar und Militär-Inspektor der freiwilligen Krankenpflege, Berlin, April 10, 1920.
Verleihung "Ehrenkreuz für Kriegsteilnehmer" Berlin, April 9, 1936.
Austritt aus der Synagogengemeinde Berlin, Bescheinigung vom May 18, 1936, Das Amtsgericht Berlin-Charlottenburg.
Hugo Marcus, Erteilung eines Einreisevisums für das Königreich Albanien, November 26, 1938.
Ungedruckte Gedichte von Kurt Hiller 1938–1947.
Bestätigung vom August 21, 1939, Der Imam der Moschee Berlin-Wilmersdorf, S. M. Abdullah.
Hugo Marcus, Kennkarte Deutsches Reich, ausgestellt: Berlin, March 16, 1939.
Unterlagen Aufenthaltsbewilligung Eidgenössische Fremdenpolizei und Polizeikommando Baselland, Polizeikommando Baselland, Aufenthaltsbewilligung Quittung, September 6, 1939; Eidgenössische Fremdenpolizei Bern, September 5, 1939, Zustimmensverfügung mit Frist zu Ausreise aus der Schweiz bis zum November 20, 1939.
Gemeinde Oberwil Baselland, Leumunds-Zeugnis vom November 10, 1942.
Unterlagen Aufenthaltsbewilligung Eidgenössische Fremdenpolizei und Polizeikommando Baselland, Gemeinde Oberwil, Baselland, Leumunds Zeugnis, November 10, 1942.
Abgangs-Zeugnis Universität Basel, Basel, May 9, 1947.
Unterlagen Aufenthaltsbewilligung Eidgenössische Fremdenpolizei und Polizeikommando Baselland, letter from Marcus, Oberwil, Baselland, bei Frau Kaiser, to the Eidgenössische Fremdenpolizei, Bern, July 1, 1947.
Unterlagen Aufenthaltsbewilligung Eidgenössische Fremdenpolizei und Polizeikommando Baselland, Letter from Marcus, Oberwil, Baselland, bei Frau Kaiser, to the Eidgenössische Fremdenpolizei, Bern, July 15, 1947.
Unterlagen Aufenthaltsbewilligung Eidgenössische Fremdenpolizei und Polizeikommando Baselland, letter from Polizeikommando Baselland, Liestal, to Dr. Hugo Markus, Bruderholzweg [today Bruderholzstrasse] 7 Oberwil, October 27, 1947.
Unterlagen Aufenthaltsbewilligung Eidgenössische Fremdenpolizei und Polizeikommando Baselland, Polizeikommando Baselland, Liestal, to Dr. Hugo Markus [*sic*], Bruderholzweg 7 Oberwil, from October 23, 1947, to June 30, 1948; Polizeikommando Baselland from July 1, 1952 to June 30, 1953; Polizeikommando Baselland from July 3, 1953, to extend to June 30, 1954; Polizeikommando Baselland, from June 23, 1954, to extend to June 30, 1955; Hugo Marcus, petition to the Fremdenpolizei des Kantons Baselland, June 15, 1956, to extend his residency; June 25, 1956, until June 30, 1957; and Polizeikommando Baselland, Niederlassungsbewilligung Quittung vom June 25, 1958.
Antrag Entschädigungszahlung, Entschädigungsamt Berlin, August 25, 1954, relating to application of Marcus from June 27, 1954; Bescheid-Nr. 130 547, August 25, 1954, Entschädigungsamt Berlin.
Antrag Entschädigungszahlung, Affidavit from Baroness Carola von Crailsheim, of Munich, March 17, 1958.
Antrag Entschädigungszahlung, Entschädigungsamt Berlin, December 10, 1958, betr. Entschädigungsanträge.
"Lebenslauf," written in Zürich at Mr. Fritz Cahn's, end of 1956.
Antrag Entschädigungszahlung, Affidavit given by Marcus on September 5, 1957, at the Notary of Basel.

"Lebenslauf," n.d. [ca. 1958].
Zeugnis (Testimony), Dr. Jur. Armin T. Wegner, German Embassy, Rome, April 15, 1958.

STIFTUNG BRANDENBURGISCHE GEDENKSTÄTTEN

Marcus's concentration camp records, 1367/1/15, Bl. 080, Russian State Military Archive, Moscow; D1 A/1015, Bl. 080, formerly R 203/M 10, Bl. 147, Stiftung Brandenburgische Gedenkstätten, Gedenkstätte und Museum Sachsenhausen.

SCHWEIZERISCHES BUNDESARCHIV

Dossier E4264#1988/2#33540*, Marcus, Hugo, 06.07.1880, Aktenzeichen: P070214, Deutsches Reich Reisepass.

Private and Official Correspondence From, to, or About Hugo Marcus

THOMAS MANN ARCHIVES, ETH ZÜRICH

Dr. Hans Marco (Hugo Marcus), Berlin, to Thomas Mann, Munich, April 18, 1902; Thomas Mann, Munich, to Dr. Hans Marco, Berlin, May 11, 1902; Thomas Mann, Munich, to Hugo Marcus, Berlin, January 1, 1904; Hugo Marcus, Berlin, to Thomas Mann, Munich, January 4, 1904; Thomas Mann, Munich, to Hugo Marcus, Berlin, January 21, 1904.

ZENTRALBIBLIOTHEK ZÜRICH, HANDSCHRIFTENABTEILUNG, NACHLASS HUGO MARCUS, KORRESPONDENZ

Roman Malicki to Hugo Marcus, summer 1922.
S. M. Abdullah to British Passport Officer, Berlin, December 1, 1938.
S. M. Abdullah to British Passport Officer, Berlin, March 16, 1939.
Sadr-ud-Din, Lahore, Ahmadiyya Buildings, to Hugo Marcus, Berlin, n.d, 1939.
Sadr-ud-Din, Lahore, to Marcus, Berlin, April 17, 1939, translated from Hindi and sent December 14, 1939, after Marcus had already left Berlin.
Secretary, Ahmadiyya Anjuman Ishaat-e-Islam, Lahore, India, to Herr Hamid Marcus, c/o Dr. S. M. Abdullah, Der Imam der Moschee, Berlin-Wilmersdorf, Germany, April 19, 1939.
J. G. Simms, Under-Secretary of the Government of India, Home Department, Simla, to British Passport Control Officer, Berlin, May 12, 1939.
Letter from Imam of the mosque S. M. Abdullah to Hugo Marcus, August 21, 1939.
Else Th. Marcus, M.D., St. George, Staten Island, N.Y., to Hugo Marcus, September 23, 1939.
Sadr-ud-Din, Lahore, to Hugo Marcus, Basel, October 24, 1939.
Hugo Marcus, Oberwil, Baselland, to Fritz Cahn, November 30, 1939.
Roman Malicki, Berlin, to Hugo Marcus, Basel, December 12, 1939.
Roman Malicki, Berlin, to Hugo Marcus, Basel, February 2, 1940.
S. M. Abdullah, Lahore, to Marcus, Basel, February 12, 1940.
S. M. Abdullah, Lahore, to Marcus, Basel, February 26, 1940

S. M. Abdullah, Lahore, to Marcus, Basel, March 20, 1940.

S. M. Abdullah, Lahore, to Hugo Marcus, Basel, May 13, 1940.

S. M. Abdullah, The Ahmadiyya Anjuman Ishaat-e-Islam, Lahore, India, to Hugo Marcus, Oberwil, Baselland, Switzerland, June 3, 1940.

S. M. Abdullah, Lahore, to Marcus, Basel, June 29, 1940.

S. M. Abdullah, Lahore, to Marcus, Basel, June 30, 1940.

Dr. S. M. Abdullah (imam), Ahmadiyya Buildings, Lahore, to Hugo Marcus, Basel, July 9, 1940.

Dr. S. M. Abdullah (imam), Ahmadiyya Buildings, Lahore, to Hugo Marcus, Basel, September 21, 1940.

S. M. Abdullah, The Ahmadiyya Anjuman Ishaat-e-Islam, Lahore, India, to Hugo Marcus, Oberwil, Baselland, Switzerland, December 1, 1940.

Leonie Cahn, Zürich, to Hugo Marcus, Basel, December 27, 1940.

Leonie Cahn, Zürich, to Hugo Marcus, Basel, January 10, 1941, and Leonie Cahn, Zürich, to Hugo Marcus, Basel, January 14, 1941.

Dr. S. M. Abdullah (imam), Ahmadiyya Buildings, Lahore, to Hugo Marcus, Basel, January 30, 1941.

Dr. S. M. Abdullah (imam), Ahmadiyya Buildings, Lahore, to Hugo Marcus, Basel, June 3, 1941.

Max Jordan (Pater Placidus), Washington, D.C., to Hugo Marcus, Basel, September 1, 1941.

Hugo Marcus, Oberwil, to M. A. Abdullah, Lahore, September 30, 1941.

Dr. S. M. Abdullah (imam), Ahmadiyya Buildings, Lahore, to Hugo Marcus, Basel, November 26, 1941.

L. Gaedicke, Berlin, to Hugo Marcus, Basel, March 11, 1942.

Amine Mosler, Berlin-Friedenau, Hauptstrasse 83, to Hugo Marcus, Basel, April 19, 1942.

Edith Landmann, Basel, Stapfelberg 4, to Hugo Marcus, April 16, 1943.

Roman Malicki, Walramsdorf (today: Stęszewko), rural district Posen, to Hugo Marcus, Baselland, August 20, 1943.

Roman Malicki, Berlin Charlottenburg Kantstrasse 30, to Hugo Marcus, Baselland, July 2, 1944.

Edith Landmann to Hugo Marcus, undated, 1944.

Michael Landmann to Hugo Marcus, letters from October 12, 1944, November 16, 1944, December 10, 1944, and February 2, 1945.

Armin Wegner, Positano, Italy, to Hugo Marcus, Baselland, August 22, 1945.

Roman Malicki, Berlin, to Hugo Marcus, Baselland, end of September 1946.

Ernst Kantorowicz, Berkeley, California, to Cäcilie Markus [*sic*], Zürich, September 26, 1946.

Leonie Cahn, Zürich, to Hugo Marcus, Basel, November 12, 1946.

Leonie Cahn, Zürich, to Hugo Marcus, Basel, November 22, 1946.

Roman Malicki, Berlin, to Hugo Marcus, Baselland, December 10, 1946.

Leonie Cahn to Cäcilie Marcus, January 16, 1947.

Edith Landmann to Hugo Marcus, March 10, 1947.

S. M. Abdullah, The Mosque, Woking, to Hugo Marcus, Baselland, April 24, 1947.

Roman Malicki, Berlin, to Hugo Marcus, Baselland, June 23, 1947.

Hugo Marcus, Oberwil, Basel, to the Eidgenössenische Fremdenpolizei, Bern, July 1, 1947.

Hugo Marcus, Oberwil, Baselland, to the Eidgenössenische Fremdenpolizei, Bern, July 15, 1947.

Hugo Marcus, Baselland, to Maulana Muhammad Ali, Lahore, undated, after 1947.

Sadr-ud-Din, Lahore, to Hamid Marcus, Oberwil, Baselland, January 2, 1952.

Sadr-ud-Din, Lahore, Ahmadiyya Buildings (West Pakistan), to Hugo Marcus, Oberwil, Baselland, January 31, 1952.

Translation into English of earlier thank you letter from Hugo Marcus to Muhammad Maulana Ali, February 20, 1952.

Hugo Marcus, Basel, to German Reparations Bureau, June 15, 1954.

Armin Wegner, Positano, Italy, to Hugo Marcus, Basel, October 18, 1955.

Armin Wegner, Positano, to Hugo Marcus, Basel, November 2, 1955.

Armin Wegner, Positano, to Hugo Marcus, Basel, undated, postmarked December 28, 1955.

Roman Malicki, Berlin, to Hugo Marcus, Basel, undated, 1955.

Felix Hepner, Zürich, to Roman Malicki, Berlin, June 3, 1956.

Mahmudal Abdullah, Mosque, Woking, to Hugo Marcus, Oberwil, Baselland, June 24, 1956.

Fritz Cahn, Zürich 6, Haldeneggsteig 7, to the Gemeindeverwaltung Oberwil, Baselland, December 4, 1956.

Father Placidus Jordan to Dr. Marcus, Zürich, January 3, 1957.

Hugo Marcus, Zürich, Haldeneggsteig 7, to Jordan, January 12, 1957.

Hugo Marcus, Zürich, Brief to the Eidgenössische Fremdenpolizei (Swiss Federal Aliens' Police), Bern, Switzerland, January 23, 1957.

Armin Wegner, Rome, Monte Verde, Viale Quattro Venti 104, to Hugo Marcus, Basel, February 2, 1957.

Sadr-ud-Din, Head of the Ahmadia Anjuman, Ahmadia Buildings, Lahore, India, to Hugo Marcus, Basel, Switzerland, August 20, 1957.

Fritz Cahn, Zürich, to Marcus, Holbeinstr. 85, Basel, August 21, 1957; Postcard, Fritz Cahn, San Francisco, to Marcus, same as above, July 17, 1957.

Hugo Marcus, Zürich, to Sadr-ud-Din, Head of the Ahmadia Anjuman, Ahmadia Buildings, Lahore, August 10, 1957.

Hugo Marcus, Basel, Switzerland, to President Theodor Heuss, Bonn, Federal Republic of Germany, October 27, 1958.

Entschädigungsamt, Berlin, to Hugo Marcus, Basel, November 2, 1959.

Armin T. Wegner, Stromboli, Italy, to Hugo Marcus, Basel, September 20, 1960.

Armin Wegner, Stromboli, Torre dei Sette Venti, Isole Eolie, to Hugo Marcus, Basel, September 20, 1960.

Armin Wegner, Rome, to Hugo Marcus, Basel, December 26, 1961.

Armin Wegner, Rome, to Hugo Marcus, Basel, December 10, 1962.

Armin Wegner, Rome, to Hugo Marcus, Basel, February 1, 1963.

Leonie Cahn, Zürich, to Bürgerspital Basel Leitung, September 26, 1965.

Leonie Cahn, Zürich, to Hugo Marcus, Basel, October 25, 1965.

Leonie Cahn, Zürich, to Hugo Marcus, Basel, November 10, 1965.

Leonie Cahn, Zürich, to Hugo Marcus, Basel, no date (1965).

Leonie Cahn to Hugo Marcus, November 16, 1965.

Armin Wegner, Rome, to Hugo Marcus, Basel, December 2, 1965.

Michael Landmann, St. Gallen, Winkelriedstr, to Leonie Cahn, Zürich, Haldeneggsteig 7, July 12, 1966.

STAATSARCHIV BASEL-STADT

PD-Reg 3a, 52516, Marcus, Hugo (1944–1966)

Akten der Fremdenpolizei des Kantons Basel-Stadt, an das Polizeikommando Abt. Fremdenpolizei, Liestal, November 27, 1944, von Kontrollbureau, Kantonale Fremdenpolizei, der Adjunkt Bickel.

Akten der Fremdenpolizei des Kantons Basel-Stadt, Michael Landmann, Präsident, Philosophische Geselleschaft Basel, Stiftsgasse 5, Basel, April 24, 1946, an den Vorsteher des Kontrollbüreaus Herrn (Fritz) Jenny, Basel, Spiegelhof.

Akten der Fremdenpolizei des Kantons Basel-Stadt, Meyer, Der Chef der Polizeiabteilung, Eidgenössisches Justiz- und Polizeidepartment, Polizeiabteilung, Bern, August 8, 1950, an Herrn Dr. H. Eckert, Basler Hilfsstelle für Flüchtlinge, Rheinsprung 1, Basel.

Akten der Fremdenpolizei des Kantons Basel-Stadt, Anmeldeformular für Ausländer, February 28, 1957.

Akten der Fremdenpolizei des Kantons Basel-Stadt, Bestätigung betr. Herrn Hugo Marcus, Basel, Frau Gertrud Kurz, Christlicher Friedensdienst Abt. Flüchtlingshilfe, Dittlingerweg 4 Bern, April 8, 1957.

Akten der Fremdenpolizei des Kantons Basel-Stadt, Binggeli, Der Chef der Polizeiabteilung, Eidgenössisches Justiz- und Polizeidepartment, Polizeiabteilung, Bern, March 12, 1958, an Kantonales Armensekretariat, Basel-Landschaft, Liestal Baselland.

Akten der Fremdenpolizei des Kantons Basel-Stadt, Kontrollbureau, Kantonale Fremdenpolizei, Der Adjunkt Schärer, April 21, 1959, an die Polizeiabteilung des Eidg. Justiz- und Polizeidepartments, Bern.

Akten der Fremdenpolizei des Kantons Basel-Stadt, Hugo Marcus an Kontrollbureau der Kantonales Fremdenpolizei, Polizei Departement, Basel, Spiegelhof, April 22, 1964.

Akten der Fremdenpolizei des Kantons Basel-Stadt, Eidgenössische Polizeiabteilung, Bern, May 27, 1964, an Kantonale Fremdenpolizei, Basel.

SCHWEIZERISCHES BUNDESARCHIV BAR/SWISS FEDERAL ARCHIVE, BERN

Dossier E4264#1988/2#33540*, Marcus, Hugo, 06.07.1880, Aktenzeichen: P070214

Kantonales Armensekretariat Basel Landschaft, Liestal, Fürsorgestelle für Auslandschweizer, an das Eidg. Justiz- und Polizeidepartement, Polizeiabteilung, Bern, December 11, 1956.

Gertrud Kurz, Christlicher Friedensdienst, Abteilung Flüchtlingshilfe, Bern, an das Kantonale Armensekretariat Baselland, Liestal, January 25, 1957.

Gertrud Kurz Christlicher Friedensdienst, Abteilung Flüchtlingshilfe, Bern, an Flüchtlingssektion der Polizeiabteilung z. Hd. Von Herrn Binggeli, Bern und Kantonales Armensekretariat Basel-Landschaft z. Hd. Von Herrn Dr. Ballmer, Liestal, February 27, 1958; Der Chef der Polizeiabteilung, i.A. sig. Binggeli, an Herrn Hugo Marcus, Privatheim Holbeinstrasse 85, Basel, March 26, 1959; and

Der Chef der Polizeiabteilung i.A. sig. Binggeli, Bern, April 28, 1959, an Kantonale Fremdenpolizei Kontrollbureau Basel.

Application for a foreigner's pass, May 13, 1964.

Published letters concerning Marcus

Letter from Rolf Meier to Kurt Hiller, March 22, 1960. Reproduced in Manfred Backhausen, *Die Lahore-Ahmadiyya-Bewegung in Europa: Geschichte, Gegenwart und Zukunft der als "Lahore-Ahmadiyya-Bewegung zur Verbreitung islamischen Wissens" bekannten internationalen islamischen Gemeinschaft* (Wembley: Ahmadiyya Anjuman Lahore Publications, 2008), 115. Backhausen obtained the citations from the letters from Zürich-based independent researcher Beat Frischknecht, who examined the originals.

Letter from Rolf Meier to Hugo Marcus, October 4, 1965, and letter from Rolf Meier to Kurt Hiller, October 18, 1965, in Backhausen, *Die Lahore-Ahmadiyya-Bewegung in Europa*, 116.

Letter from Rolf Meier to Kurt Hiller, December 16, 1965, in Backhausen, *Die Lahore-Ahmadiyya-Bewegung in Europa*, 117.

Letter from Rolf Meier to Kurt Hiller, April 21, 1966, in Backhausen, *Die Lahore-Ahmadiyya-Bewegung in Europa*, 117.

Letter from Rolf Meier to Kurt Hiller, April 26, 1966, in Backhausen, *Die Lahore-Ahmadiyya-Bewegung in Europa*, 117–18.

Letter from Rolf Meier to Kurt Hiller, April 28, 1966, in Backhausen, *Die Lahore-Ahmadiyya-Bewegung in Europa*, 118.

Letter from Rolf Meier to Kurt Hiller, May 5, 1966, in Backhausen, *Die Lahore-Ahmadiyya-Bewegung in Europa*, 118.

Additional Archival Sources

SWISS FEDERAL ARCHIVES, BERNE

Bundesratsbeschluss, August 4, 1942 [Swiss federal decree regarding refugees], Swiss Federal Archives Berne, E1004.1 1/424

NATIONAL ARCHIVES AND RECORDS ADMINISTRATION (NARA), WASHINGTON, D.C.

National Archives Collection of Foreign Records Seized (RG 242), A3340, MFOK Series (Master File, Ortsgruppenkartei, Nationalsozialistische Deutsche Arbeiterpartei) [Nazi Party membership of German Muslims]

LANDESARCHIV BERLIN

B Rep. 42, Nr. 27515, "Deutsch Muslimische Gesellschaft, Berlin e.V." [Transcripts of annual meetings of German Muslim Society and association statutes]

Protokoll und Satzungen, March 22, 1930

Protokoll und Satzungen, September 19, 1931

Protokoll und Satzungen, September 24, 1932
Protokoll und Satzungen, September 22, 1934
Protokoll und Satzungen, July 20, 1935
Protokoll und Satzungen, September 21, 1935
Protokoll und Satzungen, September 19, 1936
Protokoll und Satzungen, August 14, 1937
Protokoll und Satzungen, October 1, 1938
S.M. Abdullah an Amtsgericht Berlin, October 27, 1939

Rep. 42, Acc. 2147.

Amtsgericht Charlottenburg, Islamischer Weltkongress, Zweigstelle Berlin

A Pr. Br. Rep. 030-04, Nr. 1350

Nationalsozialistische Deutsche Arbeiterpartei, Reichsleitung, Amt für Schulung, Abteilung Verbände, Berlin, an Polizeipräsidenten in Berlin, Abteilung V, Vereine, November 24, 1936.
Sonderbeauftragten zur überwachung der geistig und kulturell tätigen Juden im deutschen Reichsgebiet, December 15, 1936.
Nationalsozialistische Deutsche Arbeiterpartei, Reichsleitung, Abteilung Verbände an den Herrn Polizeipräsidenten in Berlin, Abteilung V, Vereine, April 13, 1937.

A Pr. Br. Rep. 030-04, Nr. 2314, "Islam-Institut"

Islam-Institut (Mahad al-Islam) zu Berlin an Polizeipräsident, Abteilung V, March 21, 1939, Satzungen, "Islam Institut."
Nationalsozialistische Deutsche Arbeiterpartei, Aussenpolitisches Amt an Herrn Polizeipräsidenten in Berlin, August 8, 1939.
Vorstandsmitglieder, October 30, 1940.

BIBLIOTHEK ZENTRUM MODERNER ORIENT

Landesarchiv Berlin, Rep. 42, Acc. 2147, "Islamische Gemeinde zu Berlin, e.V.," in Bibliothek Zentrum Moderner Orient, Berlin, Nachlass Professor Dr. Gerhard Höpp, 07.05.002.

Anmeldung zur Eintragung der Islamischen Gemeinde zu Berlin, e.V., an das Preussische Amtsgericht Berlin, November 4, 1922, Akten vom Amtsgericht Charlottenburg betreffend die Islamische Gemeinde zu Berlin, e.V.
Protokoll, July 21, 1923.
Hassan (Walter) Hoffmann, Islamische Gemeinde zu Berlin, an das Amtsgericht, Berlin Mitte, Berlin, April 17, 1929.
Prof. Sattar Kheiri, Berlin, an Amtsgericht Berlin Mitte, Geschäftsstelle, Abteilung 94, August 7, 1930.
Statuten der Islamischen Gemeinde zu Berlin, e.V., Berlin, February 21, 1934.
Protokoll der konstituierenden Generalversammlung der Islamischen Gemeinde zu Berlin, February 21, 1934, in Humboldhaus Berlin.

Protokoll, Generalversammlung der Islamischen Gemeinde zu Berlin e.V., January 18, 1936.
Habibur Rahman, Islamische Gemeinde zu Berlin, an Amtsgericht Berlin, June 3, 1942.

Nachlass Höpp, 07.05.028

"Die Moschee aus der Vogelschau: Dr. Abdullah vom Fehrbelliner Platz." *Rumpelstilzchen* 38, May 31, 1934.

Nachlass Höpp, 07.05.032

Brief, Deutsches Generalkonsulat, Kalkutta, an das Auswärtige Amt, Berlin, May 14, 1935, Parch AAB, R 78242.
Brief, Geheimes Staatspolizeiamt Berlin, an das Auswärtige Amt, Berlin, June 26, 1935.

Nachlass Höpp, 07.05.033

Hauptstelle Kulturpolitisches Archiv an die Deutsche Arbeitsfront, Amt Deutsches Volksbildungswerk, Abt. II/Vortrag, Berlin, September 27, 1938, Bundesarchiv, NJ 15, Nr. 27.
Hauptstelle Kulturpolitisches Archiv an das Sicherheitshauptamt, Berlin, September 27, 1938, Bundesarchiv, NJ 15, Nr. 35.
Hauptstelle Kulturpolitisches Archiv an das Sicherheitshauptamt, Berlin, October 10, 1938.
Hauptstelle Kulturpolitisches Archiv an die Deutsche Arbeitsfront, Amt Deutsches Volksbildungswerk, Abt. II/Vortrag, Berlin, March 31, 1939, Bundesarchiv, NJ 15, Nr. 28.

Nachlass Höpp, 07.05.035

"Empfang in der Deutsch-Muslimischen Gesellschaft." *Der Tag*, January 16, 1931, 1, Beiblatt.

Nachlass Höpp, 07.05.039

Film 15205, Brief der Geheimen Staatspolizei an den Reichsminister für die kirchlichen Angelegenheiten, February 11, 1939, Bundesarchiv Berlin.
Anmeldung zur Eintragung der Islamischen Gemeinde zu Berlin.

Nachlass Höpp, 01.21.013

Brief, Der Chef der Sicherheitspolizei und des SD, Berlin, an das Auswärtige Amt, z.Hd.d. Hernn Gesandten Luther, Berlin, December 10, 1940, Politisches Archiv des Auswärtigen Amts, R 101196.
Brief, Dr. Zeki Kiram, Sanaa, Yemen, an Führer und Reichskanzler Herrn Adolf Hitler, Berlin, May 19, 1936, Politisches Archiv des Auswärtigen Amts, R 101196.

Published Archival Sources

Chronik der Erzabtei Beuron: Advent 1977–Advent 1978. Beuron, 1978
ZSg. 101/7/169/Nr. 250, March 6, 1936. In *NS-Presseanweisungen der Vorkriegszeit: Edition und Dokumentation*, ed. Hans Bohrmann. Revised by Gabriele Toepser-Ziegert, vol. 4/I: 1936. Munich, 1993, 249.

LITERARY SOURCES

Hugo Marcus's Unpublished Work

ISLAM

Zentralbibliothek Zürich, Nachlass Hugo Marcus, Vorträge

"Der religiöse Mensch und der technische Mensch" (typescript, 5 pages,undated).
"über Lessing" (1929) (typescript, 11 pages).
"Berührungspunkte zwischen den Koran und ausserislamischen Glaubensquellen" (undated).
"Was ist der Islam?" (undated)
"Was ist uns der Koran?" (typescript, undated, 26 pages)
Ansprache (1937, typescript, 5 pages).
"Goethes Begegnungen mit dem Islam" (undated, ca. 1947–1951)
"Goethe und der Islam" (undated, ca. 1947–1951)
"Warum ich Moslem wurde" (1951).

GAY FICTION AND MEMOIRS

Zentralbibliothek Zürich, Handschriftenabteilung, Nachlass Hugo Marcus

"In der Moschee zu Berlin" (typescript, 3 pages, undated, pre-1937).
"Aus fernen Tagen: Ein Blatt aus einem Nachlass" (typescript, 7 pages, undated, pre-1914)

Hugo Marcus's Published Work

FICTION

Zentralbibliothek Zürich, Handschriftenabteilung, Nachlass Hugo Marcus

Das Frühlingsglück. Die Geschichte einer ersten Liebe. Dresden and Leipzig: E. Pierson's, 1900.

Deutsche Nationalbibliothek (German National Library), Leipzig

Das Tor dröhnt zu. Berlin: Paß & Garleb, 1915.

PHILOSOPHY

Staatsbibliothek zu Berlin

Die Allgemeine Bildung in Vergangenheit, Gegenwart und Zukunft: Eine historische-kritische-dogmatische Grundlegung. Berlin: E. Ebering, 1903.
Die Fundamente der Wirklichkeit als Regulatoren der Sprache. Bonn: Bouvier, 1960.
Meditationen. Berlin: E. Ebering, 1904.

Musikästhetische Probleme auf vergleichend-ästhetischer Grundlage nebst Bemerkungen über die grossen Figuren in der Musikgeschichte. Berlin: Concordia Deutsche Verlags-Anstalt Hermann Ehbock, 1906.

Die Philosophie des Monopluralismus: Grundzüge einer analytischen Naturphilosophie und eines ABC der Begriffe im Versuch. Berlin: Concordia Deutsche Verlags-Anstalt Hermann Ehbock, 1907.

Die ornamentale Schönheit der Landschaft und der Natur als Beitrag zu einer allgemeinen Ästhetik der Landschaft und der Natur. München: Piper & Co., 1912.

Vom Zeichnerischen, Malerischen, Plastischen und Architektonischen in der Winterlandschaft: Zugl. e. Beitrag z. Klassifikation dieser Begriffe. Berlin: Paß & Garleb, 1914.

Zentralbibliothek Zürich, Handschriftenabteilung, Nachlass Hugo Marcus

Metaphysik der Gerechtigkeit: Die Äquivalenz als juristisches, ästhetisches und ethisches Prinzip. Basel: Ernst Reinhardt Verlag A.G., 1947.

Rechtswelt und Ästhetik. Bonn: Bouvier u. Co., 1952.

LITERATURE AND CULTURE

Staatsbibliothek zu Berlin

Hugo Marcus, "Mein toter Freund erzählt sich selbst seine Knabenzeit." *Das Junge Deutschland* 1, No. 7 (July 1918): 222–24.

Hugo Marcus, "Aus einem stillen Buche." [Prosa] *Das Junge Deutschland* Jg. 3, Nr. 4 (April 1920): 105–9.

Von Kurt Hiller [Rezension] *Der Feuerreiter.* Jg. 1, H. 4/5 (April 1922): 189–91.

Hugo Marcus, "Dialog vom Sinn der Güte." [Dialog] *Der Feuerreiter* Jg. 2, H. 3 (May 1923): 83–86.

ISLAM

Marcus, Hugo. "Der Islam und die Philosophie Europas." *Moslemische Revue* 1, no. 2 (1924): 84–88.

Marcus, Hugo. "Islam und Protestantismus." *Moslemische Revue* 2, no. 2 (April 1925): 17–22.

Marcus, Dr. H. "Islam and the Philosophy of Europe." Translated from the German by Abdul Majid. *Islamic Review* 13, no. 8 (August 1925): 295.

Marcus, Dr. Hugo, Ph.D. "Muhammad's Personality: The First Democrat-Prophet, The First Cavalier-Prophet." *The Light* (Lahore, India) 4, no. 17 (September 1, 1925), 1.

Marcus, Hugo. "Nietzsche und der Islam." *Moslemische Revue* 3, no. 2 (April 1926): 79–87.

Marcus, Hugo. "Spinoza und der Islam." *Moslemische Revue* 4, no. 1 (January 1929): 8–24.

Marcus, Hamid. "Die Religion und der Mensch der Zukunft." *Moslemische Revue* 6, no. 3(July 1930): 65–75.

Marcus, Hamid. "Die Religion und der Mensch der Zukunft" (Fortsetzung). *Moslemische Revue* 6, no. 4 (October 1930): 94–98.

Marcus, Dr. H. "The Message of the Holy Prophet Muhammad to Europe." Pts. 1–3, *Islamic Review* 20, no. 6 (June-July 1932): 222–39; 20, no. 8 (August 1932): 268–79; 20, no. 9

(September 1932): 281–86. Republished as Dr. H. Marcus, PhD., "Two Friends, One Muslim, the Other Christian, Discuss the Problems Facing the World." *Islamic Review* (July 1950): 5–10.

Marcus, Dr. Hamid, Ph.D. *De Boodschap van den heiligen Profeet Moehammad aan Europa*. Djokja: Kita, 1933.

Marcus, Hugo. "Moslemischer Schicksalsglaube." *Moslemische Revue* 12, no. 1 (January 1936): 6–27.

Dr. H. "Buchbesprechung." *Moslemische Revue* 15, no. 3 (Dezember 1939): 79–80.

Marcus, Dr. H. "A Bridge Between the East and the West." *Islamic Review* (March 1949): 44–45.

Marcus, Dr. H. "Islam in Switzerland." *Islamic Review* (April 1950): 46.

Marcus, Dr. H. "Switzerland and Its Relations to Islam." *Islamic Review* (June 1949): 26–28.

GAY RIGHTS MOVEMENT AND HOMOEROTIC FICTION (UNDER THE PSEUDONYM HANS ALIENUS)

ONE National Gay & Lesbian Archives at the USC libraries, Los Angeles

"Ein Paar Schuhe: Ein Kapitel aus einem Roman von Hans Alienus." *Der Kreis*, No. 1 XVI. Jahrgang (January 1948), 7–10, 22.

"Die Kirche zu den heiligen Brüsten der Jünglinge: Ein Blatt der Erinnerung an den 1. August 1914." *Der Kreis*, no. 8 XVI. Jahrgang (August 1948): 7–8.

"Licht fällt ins Fenster." *Der Kreis*, No. 5 XVI. Jahrgang (May 1948): 6–8.

"Stärker als der Tod." *Der Kreis*, No. 4 XVII. Jahrgang/Annee (April 1949): 2–11.

"Goethe und die Freundesliebe: Zu des Dichters zweihundertstem Geburtstag." *Der Kreis*, No. 8 XVII. Jahrgang/Annee (August 1949): 5–12.

"Brief eines 'Mitschuldigen.'" *Der Kreis*, no. 11 XVII. Jahrgang (November 1949), 2–4.

"In Geschäften nach Paris." *Der Kreis*, No. 7 XVIII. Jahrgang (July 1950): 8–11.

"Das Ewige und der Freund." *Der Kreis*, no. 5 XIX. Jahrgang (May 1951): 26.

"Zum 75. Geburtstage von Hans Alienus, *Die einander bei Händen und bei Sternen halten*." *Der Kreis*, No. 6 XXIII. Jahrgang (June 1955): 14–17.

"Erinnerung an Magnus Hirschfeld. Zum 30. Todestag—14. Mai 1935." *Der Kreis* 33, no. 5 (1965): 6–7.

Zentralbibliothek Zürich, Handschriftenabteilung, Nachlass Hugo Marcus

Einer sucht den Freund: Gedanken zum Thema das Ewige und der Freund. Heidelberg: L. Schneider, 1961.

PUBLISHED ABOUT MARCUS

"Hans Alienus." *Der Kreis—Le Cercle—The Circle* 34, no. 5, Jahrgang (1966): 5.

"Hugo Marcus 80 Jahre alt." *Allgemeine Wochenzeitung der Juden in Deutschland*, no. XV/16 (July 15, 1960): 6.

Other Literary Sources

ISLAM, ESPECIALLY IN GERMANY

Abdullah, O. V. "Jews Under Crescent and Cross." *Islamic Review* 27 (October 1939): 388.

Ahmad, Nasir, comp. and ed. *Eid Sermons at the Shah Jehan Mosque, Woking, England, 1931–1940.* Lahore: Aftab-ud-Din Memorial Benevolent Trust, 2002.

Ali, Muhammad. "Correspondence: Mosque in Berlin." *The Light* 2, no. 3 (February 1, 1923): 2–3.

—. "Der Beitrag des Islams zur Zivilisation." *Moslemische Revue* 10, no. 2-3 (April–July 1934): 44–46.

Asad, Muhammad. *The Message of the Quran.* Gibraltar: Dar al-Andalus, 1980.

—. *The Road to Mecca.* New York: Simon and Schuster, 1954.

Ateş, Seyran. *Der Islam braucht eine sexuelle Revolution: Eine Streitschrift.* Berlin: Ullstein, 2009.

—. *Selam, Frau Imamin: Wie ich in Berlin eine liberale Moschee gründete.* Berlin: Ullstein, 2017.

"Aus Unserer Arbeit." *Moslemische Revue* 13, no. 3 (November 1937): 69–71.

"Drei Europäerinnen bekennen sich zum Islam." *Moslemische Revue* 7, no. 2–3 (April–July 1931): 53–59.

Durrani, F.K. Khan. "Was ist Islam?" *Moslemische Revue* 4, no. 1 (January 1929): 41–45.

Editor's note, Hugo Marcus, "Muhammad's Personality: The First Democrat-Prophet, the First Cavalier-Prophet." *The Light* 4, no. 17 (September 1, 1925): 1–6.

"Die Eröffnung der Moschee." *Moslemische Revue* 2, no. 2 (April 1925): 2.

Fischer, Faruq. "Ist der Islam 'unmodern'? Eine Parallele zwischen der alten Religion und dem heutigen Europa." *Moslemische Revue* 10, nos. 2–3 (April–July 1934): 62–73.

Fisher, John. "Why Islam Appeals to Me." *Islamic Review* 22, no. 6 (March 1934), 61–63.

Gioja, Count Eduardo. "Reasons for my Acceptance of Islam." *Islamic Review* 23, no. 9 (September 1935): 329–37.

Grützmacher, R. (Richard) H. "Goethes Würdigung des Islam." *Moslemische Revue* 13, no. 3 (November 1937): 75–83.

Hobohm, Muhammad Aman. "Islam in Germany." *Islamic Review* 39 (August 1951): 16.

"Id-ul-Fitr in Berlin." *Moslemische Revue* 15, no. 3 (December 1939): 73–76.

"Islam in Germany: Great German Scholar Won, First Eid Celebrated." *The Light* 4, no. 10 (May 16, 1925): 1.

Kamal-ud-Din, Khwaja. "Note: The Berlin Mosque." *Islamic Review* 13, no. 3 (1925): 82.

Kheiri, Abdul Jabbar. "Der Untergang und die Rettung: Eine Untersuchung über Islam die Heilmittel mit aufbauender Kraft." *Islam* 1, no. 1 (1922): 2.

Khulusi, S. A., comp. *Islam Our Choice.* 1961. Reprint, Surrey: Woking Muslem Mission & Literary Trust, 1963.

Kidwai, Sheikh Mushir Hussain. "The Post-War Problems and Their Solution." *Islamic Review* 22 (March 1934): 82–83.

Kiram, Zeki. "Ein Moslem über das neue Deutschland: Hitler ist der berufene Mann." *Moslemische Revue* 14, no. 2 (August 1938): 59–60.

Der Koran Arabisch-Deutsch: Uebersetzung, Einleitung und Erklärung von Maulana Sadr-ud-Din. 2nd ed. 1939. Reprint, Berlin, 1964, 2005.

"Letter." July 14, 1940, Imam of the Mosque to the Editor of the *New Statesman and Nation*, London, reprinted in *Islamic Review* 29 (February 1941): 42–43.

Liebe im Orient: Der duftende Garten des Scheik Nefzaui. Erste vollständige deutsch Ausgabe, herausgegeben von Dr. Ferdinand Leiter und Dr. Hans H. Thal, mit Geleitworten von Hanns Heinz Ewers und Sanitätsrat Dr. Magnus Hirschfeld, Leiter des Institutes für Sexualwissenschaft. Wien: Schneider & Co., 1929.

"Mahomets Gesang." *Moslemische Revue* 1, no. 2 (July 1924): 61–62.

Marcus, Hugo. Preface, "Muhammad's Personality: The First Democrat-Prophet, the First Cavalier-Prophet." *The Light* (Lahore, India) 4, no. 17 (1926): 1–2, 6.

"Maulana Sadr-ud-Din verläßt Berlin." *Moslemische Revue* 13, no. 3 (November 1937): 71–75.

Meier, Fritz. "The Problem of Nature in the Esoteric Monism of Islam" (1947). In *Spirit and Nature: Papers from the Eranos Yearbooks*, ed. Joseph Campbell. Bollingen Series 30, no. 1 (1954): 149–203.

"Monatliche Zusammenkünfte in der Moschee." *Moslemische Revue* 2, no. 3–4 (July–October 1925): 2.

"Nachruf auf Amin Boosfeld." *Moslemische Revue* 12, no. 3 (November 1936): 67–72.

Nicholson, David Omar. "Some Reasons for Accepting Islam." *Islamic Review* 23, no. 3 (March 1935): 107–8.

Omar, David. "Goethe über die Moslems." *Moslemische Revue* 1, no. 2 (July 1924): 62–63.

Rifat, Mansur M. *Der Verrat der Ahmadis an Heimat und Religion: Ein Anhang zu der Schrift* "Die Ahmadia-Sekte" *ein Vorkämpfer für den englischen Imperialismus* (Ahmadis' Betrayal of Country and Religion: A Supplement to the Pamphlet "The Ahmadia Sect," Vanguard of British Imperialism and the Greatest Danger to Islam) (Berlin, 1923).

—. *Vollständiger Zusammenbruch der Ahmadia-Sekte: Weitere Beiweise für ihre Tätigkeit als englische Agenten. Mirza Ghulam—Der geisteskranke Mirza—ausgesprochene Paranoiac* (Berlin, 1924).

Robert, Abdullah. "Warum ich aus der römisch-katholichen Kirche austrat." *Moslemische Revue* 6, no. 4 (October 1930): 106–9.

Sabry, Mohamed. *Islam, Judentum, Bolschewismus.* Berlin: n.p., 1938.

Sadr-ud-Din. "Das Glaubensbekenntnis des Islams." *Moslemische Revue* 1, no. 2 (July 1924): 91. Note: The article was republished verbatim in every subsequent issue from 1924 to 1926. It later frequently reappeared as F. K. Khan Durrani, "Was ist Islam?" such as in *Moslemische Revue* 4, no. 1 (January 1929): 41–45.

—. "Die Christen und die Juden." *Moslemische Revue* 1, no. 1 (April 1924): 41–42.

—. "Die internationale Religion." *Moslemische Revue* 1, no. 1 (April 1924): 3–10.

—. "Eine Botschaft an die Juden." *Moslemische Revue* 2, no. 3–4 (July–October 1925): 4–7.

—. "Moses, Jesus, und Mohammed sind Brüder." *Moslemische Revue* 1, no. 1 (April 1924): 14–22.

Saunders, Fazl Karim. "Why I Embraced Islam." *Islamic Review* 23, nos. 11–13 (November-December 1935): 403.

Scharf, Hildegard Rahet, Hudah Johanna Schneider, Saffiah Irma Gohl. "Drei Europäerinnen Bekennen Sich Zum Islam." *Moslemische Revue* 7, nos. 2–3 (April–July 1931): 53–59.

Schütz, Saladin. "Wie ich Moslem wurde." *Moslemische Revue* 4, no. 1 (January 1929): 37–41.

Van Kuylenburg, A. W. L. (M. A. Rahman). "Why I Became a Muslim." *Islamic Review* 29, no. 2 (1941): 50.

von Ehrenfels, Omar Rolf Baron. "Goethe und der deutsche Islam." *Moslemische Revue* 8, nos. 1–2 (April 1932): 10–16.

—. "The *How?* and *Why?* of Conversion to Islam." *Islamic Review* 49, no. 6 (June 1961): 23–24.

Wegner, Armin, ed. *Der Prozess Talaat Pascha*. Berlin: Deutsche Verlagsgesellschaft für Politik und Geschichte, 1921.

—. *Die Austreibung des armenischen Volkes in die Wüste: Ein Lichtbildvortrag*. 1919.

"Der Zweck der Zeitschrift." *Moslemische Revue* 1, no. 1 (April 1924): 1–2.

GERMAN ART, LITERATURE, AND PHILOSOPHY

George, Stefan. *Die Transcendenz des Erkennens*. Berlin: Georg Bondi, 1923.

—. *Georgika: Das Wesen des Dichters George*. Heidelberg: Weiss, 1920.

—. *Das Jahr der Seele*. Berlin: Blätter für die Kunst, 1897.

Gerlach, Wolfgang. "Document: Armin T. Wegner's Letter to German Chancellor Adolf Hitler, Berlin, Easter Monday, April 11, 1933." Trans. by William Templer. In *Holocaust and Genocide Studies* 8, no. 3 (Winter 1994): 395–409.

Goebbels, Joseph. "Around the Gedächtniskirche." In *The Weimar Republic Sourcebook*, ed. Anton Kaes, Martin Jay, and Edward Dimendberg. Berkeley: University of California Press, 1994, 560–62. Originally published as "Rund um die Gedächtniskirche," *Der Angriff*, January 23, 1928.

Hesse, Hermann. "Die Sehnsucht unser Zeit nach einer Weltanschauung." *Uhu* 2 (1926): 3–4. Translated as "The Longing of Our Time for a Worldview." In *The Weimar Republic Sourcebook*, ed. Anton Kaes, Martin Jay, and Edward Dimendberg, 365–66. Berkeley: University of California Press, 1994.

Hirschfeld, Magnus. *Racism*. Trans. and ed. Eden and Cedar Paul. London: Victor Gollancz, 1938.

Das Junge Deutschland, Monatsschrift für Literatur und Theater—Erster Jahrgang 1918—Alfred Döblin, Walter Hasenclever, Rudolf Pannwitz, Oskar Kokoschka, Emil Orlik, Ernst Stern etc. Berlin: Emil Reiß, 1918.

Juryfreie Kunstschau Berlin 1925: Malerei, Plastik, Gartenkunst. Berlin: Gebr. Mann, 1925.

Kantorowicz, Ernst. *Kaiser Friedrich der Zweite*. Berlin: Georg Bondi, 1927. English translation 1931.

Klemperer, Victor. *I Will Bear Witness, 1933–1941: A Diary of the Nazi Years*. Trans. Martin Chalmers. New York: Random House, 1999.

Landmann, Edith. *Die Lehre vom Schönen*. Wien: Amandus, 1952.

—. *Gespräche mit Stefan George*. Düsseldorf: Küpper, 1963.

—. *Stefan George und die Griechen: Idee einer neuen Ethik*. Redaktion Michael Landmann. Amsterdam: Castrum Peregrini, 1971.

Landmann, Michael. *Erinnerungen an Stefan George: Seine Freundschaft mit Julius und Edith Landmann*. Amsterdam: Castrum Perigrini, 1980.

Mann, Klaus. *The Turning Point: The Autobiography of Klaus Mann*. 1942. London: Serpent's Tail, 1987.

Mann, Thomas. *Buddenbrooks*. 1901. Trans. H. T. Lowe-Porter. London: Alfred A. Knopf, 1924, Vintage reprint.

—. *Death in Venice*. Trans. H. T. Lowe-Porter. 1928. New York: Penguin, 1988.

—. *Doktor Faustus: Das Leben des deutschen Tonsetzers Adrian Leverkühn, erzählt von einem Freunde*. Frankfurt am Main: S. Fischer, 1947. Translated into English as Thomas Mann, *Doctor*

Faustus: The Life of the German Composer Adrian Leverkühn, as Told by a Friend, trans. H. T. (Helen Tracy) Lowe-Porter. New York: Knopf, 1948.

Meinecke, Friedrich. *Die Deutsche Katastrophe: Betrachtungen und Erinnerungen*. Wiesbaden: Eberhard-Brockhaus, 1946. Translated into English as *The German Catastrophe: Reflections and Recollections*, trans. Sidney B. Fay. Boston: Beacon Press, 1950.

JOHANN WOLFGANG VON GOETHE

Goethe, Johann Wolfgang von. *Italian Journey (1786–1788)*. Trans. W. H. Auden and Elizabeth Mayer. New York: Penguin, 1962.

—. Noten und Abhandlungen zum *West-östlichen Diwan*. Kap. Künftiger Diwan, Abschnitt *Buch des Paradieses*. Goethes Werke. Hg. Im Auftrage der Grossherzogin Sophie von Sachsen. Abth. I. Werke. 55 Bde. (in 63)–Weimar 1887–1918.

—. *Selected Poems*. Ed. Christopher Middleton. Vol. 1. Boston: Suhrkamp/Insel, 1983.

—. *Wilhelm Meister's Apprenticeship*. Ed. and trans. Eric A. Blackall in cooperation with Victor Lange. *Goethe: The Collected Works*, Vol. 9. Princeton, N.J.: Princeton University Press, 1995.

—. *Wilhelm Meister's Journeyman Years or The Renunciants*. Trans. Krishna Brown, ed. Jane Brown. *Goethe's Collected Works*, Vol. 10. New York: Suhrkamp, 1989.

Goethes Werke: Hamburger Ausgabe in 14 Bänden, ed. Erich Trunz. 11th ed. Munich: Beck, 1981.

Goethes Werke: Herausgegeben im Auftrage der Großherzogin Sophie von Sachsen. Tokyo: Sansyusya. 1975. Munich: DTV, 1987.

"Notes and Essays for a Better Understanding of the *West-East Divan*," by Johann Wolfgang von Goethe. Trans. Martin Bidney and Peter Anton von Arnim. In *West-East Divan, The Poems, with "Notes and Essays": Goethe's Intercultural Dialogues*, by Johann Wolfgang von Goethe, *Divan*, translated, with introduction and commentary poems by Martin Bidney. Albany: State University of New York Press, 2010.

West-East Divan, The Poems, with "Notes and Essays": Goethe's Intercultural Dialogues, by Johann Wolfgang von Goethe, *Divan* trans., with introduction and commentary poems by Martin Bidney. Albany: State University of New York Press, 2010.

GAY RIGHTS MOVEMENT

Hiller, Kurt. "Appeal on Behalf of an Oppressed Human Variety" [written for the Second International Congress for Sexual Reform (Copenhagen, 1928) delivered by Magnus Hirschfeld]. The speech can be found at http://paganpressbooks.com/jpl/HILLER.HTM.

—. *Leben gegen die Zeit*. Vol. 1: *Logos*. Hamburg: Rowohlt, 1969.

—. *Leben gegen die Zeit*. Vol. 2: *Eros*. Hamburg: Rowohlt, 1973.

—. *§ 175: Die Schmach des Jahrhunderts!* Hannover: Paul Steegemann, 1922.

—. "Politischer Rat geistiger Arbeiter." *Das Ziel* 3 (1919): 218–19.

—. "Philosophie des Ziels." *Das Ziel* 1 (1916): 187–218.

—. "Wo bleibt der homoerotische Roman?" *Jahrbuch für sexuelle Zwischenstufen* 14, no. 3 (1914): 338–41.

Hirschfeld, Magnus. *Die Homosexualität des Mannes und des Weibes*. Berlin: L. Marcus, 1914. Reprint: New York: de Gruyter, 2001. Translated as *The Homosexuality of Men and Women*. Reprint, Amherst, N.Y.: Prometheus Books, 2000.

—. *Sappho und Sokrates oder Wie erklärt sich die Liebe der Männer und Frauen zu Personen des eigenen Geschlechts?* Leipzig: Max Spohr, 1896.

Höchstetter, Sophie. *Lord Byrons Jugendtraum.* Leipzig: Reclam, 1920.

Isherwood, Christopher. *Christopher and His Kind: 1929–1939.* New York: Farrar, Strauss Giroux, 1976.

—. *Goodbye to Berlin.* 1939. New York: Vintage, 1998.

Rolf (Meier). Response to "Das Ewige und der Freund." *Der Kreis*, no. 5 XIX. Jahrgang (May 1951): 26.

SEXUS: Monographien aus dem Institut für Sexualwissenschaft in Berlin, herausgegeben von San.-Rat Dr. Magnus Hirschfeld, Band IV, *Paragraph 267 des Amtlichen Entwurfs eines Allgemeinen Deutschen Strafgesetzbuches "Unzucht zwischen Männern." Eine Denkschrift, gerichtet an das Reichsjustizministerium von 1925*, Herausgegeben von der Abteilung für Sexualreform (Wissenschaftlich-humanitäres Komitee) am Institut für Sexualwissenschaft zu Berlin. Stuttgart: Juluis Püttmann 1925.

SECONDARY SOURCES

Online Sources

The 1925 petition to repeal §175: http://www.schwulencity.de/Sexus_Paragraph_267.html.

1943 Berlin address book: http://digital.zlb.de/viewer/image/10089470_1943/1870.

The Adullam Foundation: http://www.adullam.ch/auftrag-struktur-stiftung.html.

The Ahmadiyya Muslim Community homepage: http://www.ahmadiyya.us/about-ahmadiyya-muslim-community.

Bundesstiftung Magnus Hirschfeld: http://mh-stiftung.de.

Das Gedenkbuch des Bundesarchivs für die Opfer der nationalsozialistischen Judenverfolgung in Deutschland (1933–1945): http://www.bundesarchiv.de/gedenkbuch/.

Grand Hotel Quisisana: http://www.quisisana.com/en/index.

Historical exchange rates: https://www.measuringworth.com/exchangeglobal/.

"Hugo Gschwind." Dr.rer.pol., Therwil, Präsident des Regierungsrats Kanton Basel, 1940/1941 and 1944/1945; Regierungsgebäude Liestal; http://www.baselland.ch/rr-praes_1832-htm.273718.0.html and https://personenlexikon.bl.ch/Hugo_Gschwind.

Jewish Museum Berlin homepage: https://www.jmberlin.de/en.

Jüdisches Adressbuch für Gross-Berlin 1931 (Berlin, 1931): https://digital.zlb.de/viewer/image/34039536_1931_1932/1/.

Kurt Hiller Gesellschaft: http://www.hiller-gesellschaft.de/.

Lahore Ahmadiyya Movement in Islam homepage, including *Moslemische Revue*, http://www.aaiil.org/.

The Lahore Mission College, Forman Christian College website: https://www.fccollege.edu.pk/about/.

Landesarchiv Berlin, Sterberegister (Register of Deaths): http://www.content.landesarchiv-berlin.de/labsa/show/index.php.

Magnus Hirschfeld Gesellschaft: http://magnus-hirschfeld.de/.

Memorial to the Homosexuals Persecuted Under the National Socialist Regime: https://www.stiftung-denkmal.de/en/memorials/memorial-to-the-homosexuals-persecuted-under-the-national-socialist-regime.html.

Memorial to the Murdered Jews of Europe: https://www.stiftung-denkmal.de/en/memorials/the-memorial-to-the-murdered-jews-of-europe.html.

Purchasing power of the past U.S. dollars: https://www.measuringworth.com/ppowerus/.

Schwules (Gay) Museum, Berlin: http://www.schwulesmuseum.de/en/the-museum/.

Şehitlik Mosque, Berlin: http://www.sehitlik-camii.de/.

Shah Jahan Mosque: http://www.shahjahanmosque.org.uk/.

Films and Interviews

Der Kreis. Dir. Stefan Haupt. Switzerland, 2014.

A Road to Mecca: The Journey of Muhammad Asad. Dir. Georg Misch, Mischief Films, 2008.

Sonderausgabe: Exclusivinterview mit Mohammed Aman Hobohm. So Gesehen TV (Germany), December 24, 2009, recorded in 2006. http://islam.de/24332.

Studies Including Media

Abdullah, Muhammad Salim. *Geschichte des Islams in Deutschland*. Graz-Wien-Köln, Styria, 1981.

Abu-r-Rida', Muhammad ibn Ahmad Ibn Rassoul. *Bruder Johann Ibn Goethe: Die unbekannte Überzeugung des deutschen Dichters zum Islam*. Köln: Islamische Bibliothek, 1998.

Achcar, Gilbert. *The Arabs and the Holocaust: The Arab-Israeli War of Narratives*. London: Saqi Books, 2011.

Aderet, Ofer. "Yad Vashem Names Egyptian First Arab Righteous Among the Nations." *Haaretz*, September 30, 2013. http://www.haaretz.com/jewish-world/jewish-world-news/.premium-1.549718.

Agamben, Giorgio. *Remnants of Auschwitz: The Witness and the Archive*. New York: Zone Books, 1999.

Ahmad, Nasir. "A Brief History of the Berlin Muslim Mission, 1922–1988." http://www.aaiil.org/text/articles/others/briefhistoryberlinmuslimmissiongermany.shtml.

—. "Brief History of the Woking Muslim Mission." http://www.wokingmuslim.org/history/woking.htm.

Al-Murabit, Schaikh 'Abdulqadir. "Goethe als Muslim." *Islamische Zeitung*, no. 5 (1995), www.islamische-zeitung.de.

Andrabi, Abroo Aman. *Muhammad Asad: His Contribution to Islamic Learning*. New Delhi: Goodword Books, 2007.

Anidjar, Gil. *The Jew, the Arab: A History of the Enemy*. Stanford, Calif.: Stanford University Press, 2003.

Ansari, Humayun. *"The Infidel Within": Muslims in Britain since 1800*. London: Hurst & Co., 2004.

—, ed. *The Making of the East London Mosque, 1910–1951: Minutes of the London Mosque Fund and East London Mosque Trust Ltd*. Cambridge: Cambridge University Press, 2011.

—. "Making Transnational Connections: Muslim Networks in Early Twentieth-Century Britain." In *Islam in Inter-War Europe*, ed. Nathalie Clayer and Eric Germain, 31–63. New York: Columbia University Press, 2008.

—. "Maulana Barkatullah Bhopali's Transnationalism: Pan-Islamism, Colonialism, and Radical Politics." In *Transnational Islam in Interwar Europe*, ed. Götz Nordbruch and Umar Ryad, 181–209. New York: Palgrave Macmillan, 2014.

—. "The Woking Mosque: A Case Study of Muslim Engagement with British Society since 1889." *Immigrants & Minorities* 21, no. 3 (2002): 1–24.

Asad, Talal. "Muhammad Asad Between Religion and Politics." *Islam & Science* 10, no. 1 (Summer 2012): 155–65.

Aschheim, Steven. *The Nietzsche Legacy in Germany, 1890–1990*. Berkeley: University of California Press, 1992.

Backhausen, Manfred. *Die Lahore-Ahmadiyya-Bewegung in Europa: Geschichte, Gegenwart und Zukunft der als "Lahore-Ahmadiyya-Bewegung zur Verbreitung islamischen Wissens" bekannten internationalen islamischen Gemeinschaft*. Wembley: Ahmadiyya Anjuman Lahore, 2008.

Baer, Marc David. *The Dönme: Jewish Converts, Muslim Revolutionaries, and Secular Turks*. Stanford, Calif.: Stanford University Press, 2010.

—. "Mistaken for Jews: Turkish PhD Students in Nazi Germany." *German Studies Review* 41, no. 1 (February 2018): 19–39.

—. "Muslim Encounters with Nazism and the Holocaust: The Ahmadi of Berlin and German-Jewish Convert to Islam Hugo Marcus." *American Historical Review* 120, no. 1 (February 2015): 140–71.

—. "Turk and Jew in Berlin: The First Turkish Migration to Berlin and the Shoah." *Comparative Studies in Society and History* 55, no. 2 (April 2013): 330–55.

Bambach, Charles. "Weimar Philosophy and the Crisis of Historical Thinking." In *Weimar Thought: A Contested Legacy*, ed. Peter Gordon and John McCormick, 133–49. Princeton, N.J.: Princeton University Press, 2013.

Barnett, Victoria. *For the Soul of the People: Protestant Protest against Hitler*. Oxford: Oxford University Press, 1992.

Bashkin, Orit. *New Babylonians: A History of Jews in Modern Iraq*. Stanford, Calif.: Stanford University Press, 2012.

—. *The Other Iraq: Pluralism and Culture in Hashemite Iraq*. Stanford, Calif.: Stanford University Press, 2008.

Bauer, Heike. "Suicidal Subjects: Translation and the Affective Foundations of Magnus Hirschfeld's Sexology." In *Sexology and Translation: Cultural and Scientific Encounters Across the Modern World*, ed. Heike Bauer, 233–52. Philadelphia: Temple University Press, 2015.

—, ed. *Queer 1950s: Rethinking Sexuality in the Postwar Years*. London: Palgrave Macmillan, 2012.

Bauknecht, Bernd. *Muslime in Deutschland von 1920 bis 1945*. Cologne: Teiresias, 2001.

Beachy, Robert. *Gay Berlin: Birthplace of a Modern Identity*. New York: Vintage, 2014.

Beinin, Joel. *The Dispersion of Egyptian Jewry: Culture, Politics, and the Formation of the Modern Diaspora*. Berkeley: University of California Press, 1998.

Beller, Steven. *Antisemitism: A Very Short Introduction*. New York: Oxford University Press, 2007.

"Benannt nach Goethe: Liberale Moschee eröffnet in Berlin." *taz*, May 12, 2017.

Bergen, Doris L. *Twisted Cross: The German Christian Movement in the Third Reich*. Chapel Hill: University of North Carolina Press, 1996.

Berghahn, Klaus, and Jost Hermand, ed. *Goethe in German-Jewish Culture*. Rochester, N.Y.: Camden House, 2001.

Berkowitz, Michael. "Rejecting Zion, Embracing the Orient: The Life and Death of Jacob Israel De Haan." In *Orientalism and the Jews*, ed. Ivan Davidson Kalmar and Derek J. Penslar. Waltham, Mass.: Brandeis University Press, 2005, 109–24.

"Berlin soll liberale Moscheegemeinde bekommen." *der Tagesspiegel*, March 4, 2017.

Biale, David. *Not in the Heavens: The Tradition of Jewish Secular Thought*. Princeton, N.J.: Princeton University Press, 2010.

Bidney, Martin. Introduction to *West-East Divan, The Poems, with "Notes and Essays": Goethe's Intercultural Dialogues*, by Johann Wolfgang von Goethe, *Divan*, trans., with introduction and commentary poems by Martin Bidney. Albany: State University of New York Press, 2010, xxv–liv.

Biess, Frank. *Homecomings: Returning POWS and the Legacies of Defeat in Postwar Germany*. Princeton, N.J.: Princeton University Press, 2006.

—. "Survivors of Totalitarianism: Returning POWs and the Reconstruction of Masculine Citizenship in West Germany, 1945–1955." In *The Miracle Years Revisited: A Cultural History of West Germany*, ed. Hanna Schissler, 57–82. Princeton, N.J.: Princeton University Press, 2001.

Bisno, Adam. "Stefan George's Homoerotic *Erlösungsreligion*, 1891–1907." In *A Poet's Reich: Politics and Culture in the George Circle*, ed. Melissa S. Lane and Martin A. Ruehl, 37–55. Rochester, N.Y.: Camden House, 2011.

Boggioni, Tom. "Anti-Muslim Long Island Blogger to Run Ads Linking Hitler to Islam on DC Area Buses." *Raw Story*, May 17, 2014. http://www.rawstory.com/rs/2014/05/17/anti-muslim-long-island-blogger-to-run-ads-linking-hitler-to-islam-on-dc-area-buses/.

Boum, Aomar. *Memories of Absence: How Muslims Remember Jews in Morocco*. Stanford, Calif.: Stanford University Press, 2013.

Boyarin, Daniel. *Border Lines: The Partition of Judaeo-Christianity*. Philadelphia: University of Pennsylvania Press, 2006.

Böer, Ingeborg, Ruth Haerkötter, and Petra Kappert, eds. *Türken in Berlin, 1871–1945: Eine Metropole in den Erinnerungen osmanischer und türkischer Zeitzeugen*. Berlin: de Gruyter, 2002.

Brann, Ross. *The Compunctious Poet: Cultural Ambiguity and Hebrew Poetry in Muslim Spain*. Baltimore: Johns Hopkins University Press, 1991.

Brann, Ross, and Adam Sutcliffe, eds. *Renewing the Past, Reconfiguring Jewish Culture: From al-Andalus to the Haskalah*. Philadelphia: University of Pennsylvania Press, 2003.

Brenner, Michael. *The Renaissance of Jewish Culture in Weimar Germany*. New Haven, Conn.: Yale University Press, 1998.

Bullough, Vern. Introduction to *The Homosexuality of Men and Women*, by Magnus Hirschfeld. Trans. Michael Lombardi-Nash. New York: Prometheus Books, 2000.

Bunzl, Matti. *Jews and Queers: Symptoms of Modernity in Late-Twentieth-Century Vienna*. Berkeley: University of California Press, 2004.

Canning, Kathleen. "Introduction: Weimar Publics/Weimar Subjects: Rethinking the Political Culture of Germany in the 1920s." In *Weimar Publics/Weimar Subjects: Rethinking the Political Culture of Germany in the 1920s*, ed. Kathleen Canning, Kerstin Barndt, and Kristin McGuire. New York: Berghahn, 2010.

Carstensen, Heike. *Leben und Werk der Malerin und Graphikerin Julie Wolfthorn (1864–1944): Rekonstruktion eines Künstlerinnenlebens*. Marburg: Tectum, 2011.

Chaghatai, M. Ikram, ed. *Muhammad Asad: Europe's Gift to Islam*. Lahore: Truth Society, 2006.

Chin, Rita. *The Guest Worker Question in Postwar Germany*. Cambridge: Cambridge University Press, 2009.

Clayer, Nathalie, and Eric Germain. Introduction to *Islam in Inter-War Europe*, ed. Nathalie Clayer and Eric Germain. New York: Columbia University Press, 2008

Cohen, Mark R. "The 'Golden Age' of Jewish-Muslim Relations: Myth and Reality." In *A History of Jewish-Muslim Relations: From the Origins to the Present Day*, ed. Abdelwahab Meddeb and Benjamin Stora. Trans. Jane Marie Todd and Michael B. Smith, 28–38. Princeton, N.J.: Princeton University Press, 2013.

—. *Under Crescent and Cross: The Jews in the Middle Ages*. Princeton, N.J.: Princeton University Press, 1994.

Cooperman, Bernard Dov, and Tsevi Zohar, ed. *Jews and Muslims in the Islamic World*. Bethesda, Md.: University Press of Maryland, 2013.

Crouthamel, Jason. "'We Need Real Men': The Impact of the Front Experience on Homosexual Front Soldiers." In *An Intimate History of the Front*, ed. Jason Crouthamel, 121–46. New York: Palgrave Macmillan, 2014.

Cwiklinski, Sebastian. "Between National and Religious Solidarities: The Tatars in Germany and Poland in the Inter-War Period." In *Islam in Inter-War Europe*, ed. Nathalie Clayer and Eric Germain, 64–88. New York: Columbia University Press, 2008.

—. *Die Wolga an der Spree: Tataren und Baschkiren in Berlin*. Berlin: Die Ausländerbeauftragte des Senats von Berlin, 2000.

Derks, Paul. *Die Schande der heiligen Päderastie: Homosexualität und Öffentlichkeit in der deutschen Literature, 1750–1850*. Berlin: rosa Winkel, 1990.

Domeier, Norman. *The Eulenburg Affair: A Cultural History of Politics in the German Empire*. Trans. Deborah Lucas Schneider. Rochester, N.Y.: Camden House, 2015.

Dose, Ralf. *Magnus Hirschfeld: Deutscher—Jude—Weltbürger*. Stiftung Neue Synagoge Berlin Centrum Judaicum, Jüdische Miniaturen, Band 15. Teetz: Hentrich & Hentrich, 2005. Translated into English as *Magnus Hirschfeld: The Origins of the Gay Liberation Movement*. New York: Monthly Review, 2014.

Dubrovic, Milan. *Veruntreute Geschichte*. Wien: Paul Zsolnay, 1985.

Efron, John M. *Germany Jewry and the Allure of the Sephardic*. Princeton, N.J.: Princeton University Press, 2016.

—. "Orientalism and the Jewish Historical Gaze." In *Orientalism and the Jews*, ed. Ivan Davidson Kalmar and Derek J. Penslar, 80–93. Waltham, Mass.: Brandeis University Press, 2005.

Egorova, Yulia. *Jews and India: Perceptions and Image*. London: Routledge, 2006.

—. *Jews and Muslims in South Asia: Reflections on Difference, Religion, and Race*. Oxford: Oxford University Press, 2018.

El-Tayeb, Fatima. "'Gays who cannot properly be gay': Queer Muslims in the Neoliberal European City." *European Journal of Women's Studies* 19, no. 1 (2012): 79–95. https://doi.org/10.1177%2F1350506811426388.

—. *European Others: Queering Ethnicity in Postnational Europe*. Minneapolis: University of Minnesota Press, 2011.

Emre, Gültekin. *300 Jahre Türken an der Spree: Ein vergessenes Kapitel Berliner Kulturgeschichte*. Berlin: Ararat, 1983.

Endelman, Todd. *Leaving the Jewish Fold: Conversion and Radical Assimilation in Modern Jewish History*. Princeton, N.J.: Princeton University Press, 2015.

—. *Radical Assimilation in English Jewish History, 1656–1945*. Bloomington: Indiana University Press, 1990.

Ercan Argun, Betigül. *Turkey in Germany: The Transnational Sphere of Deutschkei*. New York: Routledge, 2003.

Ericksen, Robert P. *Complicity in the Holocaust: Churches and Universities in Nazi Germany*. Cambridge: Cambridge University Press, 2012.

Ericksen, Robert P., and Susannah Heschel, ed. *Betrayal: German Churches and the Holocaust*. Minneapolis: University of Minneapolis Press, 1999.

Evans, Jennifer. "Seeing Subjectivity: Erotic Photography and the Optics of Desire." *American Historical Review* 118, no. 2 (April 2013): 430–62.

Evans, Richard. *The Third Reich in Power*. New York: Penguin, 2006.

Fivaz-Silbermann, Ruth. "Ignorance, Realpolitik and Human Rights: Switzerland Between Active Refusal and Passive Help." In *Bystanders, Rescuers or Perpetrators? The Neutral Countries and the Shoah*, ed. Corry Guttstadt, Thomas Lutz, Bernd Rother, and Yessica San Román, 87–99. International Holocaust Remembrance Alliance Series, Vol. 2. Berlin: Metropol, 2016.

Föllmer, Moritz, Rüdiger Graf, and Per Leo. "Einleitung: Die Kultur der Krise in der Weimarer Republik." In *Die "Krise" der Weimarer Republik: Zur Kritik eines Deutungsmusters*, ed. Moritz Föllmer and Rüdiger Graf, 9–41. Frankfurt am Main: Campus, 2005.

Freidenreich, David M., and Miriam Goldstein, eds. *Beyond Religious Borders: Interaction and Intellectual Exchange in the Medieval Islamic World*. Philadelphia: University of Pennsylvania Press, 2012.

Freimark, Peter. "Promotion Hedwig Klein—zugleich ein Beitrag zum Seminar für Geschichte und Kultur des Vorderen Orients." In *Hochschulalltag im "Dritten Reich": Die Hamburger Universität, 1933–1945*, Eckart Krause, Ludwig Huber, and Holger Fischer, eds., 851–64, Vol. 2: *Philosophische Fakultät*. Berlin, 1991.

Friedmann, Yohanan. *Prophecy Continuous: Aspects of Ahmadi Religious Thought and Its Medieval Background*. Berkeley: University of California Press, 1989.

Frisius, Hildegard, Marianne Kälberer, Wolfgang G. Krogel, and Gerlind Lachenicht, ed. *Evangelisch getauft—als Juden verfolgt: Spurensuche Berliner Kirchengemeinden*. Berlin: Wichern, 2008.

Fritzsche, Peter. "The Economy of Experience in Weimar Germany." In *Weimar Publics/Weimar Subjects: Rethinking the Political Culture of Germany in the 1920s*, ed. Kathleen Canning, Kerstin Barndt and Kristin McGuire, 374–96. New York: Berghahn, 2010.

—. "Landscape of Danger, Landscape of Design: Crisis and Modernism in Weimar Germany." In *Dancing on the Volcano: Essays on the Culture of the Weimar Republic*, ed. Thomas Kniesche and Stephen Brockmann, 29–46. New York: Camden House, 1994.

Gay, Peter. *Weimar Culture: The Outsider as Insider*. London: Secker & Warburg, 1968.

Gensicke, Klaus. *The Mufti of Jerusalem and the Nazis: The Berlin Years, 1941–1945*. Trans. Alexander Fraser Gunn. Edgware: Vallentine Mitchell, 2010.

Germain, Eric. "The First Muslim Missions on a European Scale: Ahmadi-Lahori Networks in the Inter-War Period." In *Islam in Inter-war Europe*, ed. Nathalie Clayer and Eric Germain, 89–118. New York: Columbia University Press, 2008.

Gershman, Norman H. *Besa: Muslims Who Saved Jews in World War II*. Syracuse, N.Y.: Syracuse University Press, 2008.

Gershoni, Israel. "Confronting Nazism in Egypt: Tawfiq al-Hakim's Anti-Totalitarianism, 1938–1945." *Deutschlandbilder: Tel Aviver Jahrbuch für deutsche Geschichte* 26 (1997): 121–50.

—. "'Der verfolgte Jude': Al-Hilals Reaktionen auf den Antisemitismus in Europa und Hitlers Machtergreifung." In *Blind für die Geschichte? Arabische Begegnungen mit dem Nationalsozialismus*, ed. Gerhard Höpp, Peter Wien, and René Wildangel, 39–72. Berlin: Klaus Schwarz, 2004.

—. "Egyptian Liberalism in an Age of 'Crisis of Orientation': Al-Risala's Reaction to Fascism and Nazism, 1933–39." *International Journal of Middle East Studies* 31 (1999): 551–76.

Gershoni, Israel, and James Jankowski. *Confronting Fascism in Egypt: Dictatorship Versus Democracy in the 1930s*. Stanford, Calif.: Stanford University Press, 2009.

Gershoni, Israel, and Götz Nordbruch, ed. *Sympathie und Schrecken: Begegnungen mit Faschismus und Nationalsozialismus in Ägypten, 1922–1937*. Berlin: de Gruyter 2011. Translated into English as *Arab Responses to Fascism and Nazism: Attraction and Repulsion*, ed. Israel Gershoni. Austin: University of Texas Press, 2014.

Gerwarth, Robert. *The Vanquished: Why the First World War Failed to End, 1917–1923*. London: Allen Lane, 2016.

Ghosh, Amitav. *In an Antique Land: History in the Guise of a Traveler's Tale*. New York: Vintage, 1994.

Giles, Geoffrey. "The Denial of Homosexuality: Same-Sex Incidents in Himmler's SS and Police." *Journal of the History of Sexuality* 11, nos. 1–2 (January/April 2002): 256–90.

—. "The Institutionalization of Homosexual Panic in the Third Reich." In *Social Outsiders in Nazi Germany*, ed. Robert Gellately and Nathan Stoltzfus, 233–55. Princeton, N.J.: Princeton University Press, 2001.

—. "'The Most Unkindest Cut of All': Castration, Homosexuality, and Nazi Justice." *Journal of Contemporary History* 27, no. 1 (January 1992): 41–61.

Goitein, Shlomo Dov. *Jews and Arabs: A Concise History of Their Social and Cultural Relations*. 1954. Reprint, Mineola, N.Y.: Dover, 2005.

—. *A Mediterranean Society: The Jewish Communities of the Arab World as Portrayed in the Documents of the Cairo Geniza*. 6 vols., new ed. Berkeley: University of California Press, 1999.

Göktürk, Deniz, David Gramling, and Anton Kaes, ed. *Germany in Transit: Nation and Migration, 1955–2005*. Berkeley: University of California Press, 2007.

Goldstein, Miriam. Introduction to *Beyond Religious Borders: Interaction and Intellectual Exchange in the Medieval Islamic World*, ed. David M. Freidenreich and Miriam Goldstein, 1–12. Philadelphia: University of Pennsylvania Press, 2012.

Goldman, Shalom. *Jewish-Christian Difference and Modern Jewish Identity: Seven Twentieth-Century Converts*. Lanham, Md.: Lexington, 2015.

Gossman, Lionel. *The Passion of Max von Oppenheim: Archaeology and Intrigue in the Middle East from Wilhelm II to Hitler*. Cambridge: Open Book, 2013.

Gottreich, Emily. *The Mellah of Marrakesh: Jewish and Muslim Space in Morocco's Red City*. Bloomington: Indiana University Press, 2006.

Gottreich, Emily Benichou, and Daniel J. Schroeter, ed. *Jewish Culture and Society in North Africa*. Bloomington: Indiana University Press, 2011.

Graetz, Heinrich. *History of the Jews*. 11 vols. Trans. B. Löwy. Philadelphia: Jewish Publication Society of America, 1891–1898.

Graf, Rüdiger, and Moritz Föllmer. "The Culture of Crisis in the Weimar Republic." *Thesis Eleven* 111, no. 1 (August 2012): 36–47.

Greaves, Ron. *Islam in Victorian Britain: The Life and Times of Abdullah Quilliam*. London: Kube, 2010.

Green, Nile. "Journeymen, Middlemen: Travel, Trans-Culture and Technology in the Origins of Muslim Printing." *International Journal of Middle East Studies* 41, no. 2 (2009): 203–24.

—. "Spacetime and the Muslim Journey West: Industrial Communication in the Making of the 'Muslim World.'" *American Historical Review* 118, no. 2 (April 2013): 401–29.

Groβe, Judith. "Patriotismus und Kosmopolitismus: Magnus Hirschfeld und der Erste Weltkrieg." In *Simon Dubnow Institute Yearbook* 13 (2014): 337–64.

Gross, Ahmad. "In Islam leben und sterben wir alle: Goethe, Wagner, Nietzsche, Rilke, Jünger und der Islam." *Islamische Zeitung*, Thema: Goethe (www.islamische-zeitung.de), July 5, 2001.

Gustafson, Susan E. *Men Desiring Men: The Poetry of Same-Sex Identity and Desire in German Classicism*. Detroit: Wayne State University Press, 2002.

Guttstadt, Corry. *Turkey, the Jews, and the Holocaust*. Trans. Kathleen M. Dell'Orto, Sabine Bartel, and Michelle Miles. Cambridge: Cambridge University Press, 2013.

Hamilton, Richard F. *Who Voted for Hitler?* Princeton, N.J.: Princeton University Press, 1982.

Hecht, Cornelia. *Deutsche Juden und Antisemitismus in der Weimarer Republik*. Bonn: Dietz, 2003.

Heim, Gabriel. "Fremdenpolizei-Akte 29496." *tachles: das jüdische Wochenmagazin*, April 21, 2017, 10–13.

Heine, Peter. "Die Imam-Kurse der deutschen Wehrmacht im Jahre 1944." In *Fremde Erfahrungen: Asiaten und Afrikaner in Deutschland, Österreich und in der Schweiz bis 1945*, ed. Gerhard Höpp, 229–38. Berlin: Klaus Schwarz, 1996.

Herbert, Ulrich. *Geschichte der Ausländerpolitik in Deutschland: Saisonarbeiter, Zwangsarbeiter, Gastarbeiter, Flüchtlinge*. Munich: Beck, 2001.

Herf, Jeffrey. *Nazi Propaganda for the Arab World*. New Haven, Conn.: Yale University Press, 2009.

Hermand, Jost. "German Jews Beyond Judaism: The Gerhard/Israel/George L. Mosse Case." In *The German-Jewish Dialogue Reconsidered: A Symposium in Honor of George L. Mosse*, ed. Klaus Berghahn, 233–46. New York: Peter Lang, 1996.

Hermansen, Marcia. "Roads to Mecca: Conversion Narratives of European and Euro-American Muslims." *Muslim World* 89, no. 1 (January 1999): 56–89.

Herrn, Rainer. *100 Years of the Gay Rights Movement in Germany*. New York: Goethe-Institut New York, 1997.

Hertz, Deborah. *How Jews Became Germans: The History of Conversion and Assimilation in Berlin*. New Haven, Conn.: Yale University Press, 2007.

Herzer, Manfred. *Magnus Hirschfeld: Leben und Werk eines jüdischen, schwulen und sozialistischen Sexologen*. 2nd ed. Bibliothek rosa Winkel Band 28, Schriften der Magnus-Hirschfeld-Gesellschaft Band 10. 1992. Hamburg: MännerschwarmSkript Verlag, 2001.

Herzog, Dagmar. *Sex After Fascism: Memory and Morality in Twentieth-Century Germany*. Princeton, N.J.: Princeton University Press, 2005.

Heschel, Susannah. "Abraham Geiger and the Emergence of Jewish Philoislamism." In *"Im vollen Licht der Geschichte": Die Wissenschaft des Judentums und die Anfänge der kritischen Koranforschung*, ed. D. Hartwig, W. Homolka, M. J. Marx and A. Neuwirth, 65–86. Würzburg: Ergon, 2008.

—. *Abraham Geiger and the Jewish Jesus*. Chicago: University of Chicago Press, 1998.

——. *The Aryan Jesus: Christian Theologians and the Bible in Nazi Germany*. Princeton, N.J.: Princeton University Press, 2008.

—. "German Jewish Scholarship on Islam as a Tool for De-Orientalizing Judaism." *New German Critique* 39, no. 3 (2012): 91–107.

Hindmarsh, Bruce. "Religious Conversion as Narrative and Autobiography." In *The Oxford Handbook of Religious Conversion*, ed. Lewis R. Rambo and Charles E. Farhadian, 343–68. Oxford: Oxford University Press, 2014.

Hockenos, Matthew D. *A Church Divided: German Protestants Confront the Nazi Past*. Bloomington: Indiana University Press, 2004.

Hofmann, Murad. "Muhammad Asad: Europe's Gift to Islam." *Islamic Studies* 39, no. 2 (Summer 2000): 233–45.

—. *Religion on the Rise: Islam in the Third Millenium*. Beltsville, Md.: Amana, 2001.

Höpp, Gerhard. "In the Shadow of the Moon: Arab Inmates in Nazi Concentration Camps." Germany and the Middle East, 1871–1945, Special Double Issue, Princeton Papers: *Interdisciplinary Journal of Middle Eastern Studies* 10–11 (2001): 217–40.

—. "Islam in Berlin und Brandenburg: Steinerne Erinnerungen." In *Berlin für Orientalisten: Ein Stadtführer*, ed. Gerhard Höpp and Norbert Mattes, 7–23. Berlin: Klaus Schwarz, 2001.

—. "Mohammed Essad Bey: Nur Orient für Europäer?" *Asien, Afrika, Lateinamerika* 25, no. 1 (1997): 75–97.

—, ed. *Mufti-Papiere: Briefe, Memoranden, Reden und Aufrufe Amin al-Husainis aus dem Exil, 1940–1945*. Berlin: Klaus Schwarz, 2001.

—. *Muslime in der Mark: Als Kriegsgefangene und Internierte in Wünsdorf und Zossen, 1914–1924*. Berlin: Das Arabische Buch, 1997.

—. "Muslime unterm Hakenkreuz: Zur Entstehungsgeschichte des Islamischen Zentralinstituts zu Berlin e.V." *Moslemische Revue* 70, no. 1 (1994): 16–27.

—. "The Suppressed Discourse: Arab Victims of National Socialism," with a prologue and epilogue by Peter Wien. In *The World in World Wars: Experiences, Perceptions and Perspectives from Africa and Asia*, ed. Heike Liebau, Katrin Bromber, Katharina Lange, Dyala Hamzah, and Ravi Ahuja, 167–216. Leiden: Brill, 2010.

—. "Zwischen alle Fronten: Der ägyptische Nationalist Mansur Mustafa Rif'at (1883–1926) in Deutschland." In *Ägypten und Deutschland im 19. und 20. Jahrhundert im Spiegel von Archivalien*, ed. Wajih Abd as-Sadiq Atıq and Wolfgang Schwanitz, 263–73. Cairo: Verlag Dâr ath-Thâqafa, 1998.

—. "Zwischen Entente und Mittelmächten: Arabische Nationalisten und Panislamisten in Deutschland (1914 bis 1918)." *Asien, Afrika, Lateinamerika* 19, no. 5 (1991): 827–45.

—. "Zwischen Moschee und Demonstration: Muslime in Berlin, 1922–1930." Pts. 1–3, *Moslemische Revue* 10, no. 3 (1990): 135–46; 10, no. 4 (1990): 230–38; and 11, no. 1 (1991): 13–19.

—. "Zwischen Universität und Straße: Ägyptische Studenten in Deutschland, 1849–1945." In *Die Beziehungen zwischen der Bundesrepublik Deutschland und der Republik Ägypten*, ed. Konrad Schliephake and Ghazi Shanneik, 31–42. Würzburg: Geographisches, 2002.

"Introduction." *American Historical Review* 118, no. 1 (February 2013): 45. http://www.jstor.org/stable/23425458.

Ihrig, Stefan. *Justifying Genocide: Germany and the Armenians from Bismarck to Hitler*. Cambridge, Mass.: Harvard University Press, 2016.

Jackson, Roy. *Nietzsche and Islam*. New York: Routledge, 2007.

Johnson, Ian. *A Mosque in Munich: Nazis, the CIA, and the Rise of the Muslim Brotherhood in the West.* Boston: Houghton Mifflin, 2010.

Johnston-Bloom, Ruchama. "Jews, Muslims and *Bildung*: The German-Jewish Orientalist Gustav Weil in Egypt." *Religion Compass* 8, no. 2 (February 2014): 49–59.

Jonker, Gerdien. *The Ahmadiyya Quest for Religious Progress: Missionizing Europe 1900–1965*. Leiden: Brill, 2016.

—. "A Laboratory of Modernity: The Ahmadiyya Mission in Inter-War Europe." *Journal of Muslims in Europe* 3, no. 1 (2014): 1–25.

Kaes, Anton, Martin Jay, and Edward Dimendberg. Preface to *The Weimar Republic Sourcebook*, ed. Anton Kaes, Martin Jay, and Edward Dimendberg. Berkeley: University of California Press, 1994, xvii–xx.

Kahleyss, Margot. *Muslime in Brandenburg—Kriegsgefangene im 1. Weltkrieg: Ansichten und Absichten.* Berlin: Staatliche Museen Preußischer Kulturbesitz, 1998.

Kalmar, Ivan Davidson and Derek Penslar, ed. *Orientalism and the Jews*. Waltham, Mass.: Brandeis University Press, 2005.

—. "Orientalism and the Jews: An Introduction." In *Orientalism and the Jews*, ed. Ivan Davidson Kalmar and Derek J. Penslar, xiii–xl. Waltham, Mass.: Brandeis University Press, 2005.

Kantorowicz, Ernst. *The King's Two Bodies: A Study in Medieval Political Theology*. Princeton: Princeton University Press, 1957.

Kaplan, Marion A. "When the Ordinary Became Extraordinary: German Jews Reacting to Nazi Persecution, 1933–1939." In *Social Outsiders in Nazi Germany*, ed. Robert Gellately and Nathan Stoltzfus. Princeton, N.J.: Princeton University Press, 2001, 66–98.

Karlauf, Thomas. "Stauffenberg: The Search for a Motive." In *A Poet's Reich: Politics and Culture in the George Circle*, ed. Melissa S. Lane and Martin A. Ruehl, 317–32. Rochester, N.Y.: Camden House, 2011.

Kashyap, Subhash. "Sir Mohammad Iqbal and Friedrich Nietzsche." *Islamic Quarterly* 2, no. 3 (October 1955): 175–94.

Katz, Ethan. "Did the Paris Mosque Save Jews? A Mystery and Its Memory." *Jewish Quarterly Review* 102, no. 2 (Spring 2012): 256–87.

Kaufmann, Uri. "Jüdisches Leben in der Schweiz nach 1945." Die Internationale Schule für Holocaust-Studien (ISHS), https://www.yadvashem.org/de/education/newsletter/8/jews-in-switzerland-after-1945.html.

Kazdaghli, Habib. "The Tunisian Jews in the German Occupation." In *A History of Jewish-Muslim Relations: From the Origins to the Present Day*, ed. Abdelwahab Meddeb and Benjamin Stora. Trans. Jane Marie Todd and Michael B. Smith, 367–69. Princeton, N.J.: Princeton University Press, 2013.

Keilson-Lauritz, Marita. "Stefan George's Concept of Love and the Gay Emancipation Movement." In *A Companion to the Works of Stefan George*, ed. Jens Rieckmann, 207–31. Rochester, N.Y.: Camden House, 2005.

Kenbib, Mohammed. "Mohammed V, Protector of Moroccan Jews." In *A History of Jewish-Muslim Relations: From the Origins to the Present Day*, ed. Abdelwahab Meddeb and Benjamin Stora. Trans. Jane Marie Todd and Michael B. Smith, 362–64. Princeton, N.J.: Princeton University Press, 2013.

Kennedy, Hubert. "Hiller, Kurt." *glbtq: An Encyclopedia of Gay, Lesbian, Bisexual, Transgender & Queer Culture* (2005), http://www.glbtqarchive.com/ssh/hiller_k_S.pdf.

—. *The Ideal Gay Man: The Story of 'Der Kreis'.* New York: Harrington Park, 1999.

Kermani, Navid. *Between Quran & Kafka: West-Eastern Affinities.* Trans. Tony Crawford. Cambridge: Polity, 2016.

Kontje, Todd. *German Orientalisms.* Ann Arbor: University of Michigan Press, 2004.

Koonz, Claudia. *The Nazi Conscience.* Cambridge, Mass.: Harvard University Press, 2003.

Kosnick, Kira. *Migrant Media: Turkish Broadcasting and Multicultural Politics in Berlin.* Bloomington: Indiana University Press, 2007.

Krämer, Gudrun. "Anti-Semitism in the Muslim World: A Critical Review." Anti-Semitism in the Arab World, Special Issue, *Die Welt des Islams: International Journal for the Study of Modern Islam*, new series, 46, no. 3 (2006): 243–76.

Kramer, Martin, ed. *Islam Assembled: The Advent of the Muslim Congresses.* New York: Columbia University Press, 1986.

—. *The Jewish Discovery of Islam: Studies in Honor of Bernard Lewis.* Tel Aviv: Tel Aviv University Press, 1999.

—. "The Road from Mecca: Muhammad Asad (born Leopold Weiss)." In *The Jewish Discovery of Islam: Studies in Honor of Bernard Lewis*, ed. Martin Kramer, 225–47. Tel Aviv: Tel Aviv University Press, 1999.

Kuck, Nathanael. "Anti-Colonialism in a Post-Imperial Environment: The Case of Berlin, 1914–1933." *Journal of Contemporary History* 49, no. 1 (January 2014): 134–59.

Lane, Melissa S. "The Platonic Politics of the George Circle: A Reconsideration." In *A Poet's Reich: Politics and Culture in the George Circle*, ed. Melissa S. Lane and Martin A. Ruehl, 133–63. Rochester, N.Y.: Camden House, 2011.

Lane, Melissa S., and Martin A. Ruehl. Introduction to *A Poet's Reich: Politics and Culture in the George Circle*, ed. Melissa S. Lane and Martin A. Ruehl, 1–22. Rochester, N.Y.: Camden House, 2011.

Lassner, Jacob. "Abraham Geiger: A Nineteenth-Century Jewish Reformer on the Origins of Islam." In *The Jewish Discovery of Islam: Studies in Honor of Bernard Lewis*, ed. Martin Kramer, 103–35. Tel Aviv: Tel Aviv University Press, 1999.

—. *Jews, Christians, and the Abode of Islam: Modern Scholarship, Medieval Realities.* Chicago: University of Chicago Press, 2012.

Lauzière, Henri. "The Evolution of the Salafiyya in the Twentieth Century Through the Life and Thought of Taqi Al-Din Al-Hilali." Ph.D. dissertation, Georgetown University, 2008.

—. *The Making of Salafism: Islamic Reform in the Twentieth Century.* New York: Columbia University Press, 2015.

Leck, Ralph M. *Georg Simmel and Avant-Garde Sociology: The Birth of Modernity, 1880–1920.* Amherst, N.Y.: Humanity Books, 2000.

Lepre, George. *Himmler's Bosnian Division: The Waffen-SS Handschar Division, 1943–1945.* Atglen, Pa.: Schiffer, 1997.

Levi, Primo. *If This Is a Man.* London: Abacus, 1979.

Levy, Avigdor, ed. *Jews, Turks, Ottomans: A Shared History, Fifteenth through the Twentieth Century.* Syracuse, N.Y.: Syracuse University Press, 2003.

Lewis, Bernard. *The Jews of Islam.* Princeton, N.J.: Princeton University Press, 1984.

—. "The Pro-Islamic Jews." *Judaism* 17, no. 4 (Fall 1968): 391–404.

Liebau, Heike. "The Kheiri Brothers and the Question of World Order After World War I." *Orient Bulletin: History and Cultures in Asia, the Middle East and Africa* 13 (2007): 3–4.

Lienert, Salomé. "Swiss Immigration Policies 1933–1939." In *Bystanders, Rescuers or Perpetrators? The Neutral Countries and the Shoah*, ed. Corry Guttstadt, Thomas Lutz, Bernd Rother, and Yessica San Román, 40–51. International Holocaust Remembrance Alliance Series, vol. 2. Berlin: Metropol, 2016.

Löw, Thomas. "Der 'Kreis' und sein idealer Schwuler." In *Männergeschichten: Schwule in Basel seit 1930*, ed. Kuno Trüeb and Stephan Miescher, 157–65. Basel: Buchverlag Basler Zeitung, 1988.

Löwy, Michael. *Redemption and Utopia: Jewish Libertarian Thought in Central Europe: A Study in Elective Affinity*. Stanford, Calif.: Stanford University Press, 1992.

Mallmann, Klaus-Michael, and Martin Cüppers. *Halbmond und Hakenkreuz: Das Dritte Reich, die Araber und Palästina*. Darmstadt: Wissenschaftliche Buchgesellschaft, 2006. English translation: *Nazi Palestine: The Plans for the Extermination of the Jews in Palestine*. New York: Enigma Books, 2010.

Mancini, Elena. "Boys in the City: Homoerotic Desire and the Urban Refuge in Early Twentieth Century Germany." In *Fleeing the City: Studies in the Culture and Politics of Anti-Urbanism*, ed. Michael Thompson, 91–110. New York: Palgrave Macmillan, 2009.

——. *Magnus Hirschfeld and the Quest for Sexual Freedom: A History of the First International Sexual Freedom Movement*. New York: Palgrave Macmillan, 2010.

Manjapra, Kris. *Age of Entanglement: German and Indian Intellectuals Across Empire*. Cambridge, Mass.: Harvard University Press, 2014.

——. *M. N. Roy: Marxism and Colonial Cosmopolitanism*. Delhi: Routledge, 2010.

Marchand, Suzanne. "Eastern Wisdom in an Era of Western Despair: Orientalism in 1920s Central Europe." In *Weimar Thought: A Contested Legacy*, ed. Peter E. Gordon and John P. McCormick, 341–60. Princeton, N.J.: Princeton University Press, 2013.

——. *German Orientalism in the Age of Empire: Religion, Race, and Scholarship*. New York: Cambridge University Press, 2009.

"Marcus, Hugo." In *Mann für Mann: Biographisches Lexikon zur Geschichte von Freundesliebe und mannmännlicher Sexualität im deutschen Sprachraum*, ed. Bernd-Ulrich Hergemöller, 490. Hamburg: MännerschwarmSkript Verlag, 1998, 3rd ed. Münster: Lit, 2010.

Marhoefer, Laurie. *Sex and the Weimar Republic: German Homosexual Emancipation and the Rise of the Nazis*. Toronto: University of Toronto Press, 2015.

Marti, Madeleine. "Sophie Höchstetter." FemBio. Frauen Biographieforschung. www.fembio.org.

Matar, Nabil. *Turks, Moors, and Englishmen in the Age of Discovery*. New York: Columbia University Press, 2000.

Mattar, Philip. *The Mufti of Jerusalem: Al-Hajj Amin Al-Husayni and the Palestinian National Movement*. Rev. ed. New York: Columbia University Press, 1988.

May, Yomb. "Goethe, Islam, and the Orient: The Impetus for and Mode of Cultural Encounter in the West-östlicher Divan." In *Encounters with Islam in German Literature and Culture*, ed. James Hodkinson and Jeffrey Morrison, 89–107. Rochester, N.Y.: Camden House, 2009.

Mazower, Mark. *Salonica, City of Ghosts: Christians, Muslims and Jews, 1430–1950*. New York: Vintage, 2006.

McKale, Donald M. Review of Jeffrey Herf, Nazi Propaganda for the Arab World. *Holocaust and Genocide Studies* 25, no. 1 (Spring 2011): 149–52.

McNeal, Michael. "Roy Jackson, Nietzsche and Islam." *Journal of Nietzsche Studies*, http://www.hunter.cuny.edu/jns/reviews/roy-jackson-nietzsche-and-islam. Accessed November 1, 2015.

Meddeb, Abedelwahab, and Benjamin Stora. General Introduction to *A History of Jewish-Muslim Relations: From the Origins to the Present Day*, edited by Benjamin Stora and Abedelwahab Meddeb, 13–24. Princeton, N.J.: Princeton University Press, 2013.

Meining, Stefan. *Eine Moschee in Deutschland: Nazis, Geheimdienste und der Aufstieg des politischen Islam im Westen*. Munich: C. H. Beck, 2011.

Menocal, María Rosa. *The Ornament of the World: How Muslims, Christians, and Jews Created a Culture of Tolerance in Medieval Spain*. Boston: Little, Brown, 2003.

Meri, Josef. *The Cult of Saints Among Jews and Muslims in Medieval Syria*. Oxford: Oxford University Press, 2003.

—. Introduction to *Jewish-Muslim Relations in Past and Present: A Kaleidoscopic View*, ed. Josef Meri, 1–12. Leiden: Brill, 2017.

—, ed. *The Routledge Handbook of Muslim-Jewish Relations*. London: Routledge, 2016.

Miller, Michael L. "The Contribution of Jewish Orientalists." In *A History of Jewish-Muslim Relations: From the Origins to the Present Day*, ed. Abdelwahab Meddeb and Benjamin Stora. Trans. Jane Marie Todd and Michael B. Smith, 828–35. Princeton, N.J.: Princeton University Press, 2013.

Moeller, Robert G. "Private Acts, Public Anxieties, and the Fight to Decriminalize Male Homosexuality in West Germany." *Feminist Studies* 36, no. 3 (Fall 2010): 528–52.

—. "The Regulation of Male Homosexuality in Postwar East and West Germany: An Introduction." *Feminist Studies* 36, no. 3 (Fall 2010): 521–27.

Mommsen, Katherina. "Goethe and the Arab World." *Bulletin of the Faculty of Arts, Alexandria University* 19 (1965): 77–92.

—. *Goethe and the Poets of Arabia*. Trans. Michael Metzger. Rochester, N.Y.: Camden House, 2014.

——. *Goethe und die arabische Welt*. Frankfurt am Main: Insel, 1988.

—. "Goethe's Relationship to Islam." *Muslim* 4, no. 3 (January 1967): 12–18.

—. "Zu *Goethe und der Islam*—Antwort auf die oft aufgeworfene Frage: War Goethe ein Muslim?" *Goethe Yearbook* 21, no. 1 (2014): 247–54.

Montville, Joseph V., ed. *History as Prelude: Muslims and Jews in the Medieval Mediterranean*. Lanham, Md.: Lexington, 2011.

Morsch, Günter, and Astrid Ley, ed. *Sachsenhausen Concentration Camp, 1936–1945: Events and Developments*. 4th ed. Berlin: Metropol, 2011.

Mosse, George. *German Jews Beyond Judaism*. Bloomington: Indiana University Press, 1985.

Motadel, David. "Islam and Germany's War in the Soviet Borderlands, 1941–1945." *Journal of Contemporary History* 48, no. 4 (2013): 784–820.

—. *Islam and Nazi Germany's War*. London: Belknap Press of Harvard University Press, 2014.

—. "Islamische Bürgerlichkeit-Das soziokulturelle milieu der muslimischen Minderheit in Berlin, 1918–1939." In *Juden und Muslime in Deutschland: Recht, Religion, Identität*, ed. José Brunner und Shai Lavi, 103–21. *Tel Aviver Jahrbuch für deutsche Geschichte* 37. Göttingen: Wallstein, 2009.

—. "The Making of Muslim Communities in Western Europe, 1914–1939." In *Transnational Islam in Interwar Europe: Muslim Activists and Thinkers*, ed. Götz Nordbruch and Umar Ryad, 13–43. New York: Palgrave Macmillan, 2014.

—. "The 'Muslim Question' in Hitler's Balkans." *Historical Journal* 56, no. 4 (December 2013): 1007–39.

—. "Veiled Survivors: Jews, Roma and Muslims in the Years of the Holocaust." In *Rewriting German History: New Perspectives on Modern Germany*, ed. Jan Rueger and Nikolaus Wachsmann, 288–305. Basingstoke, U.K.: Palgrave Macmillan, 2015.

Müller, Joachim. "'Wohl dem, der hier nur eine Nummer ist': Die Isolierung der Homosexuellen." In *Homosexuelle Männer im KZ Sachsenhausen*, ed. Joachim Müller and Andreas Sternweiler, 89–108. Berlin: rosa Winkel, 2000.

Münzer, Daniel. "A Twisted Road to Pacifism: Kurt Hiller and the First World War." In *Simon Dubnow Institute Yearbook* 13 (2014): 365–88.

Nawwab, Ismail Ibrahim. "A Matter of Love: Muhammad Asad and Islam." *Islamic Studies* 39, no. 2 (Summer 2000): 155–231.

Nipp, Manuela. "Hugo Marcus." *Personenlexikon des Kanton Basel-Landschaft* (2014), https://personenlexikon.bl.ch/Hugo_Marcus.

Nordbruch, Götz. "Arab Students in Weimar Germany: Politics and Thought Beyond Borders." *Journal of Contemporary History* 49, no. 2 (2014): 275–95.

—. "The Arab World and National Socialism: Some Reflections on an Ambiguous Relationship." In *Orient-Institut Studies* 1 (2012) *Rethinking Totalitarianism and Its Arab Readings*, 2–7, http://www.perspectivia.net/content/publikationen/orient-institut-studies/1-2012/nordbruch_arab-world.

—. "'Cultural Fusion' of Thought and Ambitions? Memory, Politics and the History of Arab-Nazi German Encounters." *Middle Eastern Studies* 47, no. 1 (January 2011): 183–94.

—. *Nazism in Syria and Lebanon: The Ambivalence of the German Option, 1933–1945*. New York: Routledge, 2009.

Norton, Robert E. *Secret Germany: Stefan George and His Circle*. Ithaca, N.Y.: Cornell University Press, 2002.

Novick, Peter. *The Holocaust in American Life*. Boston: Houghton Mifflin, 1999.

Oelmann, Ute. "The George Circle: From *Künstlergesellschaft* to *Lebensgemeinschaft*." In *A Poet's Reich: Politics and Culture in the George Circle*, ed. Melissa S. Lane and Martin A. Ruehl, 25–36. Rochester, N.Y.: Camden House, 2011.

—. *Frauen um Stefan George*. Göttingen: Wallstein, 2010.

Özyürek, Esra. *Being German, Becoming Muslim: Race, Religion, and Conversion in the New Europe*. Princeton, N.J.: Princeton University Press, 2015.

Peters, F. E. *The Children of Abraham: Judaism, Christianity, Islam*, new ed. Princeton, N.J.: Princeton University Press, 2006.

Portmann, Roger. "Konzepte männlicher Homosexualität in der Schweiz 1932–1967: Im Spiegel der Zeitschriften 'Freundschafts-Banner,' 'Menschenrecht' und 'Der Kreis.'" Dissertation, University of Zürich, 2000.

Potempa, Georg. "Wir Poeten und Artisten . . . Ein unbekannter Briefwechsel von Thomas Mann mit Hugo Marcus." *Neue Deutsche Hefte* 25, no. 4 (1978): 708–20.

Pretzel, Andreas. *Homosexuellenpolitik in der frühen Bundesrepublik*. Hamburg: Männerschwarm, 2010.

Pretzel, Andreas, and Gabriele Roßbach, ed. *Wegen der zu erwartenden hohen Strafe: Homosexuellenverfolgung in Berlin, 1933–1945*. Berlin: rosa Winkel, 2000.

Reetz, Dietrich. *Islam in the Public Sphere: Religious Groups in India, 1900–1947*. Oxford: Oxford University Press, 2006.

Reiss, Tom. *The Orientalist: Solving the Mystery of a Strange and Dangerous Life*. New York: Vintage, 2005. Published in the United Kingdom as *The Orientalist: In Search of a Man Caught Between East and West*. London: Vintage, 2006.

Roschewski, Heinz. "Heinrich Rothmund in seinen persönlichen Akten: Zur Frage des Antisemitismus in der schweizerischen Flüchtlingspolitik 1933–1945." *Studien und Quellen* 22 (1996): 107–36.

Rubin, Abraham. "Muhammad Asad's Conversion to Islam as a Study in Jewish Self-Orientalization." *Jewish Social Studies* 22, no. 1 (Fall 2016): 1–28.

Rubin, Barry, and Wolfgang G. Schwanitz. *Nazis, Islamists, and the Making of the Modern Middle East*. New Haven, Conn.: Yale University Press, 2014.

Rudoren, Jodi. "Netanyahu Denounced for Saying Palestinian Inspired Holocaust." *New York Times*, October 21, 2015.

Ruehl, Martin A. "Aesthetic Fundamentalism in Weimar Poetry: Stefan George and His Circle, 1918–1933." In *Weimar Thought: A Contested Legacy*, ed. Peter E. Gordon and John P. McCormick. Princeton, N.J.: Princeton University Press, 2013, 240–72.

—. "'Imperium transcendat hominem': Reich and Rulership in Ernst Kantorowicz's *Kaiser Friedrich der Zweite*." In *A Poet's Reich: Politics and Culture in the George Circle*, ed. Melissa S. Lane and Martin A. Ruehl, 204–47. Rochester, N.Y.: Camden House, 2011.

Rupp, Leila. "The Persistence of Transnational Organizing: The Case of the Homophile Movement." *American Historical Review* 116, no. 4 (October 2011): 1014–39.

Ryad, Umar. "Among the Believers in the Land of the Colonizer: Mohammed Ali van Beetem's Role among the Indonesian Community in the Netherlands in the Interwar Period." *Journal of Religion in Europe* 5, no. 2 (2012): 273–310.

—. "From an Officer in the Ottoman Army to a Muslim Publicist and Armament Agent in Berlin: Zeki Hishmat-Bey Kiram (1886–1946)." *Bibliotheca Orientalis* 63, no. 3–4 (2006): 235–68.

—. "A *Salafi* Student, Orientalist Scholarship, and Radio Berlin in Nazi Germany: Taqi al-Din al-Hilali and His Experiences in the West." In *Transnational Islam in Interwar Europe*, ed. Götz Nordbruch and Umar Ryad, 107–55. New York: Palgrave Macmillan, 2014.

—. *Wathiq Tijarat al-Silah al-Almani fi Shibh al-jazira al-Arabiyya: Qiraa fi Arshif Zeki Kiram* (Documents on the German arms trade in the Arabian peninsula: Readings in the archive of Zeki Kiram). Cairo: Dar al-Kutab al-Masriyah, 2011.

Sagaster, Börte. *Achmed Talib: Stationen des Lebens eines türkischen Schuhmachermeisters in Deutschland von 1917 bis 1983. Kaiserreich—Weimarer Republik—Drittes Reich—DDR*. Cologne: Önel, 1997.

Said, Edward. *Orientalism*. 25th anniversary edition, with a new preface. New York: Vintage, 2003.

Satloff, Robert. *Among the Righteous: Lost Stories from the Holocaust's Long Reach into Arab Lands*. New York: Public Affairs, 2006.

Schapkow, Carsten. *Role Model and Countermodel: The Golden Age of Iberian Jewry and German Jewish Culture During the Era of Emancipation*. Trans. Corey Twitchell. London: Lexington, 2016.

Schäfer, Christian. *"Widernatürliche Unzucht" (§§175, 175a, 175b, 182 a.F. StGB) Reformdiskussion und Gesetzgebung seit 1945*. Juristische Zeitgeschichte 26: Abteilung 3: Beiträge zur modernen deutschen Strafgesetzgebung-Materialien zu einem historischen Kommentar. Berlin: Berliner Wissenschafts-Verlag, 2006.

Schäfer-Borrmann, Alexandra. *Vom "Waffenbruder" zum "türkisch-deutschen Faktotum" Ekrem Rüştü Akömer (1892–1984), eine bemerkenswerte Randfigur der Geschichte.* Würzburg: Ergon, 1998.

Scheck, Raffael. "Nazi Propaganda Toward French Muslim Prisoners of War." *Holocaust and Genocide Studies* 26, no. 3 (Winter 2012): 447–77.

Scheindlin, Raymond P. *The Gazelle: Medieval Hebrew Poems on God, Israel and the Soul.* 1991. Reprint, Oxford: Oxford University Press, 1999.

—. *Wine, Women and Death: Medieval Hebrew Poems on the Good Life* 1986. Reprint, Oxford: Oxford University Press, 1999.

Shimer, David. "Germany Wipes Slate Clean for 50,000 Men Convicted Under Anti-Gay Law." *New York Times*, June 23, 2017.

Schmidtke, Sabine. "Eine doppelte Konstruktion der Wirklichkeit: Ferdinand Karsch (-Haack) (1853–1936) zu Gleichgeschlechtlichkeit im islamischen Raum." Typescript, Berlin, 2001, available at Bibliothek, Schwules Museum in Berlin, Se/111/Kar/2.

Schröder, Bernd Philipp, ed. *Deutschland und der Mittlere Osten im Zweiten Weltkrieg.* Göttingen: Musterschmidt, 1975.

Schubert, Gudrun. "Meier, Fritz." *Encyclopaedia Iranica.* Online edition, 2002, available at http://www.iranicaonline.org/articles/meier-fritz-1.

Sibold, Noëmi. "Menschen ohne Schutz: Ein Blick auf die Schweizer Flüchtlingspolitik zu Zeiten des Zweiten Weltkriegs." *tachles: das jüdische Wochenmagazin* (Zürich), April 21, 2017, 21–23.

Siddiqi, Majid Hayat. "Bluff, Doubt and Fear: The Kheiri Brothers and the Colonial State, 1904–1945." *Indian Economic and Social History Review* 24, no. 3 (1987): 233–63.

Sorkin, David. *The Transformation of German Jewry, 1780–1840.* Oxford: Oxford University Press, 1987.

Spector, Scott. *Violent Sensations: Sex, Crime & Utopia in Vienna and Berlin, 1860–1914.* Chicago: University of Chicago Press, 2016.

—. "Where Personal Fate Turns to Public Affair: Homosexual Scandal and Social Order in Vienna, 1900–1910." *Austrian History Yearbook* 38 (January 2007): 15–24.

Stein, Sarah Abrevaya. "Protected Persons? The Baghdadi Jewish Diaspora, the British State, and the Persistence of Empire." *American Historical Review* 116, no. 1 (February 2011): 80–108.

Steinfeldt, Irena. "Muslim Righteous Among the Nations." In *A History of Jewish-Muslim Relations: From the Origins to the Present Day*, ed. Abdelwahab Meddeb and Benjamin Stora. Trans. Jane Marie Todd and Michael B. Smith, 372–74. Princeton, N.J.: Princeton University Press, 2013.

Steinke, Ronen. *Der Muslim und die Jüdin: Die Geschichte einer Rettung in Berlin.* Munich: Berlin Verlag, 2017.

Steinle, Karl-Heinz. *"Der Kreis": Mitglieder, Künstler, Autoren.* Berlin: rosa Winkel, 1999.

Sternweiler, Andreas. "Er hatte doppelt so schwer zu leiden . . . Homosexuelle Juden." In *Homosexuelle Männer im KZ Sachsenhausen*, ed. Joachim Müller and Andreas Sternweiler, 172–80. Berlin: rosa Winkel, 2000.

Stillman, Norman A. "History." In *The Jews of Arab Lands: A History and Source Book*, 3–110. Philadelphia: Jewish Publication Society of America, 1979.

Stora, Benjamin. "Messali Hadj, the Refusal to Collaborate." In *A History of Jewish-Muslim Relations: From the Origins to the Present Day*, ed. Abdelwahab Meddeb and Benjamin Stora. Trans.

Jane Marie Todd and Michael B. Smith, 365–66. Princeton, N.J.: Princeton University Press, 2013.

Stromberg, Peter G. "The Role of Language in Religious Conversion." In *The Oxford Handbook of Religious Conversion*, ed. Lewis R. Rambo and Charles E. Farhadian, 117–39. Oxford: Oxford University Press, 2014.

Sutcliffe, Adam. "Religion and the Birth of Jewish Radical Politics." *AJS Perspectives*, The Religious Issue (Fall 2011): 34–35.

Taheri, Ata. *Deutsche Agenten bei iranische Stämmen, 1942–1944: Ein Augenzeugenbericht*. Berlin: Schwarz, 2008.

Taylor, Seth. *Left-Wing Nietzcheans: The Politics of German Expressionism, 1910–1920*. New York: De Gruyter, 1990.

Tobin, Robert Deam. *Peripheral Desires: The German Discovery of Sex*. Philadelphia: University of Pennsylvania Press, 2015.

——. *Warm Brothers: Queer Theory and the Age of Goethe*. Philadelphia: University of Pennsylvania Press, 2000.

van der Veer, Peter. *Imperial Encounters: Religion and Modernity in India and Britain*. Princeton, N.J.: Princeton University Press, 2001.

van Rahden, Till. "Fatherhood, Rechristianization, and the Quest for Democracy in Postwar West Germany." In *Raising Citizens in the "Century of the Child": Child-Rearing in the United States and German Central Europe in the Twentieth Century*, ed. Dirk Schumann, 141–64. New York: Berghahn, 2010.

Vena, Teresa. "Etre homosexuel en Suisse: 'Der Kreis' et l'homosexualité en Suisse entre 1930 et 1960." Dissertation, Universite de Genève, 2006.

Viswanathan, Gauri. *Outside the Fold: Conversion, Modernity, and Belief*. Princeton, N.J.: Princeton University Press, 1998.

Vitkus, Daniel. *Turning Turk: English Theater and the Multicultural Mediterranean*. London: Palgrave Macmillan, 2008.

Volkov, Shulamit. "German Jewish History: Back to *Bildung* and Culture?" In *What History Tells: George L. Mosse and the Culture of Modern Europe*, ed. Stanley Payne, David Sorkin, and John Tortorice, 223–38. Madison: University of Wisconsin Press, 2004.

von Arnim, Peter Anton. "Goethe als Leitfigur eines deutschen Islam?" Afterword in *Goethe und der Islam* by Katherina Mommsen, 431–54. Frankfurt a.M.: Insel, 2001.

Yurdakul, Gökçe. *From Guest Workers into Muslims: The Transformation of Turkish Immigrant Associations in Germany*. Newcastle upon Tyne: Cambridge Scholars, 2008.

Washburn, Dennis, and A. Kevin Reinhart. Introduction to *Converting Cultures: Religion, Ideology, and Transformations of Modernity*, ed. Dennis Washburn and Kevin Reinhart, ix–xxii. Leiden: Brill, 2007.

Wasserstrom, Steven M. *Between Muslim and Jew: The Problem of Symbiosis under Early Islam*. Princeton, N.J.: Princeton University Press, 1995.

Weitz, Eric. *Weimar Germany: Promise and Tragedy*. Princeton, N.J.: Princeton University Press, 2007.

Whisnant, Clayton J. *Male Homosexuality in West Germany: Between Persecution and Freedom, 1945–1969*. London: Palgrave Macmillan, 2012.

—. *Queer Identities and Politics in Germany: A History, 1880–1945*. New York: Harrington Park, 2016.

Widdig, Bernd. "Cultural Capital in Decline: Inflation and the Distress of Intellectuals." In *Weimar Publics/Weimar Subjects: Rethinking the Political Culture of Germany in the 1920s*, ed. Kathleen Canning, Kerstin Barndt, and Kristin McGuire, 302–17. New York: Berghahn, 2010.

Wien, Peter. "Coming to Terms with the Past: German Academia and Historical Relations between the Arab Lands and Nazi Germany." *International Journal of Middle East Studies* 42, no. 2 (May 2010): 311–21.

—. "The Culpability of Exile: Arabs in Nazi Germany." *Geschichte und Gesellschaft* 37 (2011): 332–58.

—. *Iraqi Arab Nationalism: Authoritarian, Totalitarian, and Pro-Fascist Inclinations, 1932–1941*. New York: Routledge, 2006.

Wiesenthal, Simon. *Grossmufti: Grossagent der Achse*. Vienna: Ried, 1947.

Wildangel, René. "'Der größte Feind der Menschheit': Der Nationalsozialismus in der arabischen öffentlichen Meinung in Palästina während des Zweiten Weltkrieges." In *Blind für die Geschichte? Arabische Begegnungen mit dem Nationalsozialismus*, ed. Gerhard Höpp, Peter Wien, and René Wildangel, 115–54. Berlin: Klaus Schwarz, 2004.

—. *Zwischen Achse und Mandatsmacht: Palästina und der Nationalsozialismus*. Berlin: Klaus Schwarz, 2007.

Wilson, W. Daniel. "But Is It Gay? Kissing, Friendship, and 'Pre-Homosexual' Discourses in Eighteenth-Century Germany." *Modern Language Review* 103, no. 3 (July 2008): 767–83.

—. "Enlightenment Encounters the Islamic and Arabic Worlds: The German 'Missing Link' in Said's Orientalist Narrative." In *Encounters with Islam in German Literature and Culture*, ed. James Hodkinson and Jeffrey Morrison, 73–88. Rochester, N.Y.: Camden House, 2009.

—. *Goethe Männer Knaben: Ansichten zur "Homosexualität."* Trans. Angela Steidele. Berlin: Insel, 2012.

Windhager, Günter. *Leopold Weiss alias Muhammad Asad: Von Galizien nach Arabien, 1900–1927*. Vienna: Böhlau, 2002.

Wolff, Charlotte. *Magnus Hirschfeld: A Portrait of a Pioneer in Sexology*. New York: Quartet Books, 1986.

Catalogues of Exhibits

Die Geschichte des §175: Strafrecht gegen Homosexuelle. Katalog zur Ausstellung in Berlin und in Frankfurt am Main 1990. Berlin: rosa Winkel, 1990.

Goodbye to Berlin? 100 Jahre Schwulenbewegung. Schwules Museum und Akademie der Künste, Berlin. Berlin: rosa Winkel, 1997.

Index

RELIGION, CULTURE, AND PUBLIC LIFE

Series Editor: Matthew Engelke

After Pluralism: Reimagining Religious Engagement, edited by Courtney Bender and Pamela E. Klassen

Religion and International Relations Theory, edited by Jack Snyder

Religion in America: A Political History, Denis Lacorne

Democracy, Islam, and Secularism in Turkey, edited by Ahmet T. Kuru and Alfred Stepan

Refiguring the Spiritual: Beuys, Barney, Turrell, Goldsworthy, Mark C. Taylor

Tolerance, Democracy, and Sufis in Senegal, edited by Mamadou Diouf

Rewiring the Real: In Conversation with William Gaddis, Richard Powers, Mark Danielewski, and Don DeLillo, Mark C. Taylor

Democracy and Islam in Indonesia, edited by Mirjam Künkler and Alfred Stepan

Religion, the Secular, and the Politics of Sexual Difference, edited by Linell E. Cady and Tracy Fessenden

Boundaries of Toleration, edited by Alfred Stepan and Charles Taylor

Recovering Place: Reflections on Stone Hill, Mark C. Taylor

Blood: A Critique of Christianity, Gil Anidjar

Choreographies of Shared Sacred Sites: Religion, Politics, and Conflict Resolution, edited by Elazar Barkan and Karen Barkey

Beyond Individualism: The Challenge of Inclusive Communities, George Rupp

Love and Forgiveness for a More Just World, edited by Hent de Vries and Nils F. Schott

Relativism and Religion: Why Democratic Societies Do Not Need Moral Absolutes, Carlo Invernizzi Accetti

The Making of Salafism: Islamic Reform in the Twentieth Century, Henri Lauzière

Mormonism and American Politics, edited by Randall Balmer and Jana Riess

Religion, Secularism, and Constitutional Democracy, edited by Jean L. Cohen and Cécile Laborde

Race and Secularism in America, edited by Jonathon S. Kahn and Vincent W. Lloyd

Beyond the Secular West, edited by Akeel Bilgrami

Pakistan at the Crossroads: Domestic Dynamics and External Pressures, edited by Christophe Jaffrelot

Faithful to Secularism: The Religious Politics of Democracy in Ireland, Senegal, and the Philippines, David T. Buckley

Holy Wars and Holy Alliance: The Return of Religion to the Global Political Stage, Manlio Graziano

The Politics of Secularism: Religion, Diversity, and Institutional Change in France and Turkey, Murat Akan

Democratic Transition in the Muslim World: A Global Perspective, edited by Alfred Stepan

The Holocaust and the Nabka, edited by Bashir Bashir and Amos Goldberg

The Limits of Tolerance: Enlightenment Values and Religious Fanaticism, Denis Lacorne